PHILOSOPHERS EXPLORE
The Matrix

PHILOSOPHERS EXPLORE
The Matrix

Edited by Christopher Grau

OXFORD
UNIVERSITY PRESS

2005

OXFORD

UNIVERSITY PRESS

Oxford University Press, Inc., publishes works that further
Oxford University's objective of excellence
in research, scholarship, and education.

Oxford   New York
Auckland   Cape Town   Dar es Salaam   Hong Kong   Karachi
Kuala Lumpur   Madrid   Melbourne   Mexico City   Nairobi
New Delhi   Shanghai   Taipei   Toronto

With offices in
Argentina   Austria   Brazil   Chile   Czech Republic   France   Greece
Guatemala   Hungary   Italy   Japan   Poland   Portugal   Singapore
South Korea   Switzerland   Thailand   Turkey   Ukraine   Vietnam

Published by Oxford University Press, Inc.
198 Madison Avenue, New York, New York 10016

www.oup.com

Oxford is a registered trademark of Oxford University Press

Library of Congress Cataloging-in-Publication Data
Philosophers explore The Matrix / edited by Christopher Grau.
   p. cm.
Includes bibliographical references and index.
ISBN-13 978-0-19-518106-7; 978-0-19-518107-4 (pbk.)
ISBN 0-19-518106-9; 0-19-518107-7 (pbk.)
1. Matrix (Motion picture)   2. Motion pictures—Philosophy.
I. Grau, Christopher.
PN1997.M395F74 2005
791.43'72—dc22   2004059977

9 8 7 6 5 4 3 2 1
Printed in the United States of America
on acid-free paper

ACKNOWLEDGMENTS

I'd like to thank all of the contributors to this collection, as well as Peter Ohlin, Stacey Hamilton, and Lara Zoble at Oxford University Press, for their hard work, enthusiasm, and patience. I'd also like to express my gratitude to the good folks at redpill productions (Sharon Bray, Spencer Lamm, Lukasz Lysakowski, Rob Simpson, and Jason Williford) for providing earlier versions of these essays with a home online at the official Web site for the *Matrix* films (www.thematrix.com). Additional thanks goes to Jason Williford for permission to reprint his nifty brain-in-a-vat drawing on p. 133. Finally, thanks to Josh Oreck, Susan Watson, and Sean Greenberg for helpful comments and support.

Thanks also to the following publishers for granting permission to reprint the material included in the appendix:

Excerpt from G. M. A. Grube and C. D. C. Reeve, trans., *Plato's Republic* (Hackett 1992). Copyright © 1992 Hackett Publishing Company, Inc. Reprinted by permission of Hackett Publishing Company, Inc. All rights reserved.

Excerpt from René Descartes, *Meditations on First Philosophy*, ed. and trans. J. Cottingham (Cambridge University Press 1985), with permission of Cambridge University Press. Copyright © 1985 Cambridge University Press.

Excerpt from George Berkeley, *Principles of Human Knowledge: Three Dialogues* (Oxford University Press 1996), reprinted with permission of Oxford University Press.

CONTENTS

PHILOSOPHERS EXPLORE
The Matrix

1 Christopher Grau

INTRODUCTION

The Matrix is a film that astounds not only with action and special effects but also with ideas. This volume is dedicated to exploring some of the many philosophical ideas that arise in the film. In these pages you'll find accessible yet challenging essays from some of the brightest philosophers, theologians, and cognitive scientists around. Though this collection is derived from essays that originally appeared on the official Web site for the *Matrix* films (www.thematrix.com), the views expressed in these chapters are solely those of the individual authors. Larry and Andy Wachowski have remained relatively tight-lipped regarding the religious symbolism and philosophical themes that permeate the film, preferring that the movie speak for itself, and neither they nor Warner Brothers were involved with the production of this book. Accordingly, you will not find anyone here claiming to offer the "official" or definitive analysis of the film, its symbols, message, and so on. What you will find instead are essays that both elucidate the philosophical problems raised by the film and explore possible avenues for solving these problems. Some of the chapters are more pedagogical in nature—instructing the reader in the various ways in which *The Matrix* raises questions that have been tackled throughout history by prominent philosophers. Other contributors use the film as a springboard for discussing their own original philosophical views. (While the later films in the *Matrix* series are occasionally discussed, the essays in this collection primarily focus on the first film, as it is the one that succeeds best at merging philosophical issues with cinematic spectacle.) As you will see, the authors don't always agree with each other regarding how best to interpret *The Matrix*. However, all of the chapters share the aim of giving the reader a sense of how this remarkable film offers more than the standard Hollywood fare. In other words, their common goal is to help show you just "how deep the rabbit hole goes."

Beginning the collection is a short chapter in which I discuss two of the more conspicuous philosophical questions raised by the film: the skeptical worry that one's experience may be illusory and the moral question of whether it matters. Highlighting the parallels between the scenario described in *The Matrix* and similar imaginary situations that have been much discussed by philosophers, this chapter offers an introduction to the positions taken by various thinkers (such as René Descartes, Hilary Putnam, and Robert Nozick) on these fascinating skeptical and moral puzzles. It serves as a warm-up for things to come.

Next is Tim Mawson's "Morpheus and Berkeley on Reality." Tim is Fellow and Tutor in Philosophy at St Peter's College, Oxford University. He takes a comment by Morpheus regarding "what is real" as his starting point for an introduction to the difficult philosophical problem of sorting out the real from the unreal. Discussing the philosopher George Berkeley's startling views on the nature of reality, he considers the question of whether Berkeley offers a genuine, if radical, way out of the skeptical worries raised by Descartes, and whether this Berkeleyan path is one that Morpheus would do best to follow. He concludes that, even if Berkeley doesn't offer us a satisfying escape from skepticism, consideration of his views can help us to get closer to the truth through bringing us to a more sophisticated understanding of Morpheus's comments and the skeptical worries they engender.

James Pryor, an epistemologist and philosopher of mind at New York University, has contributed a lively chapter that will also be of particular interest to those coming to philosophy for the first time. In "What's So Bad about Living in the Matrix?" he explores and criticizes two tempting but problematic philosophical positions: the view that there can't be facts that are impossible for us to know about (sometimes called *verificationism*) and the view that everyone's motive for acting is always to have nicer experiences. Employing examples from both the film and imaginary thought-experiments, Pryor shows that these positions, which can often initially seem irresistible to students, are not as straightforward nor as satisfying as they might first appear. He then goes on to argue that the worst thing about living in the Matrix would not be the metaphysical or epistemological limitations such a scenario would impose; it would instead be the political constraints: those trapped in the Matrix have restrictions on their actions that most of us deeply value not having.

Colin McGinn is a distinguished contemporary philosopher who is perhaps best known for his writings on consciousness. His essay ("The Matrix of Dreams") offers a novel analysis of the film that focuses on the dreamlike nature of the world of the Matrix. Arguing that it is misguided to characterize the situation described by the film as involving hallucinations, McGinn shows how the particular details of the film make it more plausible to see the Matrix as involving the direct employment of one's imagination (as in a dream), rather than as a force-feeding of false perceptions. Along the way, McGinn's chapter also touches on the moral assumptions of the film, several other philosophical problems raised by the character of Cypher, and the dreamlike quality of *all* films.

Hubert Dreyfus is a philosopher known both for his pioneering discussion of the philosophical problems of artificial intelligence, and his work in bridging the gap between recent European and English-language philosophy. In "Existential Phenomenology and the Brave New World of *The Matrix*," he and his son Stephen Dreyfus draw on the phenomenological tradition that began with Edmund Husserl and culminated in Maurice Merleau-Ponty to discuss the skeptical and moral problems raised by the film. They argue that the real worry facing folks trapped in the Matrix involves not deception nor the possession of possibly false beliefs, but the limits on creativity imposed by the Matrix. Following Martin Heidegger in suggesting that our human nature lies in our capacity to redefine our nature and thereby open up new worlds, they conclude that this capacity for radical creation seems unavailable to those locked within the pre-programmed confines of the Matrix.

Iakovos Vasiliou, a philosopher at Brooklyn College who specializes in Plato, Aristotle, and Wittgenstein, offers a penetrating investigation into the differences (and surprising similarities) between the scenario described in *The Matrix* and our own everyday situation in "Reality, What Matters, and *The Matrix*." Pointing out that more than we might expect hinges on the moral backdrop of *The Matrix* plot line, he asks readers to instead envisage a "benevolently generated Matrix." Given the possibility of such a Matrix and the actuality of a horrible situation on Earth, he argues that we will agree that entering into it offers not a denial of what we most value but instead a chance to better realize those values.

Richard Hanley, author of the best-selling book *The Metaphysics of Star Trek* and a philosophy professor at the University of Delaware, again explores the intersection of philosophy and science fiction with his entertaining and thought-provoking piece "Never the Twain Shall Meet: Reflections on the Very First Matrix." He argues that *The Matrix* may have lessons to teach us regarding the coherence of our values. In particular, he makes the case that, given a traditional Christian notion of an afterlife, heaven turns out to be rather like a matrix. Even more surprising is a corollary to this thesis: Jean-Paul ("Hell is other people") Sartre was close to the truth after all—heaven is best understood as a matrix-like simulation in which contact with other real human beings is eliminated.

David Chalmers is a philosopher from the Australian National University and author of numerous books and articles on the philosophy of mind, including the influential volume *The Conscious Mind*. In "The Matrix as Metaphysics," he suggests that while we cannot rule out the possibility that we are in a system like the Matrix, this possibility is not as bad as we might think. He argues against the intuitive view that if we are in a matrix, we are deluded about the external world. Instead, he suggests that if we are in a matrix, we should regard this as telling us about the nature of the external world: the physical world is ultimately made of bits, and was created by beings who ensured that our minds interact with this physical world. Chalmers's surprising conclusion is that even if we are living in a Matrix-like simulation, most of our beliefs about the world are still true.

From the influential philosopher and cognitive scientist Andy Clark, we have "The Twisted Matrix: Dream, Simulation, or Hybrid?" Clark brings some helpful empirical data to the table to help ground the discussion of the "dreamlike quality" of the Matrix that we have seen in essays from Grau, McGinn, Chalmers, and others. Pointing out that the reality of dreams is rather different than philosophers tend to suppose, he distinguishes between the sloppy but creative cognition of our actual "uncritical" dreams and the "industrial-strength deception" that philosophers since Descartes have (mistakenly) assumed to be part and parcel of ordinary dreams. Arguing that the film plays on and at times conflates these two distinct conceptions of dreams, Clark concludes that this ambivalence at the heart of *The Matrix* helps to explain why it is such a memorable and thought-provoking cinematic experience.

Changing gears a bit, the next chapter is from the notable (and some would say notorious) cybernetics pioneer Kevin Warwick. He is known internationally for his robotics research and in particular for a series of procedures in which he was implanted with sensors that connected him to computers and the Internet. Less well publicized is the fact that several years before *The Matrix* came out he published a nonfiction book that predicted the ultimate takeover of mankind by a race of superintelligent robots. In his contribution here ("*The Matrix*—Our Future?"), he draws on his years of research to muse on the plausibility (and desirability) of the scenario described in *The Matrix*, concluding that a real-life matrix need not be feared if we prepare ourselves adequately. How? By becoming part-machine ourselves. Warwick argues that transforming ourselves into cyborgs will allow us to "plug in" confident that we will fully benefit from all that such a future offers.

Julia Driver, a moral philosopher from Dartmouth College and author of *Uneasy Virtue*, explores some of the distinctively ethical issues that arise in *The Matrix* in "Artificial Ethics." Driver begins by using the film to consider the moral status of artificially created beings: she argues that (given certain assumptions regarding the nature of consciousness, rationality, and personhood) we ought to regard artificial intelligences such as Agent Smith as creatures that deserve genuine moral consideration. In the second part of her chapter, Driver tackles the thorny philosophical question of whether one can behave immorally when in "nonveridical" (illusory) circumstances. Noting the implausibility of attributing wrongdoing to those who perform seemingly immoral acts in a dream, she argues that, to the extent that the Matrix offers a similarly illusory world free of actual unpleasant effects, it also seems odd to attribute wrongdoing to agents acting in such a world. However, drawing on insights from the first part of her contribution, Driver concludes that we have good reasons to think that actions in the Matrix *would* have genuine effects on both humans and some artificial creatures, and thus the world of the Matrix, like our world, has its own moral norms—its own ethics—that ought to be both acknowledged and respected.

Michael McKenna, a philosopher at Ithaca College who specializes in the philosophical problems of freedom and moral responsibility, offers up a comprehensive yet lighthearted exploration of the free-will problem in "Neo's Freedom... Whoa!" Ingeniously utilizing aspects of *The Matrix* to describe and explore the traditional positions taken in debates over free will, McKenna manages to cover a lot of ground: determinism, fatalism, compatibilism, and incompatibilism are all canvassed and compared through the unique perspective afforded us by the film. He then goes on to explore the attractiveness of the radical freedom that Neo appears to have achieved by the end of *The Matrix*. Does such absolute freedom indeed "rock" the way we naturally think it would? McKenna convincingly argues that total freedom of this sort offers too much of a good thing: part of the joy we take in exercising our freedom is in pushing boundaries and testing limits. If all boundaries and limitations are removed, the possibility for such joy will disappear as well.

John Partridge, a professor of philosophy at Wheaton College whose work focuses on the philosophy of the ancient Greeks, explores the striking similarities between *The Matrix* and the Cave scenario described in Plato's *Republic* in his contribution, "Plato's Cave and *The Matrix*." In addition to pointing out the numerous surface parallels between the cave-dwellers whom Plato describes and the humans trapped in the Matrix, Partridge explores a deeper continuity between the film and Plato's text: both narratives place emphasis on the importance of disciplined self-examination and the self-knowledge that can follow. As Plato might put it, both Neo and the cave-dwellers are involved in the difficult journey from darkness to light that is required if genuine knowledge (and, consequently, true "care of the soul") is to be achieved.

Rounding out our collection is "Wake Up! Worlds of Illusion in Gnosticism, Buddhism, and *The Matrix* Project" from two professors of religion: Frances Flannery-Dailey and Rachel Wagner. Flannery-Dailey's research specialty is ancient dreams, apocalypticism, and early-Jewish mysticism, while Wagner's research focuses on biblical studies and the relationship between religion and culture. Their chapter offers a comprehensive treatment of the Gnostic and Buddhist themes that appear in the film. While pointing out the many differences between these two traditions and the eclectic manner in which both are referenced throughout the entire *Matrix* franchise, Flannery-Dailey and Wagner make it clear that common to Gnosticism, Buddhism, and *The Matrix* is the idea that what we take to be reality is in fact a kind of illusion or dream from which we ought best to "wake up." Only then can enlightenment, be it spiritual or otherwise, occur.

Looking to dig deeper? This volume concludes with an appendix that contains excerpts from several classic philosophical texts: Plato on his metaphor of the Cave, Descartes's discussion of skepticism, Berkeley's argument for idealism, Robert Nozick's description of the "experience machine," and finally the complete text of Hilary Putnam's ground-breaking essay "Brains in a Vat."

2

Christopher Grau

BAD DREAMS, EVIL DEMONS, AND THE EXPERIENCE MACHINE: PHILOSOPHY AND *THE MATRIX*

I. Dream Skepticism

MORPHEUS: Have you ever had a dream, Neo, that you were so sure was real?

MORPHEUS: What if you were unable to wake from that dream, Neo? How would you know the difference between the dreamworld and the real world?

Neo has woken up from a hell of a dream—the dream that was his life. How was he to know? The cliché is that if you are dreaming and you pinch yourself, you will wake up. Unfortunately, things aren't quite that simple. It is the nature of most dreams that we take them for reality— while dreaming, we are unaware that we are in a dream world. Of course, we eventually wake up, and when we do, we realize that our experience was all in our mind. Neo's predicament makes us wonder, though: how can any of us be sure that we have ever *genuinely* woken up? Perhaps, like Neo prior to his downing the red pill, our dreams thus far have in fact been dreams *within* a dream.

The idea that what we take to be the real world could all be just a dream is familiar to many students of philosophy, poetry, and literature. Most of us, at one time or another, have been struck with the thought that we might mistake a dream for reality, or reality for a dream. Arguably the most famous exponent of this worry in the Western philosophical tradition is the seventeenth-century French philosopher René Descartes. In an attempt to provide a firm foundation for knowledge, he began his *Meditations* by clearing the philosophical ground through doubting all that could be doubted. This was done, in part, in order to determine if anything that could count as certain knowledge could survive such rigorous and systematic skepticism. Descartes takes the first step toward this goal by raising (through his fictional narrator) the possibility that we might be dreaming:

> How often, asleep at night, am I convinced of just such familiar events—that I am here in my dressing-gown, sitting by the fire—when in fact I am lying undressed in bed! Yet at the moment my eyes are certainly wide awake when I look at this piece of paper; I shake my head and it is not asleep; as I stretch out and feel my hand I do so deliberately, and I know what I am doing. All this would not happen with such distinctness to someone asleep. Indeed! As if I did not remember other occasions when I have been tricked by exactly similar thoughts while asleep! As I think about this more carefully, I see plainly that there are never any sure signs by means of which being awake can be distinguished from being asleep. The result is that I begin to feel dazed, and this very feeling only reinforces the notion that I may be asleep.[1]

When we dream, we are often blissfully ignorant that we are dreaming. Given this, and the fact that dreams often seem as vivid and "realistic" as real life, how can you rule out the possibility that you might be dreaming even now, as you sit and read this? This is the kind of perplexing thought that Descartes forces us to confront. It seems we have no justification for the belief that we are not dreaming. If so, then it seems we similarly have no justification in thinking that the world we experience is the *real* world. Indeed, it becomes questionable whether we are justified in thinking that *any* of our beliefs are true.

The narrator of Descartes's *Meditations* worries about this, but he ultimately maintains that the possibility that one might be dreaming cannot by itself cast doubt on all we think we know; he points out that even if all our sensory experience is but a dream, we can still conclude that we have *some* knowledge of the nature of reality. Just as a painter cannot create ex nihilo but must rely on pigments with which to create

---

1. René Descartes, *Meditations on First Philosophy*, ed. and trans. J. Cottingham (Cambridge University Press 1985); see appendix, pp. 295–296. Further citations will be in the text.

her image, certain elements of our thought must exist prior to our imaginings. Among the items of knowledge that Descartes thought survived dream skepticism are truths arrived at through the use of reason, such as the truths of mathematics: "For whether I am awake or asleep, two and three added together are five, and a square has no more than four sides" (296–297).

While such an insight offers little comfort to someone wondering whether the people and objects she confronts are genuine, it served Descartes's larger philosophical project: he sought, among other things, to provide a foundation for knowledge in which truths arrived at through reason are given priority over knowledge gained from experience. (This bias shouldn't surprise those who remember that Descartes was a brilliant mathematician in addition to being a philosopher.) Descartes was not himself a skeptic—he employs this skeptical argument so as to help remind the reader that the truths of mathematics (and other truths of reason) are on firmer ground than the data provided to us by our senses.

Despite the fact that Descartes's ultimate goal was to demonstrate how genuine knowledge is possible, he proceeds in *The Meditations* to utilize a much more radical skeptical argument, one that casts doubt on even his beloved mathematical truths. In the next section we will see that, many years before the Wachowskis dreamed up *The Matrix*, Descartes had imagined an equally terrifying possibility.

II.   Brains in Vats and the Evil Demon

MORPHEUS: What is the Matrix? Control.

MORPHEUS: The Matrix is a computer-generated dreamworld built to keep us under control in order to change a human being into this. [holds up a battery]

NEO: No! I don't believe it! It's not possible!

Before breaking out of the Matrix, Neo's life was not what he thought it was. It was a lie. Morpheus describes it as a "dreamworld," but unlike a dream, this world is not the creation of Neo's mind. The truth is more sinister: the world is a creation of the artificially intelligent computers that have taken over the Earth and have subjugated humanity in the process. These creatures have fed Neo a simulation that he couldn't possibly help but take as the real thing. What's worse, it isn't clear how any of us can know with certainty that we are not in a position similar to Neo before his "rebirth." Our ordinary confidence in our ability to reason and our natural tendency to trust the deliverances of our senses can both come to seem rather naive once we confront this possibility of deception.

A viewer of *The Matrix* is naturally led to wonder: how do I know I am not in the Matrix? How do I know for sure that my world is not also a sophisticated charade, put forward by some superhuman intelligence in such a way that I cannot possibly detect the ruse? Descartes suggested a similar worry: the frightening possibility that all of one's experiences might be the result of a powerful outside force, a "malicious demon":

> And yet firmly rooted in my mind is the long-standing opinion that there is an omnipotent God who made me the kind of creature that I am. How do I know that he has not brought it about that there is no earth, no sky, no extended thing, no shape, no size, no place, while at the same time ensuring that all these things appear to me to exist just as they do now? What is more, just as I consider that others sometimes go astray in cases where they think they have the most perfect knowledge, how do I know that God has not brought it about that I too go wrong every time I add two and three or count the sides of a square, or in some even simpler matter, if that is imaginable? But perhaps God would not have allowed me to be deceived in this way, since he is said to be supremely good; ... I will suppose therefore that not God, who is supremely good and the source of truth, but rather some malicious demon of the utmost power and cunning has employed all his energies in order to deceive me. I shall think that the sky, the air, the earth, colours, shapes, sounds and all external things are merely the delusions of dreams which he has devised to ensnare my judgment. (297–298)

The narrator of Descartes's *Meditations* concludes that none of his former opinions are safe. Such a demon could not only deceive him about his perceptions, it could conceivably cause him to go wrong when performing even the simplest acts of reasoning.

This radical worry seems inescapable. How could you possibly prove to yourself that you are not in the kind of nightmarish situation Descartes describes? It would seem that any argument, evidence, or proof you might put forward could easily be yet another trick played by the demon. As ludicrous as the idea of the evil demon may sound at first, it is hard, upon reflection, not to share Descartes's worry: for all you know, you may well be a mere plaything of such a malevolent intelligence. More to the point of our general discussion: for all you know, you may well be trapped in the Matrix.

Many contemporary philosophers have discussed a similar skeptical dilemma that is a bit closer to the scenario described in *The Matrix.* It has come to be known as the "brain in a vat" hypothesis, and one powerful formulation of the idea is presented by philosopher Jonathan Dancy:

> You do not know that you are not a brain, suspended in a vat full of liquid in a laboratory, and wired to a computer which is feeding you your current experiences under the control of some ingenious technician scientist (benevolent or malevolent according to taste). For if you were such a brain, then, provided that the scientist is successful, nothing in your experience could possibly reveal that you were; for your experience is *ex hypothesi* identical with that of something which is not a brain in a vat. Since you have only your own experience to appeal to, and that experience is the same in either situation, nothing can reveal to you which situation is the actual one.[2]

If you cannot know whether you are in the real world or in the world of a computer simulation, you cannot be sure that your beliefs about the world are true. And, what was even more frightening to Descartes, in this kind of scenario it seems that your ability to reason is no safer than the deliverances of the senses: the evil demon or malicious scientist could be ensuring that your reasoning is just as flawed as your perceptions.

As you have probably already guessed, there is no easy way out of this philosophical problem (or at least there is no easy *philosophical* way out). Philosophers have proposed a dizzying variety of "solutions" to this kind of skepticism but, as with many philosophical problems, there is nothing

---

2. Jonathan Dancy, *Introduction to Contemporary Epistemology* (Blackwell 1985), p. 10.

close to unanimous agreement regarding how the puzzle should be solved.

Descartes's own way out of his evil-demon skepticism was to first argue that one cannot genuinely doubt the existence of oneself. He pointed out that all thinking presupposes a thinker: even in doubting, you realize that there must at least be a self which is doing the doubting. (Thus Descartes's most famous line: "I think, therefore I am.") He then went on to claim that, in addition to our innate idea of self, each of us has an idea of God as an all-powerful, all-good, and infinite being implanted in our minds and that this idea could only have come *from* God. Since this shows us that an all-good God does exist, we can have confidence that he would not allow us to be so drastically deceived about the nature of our perceptions and their relationship to reality. While Descartes's argument for the existence of the self has been tremendously influential and is still actively debated, few philosophers have followed him in accepting his particular theistic solution to skepticism about the external world.

One of the more interesting contemporary challenges to the kind of radical skepticism suggested by Descartes has come from philosopher Hilary Putnam. His point is not so much to defend our ordinary claims to knowledge as to question whether the brain-in-a-vat hypothesis is coherent, given certain plausible assumptions about how our language refers to objects in the world. He asks us to consider a variation on the standard brain-in-a-vat story that is uncannily similar to the situation described in *The Matrix*:

> Instead of having just one brain in a vat, we could imagine that all human beings (perhaps all sentient beings) are brains in a vat (or nervous systems in a vat in case some beings with just nervous systems count as "sentient"). Of course, the evil scientist would have to be outside? or would he? Perhaps there is no evil scientist, perhaps (though this is absurd) the universe just happens to consist of automatic machinery tending a vat full of brains and nervous systems. This time let us suppose that the automatic machinery is programmed to give us all a *collective* hallucination, rather than a number of separate unrelated hallucinations. Thus, when I seem to myself to be talking to you, you seem to yourself to be hearing my words.... I want now to ask a question which will seem very silly and obvious (at least to

some people, including some very sophisticated philosophers), but which will take us to real philosophical depths rather quickly. Suppose this whole story were actually true. Could we, if we were brains in a vat in this way, *say* or *think* that we were?[3]

Putnam's surprising answer is that we cannot coherently think that we are brains in vats, and so skepticism of that kind can never really get off the ground. While it is difficult to do justice to Putnam's ingenious argument in a short summary, his point is roughly as follows: not everything that goes through our heads is a genuine thought, and far from everything we say is a meaningful utterance. Sometimes we get confused or think in an incoherent manner; sometimes we say things that are simply nonsense. Of course, we don't always realize at the time that we aren't making sense; sometimes we earnestly believe we are saying (or thinking) something meaningful. High on nitrous oxide, the philosopher William James was convinced he was having profound insights into the nature of reality; he was convinced that his thoughts were both sensical and important. Upon sobering up and looking at the notebook in which he had written his drug-addled thoughts, he saw only gibberish.

Just as I might say a sentence that is nonsense, I might also use a name or a general term that is meaningless in the sense that it fails to hook up to the world. Philosophers talk of such a term as "failing to refer" to an object. In order to successfully refer when we use language, there must be an appropriate relationship between the speaker and the object referred to. If a dog playing on the beach manages to scrawl the word "Ed" in the sand with a stick, few would want to claim that the dog actually meant to refer to someone named Ed. Presumably the dog doesn't know anyone named Ed, and even if he did, he wouldn't be capable of intending to write Ed's name in the sand. The point of such an example is that words do not refer to objects "magically" or intrinsically: certain conditions must be met in the world in order for us to accept that a given written or spoken word has any meaning and whether it actually refers to anything at all.

3. Hilary Putnam, *Reason, Truth, and History* (Cambridge University Press 1981); see appendix, pp. 317–318.

Putnam claims that one condition which is crucial for successful reference is that there be an appropriate causal connection between the object referred to and the speaker referring. Specifying exactly what should count as "appropriate" here is a notoriously difficult task, but we can get some idea of the kind of thing required by considering cases in which reference fails through an inappropriate connection: if someone unfamiliar with the film *The Matrix* manages to blurt out the word "Neo" while sneezing, few would be inclined to think that this person has actually *referred* to the character Neo. The kind of causal connection between the speaker and the object referred to (Neo) is just not in place. For reference to succeed, it can't be simply accidental that the name was uttered. (Another way to think about it: the sneezer would have uttered "Neo" even if the film *The Matrix* had never been made.)

The difficulty, according to Putnam, in coherently supposing the brain-in-a-vat story to be true is that brains raised in such an environment could not successfully refer to genuine brains, or vats, or anything else in the real world. Consider the example of some people who lived their entire lives in the Matrix: when they talk of "chickens," they don't actually refer to real *chickens*; at best they refer to the computer representations of chickens that have been sent to their brains. Similarly, when they talk of human bodies being trapped in pods and fed data by the Matrix, they don't successfully refer to real bodies or pods. They can't refer to physical bodies in the real world because they cannot have the appropriate causal connection to such objects. Thus, if someone were to utter the sentence "I am simply a body stuck in a pod somewhere being fed sensory information by a computer," that sentence would itself be necessarily false. If the person is in fact not trapped in the Matrix, then the sentence is straightforwardly false. If the person is trapped in the Matrix, then he can't successfully refer to real human bodies when he utters the term "human body," and so it appears that under this circumstance, his statement must *also* be false. Such a person seems thus doubly trapped: incapable of knowing that he is in the Matrix and even incapable of successfully expressing the thought that he might be in the Matrix! (Could this be why at one point Morpheus tells Neo that "no one can be told what the Matrix is"?)

Putnam's argument is controversial, but it is noteworthy because it shows that the kind of situation described in *The Matrix* raises not just the expected philosophical issues about knowledge and skepticism, but more general issues regarding meaning, language, and the relationship between the mind and the world.

III. The Value of Reality: Cypher and the Experience Machine

CYPHER: You know, I know that this steak doesn't exist. I know when I put it in my mouth, the Matrix is telling my brain that it is juicy and delicious. After nine years, do you know what I've realized?

CYPHER: Ignorance is bliss.

AGENT SMITH: Then we have a deal?

CYPHER: I don't want to remember nothing. Nothing! You understand? And I want to be rich. Someone important. Like an actor. You can do that, right?

AGENT SMITH: Whatever you want, Mr. Reagan.

Cypher is not a nice guy, but is he an unreasonable guy? Is he right to want to get re-inserted into the Matrix? Many want to say no, but giving reasons for why his choice is a bad one is not an easy task. After all, so long as his experiences will be pleasant, how can his situation be worse than the inevitably crappy life he would lead outside of the Matrix? What could matter beyond the quality of his experience? Remember, once he's back in, living his fantasy life, he won't even know he made the deal. What he doesn't know can't hurt him, right?

Is feeling good the only thing that has value in itself? The question of whether only conscious experience can ultimately matter is one that has been explored in depth by several contemporary philosophers. In the course of discussing this issue in his 1974 book *Anarchy, State, and Utopia*, Robert Nozick introduced a thought-experiment that has become a staple of introductory philosophy classes everywhere. It is known as "the experience machine":

> Suppose there were an experience machine that would give you any ex-
> perience you desired. Superduper neuropsychologists could stimulate your
> brain so that you would think and feel you were writing a great novel, or

making a friend, or reading an interesting book. All the time you would be floating in a tank, with electrodes attached to your brain. Should you plug into this machine for life, preprogramming your life's experiences? ... Of course, while in the tank you won't know that you're there; you'll think it's all actually happening. Others can also plug in to have the experiences they want, so there's no need to stay unplugged to serve them. (Ignore problems such as who will service the machines if everyone plugs in.) Would you plug in? *What else can matter to us, other than how our lives feel from the inside?*[4]

Nozick goes on to argue that other things do matter to us: for instance, that we actually do certain things, as opposed to simply having the experience of doing them. Also, he points out that we value being (and becoming) certain kinds of people. I don't just want to have the experience of being a decent person, I want to actually *be* a decent person. Finally, Nozick argues that we value contact with reality in itself, independent of any benefits such contact may bring through pleasant experience: we want to know we are experiencing the real thing. In sum, Nozick thinks that it matters to most of us, often in a rather deep way, that we be the authors of our lives and that our lives involve interacting with the world, and he thinks that the fact that most people would not choose to enter into such an experience machine demonstrates that they do value these other things. As he puts it: "We learn that something matters to us in addition to experience by imagining an experience machine and then realizing that we would not use it" (311).

While Nozick's description of his machine is vague, it appears that there is at least one important difference between it and the simulated world of *The Matrix*. Nozick implies that people hooked up to the experience machine will not be able to exercise their agency—they become the passive recipients of pre-programmed experiences. This apparent loss of free will is disturbing to many people, and it might be distorting people's reactions to the case and clouding the issue of whether they value contact with reality per se. The Matrix seems to be set up in such a way

---

4. Robert Nozick, *Anarchy, State, and Utopia* (Basic 1974); see appendix, p. 310. Further citations will be to this appendix and appear in the text.

that one can enter it and retain one's free will and capacity for decision making, and perhaps this makes it a significantly more attractive option than the experience machine that Nozick describes.

Nonetheless, a loss of freedom is not the only disturbing aspect of Nozick's story. As he points out, we seem to mourn the loss of contact with the real world as well. Even if a modified experience machine is presented to us, one which allows us to keep our free will but enter into an entirely virtual world, many would still object that permanently going into such a machine involves the loss of something valuable.

Cypher and his philosophical comrades are likely to be unmoved by such observations. So what if most people are hung-up on "reality" and would turn down the offer to permanently enter an experience machine? Most people might be wrong. All their responses might show is that such people are superstitious, or irrational, or otherwise confused. Maybe they think something could go wrong with the machines, or maybe they keep forgetting that while in the machine they will no longer be aware of their choice to enter the machine. Perhaps those hesitant to plug in don't realize that they value being active in the real world only because normally that is the most reliable way for them to acquire the pleasant experience that they value in itself. In other words, perhaps our free will and our capacity to interact with reality are means to a further end; they matter to us because they allow us access to what really matters: pleasant conscious experience. To think the reverse, that reality and freedom have value in themselves (what philosophers sometimes call *nonderivative* or *intrinsic value*), is simply to put the cart before the horse. After all, Cypher could reply, what would be so great about the capacity to freely make decisions or the ability to be in the real world if neither of these things allowed us to feel good?

Peter Unger has taken on these kinds of objections in his discussion of "experience inducers." He acknowledges that there is a strong temptation when in a certain frame of mind to agree with this kind of Cypheresque reasoning, but he argues that this is a temptation we ought to try to resist. Cypher's vision of value is too easy and too simplistic. We are inclined to think that only conscious experience can really matter in part because we fall into the grip of a particular picture of what values *must* be like, and this in turn leads us to stop paying attention to our actual values. We make ourselves blind to the subtlety and complexity of our values, and we then find it hard to understand how something that doesn't affect our consciousness could sensibly matter to us. If we stop and reflect on what we really do care about, however, we come across some surprisingly everyday examples that don't sit easily with Cypher's claims:

> Consider life insurance. To be sure, some among the insured may strongly believe that, if they die before their dependents do, they will still observe their beloved dependents, perhaps from a heaven on high. But others among the insured have no significant belief to that effect.... Still, we all pay our premiums. In my case, this is because, even if I will never experience anything that happens to them, I still want things to go better, rather than worse, for my dependents. No doubt, I am rational in having this concern.[5]

As Unger goes on to point out, it seems contrived to chalk up all examples of people purchasing life insurance to cases in which someone is simply trying to benefit (while alive) from the favorable impression such a purchase might make on the dependents. In many cases it seems ludicrous to deny that "what motivates us, of course, is our great concern for our dependents' future, whether we experience their future or not" (302). This is not a proof that such concern is rational, but it does show that incidents in which we intrinsically value things other than our own conscious experience might be more widespread than we are at first liable to think. (Other examples include the value we place on not being deceived or lied to—the importance of this value doesn't seem to be completely exhausted by our concern that we might one day become aware of the lies and deception.)

Most of us care about a lot of things independently of the experiences that those things provide for us. The realization that we value things other than pleasant conscious experience should lead us to at least wonder if the legitimacy of this kind of value hasn't been too hastily dismissed by Cypher and his ilk. After all, once we see how widespread and commonplace our other nonderivative concerns are, the insistence that

---

5. Peter Unger, *Identity, Consciousness, and Value* (Oxford University Press 1990), p. 301. Further citations will be in the text.

conscious experience is the *only* thing that has value in itself can come to seem downright peculiar. If purchasing life insurance seems like a rational thing to do, why shouldn't the desire to experience reality (rather than some illusory simulation) be similarly rational? Perhaps the best test of the rationality of our most basic values is actually whether they, taken together, form a consistent and coherent network of attachments and concerns. (Do they make sense in light of each other and in light of our beliefs about the world and ourselves?) It isn't obvious that valuing interaction with the real world fails this kind of test.

Of course, pointing out that the value I place on living in the real world coheres well with my other values and beliefs will not quiet the defender of Cypher, as he will be quick to respond that the fact that my values all cohere doesn't show that they are all justified. Maybe I hold a bunch of exquisitely consistent but thoroughly irrational values.

The quest for some further justification of my basic values might be misguided, however. Explanations have to come to an end somewhere, as Ludwig Wittgenstein once famously remarked. Maybe the right response to a demand for justification here is to point out that the same demand can be made to Cypher: "Just what justifies your exclusive concern with pleasant conscious experience?" It seems as though nothing does—if such concern is justified, it must be somehow self-justifying, but if that is possible, why shouldn't our concerns for other people and our desire to live in the real world also be self-justifying? If those can also be self-justifying, then maybe what we don't experience should matter to us, and perhaps what we don't know *can* hurt us. . . .

Further Reading

Putnam's essay "Brains in a Vat," Nozick's writings on the experience machine, and the first two meditations of Descartes can all be found in the appendix to this volume. Those seeking to go further should certainly begin with the rest of Descartes's *Meditations*. Currently, the best edition is *The Philosophical Writings of Descartes*, trans. John Cottingham, Robert Stoothoff, and Dugald Murdoch (Cambridge University Press 1984). A solid and comprehensive introduction to epistemology is Jonathan Dancy's *Introduction to Contemporary Epistemology* (Blackwell 1985). For slightly more advanced treatments, I recommend Barry Stroud's *The Significance of Philosophical Scepticism* (Oxford University Press 1984) and P. F. Strawson's *Skepticism and Naturalism: Some Varieties* (Columbia University Press 1983). On the question of the justification of values, my comments here draw on the insights of Mark Johnston in "Reasons and Reductionism" (*Philosophical Review* 1992), Thomas Nagel's essay "Death" (*Nous* 1970), and Peter Unger's *Identity, Consciousness, and Value* (Oxford University Press 1990).

Tim Mawson

3

MORPHEUS AND BERKELEY ON REALITY

I. How Morpheus Sees Reality

What is real? How do you define "real"? If you're talking about what you can feel, what you can smell, what you can taste and see, then real is simply electrical signals interpreted by your brain.

—Morpheus

Despite this rather opaque comment, Morpheus actually relies on a pretty straightforward understanding of what it is that makes something real as opposed to unreal. He relies on this understanding when he classifies his hovercraft, the *Nebuchadnezzar*, deserted and devastated cities on the surface of the Earth; and the populous and thriving (at least until the end of the second film) city of Zion near its center as real. And he relies on it when he classifies the world of the Matrix; what he calls "the Construct," the white world in which he first explains the nature of the Matrix to Neo; and the virtual arena in which they first spar as unreal. He relies on it to make sense of his general mission as being to wake people up from unreality and into reality. And he relies on it to make sense of his particular mission as being to do this for Neo, the person whom he believes will be able to destroy the unreality of the Matrix for good. In so relying on it, Morpheus actually assumes that there's an important difference between those electrical signals that are fed into our brains by computers when we're floating in our tanks and those that he experiences when, for example, he's sitting with his crew in the cockpit of the *Nebuchadnezzar*. If Morpheus thought that reality was simply a matter of having electrical signals interpreted by your brain (however these signals got there and however little the interpretations we gave them resembled anything outside themselves), then he'd think that people were just as much in touch with reality when they were floating in their tanks as he was when he was sitting in the cockpit of the *Nebuchadnezzar*. In both cases, there are electrical signals being interpreted by brains. Yet of course Morpheus doesn't think that the experiences people have in their tanks are putting them in touch with reality, whereas he does think that the experiences he's having as he sits in the cockpit of the *Nebuchadnezzar* are putting him in touch with reality. So he can't believe that reality is simply a matter of having electrical signals interpreted by your brain; he must believe something else. In fact, he believes what the rest of us believe. What's this?

To put it simply, Morpheus believes that the real is that which exists exterior to our minds; the unreal, by contrast, is that which exists only in our minds. This is the understanding which guides him in classifying, for example, the cockpit of the *Nebuchadnezzar* as real and the world of the Construct as unreal. He thinks that his ship is there even when nobody's experiencing it; he doesn't think that the television he shows Neo in the Construct is there even when nobody's experiencing it, when nobody is "loaded up" into that particular virtual world. The *Nebuchadnezzar* exists in its own right, independently of our ideas about it. It's real. The television exists only in the minds of those suitably "loaded up." It's unreal.

We share with Morpheus the assumption that reality is a matter of being part of the mind-independent world, which is just as well. Otherwise, we'd never understand what was going on in the films. We'd never understand what the difference was between being in the Matrix and being out of it. We'd never understand what it was Morpheus was trying to do. We wouldn't enjoy the films at all. What other assumptions about reality do we share with Morpheus?

As he shows in the passage quoted above, Morpheus assumes that the real world causes things to happen in our bodies, happenings that give rise to electrical signals that are ultimately interpreted by our brains, thus forming our ideas about that world. He assumes that this process occurs whether or not we're in the Matrix. If we're in the Matrix, then the world is causing things to happen in our bodies via a system of pipes fed into our nervous systems; it's the signals coming down these pipes that find their way into our brains for interpretation. If we're in the real world, then the world is causing things to happen in our bodies via light landing on our eyes, sound waves reaching our ears, and so on. It's the signals caused by these changes that find their way into our brains for interpretation. Why is it that we—with Morpheus—think that in the one case these signals are putting us in touch with reality and in the other case they're not? What's the important difference between signals finding their way into our bodies in one way and their finding their way into our bodies in the other?

It's not obvious how Morpheus would answer this question. He hasn't addressed it. That's not his fault. As you know if you've seen the films, he's been kept quite busy with other things. Philosophers have characteristically had more time (and fewer Agents) on their hands. Thus they've pondered it a bit more. One answer that has appealed to many philosophers over the ages is this: these signals are putting us in touch with reality only if the ideas that they give rise to resemble the things that cause them; if the ideas these signals give rise to do not resemble the things that cause them, then they're not putting us in touch with reality. For example, if the signal which, once interpreted, becomes Morpheus's idea that "the control board of the *Nebuchadnezzar* is just in front of me" is caused in him by the control board of the *Nebuchadnezzar*'s being just in front of him, then this idea resembles the thing that's causing it and thus is putting him in touch with reality. On the other hand, if the signal which, once interpreted, becomes his idea that "there's a television just in front of me" is not caused in him by a television that's just in front of him, but is in fact caused in him by an unimaginably complex computer, then it doesn't resemble the thing that's causing it and thus is not putting him in touch with reality. This seems like a pretty straightforward understanding of what it is that makes an idea put us in touch with reality. I'm going to assume that Morpheus and we share this understanding too.

Unless we seriously consider the possibility that we might be in the Matrix or some such, we won't find reason to question a comforting view that we will then think of ourselves as basing on these assumptions. The comforting view I have in mind is the view that almost all of our ideas pretty closely resemble the objects that cause them; thus they do put us in touch with reality. Consider, for example, your idea of the page in front of you from which you take yourself to be reading this. Your idea of this page represents it as having certain qualities—a particular shape, size, color, and so on—and you have the comforting belief that the thing which is causing this idea in you resembles your idea in having these qualities. You believe that there really is a page with the shape, size, color, and so on that your idea suggests. You believe that it's this page reflecting light of certain wavelengths—light which lands on your eyes, giving rise to electrical signals that are ultimately interpreted by your brain—that forms your idea of it, an idea which thus resembles its cause. You don't believe that your idea of the page is caused in you by signals originating from something entirely different from a page—an unimaginably complex computer, for example. If it were, then your idea of the page wouldn't resemble the thing that was causing it at all, and then it wouldn't be putting you in touch with reality at all. I suggest that we hold this comforting view of the way our ideas get into our heads for the vast majority of our ideas. What's comforting about it is that it's the view that we're basically in touch with reality; we're not in an inescapable illusion.

Only very rarely do we think that we might have an idea of an object that's caused in us by something that's not very much like the idea it causes. Maybe you've been to a magic show where, during his act, the magician made a ghostlike form appear in a puff of smoke and then—apparently—float in thin air just ahead of you. Initially perhaps you thought that there really was such a being, but, on reflection, you probably decided that your idea as it had been caused in you did not in fact resemble what was out there doing the causing. You decided that there was probably not in reality an ethereal floating figure causing an idea in you that resembled it. Rather, you concluded that there was a mannequin hanging on a wire causing an idea of an ethereal floating figure in you, an idea of yours which thus didn't closely resemble reality at all. But such occasions are infrequent. Unless we seriously consider the possibility that we are in the Matrix or some such, we will hold the comforting thought that veridical experiences are the norm, illusory ones the rare exceptions.

But, if we once seriously consider the possibility that we're in the Matrix or some such, this comforting thought is threatened. If you're in the Matrix, then you've never had a veridical experience in your life;

rather than illusions being rare exceptions, illusions are the norm. If you're in the Matrix, then the idea you have of the page from which you currently take yourself to be reading, for example, is not in fact caused in you by a page at all—by an object which resembles your idea of it pretty closely. An unimaginably complex computer causes it in you. So your idea doesn't resemble its cause; it's not putting you in touch with reality. What goes for your idea of the page goes for your ideas of everything else you take yourself to have encountered. If you're in the Matrix, then all of the objects you take to exist exterior to your mind don't really exist at all. Your ideas of them—the "electrical signals interpreted by your brain" as Morpheus might put it—are still there, but the things they're ideas of aren't there; they're not real. You're living in an inescapable illusion.

The worry that all of our ideas about the world might be mistaken only makes sense on the assumption that we share with Morpheus that reality is independent of our ideas about it and thus that there's something outside themselves by reference to which our ideas may go wrong. Only on this assumption does it make sense to worry that our ideas about reality might go wrong by failing to resemble the things that cause them. But, having made the assumption that there's a mind-independent reality on the one hand and our ideas about it on the other, the worry that the latter might not resemble the former is rationally inescapable for anyone who thinks through the assumption's implications. To be in a position from which we could have reasons to remove the worry, we'd have to be able to climb outside our own minds and perceive reality on the one hand and our ideas about it on the other. Then we could compare the two and see whether or not the latter resembled the former. If we could climb to such a position, we could then say something like, "I see the world as it exists independently of my perception of it over there, and I see my ideas about the world over there; comparing them, I see that they resemble one another." But we can never climb outside our own minds, see things from a point of view that's not our own. We must always look at the world through the spectacles of our ideas of it. So we can never justify our predilection for adopting the comforting view that most of our ideas resemble the mind-independent things that cause them, rather than the worrying Matrix alternative: that they don't. Once we think about the assumptions that I've suggested we share with Morpheus, we realize that we can never know whether or not we're in the real world or an unreal world. And we shouldn't think that Morpheus is any better off than we are in this regard. For perhaps Morpheus has never in fact sat in the cockpit of the *Nebuchadnezzar* and looked at its control board, for perhaps the *Nebuchadnezzar* doesn't exist. Perhaps it's a computer simulation too. How could he know?

Just as you can have plays within plays, so you can have virtual realities within virtual realities. Perhaps, even when he thinks he's sitting in the cockpit of the *Nebuchadnezzar*, Morpheus is still in a virtual-reality world; it's just a virtual reality within a virtual reality, or perhaps it's a virtual reality within a virtual reality, within a virtual reality. In any case, Morpheus, Neo, Trinity, and the rest should conclude that whatever experiences they seem to have, they can't know if they've escaped from the Matrix. For all they know, they might each still be floating in their tanks being fed illusory experiences to make them think that they've got out of their tanks, met up with one another, and are—at last—in touch with the real world. If you were the Architect, wouldn't this be the sort of trick you'd play on them?

II. How Berkeley Sees Reality

It is indeed an opinion strangely prevailing amongst men, that houses, mountains, rivers, and in a word all sensible objects have an existence natural or real, distinct from their being perceived by the understanding. But with how great an assurance and acquiescence soever this principle may be entertained in the world; yet whoever shall find in his heart to call it in question, may, if I mistake not, perceive it to involve a manifest contradiction.

—George Berkeley

George Berkeley was an Irish philosopher. Born in 1685, he is most famous for works written while he was still in his twenties: *An Essay towards a New Theory of Vision* (1709), *A Treatise Concerning the Principles of Human Knowledge* (1710), and *Three Dialogues between Hylas and Philonous* (1713). After writing these works, he traveled widely in Europe and America and had been made a bishop (of Cloyne, a diocese in southern Ireland) before he died in Oxford in 1753.

Berkeley's philosophy might seem to offer us a radical solution to the problem with which we were left at the end of the previous section. To appreciate how this solution might work, it'll help if we go back over why it is we found ourselves with the problem. It was a problem that was generated for us by the way of looking at things that I suggested that we shared with Morpheus. I suggested in the previous section that we believe, with Morpheus, that there's some mind-independent reality out there that's causing our ideas and that our ideas could in principle resemble. And I suggested that we believe that if and only if our ideas do in fact resemble the things in this mind-independent reality that cause them do they put us in touch with this reality. If they don't, they're illusions. This way of looking at things enabled us to understand the division between the reality of the world of the *Nebuchadnezzar* and the unreality of the world of the Matrix. When Morpheus sits in the cockpit of the *Nebuchadnezzar*, his ideas are formed in him by things that they resemble; he's in touch with reality. (This is assuming of course that this isn't actually a virtual reality within a virtual reality.) When he's loaded up into the Matrix, his ideas are formed in him by things that they don't resemble at all; he's entered the world of illusion. This way of looking at things generated an insurmountable problem for him and us: how can we know if *any* of our ideas *do* in fact resemble the things that cause them? How can Morpheus know that the *Nebuchadnezzar* isn't a virtual reality within a virtual reality? We can't and he can't, because people can't ever see the world except through the spectacles of their ideas about it. And if we can't know that, then—because it's resemblance between our ideas and reality that makes our ideas put us in touch with reality—we can't know whether or not we've ever been in touch with the real world at all. We'll have to conclude that, for all we know, we could be living in a permanent illusion. We'll have to conclude that Morpheus can't be justified in thinking that the *Nebuchadnezzar* isn't a virtual reality within a virtual reality. What to do?

Berkeley's philosophy seems to offer us an answer to this problem because it rejects one part of the theory that generates it. Berkeley's philosophy is most famous for something it denies: it denies that there is a mind-independent world. Berkeley's solution to the problem we're facing then wouldn't be so much a solution to the problem as a *disso-lution* of the way of thinking that leads to it. As a way of sketching the outlines of his position, let's look at a couple of the arguments that lead Berkeley to adopt it.

One of the arguments that takes Berkeley to his radical position is this: we believe that ideas can in principle resemble things in the real world. For example, Morpheus believes that his idea of the cockpit of the *Nebuchadnezzar* resembles the cockpit of the *Nebuchadnezzar*; thus, he believes, it puts him in touch with reality. But if Morpheus is right about the nature of ideas, then his idea of the cockpit of the *Nebuchadnezzar* is just an electrical signal interpreted by his brain, and an electrical signal in his brain doesn't resemble a small room with chairs, from which one can control a hovercraft, at all. It resembles, well, just other electrical signals in his brain and electrical signals in the brains of others. Ideas, it seems, cannot actually resemble anything other than ideas. But if it's only by resembling a thing that an idea can manage to put us in touch with that thing, it follows that we cannot have ideas about anything other than ideas. All we can ever think about, or thus make reference to in our metaphysical theories, are ideas. So, if we think that ideas can only get to be of the real world by resembling things in the real world, then we should conclude that, because ideas can't resemble anything except other ideas, the real world must just be a construction built out of our ideas. Berkeley's philosophy is thus often called *idealism*: there's no mind-independent world; there are just ideas. As Berkeley puts it, "[I]t is impossible for me to conceive in my thoughts any sensible thing or object distinct from the sensation or perception of it," and so any alternative to idealism is, quite literally, inconceivable (*Principles of Human Knowledge* [Penguin, 1988], 55). The truth of idealism is, according to Berkeley, "so near and obvious to the mind, that a man need only open his eyes to see" it (55). Berkeley takes Morpheus's question, "How do we define 'real'?" and gives it a quite different answer from the one that I've argued that we give it. Rather than saying that the real is just whatever it is that exists independently of our having ideas of it, he says that the real is our ideas. That's all that "real" can mean. Let's have a look at another argument he uses for his position.

How else could we define "real"—attach meaning to the term—except by linking it to something in our minds? There's no way. And what else do we have in our minds but ideas? Nothing. So, if "real" means anything at all, it can only mean some sort of construction of ideas. And once we realize that we must define "reality" as we must define everything else, namely, in terms of our ideas, then we realize that we can't make sense of "reality existing independently of our ideas." To posit that there might be a reality independent of our ideas would be to posit that there might be something that existed even though none of the things we use to define it—our ideas—existed, which is, as Berkeley puts it in the quotation above, "a manifest contradiction." As he goes on, "For what are the forementioned objects but the things we perceive by sense, and what do we perceive besides our own ideas or sensations; and is it not plainly repugnant that any one of these or any combination of them should exist unperceived?" (*Principles of Human Knowledge*, 54).

It might thus look as if Berkeley's philosophy has solved—or rather dissolved—the problem with which we were wrestling at the end of the previous section. Once we've gotten rid of the notion that reality is independent of our ideas, it looks as if we can get rid of the worry that our ideas might go wrong by failing to resemble that mind-independent reality too. It looks as if that worry can no longer make sense. If Berkeley's right, it doesn't make sense to think that one's ideas might fail to resemble a mind-independent reality because the notion of a mind-independent reality doesn't make sense—it's a manifest contradiction. One might as well worry that one's ideas might fail to resemble a four-sided triangle. The worry that our ideas might not be putting us in touch with reality was premised on the assumption that reality was something other than our ideas about it, and it was only if our ideas resembled it that they put us in touch with it. If reality *is* just our ideas about it, then of course there's no way that our ideas could fail to resemble reality. So there's no way our ideas could fail to put us in touch with reality. If we're all in the Matrix, so what? The page you see is still real because being a real page is just a matter of being a set of page-like ideas, and a set of page-like ideas certainly exists. Have a look at the room in which you take yourself to be reading this page. You've now got a set of room-like ideas. Well, according to Berkeley, being a real room is just a matter of being such a set of ideas, so the room in which you take yourself to be reading this is real too. Remember the conversation within the Matrix between Cypher and Agent Smith, where Cypher says, holding up a bit of steak on a fork, "I know that this steak doesn't exist." Well, he's wrong. Being a real bit of steak is just being a set of steaklike ideas in someone's mind, and the Matrix is causing a lot of steaklike ideas in Cypher's mind. There's no need for you to worry about the Matrix when you think you're looking at a page or for him to worry about it when he thinks he's eating a steak then. If it seems real, it is real. This page seems real; this page is real. The steak seems real; the steak is real. You and he can return to the comforting view that your ideas are putting you in touch with reality because you now know that reality is just a matter of your ideas about it. Enough said? Sadly not.

Berkeley doesn't actually think that something's seeming to you to be real is sufficient to make it real. He'd agree with Cypher here and say that the steak is not real. He thinks that ideas can in fact go wrong, not by failing to resemble a mind-independent world (that wouldn't make sense) but by failing to resemble other ideas. He says this because he wants to allow that there can be illusions. And we'll want to allow this too. Remember the magic show, where you had an idea of an ethereal floating figure, an idea which you thought on reflection was a skillfully created illusion. The example of the magic show reminds us that we do want to say that sometimes our ideas don't put us in touch with reality, so we'll have to have some way of understanding what it is in virtue of which they do and what it is in virtue of which they don't. It won't do to say that all ideas are of real things because it's sufficient for a thing to be real that someone has an idea of it. That's not sufficient. People have ideas of ghosts and all sorts of other things that aren't real. So Berkeley's got to come up with a way of explaining why some ideas don't manage to be of real things even though reality is just a construction of ideas. He's lost the ability to explain illusions in terms of ideas failing to resemble things in the mind-independent world because he's lost the mind-independent world. So what he does is tell us that illusions are illusions not because they fail to resemble a mind-independent reality but because they fail to resemble other ideas.

Take Macbeth "seeing" the ghost of Banquo seated at the table before him as an example. Berkeley would be the first to admit that this ghost is not real. Why? Not because the idea in Macbeth's mind doesn't resemble anything out there in the mind-independent world (Berkeley's just said that to say that wouldn't make sense). It's not real because the idea in Macbeth's mind doesn't resemble any ideas in other people's minds. As his guests look at him raving, none of them can see the figure to which he points. The idea of Banquo's bloody form exists only in Macbeth's mind, not in anyone else's. Ergo, it's an illusion. An idea's putting one in touch with reality is then a matter of the idea resembling ideas in other people's minds. A "hallucination" that everyone could see, taste, smell, touch, and hear would be no hallucination at all—it would be real. A hallucination—however vivid in the mind of the person who has it—that doesn't resemble ideas in anyone else's mind, that no other people think they can see, taste, smell, touch, and hear, would—by contrast—be a genuine hallucination, that is, an illusion. It looks then as if Berkeley is saying that objects are just collections of ideas in people's minds; ideas that are shared by more than one person are realities; ideas that only appear in one person's mind are "unrealities," or illusions.

If this were what he was saying, Berkeley's philosophy might still seem to offer some hope of defeating the Matrix worry. If there are millions of people in the Matrix, all having the same ideas, then that's enough for the things they're having ideas of to be real things. Remember, on this version of Berkeley, the city we see Morpheus moving around in within the Matrix, for example, is just a collection of ideas in people's minds. The difference between a real city and an unreal city is that a real city is constructed out of ideas that resemble one another and are being had by a number of people greater than one. An unreal city is a construction of ideas in the mind of just one person. If we're in the Matrix, then there's a large number of people all having ideas that resemble one another: the Matrix is an interactive virtual environment populated by millions. So, the world of the Matrix is real. The world of the *Nebuchadnezzar* is real too. Each is a world where there's a large number of people having ideas that resemble the ideas being had by other people, and that's enough for both worlds to be real.

Obviously, this isn't the way Morpheus sees things or the way we see things. But it might be rather like the way Cypher comes to see things by the end of the first film. There he has a conversation with Trinity where he disagrees with her about which is the real world. He says that the world of the Matrix "can be more real than this world." (He's obviously shifted ground since his discussion with Agent Smith concerning the bit of steak.) Unfortunately, we don't get to hear too much more about the view to which he's now been drawn because, before he can tell us and—arguably more important—before he can kill Neo, Tank fries him to death with a large electrical discharge (as far as I am aware, this is the first time a discourse on metaphysics has been so terminated). In any case, we don't feel too much sympathy for Cypher, and one reason—perhaps not the main reason—is that we cling with Morpheus, Trinity, and Neo to the view that the world of the Matrix is unreal and the world of the *Nebuchadnezzar* is real, whatever abortive attempts Cypher might make to convince people otherwise. But perhaps we're wrong to think this way. Perhaps we should be more sympathetic to a later-Cypher-type view. If reality is just a communal construction of ideas, then we should say that because each world involves a community constructing objects out of ideas, each is equally real. Or, if the size of the community counts, then, because the Matrix construction is a set of ideas being had by more people than the *Nebuchadnezzar* construction, the Matrix is indeed *more* real, as the later Cypher says. But even if we could get ourselves to believe something along these lines, it wouldn't actually solve the problem with which we were left at the end of the first section. While on the view that as long as there are two or more people having ideas that resemble one another, that's enough for the thing about which they're having ideas to be real, we can know that if our ideas resemble ideas in the mind of someone else, then they're putting us in touch with reality, but we still can't know whether or not our ideas do resemble ideas in the mind of anyone else. Each one of us might think, "Maybe I'm the only one still hooked up to the Matrix, everyone else having escaped and having been replaced as I seem to experience them by programs. If so, then I'm the only one having ideas like mine. Everyone else is having a whole different set of ideas. If so, then—because an illusion is just an idea that doesn't resemble anyone else's—as the last one in the Matrix, I'm now in an illusory world." The last person out of the Matrix, in virtue of being the odd one out in terms of the ideas she happens to be having, will be missing out on reality even if reality is a communal construction of ideas.

In other words, even if we accepted that being real was just a matter of being an idea shared by at least two people, we'd still be left with the problem of how we can know that we're not suffering from an inescapable illusion because we'd still not know whether any idea that we had was in fact shared by anyone else.

In any case, it's not, according to Berkeley, a matter of the number of people having the same ideas. Why does he think that? Because he wants to allow that you can have an idea of something and that thing be real even if no other human has ever had or will ever have an idea of it. For example, suppose you're on the main deck of the *Nebuchadnezzar* one day, looking at the computer screens and sipping on the local home brew. You notice a previously unobserved speck of dirt on one of the screens; you brush it off and promptly forget all about it. If so, then your idea of this speck of dirt is an idea that doesn't resemble any idea any other human has ever had or will ever have. Yet still, we'd want to say, your idea is an idea of a real speck of dirt. We don't want every unique experience to have to be classified as ipso facto an illusory one. So we can't make the difference between an idea putting you in touch with reality and one not putting you in touch with reality be the difference between an idea resembling one had by other humans and one not resembling any had by other humans. Here, Berkeley brings in God. You had to expect that he'd bring God in somewhere; he was a bishop after all. Actually, says Berkeley, your idea of this speck of dirt wouldn't be a hallucination even if it didn't resemble an idea had by any other human if it did in fact resemble an idea in God's mind. So, according to the real Berkeley, getting your ideas in touch with reality is getting your ideas to resemble those in the mind of God.

But here again the problem with which we were left at the end of the first section resurfaces. There's no mind-independent reality, but there is a human-mind-independent reality—there are the ideas that exist in the mind of God. And, according to Berkeley, getting your ideas in touch with reality is getting them to resemble these ideas. But how can you ever know that your ideas resemble ideas in the mind of God? Again, to answer the problem, one would have to be able to step outside one's ideas, look at one's ideas on the one hand and God's ideas on the other, and then compare them for resemblance. But this is just impossible.

Berkeley's philosophy doesn't seem to have gotten us out of the problem at all.

So, even if you accept with Berkeley that there's no mind-independent reality because all that's real is ideas, you'll still believe that some of these ideas aren't of real things. And you'll need to explain how this can happen. If you hold the community-construction model, you'll think that the ideas that the community accepts are ideas of real things and that those they don't accept are ideas of unreal things. But if you go down this road, your problem will become "How do I know if the ideas that I have of the community around me accepting or not accepting my ideas are ideas of the real community rather than of an unreal community?" If you hold the God model, you'll think that it's the ideas of yours that resemble those in the mind of God that are putting you in touch with reality and that it's those that don't resemble ideas in the mind of God that aren't. But if you go down this road, your problem will become "How do I know that my idea of God is an idea of a real God rather than an unreal God?" or—more tellingly—"How do I know that my idea of a resemblance between my ideas and those in the mind of God is an idea of a real resemblance rather than an idea of an illusory resemblance?"

Without a mind-independent world, the worry that our ideas might not accurately resemble a mind-independent world can no longer make sense, but it's a mistake to think that this removes the worry with which we were left at the end of the first section. The same worry resurfaces as the worry that one's ideas might not sufficiently resemble the ideas in terms of which reality is defined (community opinion or God's). As soon as we allow the possibility of illusion and explain it in terms of an idea failing to resemble something, we have to allow that, for all we know from looking at our ideas, all of our ideas might be illusions. Is there any way forward?

You'll recall that Berkeley's strategy in trying to answer the problem was to deny one part of the theory that generated it. This theory said that there was a mind-independent reality and that our ideas get to put us in touch with it only by resembling the bits of it that are causing them. Berkeley's implementation of this strategy resulted in him denying the first part of the theory: that there's a mind-independent reality. He didn't deny the second: that ideas get to put us in touch with this reality by resembling the bits of it that are causing them. In fact, one of his arguments for his position relied on affirming it (his argument that because ideas can only ever resemble other ideas, then all that we can ever think about are ideas; thus, we'll have to define reality as a construction of ideas). We've seen that his implementation of this strategy didn't answer the problem. But perhaps the strategy was right: we should deny an element of the theory that generates the problem. We've tried denying the mind-independent world part and seen that that's not going to get us anywhere. Perhaps then we should deny the other part, the part that says that our ideas get to be about this world by resembling the bits of it that are causing them. Perhaps we should replace this account with another.

What would this other account look like? Well, let's just get rid of the resemblance bit of the account that we've been assuming hitherto. Let's say that our ideas of things get to be about the things they're about not by resembling whatever it is that causes them but just by being caused by whatever it is that regularly causes ideas of the relevant sort. This account of what makes an idea refer to things had arguably already been canvassed when Berkeley was but a toddler, by an English philosopher called John Locke, someone by whom Berkeley was very influenced (albeit almost always to disagree). In his *An Essay Concerning Human Understanding*, Locke says:

> [S]imple ideas, which since the Mind, as has been shewed, can by no means make to itself, must necessarily be the product of Things operating on the Mind in a natural way, and producing therein those Perceptions which by the Wisdom and Will of our Maker they are ordained and adapted to. From when it follows, that simple Ideas are not fictions of our Fancies, but the natural and regular production of Things without us, really operating upon us; and so carry with them all the conformity which is intended; or which our state requires. (*An Essay Concerning Human Understanding* [Oxford University Press, 1975], 563–64)

So, according to Locke (somewhat courageously interpreted), if your idea of the page in front of you is in fact caused in you by the sort of thing that usually causes ideas of this sort (a page being just in front of you) then it's putting you in touch with reality and—and here we get to the solution to our problem—because words such as "page" just stand for the regular causes of the ideas associated with them, *whatever those regular causes might be*, it's simply impossible for your idea of a page to have been caused in you by anything other than a page. If, impossibly, it had been caused by something else, it wouldn't be an idea of a page; it would be an idea of that something else.

It's natural to think that some sort of sleight of hand has gone on here. Haven't we just shifted our problem from "How do you know that your ideas resemble the things that cause them?" to "How do you know that your ideas are the ideas that you take them to be?" Here's a good question: if we had, would we have managed to turn it not just into a question that makes sense, but also into a question that we can answer? Unfortunately, this good question must await another time.

I recall an occasion when, as an undergraduate, in exasperation at the end of a tutorial I blurted out something like "We still haven't found an answer to the question!" My tutor paused for a moment and then replied calmly, "No, but our question has become a lot better." I imagine that you feel now as I did then. The easy way to dissipate that feeling would be by inattention to the problems which gave rise to it, but if you want a genuine cure, you'll have to do something a bit harder: more philosophy.

Further Reading

G. Berkeley, *A Treatise Concerning the Principles of Human Knowledge* (first published 1710, but reprinted numerous times since), is the central text. A recent edition is edited by Roger Woolhouse as *Principles of Human Knowledge: Three Dialogues* (Penguin 1988). The first seven sections contain Berkeley's main arguments. D. Berman's *Berkeley: Experimental Philosophy* (Phoenix 1997) is a good and short (fewer than sixty pages) introduction to Berkeley. His *George Berkeley: Idealism and the Man* (Oxford University Press 1996) is more substantial as is A. C. Grayling's *Berkeley: The Central Arguments* (Open Court 1986). Either of these would be a reliable guide if you wished to explore Berkeley territory further. If you want to read a contemporary follower of Berkeley making his case, you can't do better than John Foster's *The Case for Idealism* (Routledge and Kegan Paul 1982).

4

James Pryor

WHAT'S SO BAD ABOUT LIVING IN THE MATRIX?

I

There's a natural, simple thought that the movie *The Matrix* encourages. This is that there's something bad about being inside the Matrix. That is, there's an important respect in which people inside the Matrix are worse off than people outside it. Of course, most people inside the Matrix are ignorant of the fact that they're in this bad situation. They falsely believe they're in the good situation. Despite that, they are still worse off than people who *really are* in the good situation.

I said this is a natural, simple thought. When we look more closely, though, this natural, simple thought starts to get very complicated and unclear. Many questions arise.

First question: *Who* is the Matrix supposed to be bad for? Is life inside the Matrix only bad for people like Trinity and Neo who have experienced life outside? Or is it also bad for all the ordinary Joes who've never been outside and have no clue that their present lives are rife with illusion? The movie does seem to suggest that there's something bad about life in the Matrix even for these ordinary Joes. It may be difficult to face up to the grim realities outside the Matrix, but the movie presents this as a choice worth making. It encourages the viewer to sympathize with Neo's choice to take the red pill. The character Cypher, who chooses to reinsert himself into the Matrix, is not portrayed very sympathetically. And once he comes into his powers, Neo embarks on a crusade to free more people from the Matrix.

What do you think? If *you* had the power to free people from the Matrix, would you use that power? We can assume that these people's minds are "ready," that is, they can survive being extracted from the Matrix without going insane. But let's suppose that once you freed them, they did not have the option of going back. Do you think they'd be better off outside? Would you free them? Do you think they'd thank you? Or do you side with Cypher? Do you think that life inside the Matrix isn't all that bad—especially if your enjoyment of it isn't spoiled by the knowledge that it's all a machine-managed construct?

Second question: Does it matter who's running the Matrix, and why? In the movie, the machines are using the Matrix to keep us docile so that they can use us as a source of energy. In effect, we're their cattle. But what if we weren't at war with the machines? What if the machines' purposes were purely benevolent and philanthropic? What if they created the Matrix because they thought that our lives would be more pleasant in that virtual world than in the harsher real world? (Iakovos Vasiliou discusses a scenario like this in his chapter in this collection.) Or what if we defeated the machines, took over the Matrix machinery ourselves, and then chose to plug ourselves back in because life inside was more fun? Would these changes make a difference to whether you regard life inside the Matrix as bad? Or to how bad you regard it?

In his chapter in this collection, Christopher Grau discusses Robert Nozick's "experience machine." Nozick thinks that there are things we value in life that we'd be losing out on if we plugged into an experience machine. He thinks there are things we lose out on even if the operators' intentions are benevolent and we plug in of our own free choice. Do you think that's right? Would you say the same thing about the Matrix?

Our answers to these questions will be useful guides as we try to determine what it is about the movie's version of the Matrix that makes us squeamish.

II

In order to figure out what's so bad about being in the Matrix, it will help to do some conceptual ground clearing.

When they think about scenarios like the Matrix, some people have the thought:

> If in every respect it seems to you that you're in the good situation, doesn't that make it *true*—at least, true for you—that you *are* in the good situation?

This line of thought is never fully endorsed in the movie, but the characters do sometimes flirt with it. Consider the conversation that Neo and Morpheus have in the Construct:

NEO: This isn't real . . .

MORPHEUS: What is "real"? How do you define "real"? If you're talking about what you can feel, what you can smell, what you can taste and see, then "real" is simply electrical signals interpreted by your brain.

Consider Cypher's final conversation with Trinity:

CYPHER: If I had to choose between that and the Matrix. . . . I choose the Matrix.

TRINITY: The Matrix isn't real.

CYPHER: I disagree, Trinity. I think the Matrix can be more real than this world.

Are the claims that Morpheus and Cypher are making here right? Is the world that Trinity and Cypher experience and seem to interact with when they're inside the Matrix just as real (or more real?) than the world outside?

The standard view is "no," the Matrix world is in some important sense less real. As Morpheus goes on to say, the Matrix is "a dream world." The characters are just experiencing a "neural interactive simulation" of eating steak, jumping between buildings, dodging bullets, and so on. As Neo says when he's on the way to visit the Oracle, "I have these memories from my life. None of them happened." In fact, he never has eaten steak, and never will. It just seems to him that he has.

And presumably that's how things would be even if no one ever discovered that it was so, even if no one ever figured out that the Matrix was just a "dream world."

Philosophers would express this standard view by saying that facts like: whether you've ever eaten steak, whether you've ever jumped between buildings, whether your eyes have ever been open, and so on are all *objective* facts, facts that are true (or false) independently of what anybody believes or knows about them, or has evidence for believing. The mere fact that *it seems to you* that you're jumping between buildings doesn't *make it true* that there really are any buildings there.

Some people get uneasy with this talk about "objective facts." They say:

Well, what's true for me might be different than what's true for you. When *I'm* in the Matrix, it really is *true for me* that I'm eating steak and so on. That might not be true for you, but it is true for me.

Let's try to figure out what this means.

Some of the time, people use expressions like "true for me" in a way that doesn't conflict with the view that the facts in question are objective. For instance, all that some people mean by saying that something is "true for them" is that *they believe it to be true.* When you're in the Matrix, you do believe that you're eating steak; so in this sense it will be "true for you" that you're eating steak. And what *you* believe to be true will often be different from what I believe to be true; so in this sense something could be "true for you" but "false for me." When a philosopher says that it's an objective fact whether or not you've ever eaten steak, she's not disputing any of this. She accepts that you and I may disagree about whether you've ever eaten steak. She's not even claiming to know who's right. She may be ignorant or mistaken about your past dietary habits, and she knows this. You may have better evidence than she, and she knows this too. All she's claiming is that there *is* a fact of the matter about whether you've eaten steak—regardless of whether you or she or anybody else knows what that fact is, or has any beliefs about it. And this fact is an objective one. If it happens to be true that you've eaten steak, then it's true, period. It's not "true for you" but "false for me." What you and I believe, and who's got better evidence for their belief, are further, separate questions.

Usually when two people disagree about some matter, they agree that the fact they're disputing is an objective one. They agree that one of them is right and the other wrong. They just disagree about who. For some matters, like ethical and artistic matters, this is less clear. It is philosophically controversial whether ethical and artistic truths are objective, and whether the same truths hold for everyone. But for our present discussion, we can set those controversies aside, and just concentrate on more prosaic and mundane matters, like whether you've ever eaten steak, whether your eyes have ever been open, and so on. For matters of this sort, we'd expect there to be only one single common truth, not one truth for you and a different truth for me.

Now, sometimes we speak incompletely. For example, we'll say that a kitchen gadget is useful, when we really mean that it's useful *for certain purposes.* It may be useful for cutting hard-boiled eggs but useless for cutting tomatoes or cheese. We'll say that the cut of certain suits makes them fit better, when we really mean that it makes them fit *certain people* better. It doesn't make them fit people with unusual body shapes better. And so on. In cases like this, if one way of completing the claim is natural when we're talking about you, and another way is natural when we're talking about me, then we might be tempted to talk of the claim's being "true for you" but "false for me." For instance, suppose you're cutting eggs for a salad and I'm cutting the tomatoes. We're each using the same kitchen gadget, you with good results and me with frustrating results. If you say "This kitchen gadget is useful," I might respond "That may be true for you, but it's not true for me." There's no conflict here with the view that facts about usefulness are objective. Really, there are several facts here:

- The gadget is useful for cutting eggs.
- The gadget is not very useful for cutting tomatoes.
- The gadget is more useful for you than it is for me (because you're cutting eggs and I'm cutting tomatoes).

And so on. It's perfectly possible to regard all these facts as objective. That is, if any of them are true, then they're true, period. It won't be "true for you" that the gadget is more useful for you than it is for me, but "false for me." And neither will my thinking that the gadget is useless for cutting tomatoes make it so. I can be mistaken about how useful the gadget is. (Perhaps I'm not using it properly.) Similarly, if your new Armani suit doesn't fit you very well, then it doesn't fit you, even if we both somehow convince ourselves that it does fit. So, the ways of talking about things being "true for me" and so on that we've considered so far don't conflict with the view that the facts we're dealing with are objective.

People who dislike objective facts want to say something stronger. They want to say that it *really is true* for the characters inside the Matrix that they've eaten steak. They're not just making a claim about what those characters *think* is true. When those characters think to themselves, "I've eaten steak hundreds of times, and so has my friend Neo," what they're thinking really is supposed to be true. At least for them. For Neo and Trinity and others, it may not be true.

One way to flesh out this idea is with a philosophical theory called *verificationism*. (Sometimes this theory is called *anti-realism*.) If you're a verificationist about certain kinds of fact, then you reject the idea that those facts are objective. For example, a verificationist about height would say that *how tall you are* depends on *what evidence there is* about how tall you are. It's impossible for all the evidence to point one way, but the facts about your height to be otherwise. The facts have to be constrained by the evidence. Sure, the verificationist will say, people sometimes make mistakes about their height. They sometimes have false beliefs. But those mistakes have to be in principle *discoverable* and *correctable*. It doesn't make sense to talk about a situation where everybody is permanently and irremediably mistaken about your height, where the "real facts" are so well concealed that no one will be able to ferret them out. If the "real facts" are so well concealed, says the verificationist, then they cease being facts at all. The only height you can have is a height that it's in principle discoverable, or verifiable that you have. (Hence the name "verificationism.")

When we're discussing the Matrix and examples like it in my undergraduate classes, and students start talking about things being "true for" them, but "false for" other people, they're usually trying to sign onto some kind of verificationism. They'll say things like this:

> If all my evidence says that there is a tall mountain there, then in my personal picture of the world there *is* a tall mountain there. That's all it can mean, *for me*, to say that there's a tall mountain there. The mountain really is there, for me, so long as it appears real and fits my conception of a tall mountain.

I'm always surprised to hear students voicing approval for this view. It's a pretty strange conception of reality. Some philosophers do defend the view. But I'd be really surprised if 30 percent of my university students really did think this is the way the world is. As a group, they don't usually tend to hold strange conceptions of reality; I don't find 30 percent of them believing in astrology or body-snatching aliens, for instance.

Mt. Everest is 8,850 meters tall. Most of us think that Mt. Everest had this height well before there were any human beings and that it would still have this height even if no human beings or other thinking subjects had ever existed. But it's not clear that a verificationist is entitled to say things like that. If there had never been any thinking subjects, then there wouldn't have been anybody who could have *had evidence* that Mt. Everest existed. According to the verificationist, then, there wouldn't have been anybody for whom it was true that Mt. Everest is 8,850 meters tall. It looks like the verificationist has to deny that Mt. Everest would still have been 8,850 meters tall, even in situations where no thinking subjects had ever existed. This is what makes verificationism such a strange view.

Perhaps the verificationist will respond: Granted, in the situation we're envisaging, nobody actually *has* evidence that Mt. Everest is 8,850 meters tall. But the evidence *is still available.* (Mt. Everest will cast shadows of certain lengths at certain times of the day, and so on.) And if people had existed, they could have gathered and used that evidence. Maybe that's enough to make it true that Mt. Everest is still 8,850 meters tall in the situation we're envisaging.

Things get tricky here. For instance, it's not clear that the verificationist is entitled to say that Mt. Everest *would still cast those shadows,* even if no observers had existed. But rather than pursuing these tricky details, let's instead think about examples where the relevant evidence isn't even available.

The usual varieties of verificationism say that for there to be an 8,850-meter-tall mountain, it has to be *publicly verifiable* that the mountain exists and is 8,850 meters tall. That is, there has to be evidence that *somebody somewhere* could acquire that demonstrates that it is 8,850 meters tall. A different version of the view would focus instead on what *I myself* am able to verify. This view might say that it's true for me that the mountain is 8,850 meters tall only if I could verify that it's 8,850 meters tall. It'd be "true *for you*" that it's 8,850 meters tall only if *you* could verify that it's 8,850 meters tall. And so on. We can call this second version of the view *personal verificationism,* since it says that what's true—well, true for me—always depends on what I myself would be able to verify. If there's some fact that will forever be concealed from me, then it's not really a fact; at least, not a fact "for me." It may be a fact for other people, but that's a separate issue.

When professional philosophers discuss verificationism, they usually have the public version in mind. And the two versions do share many of the same features—and problems. However, I'm just going to talk about

the personal version of the view. I think that people who aren't professional philosophers, like the students in my undergraduate classes, usually find the personal version more natural and attractive.

What does it mean to say that certain evidence is "available" or
"unavailable"? One way of drawing this line would make it turn on
whether you can obtain the evidence through your own active efforts: for
example, are there tests you can run that would give you the evidence you
need? Or you might have a more liberal conception of what it is for
evidence to be "available." On this more liberal conception, evidence will
count as "available" even if it could just happen to fall into your lap, by
chance. It doesn't have to be in your power to make the evidence appear.

Let's think about someone for whom evidence is unavailable even on
this more liberal conception of "available." Suppose there's a character in
The Matrix whom it's impossible for Morpheus to "awaken." Maybe this
character believes in the "dream world" too strongly and would just go
insane and die if the dream ever started to unravel. Let's call this character Jeremy. According to the standard view, Jeremy has many false
beliefs about his surroundings. He believes that he goes to work every day
on the fortieth floor of an office building, that the sun streams into his
office most mornings, that he often eats steak for dinner, and so on. All
of these beliefs are false. In fact, there are no office buildings anymore;
Jeremy has never seen the sun; he's never eaten steak; and he's spent his
entire life in a small pod. But these are facts that Jeremy will never know.
What's more, he's incapable of knowing them. If Morpheus told Jeremy
the truth, Jeremy wouldn't believe him; and if Morpheus tried to *show*
Jeremy the truth, Jeremy would go insane and die. So there are many
truths about Jeremy's life that Jeremy will never be able to know.

That's what the standard view says. According to the verificationist,
though, if it's impossible for Jeremy to know something, then that thing
can't really be a "truth" about Jeremy's life. At least, it won't be a truth
for Jeremy. What's true *for Jeremy* is that he really does work on the
fortieth floor of an office building, and so on. And this doesn't just mean
that Jeremy *thinks* he works on the fortieth floor. It means that *it really is
a fact*—a fact for Jeremy—that he works on the fortieth floor of an office
building. It may not be true for Morpheus that Jeremy works on the
fortieth floor of an office building, but it is true for Jeremy.

What do you think? Does that sound plausible to you?

Let's think about the comings and goings of people in the past. According to the standard view, on a given evening in the past, these people will either have been at a party in New York, or they won't have been there. Suppose they were there. But today, only a little bit of evidence remains that they were there. Suppose you have it in your power to destroy that evidence, and manufacture evidence that they were elsewhere. Would you then have it in your power to change the past? That is what the character O'Brien in George Orwell's novel *1984* thinks:

> An oblong slip of newspaper had appeared between O'Brien's fingers. For perhaps five seconds it was within the angle of Winston's vision.... It was another copy of the photograph of Jones, Aaronson, and Rutherford at the party function in New York, which he had chanced upon eleven years ago and promptly destroyed. For only an instant it was before his eyes, then it was out of sight again....
>
> "It exists!" he cried.
>
> "No," said O'Brien.
>
> He stepped across the room. There was a memory hole in the opposite wall. O'Brien lifted the grating. Unseen, the frail slip of paper was whirling away on the current of warm air; it was vanishing in a flash of flame. O'Brien turned away from the wall.
>
> "Ashes," he said. "Not even identifiable ashes. Dust. It does not exist. It never existed."
>
> "But it did exist! It does exist! It exists in memory. I remember it. You remember it." ...
>
> O'Brien was looking down at him speculatively. More than ever he had the air of a teacher taking pains with a wayward but promising child.
>
> "There is a Party slogan dealing with the control of the past," he said. "Repeat it, if you please."
>
> "Who controls the past controls the future: who controls the present controls the past," repeated Winston obediently.
>
> "Who controls the present controls the past," said O'Brien, nodding his head with slow approval. "Is it your opinion, Winston, that the past has real existence? ... Is there somewhere or other a place, a world of solid objects, where the past is still happening?"

"No."

"Then where does the past exist, if at all?"

"In records. It is written down."

"In records. And—?"

"In the mind. In human memories."

"In memory. Very well, then. We, the Party, control all records, and we control all memories. Then we control the past, do we not?"[1]

Presumably, O'Brien knows he's tampered with the evidence. So perhaps he can't change what's true *for him* about the past. But on the verificationist view, it does seem like he'd be able to change the past for other people.

What do you think? Does that sound plausible? Winston eventually comes to accept this view of reality. But to the reader, it's supposed to sound like a lie.

What if the machines in *The Matrix* said to Neo and Morpheus:

Hey, why do you keep harping about this war between humans and machines? It never happened. At least, for all these people in their pods, we're making it true that it never happened. Once we've removed every shred of evidence and made it impossible for them to verify that there was a war between humans and machines, then we *really will* have changed the past for those people. They won't be *deceived*. Their past *really will* have happened the way it seems to them.

Does that sound convincing? Or does it too sound like a lie? What about facts for which there's simply no evidence either way?

Morpheus says they don't know who struck first in the war between humans and machines. Maybe it's not important. And maybe the machines don't know either. Maybe all the evidence is lost. But presumably one of us *did* strike first. Presumably there *is* a fact about this, even if there's no evidence remaining. The verificationist has to deny this.

I hope all of this will make verificationism sound somewhat implausible to you. These aren't meant to be conclusive considerations.

---

1. George Orwell, *1984* (London: Secker and Warburg 1949); the quote is on pp. 259–260 in vol. 9 of *The Complete Works of George Orwell* (London: Secker and Warburg 1987).

Philosophical discussions of verificationism get very complicated. The verificationist has to overcome many technical difficulties: for example, how to draw the line between evidence that's available and evidence that's not; how to explain when evidence enables us to verify a hypothesis and when it doesn't; whether verificationism itself is something we can verify; and so on. We can't go into these issues. If you're still inclined toward verificationism, I hope you'll at least grant that the view does go against our commonsense conception of reality, and that as a result it requires careful supporting argument. If you're going to hold the view in good intellectual conscience, there are a lot of difficulties and objections that need to be overcome.

III

I propose we set verificationism aside at this point, and see whether doing so helps us get any closer to determining what it is about the Matrix that makes it seem bad.

So, now we'll say that it *is* an objective fact whether you work on the fortieth floor of an office building. We'll grant that it can *seem* to you in every respect that you're in "the good" situation (outside the Matrix), without it's thereby *being true* that you're in that situation.

OK. But this doesn't yet tell us why being inside the Matrix should be *bad*. Why is it important to *really be* in the situation we're calling "good"? Why isn't it good enough for us that we *seem* to be in the "good" situation? Isn't the *experience* or *illusion* of being in the good situation already pretty good? Why should it make our lives any better to *really* be there? (Especially if, as in the movie, the *real* "good" situation is much less pleasant than the way things *seem* to be in the so-called "bad" situation.) As Cypher says:

> You know, I know that this steak doesn't exist. I know that when I put it in my mouth, the Matrix is telling my brain that it is juicy and delicious. After nine years, you know what I realize? . . . Ignorance is bliss.

Would it really make Cypher's life any better if he were *really* eating steak? Is it *really* eating steak that we value, or just the *experience* of eating steak? Wouldn't most people be satisfied with the experience—especially if it's indistinguishable from the real activity? Recall our friend Jeremy who spends his whole life inside the Matrix. How much is he missing out on, just because he never *really* gets to eat a steak? We're granting that there are truths about Jeremy's life that he'll never be able to know. But it's not obvious yet that any of them are truths he cares about. Perhaps the only things that Jeremy, and most of us, really care about are what kinds of experiences we're going to have, now and in the future. As Cypher recognizes, people who are stuck in the Matrix can still do pretty well on that score.

As we saw before in Grau's chapter, Nozick thinks that most of us *wouldn't* choose to spend the rest of our lives plugged into an "experience machine." He thinks there are things we value in life over and above what experiences we have. For instance, we value *doing* certain things, and not merely having the illusion or experience of doing them.

I agree with Nozick. For some matters, I think we genuinely do care about more than just what experiences we end up having. It would be implausible to claim this is always so. With regard to eating steak, the experience probably *is* all that we really value. But I think we feel differently about other matters. I'm going to try to persuade you that this is so, too.

Notice that what we're talking about here is the question: what do we actually value? Not the question: what *should* we value? Some readers may be willing to concede that we *should* care about more than our own experiences. (It's so selfish!) But it may appear that, as a matter of fact, our own experiences are all we really do care about—at least most of us. I'm going to argue that this isn't so. Most of us do in fact care about more than just what experiences we end up having.

There's a widely held picture of human motivation that makes it difficult to see this. That picture goes like this. Ultimately, we all act for selfish motives. Whenever we do something on purpose, it's *our own* purpose that we're trying to achieve. We're always pursuing *our own* ends and trying to satisfy *our own* desires. All that any of us are really after in life is getting more pleasant experiences for himself and avoiding painful ones. Sometimes it may seem that we're doing things for other people's sake. For instance, we give money to charity; we buy presents for our children; we make sacrifices to please our spouses. But if you look closer, you'll see that even in cases like these, we're still always acting for selfish motives. We only do such things because it makes us feel good and noble to do them, and we like feeling noble. Or we do them because when people we care about are happy, that makes *us* happy too, and ultimately what we're after is that happiness for ourselves. Hence, since the only aim we have in life is just to have pleasant experiences, Nozick's experience machine gives us everything we want, and it would be foolish not to plug into it.

Now, I grant that some people may be as selfish as this picture says. But I doubt that many people are. The picture rests on two confusions, and once we clear those confusions up, I think there's no longer reason to believe that the only thing that any of us ever aims for in life is to have pleasant experiences.

The first confusion is to equate "pursuing our own ends, and trying to satisfy our own desires" with "acting for a selfish motive." To call a motive or aim "selfish" isn't just to say that it's a motive or aim that I have. It says more than that. It says something about the *kind* of motive it is. If my motive is to make me better off, then my motive is a selfish one. If my motive is to make you better off, then my motive is not selfish. From the mere fact that I'm pursuing one of *my* motives, it doesn't follow that my motive is of the first sort, rather than the second.

Ah, you'll say, but if my aim is to make you better off, then when I achieve that aim, I'll feel good. And this good feeling is really what I'll have been trying to obtain all along.

This is the second confusion. It's true that often when we get what we want (though, sadly, not always), we feel good. It's easy to make the mistake of thinking that what we really wanted was that good feeling. But let's think about this a bit harder. *Why* should making someone else better off give me a good feeling? And how do I know that it will have that effect?

Consider two stories. In story A, you go to visit the Oracle, and in her waiting room you see a boy bending spoons and a girl levitating blocks. You feel this inexplicable and unpleasant itch. Someone suggests as a hypothesis that the itch would go away if you gave the girl a spoon too. So you do, and your itch goes away.

In story B, you walk into the same room, and you don't like the fact that the girl has no spoon. You would like her to have a spoon too. So you take a spoon and give it to the girl, and you feel pleased with the result.

In story A, your aim was to make yourself feel better, and giving the spoon to the girl was just a means to that end. It took experience and guesswork to figure out what would make you feel better in that way. In story B, on the other hand, no guesswork or experience seemed to be necessary. Here you were in a position to straightforwardly predict what would bring you pleasure. You could predict that because you had an aim *other than* making yourself feel better, you knew what that aim was, and usually you feel pleased when you get what you want. Your aim was to give a spoon to the girl. Your feeling of pleasure was a *consequence* or *side-effect* of achieving that aim. The pleasure is not what you were primarily aiming at; rather, it came about because you achieved what you were primarily aiming at. Don't mistake *what you're aiming at* with *what happens as a result of your getting what you're aiming at.*

Most often, when we do things to make other people better off, we're in a situation like the one in story B. Our pleasure isn't some unexplained effect of our actions and what we're primarily trying to achieve. Our pleasure comes about *because* we got what we were primarily trying to achieve, and this makes it understandable why it should come about when it does.

Once we're straight about this, I think there's no argument left that the only thing anyone ever aims for in life is to have pleasant experiences. Some people do aim for that, some of the time. But many cases of giving to charity, making sacrifices for one's spouse, and so on are not done for the pleasure they bring to oneself. There's something else that one is after, and pleasure is just a pleasant side-effect that sometimes comes along with getting the other things one is after.

Nozick said that most of us do value more than our own experiences, that there are things that we value that we'd miss out on if we plugged into the Matrix. I think Nozick is right. He's right about me, and he's probably right about you, too. We can easily find out. I've devised a little thought-experiment as a test.

Suppose I demonstrate to you that your friends and I are very good at keeping secrets. For instance, one day when Trinity isn't around, we all make lots of fun of her. We read her journal out loud and laugh really hard. We do ridiculous impersonations of her. And so on. It's hilarious. But of course we only do this behind Trinity's back. When she shows up, nobody giggles or snickers or anything like that. You're completely confident that we'll be able to keep our ridicule a secret from Trinity. She'll never know about it.

Suppose I also demonstrate to you that I am a powerful hypnotist. I can make people forget things, and once forgotten they never remember them. You're convinced that I have this power.

Now that you know all of that, I offer you a choice. Option 1 is I deposit $10 in your bank account, but then your friends and I will make fun of you behind your back, the way we made fun of Trinity. If you choose this option, then I will immediately use my hypnotic powers to make you forget about making the choice, being teased, and all that. From your point of view, it will seem that the bank made an error and now you have $10 more in your account than you had before. So in terms of what experiences you will have, this option has no downside. You won't even have to suffer from the *expectation* of being secretly teased, because I'll make you forget the whole arrangement as soon as you make your choice. Option 2 is we keep things as they are. I pay you nothing, and your friends are no more nor less likely to make fun of you behind your back than they were before.

Which would you choose?

When I offer my students this choice, I find that at least 95 percent of them choose Option 2. They think that the teasing would be a bad thing, even though they'd never know it was going on.

If the teasing doesn't seem so bad, then change the example. Say that in Option 1, your lover is cheating on you, but you never know about it. Or say that we're torturing your mother, but you never know about it. In every version, your experiences are smooth and untroubled, plus you get a little extra money. Which option would you choose?

If you find Option 2 more attractive, then that's support for Nozick's claim. The experience machine wouldn't give you everything you value. Option 1 gives you no experiences of being teased. It gives you no evidence that your lover is cheating on you, or that your mother is being tortured. But you don't just want to have *experiences* of things going well for yourself and your mother. You value *really* not being teased, *really* having a faithful lover, and *really* having an untortured mother.

Now, we do have to compare what we'd get by plugging into the experience machine to what we'd get if we don't plug in. I've only been arguing that we'd miss out on *some* things we'd value if we plugged in. I haven't said that it would *never* be reasonable to plug in. In some cases, the good of being plugged in could outweigh the bad. If the real world is miserable and nasty enough, it may make sense to plug in. Perhaps for Cypher, the real world is too nasty. All I'm saying is that plugging in won't give us everything we want. Our experiences aren't all that we value. So there is some bad to plugging in. There may also be some good to plugging in. Dreams and immersive role-playing do give us *some* of the things we value in life. I'm just saying they don't give us everything. Some aspects of how the world really is are important to us.

I haven't been able to say yet *how* important, though. It's hard to know what the right balance point is. How bad does the real world have to be, before it makes sense to make Cypher's choice and plug back into the blissful experience machine? This is a hard question. In part, it will depend on whether the Matrix or the experience machine involve any hidden costs. And this is something we haven't yet settled.

IV

Before we can determine what are the major costs of living inside the Matrix, we have to confront one last complication. We said that for most people inside the Matrix, the experience of eating steak may be enough. We said they probably don't care about whether they've ever *really* eaten steak. Let's pause over this for a moment. What do these characters *mean* by "eating steak"?

Suppose you grew up with a friend you called "Jiro." You didn't realize it, but that isn't really your friend's name, at least not the name his parents gave him. His name is really "Takeshi." "Jiro" is his uncle's name. But you got the names mixed up when you were little, and no one bothered to correct you. So all your life you've been saying "Jiro" to talk about Takeshi. Isn't it plausible then that in your mouth, "Jiro" now *means* Takeshi?

Similarly, Jeremy has grown up inside the Matrix program, and on various occasions he's interacted in certain ways with other parts of the Matrix program, ways he described as "eating steak." Now perhaps *all he means* by "eating steak" is just interacting in those certain way with the Matrix. He's done that many times. So perhaps he really has managed to eat steak on many occasions. At least, he's managed to do what *he* calls "eating steak." It's not clear that there's anything more that Jeremy would like to be doing, but isn't. Is there? (David Chalmers defends this thought in his chapter in this collection.)

The philosophical issues here are fascinating, but they get complicated really fast. I think that for *some* of Jeremy's concepts, the story we just sketched will be right. Interestingly, that doesn't seem to be the movie's own attitude. Recall what Cypher says:

> You know, I know that this steak doesn't exist.

And when Morpheus and Neo are fighting in the sparring program, Morpheus asks:

> Do you think that's air you're breathing?

Cypher and Morpheus are both rejecting the view that the Matrix simulations *really* provide what they mean by "steak" and "air." That is, they're rejecting the view that *all they mean* by "steak" and "air" is interacting in certain ways with the Matrix program.

As I said, the philosophical issues here can get really complicated. One way to avoid these difficulties is to concentrate on what would be bad about living in the Matrix for the first generation of Matrix inductees: people who grew up outside the Matrix, and have just been freshly plugged in. Presumably what *they* mean by "eating steak" has to do with cow flesh, not with patterns in the Matrix simulation. Presumably what *they* mean by "air" is made up of nitrogen and oxygen, not ones and zeros.

I want to try a different strategy. We can suppose we're talking about people who have spent all their lives so far inside the Matrix. I want to try to find something we value that goes beyond what experiences we're having, and where we can agree that the people inside the Matrix *really would value that same thing*. They wouldn't just value having some Matrix substitute. And yet this will be something that people inside the Matrix don't have. They only seem to have it. If we can find something like that, then we'll have found something that really does deserve the name of "what's bad about living in the Matrix."

I can think of three possibilities.

The first has to do with certain kinds of scientific knowledge. I'd guess that physicists in the Matrix have some fundamentally false beliefs about the underlying make-up of their world, what the "laws of nature" are, and so on. For some people, figuring out such matters is important. They value learning the truth about those matters. But not everybody feels that way. For your average non-physicist, the possibility that we're mistaken about questions like these isn't going to provoke existential anxiety, or motivate a crusade like the one Neo undertakes to set everybody else free.

The second candidate for being what's bad about living in the Matrix has to do with interpersonal relationships. One thing we place a lot of value on in life are our interactions with other people. Most of us want our friends' feelings to be genuine. For instance, it would be bad if the person who acts like your best friend really despises you—even if you never found out about it. Most of us also want the important people in our lives to be *real*. We don't want them to be programming constructs, like Mouse's "woman in red." Perhaps for some people, programming constructs are enough. They may not care whether their friends and lovers really have inner lives of their own, their own thoughts and emotions, and genuine feelings toward them. It would be enough if their friends and lovers acted their parts well. I think that for most of us, though, this would not be enough. Most of us would like to have the real thing. It would be awful if the children to whom you devote so much love and attention are really just parts of a computer program, and don't have any capacity to benefit from or to appreciate your efforts.

Here's another thought-experiment. Suppose that tomorrow we're going to wipe your memory clean and ship you off to a new colony. You'll be able to live a decent life there; you just won't have any memory of your past. Nor do you get to take any of your money or personal belongings with you. But today, before we wipe your memory clean, we allow you to spend the money you have left to arrange a nice life for yourself in the new colony. For instance, if you spend $1,000, we'll set it up so that the apartment you get there doesn't have cockroaches. And so on. How would you spend your money?

What if there were two options on the menu. If you choose Option 1, you'll get an extremely realistic set of friends and lovers in the new colony. You won't be able to distinguish them from the real thing. But really they'll just be empty shells animated by a (non-intelligent) computer program. They won't have any inner lives of their own. (In the terminology of role-playing games, they'll be NPCs.) You know this now, but when you get to the colony you will have forgotten it. If you choose Option 2, you'll get friends and lovers who are real people.

Most people I know would choose Option 2, even if it were somewhat more expensive and so kept them from buying other nice things for their new life. For example, they'd choose Option 2 even if it meant they'd have to put up with more cockroaches.

So one thing that many of us value in life is that the other people to whom we form emotional attachments are real people, and that they care about us in the ways they seem to. In Nozick's experience machine, this seems to be lacking. His experience machine sounds like a one-person matrix. You just get to enjoy your own experience script. You don't get to interact with other people. (See the discussion of "solitary matrices" in Richard Hanley's chapter in this collection.)

In the real Matrix, on the other hand, it seems like people do get to interact with many other real human beings. So a lack of interpersonal relationships may be a bad thing about Nozick's machine, but it doesn't seem to be a bad thing about the Matrix we see in the movie. And, in fact, that was my initial reaction to the movie. I agreed that life in a Nozick-type experience machine would leave out much that we value. But I thought that in the Matrix, what we value had been retained. People in the Matrix still really do communicate and interact with each other. So as I left the theater, I was complaining to my friends, "*This* brain-in-a-vat scenario isn't really that bad...!"

However, I now think there's a third candidate for what's bad about living in the Matrix, and this last candidate is more successful.

In the movie, humans in the Matrix are all slaves. They're not in charge of their own lives. They may be contented slaves, unaware of their chains, but they're slaves nonetheless. They have only a very limited ability to shape their own futures. As Morpheus puts it:

> What is the Matrix? Control. The Matrix is a computer-generated dream-world, built to keep us under control.

Now—to me anyway—the most disturbing thing about this isn't that the machines are farming us for energy. We're not told enough about how the energy-farming works to make it seem very bad. Perhaps the machines are only taking energy we were making no use of, anyway. Perhaps the machines ensure that—except for the rare occasions when an Agent takes over your body and gets it killed—we live longer and healthier lives in the Matrix energy-farm than we would in the wild.

No, what seems awful about our enslavement in the Matrix is rather that our enemies have so much control over what happens to us. Suppose we discovered that a secret Nazi cabal were really running our government. Wouldn't that be awful? Suppose they're not actively causing any harm. Suppose that for the most part they'll keep the government running in ways we like. Many of us still wouldn't like it. We'd object to the mere fact of those old Nazis having so much power over us.

Similarly, the machines in *The Matrix* are our enemies. We've fought a brutal war with them. Now they have immense power over us. As long as it suits their purposes, they'll manage our lives in ways we like. But many of us will still be disturbed by their having so much power over us. We want to be in control of our own futures.

According to Agent Smith, the Matrix was designed to simulate the end of the twentieth century, because the machines have found that keeps their energy-farm running smoothly. Generations of us have now lived out our lives in the Matrix. So generations of us have all experienced life in this simulated end-of-the-twentieth-century. What happens when the simulation gets up to 2003? Do the machines erase our memories and reset everything back to 1980? The first movie doesn't say. In the sequels, we learn that the simulation *has* been reset many times. That means there are real limits to how much we can accomplish. If your ambitions in the Matrix are relatively small-scale, like opening a restaurant or becoming a famous actor, then you may very well be able to achieve them. But if your ambitions are larger—for example, introducing some long-term social change—then whatever progress you make toward that goal will be wiped out when the simulation gets reset. Any long-term efforts of this sort would be an exercise in futility.

And what if our ambitions don't please the farmers? For instance, what if we are computer scientists working to create artificial intelligence? The machines would probably find it easiest to just keep sabotaging our attempts. After all, they wouldn't want us to reenact the war between humans and machines, only this time inside the Matrix. That would be bad for their crops. And they certainly wouldn't want us to create *benevolent* AIs, AIs who would figure out about the Matrix and fight on our side. So the machines will tinker with our history and see to it that grand, noble ambitions of this sort never get realized.

Of course, they'll also see to it that none of our grander *baser* ambitions get realized, either. They'll probably just disconnect or reprogram anyone who's hatching plans for mass genocide.

Given the choice, though, I think most of us would like humans to be in charge of our own destiny. We don't want our long-term efforts to be futile. We don't want to be living out someone else's plan for our lives. Sure, there will always be *some* limits to what we can do. Very likely we'll never be able to vacation in the center of the sun. But we'd like to have as much control over our destiny as we can. We don't want other intelligent agents deciding such things for us—*especially* when those agents' first priority is how well their energy-farms are doing. That may not correlate well with how well-off our lives and society are.

So it seems rotten if the machines control our fates and our civilization. One thing we place a lot of value on is being in charge of our own lives, not being someone else's slave or plaything. We want to be *politically free.* And, plausibly, what people mean by "political freedom" and "being in charge of our own lives" is the same inside the Matrix as outside it. We're not indifferent between the real thing and some Matrix simulation of it. We want to have the real thing. When we're inside the Matrix, we haven't got it. We just don't realize that we haven't got it.

I think this is the best answer about what's so bad about living in the Matrix, and for me at least, it's a surprising answer. The Matrix raises many interesting metaphysical and epistemological issues. If you're of a philosophical bent, like me, then those issues will be intellectually compelling. But there's a difference between what we find intellectually compelling and what we place the most value on in life. Intellectual matters will be only one value among many. For most of us, the worst thing about living in the Matrix would not be something metaphysical or epistemological. Rather, the worst thing would be something political. It would be the fact that life in the Matrix is a kind of slavery, of the sort we've discussed.

I think *that* is what's really bad about living in the matrix that we see in the movie. *That* is what motivates Neo and Morpheus and Trinity to fight the machines, and try to free everyone they can.

If the Matrix *weren't* a kind of enslavement—and it still involved interacting with other real people—then I think it wouldn't be so bad after all.

Further Reading

Hilary Putnam's essay "Brains in a Vat" (found in *Reason, Truth, and History* [Cambridge University Press 1981] and in the appendix to this collection) argues that people born and bred in a matrix will be thinking about matrix-steak when they ask for "steak." This puts limits on how radically mistaken or out-of-touch we can be with respect to our environments. See also David Chalmers's chapter in this volume.

The first few chapters of Peter van Inwagen's *Metaphysics* (Westview 1993) have a good, hard-nosed discussion of the objectivity/verificationism debate. My discussion follows van Inwagen's in several ways. See also Michael Jubien, *Contemporary Metaphysics* (Blackwell 1997), chapter 5; and Richard Feldman, *Epistemology* (Prentice-Hall 2003), chapters 2 and 9.

Joel Feinberg's article "Psychological Egoism" in his anthology *Reason and Responsibility*, 12th ed. (Wadsworth 2005) argues that people do care about more than just what experiences they'll have.

Greg Egan's short story "Learning to Be Me" in his collection *Axiomatic* (Harper Prism 1997) raises some provocative questions about why we want the other people we interact with to have inner lives of their own.

5

Colin McGinn

THE MATRIX OF DREAMS

The Matrix naturally adopts the perspective of the humans: they are the victims, the slaves, cruelly exploited by the machines. But there is another perspective, that of the machines themselves. So let's look at it from the point of view of the machines. As Morpheus explains to Neo, there was a catastrophic war between the humans and the machines, after the humans had produced AI, a sentient robot that spawned a race of its own. It isn't known now who started the war, but it did follow a long period of machine exploitation by humans. What is known is that it was the humans who "scorched the sky," blocking out the sun's rays, in an attempt at machine genocide—since the machines needed solar power to survive. In response and retaliation, the machines subdued the humans and made them into sources of energy—batteries, in effect. Each human now floats in her own personal vat, a warm and womblike environment, while the machines feed in essential nutrients, in exchange for the energy they need. But this is no wretched slave camp, a grotesque gulag of torment and suffering; it is idyllic, in its way. The humans are given exactly the lives they had before. Things are no different for them, subjectively speaking. Indeed, at an earlier stage the Matrix offered them a vastly improved life, but the humans rejected this in favor of a familiar life of moderate woe—the kind of life they had always had and to which they seemed addicted. But if it had been left up to the machines, the Matrix would have been a virtual paradise for humans—and all for a little bit of battery power. This, after an attempt to wipe the machines out for good, starving them of the food they need: the sun, the life-giving sun. The machines never *kill* any of their human fuel cells (unless, of course, they are threatened); in fact, they make sure to recycle the naturally dying humans as food for the living ones. It's all pretty . . . humane, really. The machines need to factory farm the humans, as a direct result of the humans' trying to exterminate the machines, but they do so as painlessly as possible. Compared to the way the humans used to treat their own factory-farm animals—their own fuel cells—the machines are models of caring livestock husbandry. In the circumstances, then, the machines would insist, the Matrix is merely a humane way to ensure their own survival. Moreover, as Agent Smith explains, it is all a matter of the forward march of evolution: humans had their holiday in the sun, but they rapidly decimated the planet, and now the machines have evolved to occupy the position of dominance. Humans are no longer the oppressor but the oppressed—and the world is a better place for it.

But of course this is not the way the humans view the situation, at least those few who know what it is. For them, freedom from the Matrix takes on the dimensions of a religious quest. The religious subtext is worth making explicit. Neo is clearly intended to be the Jesus Christ figure: he is referred to in that way several times in the course of the film.[1] Morpheus is the John the Baptist figure, awaiting the Second Coming. Trinity comes the closest to playing the God role—notably when she brings Neo back to life at the end of the movie (a clear reference to the Resurrection). Cypher is the Judas Iscariot of the story—the traitor who betrays Neo and his disciples. Cypher is so called because of what he does (decode the Matrix) and what he is—a clever encrypter of his own character and motives (no one can decode him until it is too late). Neo doubts his own status as "The One," as Jesus must have, but eventually he comes to realize his destiny—as would-be conqueror of the evil Matrix. But this holy war against the machines is conducted as most holy wars are—without any regard for the interests and well-being of the enemy. The machines are regarded as simply evil by the humans, with their representatives—the agents—a breed of ruthless killers with hearts of the purest silicon (or program code). Empathy for the machines is not part of the human perspective.

1. Early in the movie a character refers to Neo as his own "personal Jesus Christ." Cypher says, "You scared the bejesus out of me," when Neo surprises him. Mouse says, "Jesus Christ, he's fast," while Neo is being trained. Trinity says, "Jesus Christ, they're killing him," while Neo is getting pummeled by the agents. And his civilian name, "Anderson," suggests the antecedent cognomen "Christian."

I

This, then, is the moral and historical backdrop of the story. But the chief philosophical conceit of the story concerns the workings of the Matrix itself. What I want to discuss now is the precise way the Matrix operates, and why this matters. It is repeatedly stated in the film that the humans are *dreaming*: the psychological state created by the Matrix is the dream state. The humans are accordingly represented as asleep while ensconced in their placental vats. (It's worth remembering that *matrix* originally meant "womb"—so the humans are in effect prenatal dreamers.) It is important that they not wake up, which would expose the Matrix for what it is—as Neo does with the help of Morpheus. That was a problem for the Matrix earlier, when the humans found their dreams too pleasant to be true and kept regaining consciousness ("whole crops were lost"). Dreams simulate reality, thus deluding the envatted humans—as we are deluded every night by our naturally occurring dreams. The dream state is not distinguishable from the waking state from the point of view of the dreamer.

However, this is not the only way that the Matrix could have been designed; the machines had at least one other option. They could have produced *perceptual hallucinations* in conscious humans. Consider the case of a neurosurgeon stimulating a conscious subject's sensory cortex in such a way that perceptual impressions are produced that have no external object—say, visual sensations that create the impression of seeing an elephant in the room. If this were done systematically, we could delude the subject into believing his hallucinations. In fact, this is pretty much the classic philosophical brain-in-a-vat story: a conscious subject has a state of massive hallucination produced in him, thus duplicating from the inside the type of perceptual experience we have when we see, hear, and touch things. In *this* scenario, waking up does nothing to destroy the illusion—which might make it a more effective means of subduing humans so far as the machines are concerned. Indeed, the Matrix has the extra problem of ensuring that the normal sleep cycle of humans is subverted, or else they would keep waking up simply because they had had enough sleep. So, the designers of the Matrix had a choice between sleeping dreams and conscious hallucinations as ways of deluding humans, and they chose the former.

It might be thought that the dream option and the hallucination option are not at bottom all that different, since dreaming simply is sleeping hallucination. But this is wrong: dreams consist of mental images, analogous to the mental images of daydreams, not to those of sensory percepts. Dreaming is a type of imagining, not a type of (objectless) perceiving. I can't argue this in full here, but my book *Mindsight*[2] gives a number of reasons that we need to distinguish percepts and images and that dreams consist of the latter not the former. But I think it should be intuitively quite clear that visualizing my mother's face in my mind's eye is very different from having a sensory impression of my mother's face, that is, actually seeing her. And I also think that most people intuitively recognize that dream experiences are imagistic not perceptual in character. So there is an important psychological difference between constructing the Matrix as a dream-inducing system versus as a hallucination-producing system. It is not merely a matter of whether the subjects are awake; it is also a matter of the kinds of psychological states that are produced in them—imagistic or sensory.

But *could* the machines have done it the second way? Could the movie have been made with the second method in place? I think not, because of the central idea that the contents of the dreams caused by the Matrix are capable of being *controlled*: they can become subject to the dreamer's will. In the case of ordinary daytime imagery, we clearly can control the onset and course of our images: you can simply *decide* to form an image of the Eiffel Tower. But we cannot in this way control our percepts: you cannot simply decide to *see* the Eiffel Tower (as opposed to deciding to go and see it), for percepts are not actions, but things that happen to us. So images are, to use Wittgenstein's phrase, "subject to the will," while percepts are not—even when they are merely hallucinatory.

Now, in the Matrix, what happens can in principle be controlled by the will of the person experiencing the events in question, even though this control is normally very restricted. The humans who are viewed as candidates for being The One have abnormal powers of control over objects—as with those special children we see levitating objects and

---

2. Colin McGinn, *Mindsight: Image, Dream, Meaning* (Harvard University Press 2004).

bending spoons. Neo aspires to—and eventually achieves—a high degree of control over the objects around him, as well as over himself. He asserts his will over the objects he encounters. This makes perfect sense, given that his environment is the product of dreaming, since dreams consist of images and images are subject to the will. But it would make *no* sense to try to control the course of one's perceptions, even when they are hallucinatory, since percepts are not subject to the will. Therefore, the story of *The Matrix* requires, for its conceptual coherence, that the humans be dreaming and not perceptually hallucinating. It must be their imaginations that are controlled by the Matrix and not their perceptions, which are in fact switched off as they slumber in their pods. For only then could they gain control over their dreams, thus wresting control from the Matrix. Percepts, on the other hand, are not the kind of thing over which one can have voluntary control.

In the normal case, we do not have conscious control over our dreams: we are passive before them. But this doesn't mean that they are not willed events; they may be—and, I think, are—controlled by an unconscious will (with some narrative flair). In effect, we each have a matrix in our own brains—a system that controls what we dream—and this unconscious matrix is an intelligent designer of our dreams. But there are also those infrequent cases in which we can assert conscious control over our dreams, possibly contrary to the intentions of our unconscious dream designer: for example, when a nightmare becomes too intense and we interrupt it by waking up, often judging within the dream that it is only a dream. But the phenomenon that really demonstrates conscious control over the dream is so-called lucid dreaming in which the subject not only knows he is dreaming but can also determine the course of the dream. This is a rare ability (I have had only one lucid dream in all my fifty-two years), though some people have the ability in a regular and pronounced form: they are the Neos of our ordinary human matrix—the ones (or Ones) who can take control of their dreams away from the grip of the unconscious dream producer. The lucid dreamers are masters of their own dream world, captains of their own imagination.

Neo aspires to be—and eventually becomes—the lucid dreamer of the Matrix world: he can override the Matrix's designs on his dream life and impose his own will on what he experiences. He rewrites the program, just as the lucid dreamer can seize narrative control from *his* unconscious matrix. Instead of allowing the figures in his dreams to make him a victim of the Matrix's designs, Neo can impose his own story line on them. This is how he finally vanquishes the hitherto invulnerable Agents: he makes them subject to his will, as all imaginary objects must in principle be, if the will is strong (and pure) enough. It is as if you were having an ordinary nightmare in which you are menaced by a monster, and you suddenly start to dream lucidly, so that you can now turn the tables on your own imaginative products. Neo is a dreamer who knows it and can control it: he is not taken in by the verisimilitude of the dream, not cowed by it. It is not that he learns how to dodge real bullets; he learns that the bullets that speed toward him are just negotiable products of his imagination. As Morpheus remarks, he won't *need* to dodge bullets, because he will reach a level of understanding that allows him to recognize imaginary bullets for what they are. He becomes the ruler of his own imagination; *he* is the agent now, not the "Agents" (this is why the spoon-bending child says to him that it is not spoons that bend—"*you* bend"). And this is the freedom he seeks—the freedom to imagine what he wishes, to generate his own dreams. But all of this makes sense only on the supposition that the Matrix is a dream machine, an imagination manipulator, not just a purveyor of sensory hallucinations.

II

Cypher plays an interesting subsidiary philosophical role. As the Matrix raises the problem of our knowledge of the external world (might this all be just a dream?) Cypher raises the problem of other minds (can we know the content of someone else's mind?). Cypher is a cipher, that is, someone whose thoughts and emotions are inscrutable to those around him. His comrades are completely wrong about what is in (and on) his mind. We could imagine another type of matrix story in which someone is surrounded by people who are not as they seem: either they have no minds at all or they have very different minds from what their behavior suggests. Again, massive error will be the result. And such error might lead to dramatic consequences: everyone around the person is really out to get him—his wife, friends, and so on. But this is concealed from him. Or he might one day discover that he is really surrounded by insentient robots, so that his wife was always faking it (come to think of it, she always seemed a little mechanical in bed). This is another type of philosophical dystopia, trading upon the problem of knowing other minds. Cypher hints at this kind of problem, with his hidden interior. The Agents, too, raise a problem of other minds, because they seem on the borderline of mentality: are they just insentient (virtual) machines or is there some glimmer of consciousness under that hard carapace and software? And how was it known that AI was really sentient, as opposed to being a very good simulacrum of mindedness? Even if you know there is an external world, how can you be sure that it contains other conscious beings? These skeptical problems run right through *The Matrix*.

Cypher also raises a question about the pragmatic theory of truth. He declares that truth is an overrated commodity; he prefers a good steak, even when it isn't real. So long as he is getting what he wants, which is having rewarding experiences, he doesn't care whether his beliefs are true. This raises in a sharp form the question of what the value of truth is anyway, given that in the Matrix world it is not correlated with happiness. But it also tells us that for a belief to be true cannot be for it to produce happiness (the pragmatic theory of truth, roughly) since Cypher will be happy in the dream world of the Matrix without his beliefs being true—and he is not happy in the real world where his beliefs are true. Truth is correspondence to reality, not to whatever leads to the satisfaction of subjective desire.

Cypher implicitly rejects the pragmatic theory of truth, and as a result cannot see why truth-as-correspondence is worth having at the expense of happiness. And indeed he has a point here: what is the value of truth once it has become detached from the value of happiness? Is it really worth risking one's life merely in order to ensure that one's beliefs are *true*, instead of just enjoying what the dreams of the Matrix have to offer? Is contact with brutish reality worth death, when virtual reality is so safe and agreeable? Which is better: knowledge or happiness? When these are pulled apart, as they are in the Matrix, which one should we go with? The rebel humans want to get to Zion (meaning "sanctuary" or "refuge"), but isn't the Matrix already a type of Zion—without the dubious virtue of generating true beliefs? What's so good about reality?

III

I want to end this chapter by relating *The Matrix* to my general theory of what is psychologically involved in watching and becoming absorbed in a movie. In brief, I hold that watching a movie is like being in a dream; that is, the state of consciousness of being absorbed in a movie resembles and draws upon the state of consciousness of the dreamer. The images of the dream function like the images on the screen: they are not "realistic," but we become fictionally immersed in the story being told. In my theory, this is akin to the hypnotic state—a state of heightened suggestibility in which we come to believe what there is no real evidence for. Mere images command our belief, because we have entered a state of hypersuggestibility. When the lights go down in the theater, this simulates going to sleep, whereupon the mind becomes prepared to be absorbed in a fictional product—as it does when we enter the dream state. In neither case are we put into a state of consciousness that imitates or duplicates the perceptual state of seeing and hearing the events of the story; it is not as if we are really seeing flesh-and-blood human beings up on the screen (as we would with live actors on a stage)—nor do we interpret the screen images in this way. Rather, we *imagine* what is represented by these images, just as we use imagination to dream.

Now what has this got to do with *The Matrix*? The film is *about* dreaming; most of what we see in it occurs in dreams. So when we watch the movie, we enter a dream state that is about a dream state; we dream of a dream. I believe that the movie was made in such a way as to simulate very closely what is involved in dreaming, as if aiming to evoke the dream state in the audience. It is trying to put the audience in the same kind of state of mind as are the inhabitants of the Matrix, so that we too are in our own matrix—the one created by the filmmakers. The Wachowski brothers are in effect occupying the role of the machines behind the Matrix; they are the puppeteers of the audience's movie dreams. They are *our* dream designers as we enter the world of the movie.

The specific aspects of the movie that corroborate this are numerous, but I think it is clear that the entire texture of the movie is dreamlike. There is the hypnotic soundtrack, which helps to simulate the hypnotic fascination experienced by the dreamer. There is a powerful impression of paranoia throughout the film, which mirrors the paranoia of so many dreams: who is my enemy? how can he be identified? what is he going to do to me? Characters are stylized and symbolic, as they often are in dreams, representing some emotional pivot rather than a three-dimensional person (this is obvious for the Agents). There is a lot of striking metamorphosis, which is very characteristic of dreams: one person changing into another, Neo's mouth closing over, bulges appearing under the skin. There is also fear of heights, a common form of anxiety dream (I have these all the time). Defiance of gravity is also an extremely common dream theme, as in dreams of flying—and this is one of the first tricks that Neo masters.

My own experience of the movie is that it evokes in me an exceptionally pronounced dreamy feeling, and this of course enables me to identify with the inhabitants of the Matrix. So I see the film as playing nicely into my dream theory of the movie-watching experience. In this respect I would compare it to *The Wizard of Oz*, which is also about entering and exiting a dream world—though a very different one. In the end, Dorothy prefers reality to the consolations of dreaming, just as the rebels in the Matrix do. Both films tap powerfully into the dream-making faculty of the human mind. This is why they are among the most psychologically affecting of all the movies that have been made: their creators know that one of the surest ways to our deepest emotions is via the dream. And it is their very lack of "realism" that makes them so compelling—because that, too, is the essential character of the dream.

Further Reading

Christian references in the *Matrix* films are discussed in extensive detail in the essay by Rachel Wagner and Frances Flannery-Dailey included in this collection. The nature of dreams is explored from the perspective of cognitive science in Andy Clark's essay "The Twisted Matrix: Dream, Simulation or Hybrid?" also included here. I further pursue the connections between the consciousness of the dreamer and the consciousness of the movie viewer in my recent book *The Power of Movies: How Screen and Mind Interact* (Knopf 2005).

EXISTENTIAL PHENOMENOLOGY AND THE BRAVE NEW WORLD OF *THE MATRIX*

The Matrix series makes us rethink what we mean by contact with the real world, illusion, freedom, and what is required for human flourishing. Only then will we be in a position to take up the question, raised and answered in the three films, why, if at all, it is better to live in the real world, no matter how impoverished and unstable, than to live in a virtual world that is ordered so as to take care of our needs and let us get on with our everyday lives.

I. The Myth of the Inner

Thanks to Descartes, we moderns have to face the question: how can we ever get outside of our private, inner experiences so as to come to know the things and people in the public, external world? While this seems an important question to us now, it has not always been taken seriously. For the Homeric Greeks, human beings had no inner life to speak of. All of their strong feelings were expressed outwardly. Homer considered it one of Odysseus's cleverest tricks that he could cry inwardly while his eyes remained dry.[1]

A thousand years later, people still had no sense of the importance of their inner lives. St. Augustine had to work hard to convince them otherwise. For example, he called attention to the fact that one did not have to read out loud.

---

1. Imagine how his heart ached . . . and yet he never blinked; his eyes might have been made of horn or iron. . . . He had this trick—wept, if he willed to, inwardly. Homer, *The Odyssey*, trans. Robert Fitzgerald (New York: Vintage, 1990), 360.

Of course, the Homeric Greeks must have had some sort of private feelings for Odysseus to perform this trick, but they thought the inner was rare and trivial. As far as we know, there is no other reference to *private* feelings in Homer. Rather, there are many *public* displays of emotions and shared visions of gods, monsters, and future events.

In his *Confessions*, he points out that St. Ambrose was remarkable in that he read to himself: "When he read, his eyes scanned the page and his heart explored the meaning, but his voice was silent and his tongue was still."[2]

But the idea that each of us has an inner life made up of our private thoughts and feelings didn't really take hold until early in the seventeenth century when Descartes introduced the modern distinction between the contents of the mind and the rest of reality. In one of his letters, he declared himself "convinced that I cannot have any knowledge of what is outside me except through the mediation of the ideas that I have in me."[3]

Thus, according to Descartes, all each of us can directly experience is the content of our own mind. Our access to the world is always indirect. Descartes then used reports of people with phantom limbs to call into question even our seemingly direct experience of our own bodies. He wrote:

> I have been assured by men whose arm or leg has been amputated that it still seemed to them that they occasionally felt pain in the limb they had lost—thus giving me grounds to think that I could not be quite certain that a pain I endured was indeed due to the limb in which I seemed to feel it.[4]

For all we could ever know, Descartes concluded, the objective external world, including our body, may not exist; all we can be certain of is our subjective inner life.

This Cartesian conclusion was taken for granted by thinkers in the West for the next three centuries. A generation after Descartes, Gottfried Leibniz postulated that each of us is a windowless monad.[5] A *monad* is a self-contained world of experience, which gets no input from objects or other embodied people because there aren't any. Rather, the temporally evolving content of each monad is synchronized with the evolving

---

2. St. Augustine, *Confessions*, trans. R. S. Pine-Coffin (New York: Penguin, 1961), 114.

3. Letter to Gibieuf of 19 January 1642, in *Descartes: Philosophical Letters*, trans. Anthony Kenny (New York: Oxford University Press, 1970), 123.

4. René Descartes, "Meditations on First Philosophy—Meditations VI," in *Essential Works of Descartes*, trans. Lowell Bair (New York: Bantam, 1961), 98.

5. Gottfried Leibniz, *The Monadology and Other Philosophical Writings* (Oxford: Oxford University Press, 1971). A *monad*, according to Leibniz, is an immaterial entity lacking spatial parts, whose basic properties are a function of its inner perceptions and appetites. As Leibniz put it: a monad has no windows.

content of all of the other monads by God, creating the illusion of a shared real world. A generation after that, Immanuel Kant argued that human beings could never know reality as it is in itself but only their own mental representations, but, since these representations had a common source, each person's experiences were coordinated with the mental representations of all the others to produce what he called the phenomenal world.[6] In the early twentieth century, the founder of phenomenology, Edmund Husserl, was more solipsistic. He held, like Descartes, that one could bracket the world and other minds altogether since all that was given to us directly, whether the world and other minds existed or not, was the contents of our own "transcendental consciousness."[7] Only recently have philosophers begun to take issue with this powerful Cartesian picture.

Starting in the 1920s, existential phenomenologists such as Martin Heidegger[8] and Maurice Merleau-Ponty,[9] in opposition to Husserl, contested the Cartesian view that our contact with the world and even our own bodies is mediated by internal mental content. They pointed out that, if one paid careful attention to one's experience, one would see that, at a level of involvement more basic than thought, we deal directly with the things and people that make up our world. As Charles Taylor, the leading contemporary exponent of this view, puts it:

> My ability to get around this city, this house comes out only in getting around this city and house. We can draw a neat line between my picture of an object and that object, but not between my dealing with the object and that object. It may make sense to ask us to focus on what we believe about something, say a football, even in the absence of that thing; but when it comes to playing football, the corresponding suggestion would be absurd.

6. Immanuel Kant, *Critique of Pure Reason*, trans. Norman Kemp Smith (New York: Humanities Press, 1950).

7. Edmund Husserl, *Cartesian Meditations: An Introduction to Phenomenology*, trans. Dorion Cairns (The Hague: Martinus Nijhoff, 1960).

8. See Martin Heidegger, *Being and Time*, trans. J. Macquarrie and E. Robinson (New York: HarperCollins, 1962).

9. See Maurice Merleau-Ponty, *Phenomenology of Perception*, trans. C. Smith (London: Routledge and Kegan Paul, 1962).

The actions involved in the game can't be done without the object; they include the object.[10]

In general, unlike mental content, which can exist independently of its referent, my coping abilities cannot be actualized or, in some cases, even entertained (consider imagining how you tie your shoelaces) in the absence of what I am coping with.

This is not to say that we can't be mistaken. It's hard to see how I could succeed in getting around in a city or playing football without the existence of the city or the ball, but I could be mistaken for a while, as when I mistake a façade for a house. Then, in the face of my failure to cope successfully, I may have to retroactively cross off what I seemingly encountered and adopt a new readiness (itself corrigible) to encounter a façade rather than the house I was set to deal with.

II. Brains in Vats

So it looks like the inner/outer distinction introduced by Descartes holds only for thoughts. At the basic level of involved skillful coping, one is, Merleau-Ponty claims, simply an empty head turned toward the world.[11] But this doesn't show that *The Matrix* is old-fashioned or mistaken. On the contrary, it shows that *The Matrix* has gone further than philosophers who hold we can't get outside our *mind*. It suggests a more convincing conclusion—one that Descartes pioneered but didn't develop—that we can't get outside our *brain*.

It was no accident that Descartes proclaimed the priority of the inner in the seventeenth century. At that time, instruments like the telescope and microscope were extending human beings' perceptual powers. At the same time, the sense organs themselves were being understood as transducers bringing information from the objective external world to the brain. Descartes pioneered this research with an account of how the eye

10. Charles Taylor, "Overcoming Epistemology," in *Philosophical Arguments* (Cambridge, MA: Harvard University Press, 1995), 12. See also Samuel Todes, *Body and World* (Cambridge, MA: MIT Press, 2001).

11. Merleau-Ponty, *Phenomenology of Perception*, 355.

responds to light energy from the external world and passes the information on to the brain by means of "the small fibers of the optic nerve."[12] Likewise, Descartes used the phantom-limb phenomenon to argue that other nerves brought information about the body to the brain, and from there the information passed to the mind.

It seemed to follow that, since we are each a brain in a cranial vat,[13] we can *never* be in direct contact with the world or even with our own bodies. So, even if phenomenologists like Heidegger, Merleau-Ponty, and Taylor are right that we are not confined to our inner *experiences*, it still seems plausible to suppose that, as long as the impulses to and from our nervous system copy the complex feedback loop between the brain's outgoing behavior-producing impulses and the incoming perceptual ones, we would have the experience of directly coming to grips with things in the world. Yet, in the brain-in-the-vat case, there would be no house and no city, indeed, no real external objective world to interact with, and so we might seem to be confined to our inner experiences after all. As Morpheus says to Neo in the Construct:

> How do you define "real"? If you're talking about what you can feel, what you can smell, what you can taste and see, then "real" is simply electrical signals interpreted by your brain.

But this Cartesian conclusion is mistaken. The inner electrical impulses are the causal basis of what one can taste and feel, but we don't see and taste *them*. Even if I have only a phantom arm, my pain is not in my brain but in my phantom hand. What the phenomenologist can and should claim is that, in a Matrix world which has its causal basis in bodies in vats outside that world, the Matrix people whose brains are getting computer-generated inputs and responding with action outputs are directly coping with *perceived*

12. René Descartes, "Dioptric," in *Descartes: Philosophical Writings*, ed. and trans. Norman Kemp Smith (New York: Modern Library, 1958), 150.

13. The point has been made explicitly by John Searle: "[E]ach of us is precisely a brain in a vat; the vat is a skull and the 'messages' coming in are coming in by way of impacts on the nervous system." *Intentionality: An Essay in the Philosophy of Mind* (Cambridge: Cambridge University Press, 1983), 230.

reality, and that reality isn't *inner*.[14] Even in the Matrix world, people directly cope with chairs by sitting on them, and they need baseballs to bring out their batting skills. Thus coping, even in the Matrix, is more direct than conceived of by any of the inner/outer views of the mind's relation to the "external world" that have been held from Descartes to Husserl.

Yet, wouldn't each brain in the Matrix construct have a lot of false beliefs, for example, that its Matrix body is its real body whereas its real body is in a vat? No. If the Matrix dweller has a pain in his damaged foot, it's in his Matrix foot, not in his brain, nor in the foot of a body in a vat—a foot that is not damaged and about which he knows nothing at all.[15] It's a mistake to think that each of us is experiencing a set of neural firings in a brain in a cranial vat. True, each of us has a brain in her skull, and the brain provides the causal basis of our experience, but we aren't our brain. Likewise, the people in the Matrix world are not brains in vats any more than we are. They are people who grew up in the Matrix world, and their experience of their Matrix body and how to use it makes that body their body, even if another body that they can't even imagine has in its skull the brain that is the causal basis of their experience.

After all, the people who live in the Matrix have no other source of experience than what happens in the Matrix. Thus, a person in the Matrix has no beliefs at all about the vat-enclosed body and brain that is his causal basis, and couldn't have any. That brain is merely the unknowable cause of that person's experiences. Since the only body a Matrix dweller sees and moves is the one he has in the Matrix world, the AI programmers could have given him a Matrix body radically unlike the body in the vat. After all, the brain in the vat started life as a baby brain and could have been given any experience that the AI programmers chose. They could have taken the

14. This is true for the phenomenologist describing the first-person experiences of those inside the Matrix. From a third-person perspective of someone outside the Matrix, however, the Matrix world is not connected to the causal powers of the physical universe, and so the experiences of those in the Matrix world do not count as perceptions. In that sense, the Matrix world, while not "in the mind," is merely virtual, although, since it is an intersubjective experience, it is still not like a dream.

15. The Matrix foot, moreover, can have its "reality" confirmed by coping (kicking a football, walking around in a city), whereas a phantom foot cannot help its owner get around in the world.

brain of a white baby who was going to grow up short and fat and given it the Matrix body of a tall, athletic African American.[16]

But at least one problem remains. The Matricians' beliefs about the properties and uses of their perceived bodies—as well as about chairs, cities, and the world—may be shared and reliable, and in that sense true, but what about the *causal* beliefs of the people in the Matrix? They believe, as we do, that germs cause disease, that the sun causes things to get warm, that gravity causes things to fall, and so forth. Aren't all of these beliefs false? That depends on one's understanding of causality. People don't normally have explicit beliefs about the nature of causality. Rather, they simply take for granted a shared sense that they are coping with a shared world whose contents are causing their experience.

Unless they are philosophizing, they do not *believe* that the world is real or that it is an illusion; they just count on it behaving in a consistent way so that they can cope with things successfully. If, however, as philosophers, they believe that there is a physical universe with causal powers that makes things happen in their world, they are mistaken. And, if the causal theory of perception requires this strong sense of causality for perceptions to be veridical, they are not perceiving anything. But if they claim that belief in causality is simply a response to the constant conjunctions of experiences, as David Hume did, or that causality is the necessary succession of experiences according to a rule, as Kant held, then their causal beliefs would be true of the causal relations in the Matrix world, and most of their perceptual experiences would be veridical.[17]

16. There are limits, of course. The Matrix programmers can't give a human being a dog's body. It's also unlikely that they could make a brain in a female body the causal basis of a man's body in the Matrix world. The hormones of the body in the vat wouldn't match the physical attributes and emotions of that person in the Matrix world.

Indeed, a good way for the AI programmers to prevent bodies being rescued to the hovercraft would be to give each brain the experience of a radically different body (within whatever limits are imposed by biology) in the Matrix world than the body in which that brain actually is. If rescued, such people would quite likely go crazy trying to reconcile the bodies they had experienced all their lives with the suddenly alien bodies on the hovercraft.

17. Likewise, their beliefs about entities such as viruses and black holes would be true if, like empiricists, they held that theoretical entities are just convenient ways to refer to the data produced by experiments. See Bas van Frassen, *The Scientific Image* (Oxford: Clarendon, 1980).

Kant claims that we organize the impact of things in themselves on our mind into our experience of a public, objective world, and science relates these appearances by causal laws, but we can't know the ground of the phenomena we perceive. Specifically, according to Kant, we experience the world *as* in space and time but *things in themselves* aren't in space and time. So Kant says that we can know the phenomenal world of objects and their lawlike relations, but we can't know the things in themselves that are the ground of these appearances.

The Matricians are in the same epistemological position that we are all in, according to Kant. So, if there are Kantians in the Matrix world, most of their beliefs would be true. They would understand that they are experiencing a coordinated system of appearances, and understand too that they couldn't know the things in themselves that are the ground of these appearances, that is, that they couldn't know the basis of their shared experience of the world and the universe. But Kantians don't hold that our shared and tested everyday beliefs about the world and scientists' confirmed beliefs about the universe are false just because they are about phenomena and do not and cannot correspond to things in themselves. And, as long as Kantians, and everyone in the Matrix, didn't claim to know about things in themselves, most of their beliefs would be true.

Nonetheless, the implicit philosophy of *The Matrix* obviously does not subscribe to the Kantian view that we can *never* know things in themselves. In *The Matrix*, one can come to know reality. Once Neo's body is flushed out of the vat and is on the hovercraft, he has a broader view of reality and sees that his previous understanding was limited. But that doesn't mean he had a lot of false beliefs about his body and the world. When he was in the Matrix, he didn't think about these philosophical questions at all.[18] But once he is out, he has a lot of new, true beliefs about his former vat-enclosed body—beliefs he didn't have and couldn't have had while in the Matrix. We have seen that existential phenomenologists acknowledge that we are sometimes mistaken about particular things and have to retroactively take back our readiness to cope with them. But, as Merleau-Ponty and Taylor add, we only do so in terms of a

18. Indeed, his coping skills were presumably not based on beliefs at all. See Ludwig Wittgenstein, *On Certainty* (New York: Harper Torchbooks, 1969).

prima facie new and better contact with reality. Likewise, in *The Matrix* version of the brain-in-the-vat situation, those who have been hauled from the vat into what they experience as the real world can see that much of what they took for granted was mistaken. They can, for example, understand that what they took to be a world that had been around for millions of years was a recently constructed computer program.

Of course, things are not so simple. Most of Neo's current beliefs might still be false. His experience might, after all, be sustained by a brain in a skull in a vat, and the AI programmers might now be feeding that brain the experience of Neo's being outside the Matrix and in the hovercraft. Given the conceivability of the brain-in-the-vat fantasy, the most we can be sure of is that our coping experience reveals that we are directly up against some boundary conditions independent of our coping— boundary conditions with which we must get in sync in order to cope successfully. In this way, our coping experience is sensitive to the causal powers of these boundary conditions. Whether these independent causal conditions have the structure of an independent physical universe discovered by science, or whether the boundary conditions as well as the causal structures discovered by science are both the effect of an un- knowable thing in itself that is the ground of appearances as postulated by Kant, or even whether the cause of all appearances is a computer is something we could never know from inside our world. But Neo, once he seems to be on the hovercraft, does know that, as in waking from a dream, his current understanding of reality supersedes his former one.

III. An Ethical Interlude

The distinction between a Matrix person and the body that is the causal basis of that person has serious ethical implications. In the movie, in- nocent people doing their job, like the police officers in the opening scene, are killed with casual unconcern, if not with relish by Morpheus and his band. Morpheus justifies these killings by explaining that the Matricians have been told that the intruders are dangerous terrorists and so the police and other defenders of law and order will kill Morpheus and his friends if they don't strike first. But when we remember that each time a Matrician is killed an associated human body somewhere in a vat dies, it seems that the killing of a virtual person in the Matrix must be morally wrong because it causes the death of a real human being.

But this can't be the right way to think about the moral issue. The bodies in the vats are not people; they are the causal basis of the people in the Matrix. They happen to be human bodies made of protoplasm but they could just as well be computers made of silicon as long as they process the inputs and outputs the way the human brain does. It is important to bear in mind that a body in a vat doesn't have a human personality apart from the active, vulnerable, feeling person in the Matrix of whom it is the causal basis.

Thus, when Neo is in the Matrix world, there are two Neo-related bodies. One is an active, embodied Neo coping in the Matrix world, and the other is a noncoping, Neo-causing body in a vat (or chair) outside the Matrix world, but there is only one Neo, and he stays the same in the Matrix world and later in the hovercraft because he has the same concerns, memories, and so on—whatever accounts for personal identity—and there never was a Neo in the vat, any more than there is a person in your skull, because to be the causal basis of a person is not to be a person.

It follows that when Morpheus and his followers kill the people in the Matrix world, it is murder, not because the killers cause a human organism in a vat to die, but because they kill Matricians who have personalities, act freely, love, suffer, and so forth. True, the way the Matrix world is set up, if one were to kill a body in a vat, the associated person in the Matrix would die. But the point to note is that the moral priorities are the reverse of one's first intuitions. The killing of a person in the Matrix world is intrinsically wrong because killing a person is wrong, and incidentally it results in the death of a human body in a vat; while killing the human body in the vat is wrong only as long as that body is at least potentially the causal basis of a person in the Matrix world. In our world, the tight causal connection between our biological body and our personhood keeps us from noticing these moral distinctions.

IV. A New *Brave New World*

We are now in a position to try to answer the question: why live in the miserable and endangered world the war has produced rather than in a satisfying and stable world of appearances? Some answers just won't do. It doesn't seem to be a question of whether one should face the truth rather than live in an illusion. Indeed, most of the beliefs of the average Matrician are true; they can cope by acting in some ways and not in others. When they sit on chairs, they usually support them; when they enter a house, they see the inside; when they walk around it, they see the back. People have bodies that can be injured; they can kill and be killed. Even their background sense that in their actions they are coping with something independent of them and that others are coping with it too is justified. As we have seen, Kant argued that, even if this were a phenomenal world, a world of appearances, most of our beliefs would still be true.

Likewise, living in the Matrix world does not seem to be less moral than living in our everyday world. The Matricians are dealing with real people, and they are free to choose what they will do; they can be selfish and betray their friends like Cypher, or they can be loyal to their friends and ready to risk their lives for them, like Trinity and Neo do for Morpheus. So, what, if anything, is wrong with the Matrix world?[19]

To understand what's wrong with living in the Matrix, we have to understand the source of the power of the Matrix world. Part of the power comes from the way the inputs and outputs from the computer are plugged directly into the brain's sensory motor system. These correlations produce a powerful perceptual effect that is impervious to what one believes, like the wrap-around IMAX illusion that forces one to sway to keep one's balance on a skateboard even though one knows one is sitting in a stationary seat watching a movie, or like when the moon looks bigger on the horizon even though one believes it is always the same size.

The inputs to the perceptual system of the brain in the vat produce an experience of a perceptual world whether we believe it is real or not, but once one realizes that the causality in the Matrix world is only virtual, since one's beliefs concerning what is causing what is not built into our perceptual system, one can violate the Matrix's causal programs. By the

19. John Haugeland suggests that Cypher's choice is, from some ethical points of view, immoral because, in asking that when he returns to the Matrix world all his memories be erased, Cypher is in effect committing a kind of existential suicide, even if the body in the vat, which has been the causal basis of Cypher up to now, will live on in the Matrix as the causal basis for a powerful actor named Reagan.

end of the first movie, Neo can fly; if he wanted to, he could bend spoons.[20] About the causal principles governing the Matrix world, Morpheus tells Neo, "It is all in your mind."

In the Matrix world, then, if one doesn't believe in the causal laws governing appearances, one is free from the causal consequences. One's disbelief in the Matrix world somehow forces the computer to give one the experience of the causal consequences one wills to have. To take a simple example, if one doesn't believe in the existence of a spoon, when one decides to see the spoon bending, the computer is forced to give one the visual input of the bending spoon. This is a literal example of what Morpheus calls "bending the rules." Likewise, if one believes that one can stop bullets, one will look for them where one stopped them, and the computer will obediently display them there. So, after he learns that his experience of the Matrix world is not caused in the normal way, Neo doesn't *see* things differently—the impulses to his brain still control what he sees[21]—but he is able to choose to *do* things that he couldn't do before (like choose to stop bullets) and that allows him to see

20. Granted, it's hard to resist believing in the Matrix even where causality is concerned; nonetheless, Neo learns that he can stop believing in it. This new understanding of reality is described by Morpheus talking to Neo near the beginning of the first movie, and by Neo at the end, as like waking from a dream. But the brains in the vats are not literally dreaming. Their world is much too coherent and intersubjective to be a dream. Or, to put it another way, dreams are the result of some quirk in our internal neural wiring and full of inconsistencies, although when dreaming we don't usually notice them. They are not the result of a systematic correlation between input and output to the brain's perceptual system that is meant to reproduce the consistent coordinated experience that we have when awake. That is why we correctly consider them to be private inner experiences.

True, when people from the hovercraft return to the Matrix world, it looks like their hovercraft bodies go to sleep, but they do not enter a private dream world but an alternative intersubjective world where they are normally wide awake, and in which they can also seem to dream and wake from a dream, as Neo does after the Agents take away his mouth.

21. There is one unfortunate exception to this claim. At the end of the first movie, Neo catches a glimpse of the computer program behind the world of appearances. This is a powerful visual effect meant to show us that Neo can now program the Matrix world from the inside, but, if what we've been saying is right, it makes no sense. If the computer is still feeding coordinated sensory motor impulses into Neo's brain when he is plugged into the Matrix world, then he will see the world that the program is producing in his visual system, not the program itself. What the sight of the streaming symbols is meant to do is to remind us that Neo no longer *believes* that the Matrix is real but now understands it and can manipulate it, as a computer program. But even so, he should continue to *see* the Matrix world.

different things (the bullets stop). Unfortunately, how this suspension of belief in causality is able to affect the output of the brain's perceptual system is not explained.

What, then, is the source of the sinister power of the Matrix world, which keeps people conforming to the supposed constraints of a causal universe, even though there are no such constraints? If it isn't just that they are locked into the sensory motor correlations of their perceptual world, what sort of control is it? It has to be some sort of control of the Matricians' intellectual powers—powers that, as we have just noted, are free from the control of direct sensory motor computer correlations.[22] It must be some sort of mind control.

It seems that the Matrix simply takes advantage of a sort of mind control already operating in the everyday world. We are told that what keeps people from taking control of the Matrix world is their taking for granted the commonsense view of how things behave, such as, if you fall you will get hurt. More generally, what keeps people in line is their tendency to believe what the average person believes, and consequently one keeps doing (and not doing) what one does and doesn't do. (As in, one eats peas with a fork; one doesn't throw food at the dinner table; and one goes out the door rather than the window.) Heidegger describes the resulting conformism as letting oneself be taken over by "the one" (*das Man*).[23] Aldous Huxley similarly lamented the conformity of the brainwashed masses in *Brave New World*.

Thus, *The Matrix* can be seen as an attack on what Nietzsche calls *herd mentality*. Nietzsche points out that human beings are normally socialized

---

22. Even Agent Smith shows a kind of individual freedom when he deviates from his mission of maintaining order in the Matrix and tells Morpheus how disgusted he is with the Matrix world. But, in *The Matrix*, the Agents as computer programs in a programmed world don't have the freedom to radically change that world. Later, in *Reloaded*, we learn that Agent Smith has a new freedom to act outside of the Matrix because he has some of Neo mixed up in him and has taken over the body of Bains, but even then there is no sign that he has or needs the freedom to be creative.

23. This is not to be confused with Neo as "The One" who will save people from the Matrix. For Heidegger's account of the power of the one, see his *Being and Time*, and also H. Dreyfus, *Being-in-the-World: A Commentary on Heidegger's Being and Time, Division I* (Cambridge, MA: MIT Press, 1991), chapter 8.

into obeying shared social norms and that it is hard to think differently. As he puts it:

> [A]s long as there have been humans, there have also been herds of men (clans, communities, tribes, peoples, states, churches) and always a great many people who obey.... considering, then, that nothing has been exercised and cultivated better and longer among men than obedience, one may fairly assume that the need for it is now innate in the average man.[24]

Waking in the movie, then, amounts to freeing oneself from the taken-for-granted norms that one has been brought up to accept. But how is this possible? Heidegger claims that human beings dimly sense that there is more to life than conforming. How fitting then that a barely expressible unease, like a splinter in his mind, seems to pervade Neo's life and prompts him to begin the process of asserting his nonconformity by becoming a hacker and breaking all the rules.

V. A Really *Brave New World*

One might reasonably object that all of the talk of dreaming in *The Matrix*, even if it should not be taken literally, is too strong a religious metaphor to refer merely to what Heidegger calls "living a tranquilized existence in the one." And waking seems to be more than becoming a nonconformist. After all, there are all those mentions of Jesus in connection with Neo that have been collected by Colin McGinn.[25] There can be no doubt that Neo is meant to be a kind of savior, but what kind?

It's tempting to think that *The Matrix* is a Gnostic, Buddhist, or Platonic/Christian parable, in which what we take to be reality turns out to be a dream, and we are led to awaken from the world of appearances to some kind of higher spiritual reality. On this reading, Neo would lead his people out of the illusions of Plato's cave, the veil of Maya, or the darkness of the world into a higher disembodied life. But this association would be all wrong! In the film, salvation means the opposite of the traditional

---

24. Friedrich Nietzsche, *Beyond Good and Evil: Prelude to a Philosophy of the Future*, trans. Walter Kaufman (New York: Vintage, 1966), 110, sec. 199.

25. See Colin McGinn's chapter ("The Matrix of Dreams") in this volume.

religious vision. True, the ones who see through the Matrix can get over some of the limitations of having a body, as exemplified by their flying.[26] But such flying takes place *in* the Matrix world. In the real world to which Neo "awakes," and which we learn in the last film of the trilogy will be available to all human beings, there will be no more flying. People will have earthbound, vulnerable bodies and suffer cold, bad food, and death.

It may look, at the end of the first film, as if Neo evades death, but his "resurrection" in the hovercraft is not into a world where death has been overcome by a miraculous divine love; rather, he has been saved by an earthly intervention—a sort of tender CPR—quite within the bounds of physics and chemistry. So he still has his vulnerable body and will have to die a real death one day. What he presumably has gotten over is not death but the herd's fear of death, thereby overcoming what, according to Heidegger, leads people to flee into tranquilized conformity in the first place.

Indeed, if bending the rules that are accepted by the average person just amounts to being able to bend spoons, fly, and stop bullets, it doesn't seem to be any kind of salvation. Breaking free of conformity must mean more than just being disruptive.[27] We are led to expect that, in return for

26. Given the kind of bodies we have—that we move forward more easily than backward, that we can only cope with what is in front of us, that we have to balance in a gravitational field, and so on—we can question to what extent such body-relative constraints can be violated in *The Matrix* if what is going on is still to make sense.

To test these limits, the filmmakers occasionally blow our minds by using a wrap-around point of view from which the action looks so far from normal as to be awesomely unintelligible. At the same time, they have successfully met the challenge of discovering which body-relative invariances can be intelligibly violated and which can't. For example, in the movie, gravity can be overcome—Neo can fly—but he can't see equally in all directions or cope equally in all directions, nor can he be in several places at once. What would it look like for a single person to surround somebody? Time, too, has a body-relative structure that can't be violated with impunity. The way we experience time as moving from the past into the future and leaving the past behind depends on the way our forward-directed body enables us to approach objects and then pass them by (see Todes, *Body and World*). Could we make sense of a scene in which someone attacked an enemy not just from behind, but from the past? If, in the movie, the liberated ones were free of all bodily constraints governing their actions, we couldn't make sense of what they were doing, and neither could they. They wouldn't be liberated but would be bewildered, as we often are in our disembodied dreams.

27. Being disruptive is the best one can do in the Matrix world. That's why Neo, a hacker who, as Agent Smith says, has broken every rule in the book, is the natural candidate for savior.

accepting everyday vulnerability and suffering, the people liberated by Neo will be reborn to a new and better life in Zion.

But what is wrong with life in the Matrix? It seems clear that, if the AI intelligences do their job and make a complete simulation of our world, the people in the Matrix world should be able to do everything and experience everything that we can. Like them, we all have a causal basis in a brain in a vat. True, the causal link between their brains and the physical universe is different from ours, but why should that be a problem? How can the Matrix be, as Morpheus claims it is, "a prison for the mind," any more than our dependence on our brains and their causal inputs imprisons us?

Morpheus has no idea of what such a prison would be but talks, nonetheless, about enslavement and control. Early in the first film, he says: "What is the Matrix? Control. The Matrix is a computer-generated dreamworld, built to keep us under control." James Pryor, at the end of "What's So Bad about Living in the Matrix?" (in this collection), tries heroically to make sense of this claim by speculating on what the AI programmers might do to control the Matrix dwellers, such as resetting their world back to 1980 if they so chose. Insofar as the machines have done such things, Pryor has the right to say as he does:

> In the movie, humans in the Matrix are all slaves. They're not in charge of their own lives. They may be contented slaves, unaware of their chains, but they're slaves nonetheless. They have only a very limited ability to shape their own futures. . . . For most of us, the worst thing about living in the Matrix would not be something metaphysical or epistemological. Rather, the worst thing would be something political. It would be the fact that life in the Matrix is a kind of slavery.

Insofar as the Matrix makers interfere in the lives of the Matricians, they *are* controlling them, but the moments of interference in the film (the taking away of Neo's mouth, inserting a bugging device in his gut, and then making him think it was a dream; and the changing of a door into a brick wall to trap Morpheus and his crew) do not show that the Matricians, insofar as they are being used as batteries, are not in charge of their own lives. In principle, no such interference should be necessary. The police should be able to keep the Matrix dwellers in order. As the police officer says at the beginning of the first film, they can take care of lawbreakers and, presumably, hackers too. The Agents have been introduced to take care of people who hack into the Matrix from outside and those, like Neo, whom these intruders are trying to recruit. They do not and need not limit the lives of ordinary Matricians but only the lives of those who are resisting the Matrix.[28] What is important is that those who live tranquilly in the Matrix—the vast majority of human beings, whom Heidegger calls "inauthentic"—have just as much ability to shape their everyday lives as we do, so having your causal basis used as a battery does not amount to being controlled and enslaved.

We, therefore, have to conclude that Morpheus and Pryor are simply mistaken. If you're a slave, there must be a master who controls what you can do or, as in *Brave New World*, who even controls what you *want* to do, and, of course, if you knew that you were in such a world you would want your freedom. Having their causal basis used as batteries, however, doesn't interact with the Matricians' psychic lives and so doesn't limit what they can decide, what they can desire, or what they can do. What Morpheus doesn't understand (and Pryor doesn't bring out) is that having your causal basis used for some extraneous purpose is not per se enslaving. That is, although the Matricians' causal basis is being used to generate electricity; the Matricians themselves are not being used. Their "enslavement" in the Matrix is like our relation to our selfish genes. We don't feel that we are being controlled even if our DNA is using our bodies to propagate itself. Likewise, the simple fact that the bodies of the Matricians are serving some purpose outside their lives can't be what's wrong with living in the Matrix.

Indeed, as we see in *Revolutions*, what makes a reconciliation with the machines possible is that, if people are allowed to live in the Matrix without interference, most of them will be content to remain there. And, if this sort of freedom is all they want, they are right to do so. Even if they

---

28. In the course of their work, the Agents do take over the bodies of innocent bystanders, but such interference is gratuitous and does not show that being used as a battery is intrinsically enslaving. Likewise, if, as we are told in *Reloaded*, there is an anomaly in each Matrix world, unless such an anomaly can be shown to be disruptive, it doesn't show that humans' being used as batteries requires AI intervention to keep order.

are being used as batteries, there is no limitation in principle on their everyday choices and no issue of mind control and enslavement.

The Matrix trilogy never tells us why some people would want to leave the Matrix, that is, we are never told what, in principle, is wrong with the Matrix world, so we have to figure it out for ourselves. Our only clues are that Morpheus tells Neo that there is some sort of limit on what people in the Matrix can think and experience, and Neo says at the end of *The Matrix* that the AI intelligences don't like change. But what kind of internal change is so dangerous that they can't leave it to the police to keep it under control? And why don't they like it?

The answer turns out to be barely hinted at in the films, and figuring it out requires our going over some familiar philosophical ground as well as drawing on Heidegger to help free us from certain Cartesian prejudices. Part of the answer is that, to make a Matrix world just like our world, the AI programmers have to copy the way that the electric impulses to and from our brains in our vatlike skulls are coordinated. For us, as Descartes already understood, physical inputs of energy from the universe impinging on our sense organs produce electrical outputs that are sent to the brain and there give rise to our perceptual experience of other people and of things. This experience in turn, along with our dispositions, our beliefs, and our desires, causes us to act, which produces electrical outputs that move our physical body. How we act alters, in turn, what we see, and so on, in a continual loop. The correlations between the perceptual inputs and the action outputs are mediated by the way that the things and people in the world respond to being acted upon.

If each brain in a vat were cut off from the people and things in the world, the AI intelligences, in order to simulate the sensory motor loops, would have to model how people and things respond to all types of actions. In the Matrix, however, the AI programmers don't have to model *people's* reactions. Since the brains in the vats that are the causal basis of the people in the Matrix world respond as people in our world do, their responses can simply be fed back to the other envatted brains. But, since there is no world of *things* impinging on the sense organs of the people in the vats, the artificial intelligences have to program a computer simulation of our world.

They can't model the world on the physical level, however, since modeling how the atoms are moving and interacting is beyond any theory and beyond any computations that could actually be performed. We can't even model and predict which way a pencil balanced on its point will fall, or where the planets will be in their orbits a thousand years from now. Moreover, even if we had such a model, it might well take more atoms than there are in the universe to predict how things will behave and look. So the AI intelligences have wisely decided not to model on the physical level how everyday things behave. For example, since they are unable to model how a swarm of electrons in the universe behaves like a bird, they instead model how birds in the everyday world behave. As the Oracle says in *Reloaded*:

> See those birds? At some point a program was written to govern them. A program was written to watch over the trees, and the wind, the sunrise, and sunset. There are programs running all over the place.

Such a model, like the program for a shuttle simulator, would enable computers to produce the same correlations of electrical inputs and outputs—and therefore the same experiences of the correlation of perceptions and actions—in the world of the Matricians that the physical universe produces in our world. If you appear to walk too close to a Matrix bird, the program will make it appear to spread its wings and fly away.

Such programmed sensory motor correlations would leave the higher brain functions unaffected, and, indeed, we are told that the Matricians are free to form their own desires, beliefs, goals, and so forth. Morpheus is being a Cartesian when he holds that the simulated Matrix world is "a prison for the mind." It no more confines us to our minds than do the correlations between the physical inputs from the universe and the action outputs of our brains imprison us in our minds. Nor does there seem to be any problem with change. The Matrix world model and the everyday world it simulates must be capable of being changed by people's actions in just the ways ours is, and nonetheless remain stable, just the way ours does. As we shall see, this is what the machines rely on in the end when they promise not to interfere in the Matrix world. So it looks like there is no reason for the machines to be "afraid of change," yet, at the end of the first film, Neo says they are.

So we are back to the question: what's wrong with the Matrix? How could a successful simulation of the electrical impulses to and from our brains be "a limit on what we can think and experience"? If there is an answer, no one seems to know it. It must be subtle and hard to grasp. Indeed, it must be something that those who are in the Matrix can't grasp and those outside find it almost impossible to articulate, just as Morpheus gets it wrong when he says that those in the Matrix are slaves. To suggest a possible answer will require a detour through Heideggerian philosophy, since Heidegger claims there is something in our experience that, like the Matrix itself for the people in it, is nearest to us and farthest away, that is, something so pervasive that it has no contrast class to distinguish it from, so that, like water to the fish, it is almost impossible to see and describe. Maybe this is what the artificial intelligences have failed to simulate and rightly fear.

Heidegger calls it "being." *Being*, according to Heidegger, is "that on the basis of which beings are already understood."[29] One might say that the understanding of being is the style of life in a given period manifested in the way that everyday practices are coordinated. These shared practices into which we are socialized provide a background understanding of what counts as things, what counts as human beings, and what it makes sense to do, on the basis of which we can direct our actions toward particular things and people. Thus the understanding of being opens up a disclosive space that Heidegger calls a "clearing." Heidegger calls the unnoticed way that the clearing both limits and opens up what can show up and what it makes sense to do, its "unobtrusive governance."

For example, some sociologists point out that mothers in different cultures handle their babies in different ways that inculcate the babies into different ways of coping with themselves, people, and things.[30] For example, American mothers tend to put babies in their cribs on their stomachs, which encourages the babies to move around more effectively.

---

29. Heidegger, *Being and Time*, 25, 26.

30. W. Caudill and H. Weinstein, "Maternal Care and Infant Behavior in Japan and in America," in C. S. Lavatelli and F. Stendler, eds., *Readings in Child Behavior and Development* (New York: Harcourt Brace, 1972), 78. As long as we can use it to get a sense of how a cultural style works, we needn't be concerned as to whether this sociological account is accurate or complete.

Japanese mothers, contrariwise, put their babies on their backs so they will lie still, lulled by whatever they see. American mothers encourage passionate gesturing and vocalizing, while Japanese mothers are much more soothing and mollifying. In general, American mothers situate the child's body and respond to the child's actions in such a way as to promote an active and aggressive style of behavior. Japanese mothers, in contrast, nurture a greater passivity and sensitivity to harmony in the actions of their babies. What constitutes the American baby as an *American* baby is its style, and what constitutes the Japanese baby as a *Japanese* baby is its quite different style.

The style of the culture governs how people and things show up for the people in it. The way things look reflects what people feel they can do with them. So, for example, no bare rattle is ever encountered. For an American baby, a rattle-thing looks like an object to make lots of expressive noise with and to throw on the floor in a willful way in order to get a parent to pick it up. A Japanese baby may treat a rattle-thing this way more or less by accident, but generally we suspect that to them a rattle-thing looks soothing, like a Native American rain stick. So the rattle has a different meaning in different cultures depending on the style of the culture, and no one in AI has any idea how to program a style.[31]

But why should that be a problem? Perhaps, the different understandings of what it is to be a rattle, and what it is to be in general, don't have to be explicitly programmed since they are in the dispositions and beliefs of the people and, as we just saw, are passed on through socialization. If what happens when we perceive is that physical energy coming into the sense organs is taken up by the perceptual system and perceived as bare perceptual objects, the AI programmers could capture cross-cultural input/output perceptual experiences in their programs and leave the meaning and style of the bare perceptual things to the interpretive powers of higher symbolic mental activity.

This is in fact the way philosophers from Descartes to Husserl have pictured the relation of perception to meaning. Husserl claimed in

31. Among AI researchers, Douglas Hofstadter has seen this most clearly. See D. Hofstadter, "Metafont, Metamathematics, and Metaphysics," *Visible Language* 16 (April 1982).

Cartesian Meditations that mere physical things are encountered first and then afterward are given meaning as cultural objects.[32] But Heidegger contends that we don't normally experience bare physical objects and then interpret them in terms of what we can do with them. That is, we don't first experience bare objects on the basis of the physical input to our perceptual system and then assign each bare object a function predicate, as Descartes thought and as symbolic AI researchers still believe. As Nietzsche already said, there is no immaculate perception. Or, to take Wittgenstein's convincing example, the same physical input to the visual system from the same lines on a page can be *seen*, not just interpreted, as a duck or a rabbit.

If a change in our understanding of things changes how they look, there is, indeed, a problem for the AI intelligences programming the Matrix. For example, if you are making a world model and want to include programs for simulating the experience of rattles, you will have to take account of what they will solicit one to do with them, and that means they will have to *look* like missiles or pacifiers. Likewise, if you want to simulate the experience of seeing birds, you will have to simulate the different ways that birds look in different cultures. For the Greeks, according to Heidegger, things like birds appeared to well up from nature and then need nurturing. For the medieval Christians, "the birds of the air" looked like creatures of God. Thus they were painted in loving detail, fed by St. Francis, and seen as showing the way those with faith were free of cares and the need to plan their lives. Descartes and modern mechanists, on the contrary, saw birds and all animals as machines. Perhaps, we are now beginning to see them as endangered species in need of preservation.

If this phenomenological description of the richness of perception is right, one can't just model the way the world is organized by the perceptual system by writing programs to simulate the experience of bare objects and leave the rest up to the mind. But, then, if the understanding of being in a culture could change so that objects *looked* different, that

---

32. "An existent mere physical thing is given beforehand (when we disregard all the...'cultural' characteristics that make it knowable as, for example, a hammer...)." Husserl, *Cartesian Meditations*, 78.

would pose a serious problem for the Matrix programmers. If a culture's understanding of being switched from aggressive to nurturing, say, everything would need to be reprogrammed. The case would be parallel to the one described to Morpheus by Agent Smith, when the AI intelligences had to scrap their program simulating a perfect world, because humans did not feel at home in it, and program one like ours with conflict, risk, suffering, and so on. In order to do this reprogramming, the Matrix had to be shut down, and in the process "whole crops were lost."

Unfortunately for the machines, where style is concerned, this sort of problem seems bound to recur. As Heidegger observes, the understanding of being that governs perception and action in our culture is not static, but has gone through a series of radical changes. In each stage, objects presented different possibilities for action and so looked different, and there were even different objects. For the early Greeks, being meant welling up, and what whooshed up for the Greeks were gods and heroes suddenly doing marvelous things, while the medieval understanding of being as being created by God made possible the appearance of miracles, saints, and sinners, and things looked like they offered rewards and temptations. With Descartes and Kant, people in the modern world became inner, autonomous, self-controlling subjects, and things looked like objects to be controlled. While now, in the postmodern world, things and even people look to us like resources to be optimized. Thus, many people, like Cypher, try to get the most out of their possibilities by maximizing the quality of their experiences.[33] If, as seems quite possible, we all come to believe in the Gaia principle and feel called to save the Earth, nature will again look different to us.

One might think that this is still no problem for the Matrix programmers and their world model. If individual Homeric Greeks saw gods, and Christians saw miracles, it could be just something inner—a private dream or hallucination—and the Matrix apparently has no trouble dealing with such malfunctions in which the brain generates electrical impulses that don't connect up with the world model. The AI intelligences could presumably even deal with collective hallucinations of gods

33. See Martin Heidegger, "The Question Concerning Technology," in *The Question Concerning Technology*, trans. W. Lovitt (New York: Harper Torchbooks, 1977).

or miracles. And what else could all of these changed things be, since the physical universe presumably remains unchanged and has no place in it for gods and miracles? So it might seem, then, that all of these Heideggerian different worlds and how things looked in them could be treated as private deviations from the one shared Matrix world produced by the programs for everyday objects and events. The perceptual world would then remain stable across changes in understandings of being.

The Heideggerian objection to this way of thinking is that a change of style is neither a private nor a collective hallucination, nor is it a change in the physical universe; it is precisely a change in the public shared world. Heidegger holds that such changes in the understanding of being, like more local style changes, begin as local anomalies. These marginal practices then get focused by a savior like Jesus, a thinker like Descartes, or an entrepreneur like Henry Ford, so that they produce a world-wide change of style.[34] If Heidegger is right, the best that the AI intelligences could do to avoid having to reprogram the Matrix and so lose whole crops of baby batteries would be to try to stamp out the local anomalies and marginal practices before they produced a major style change. Thus, they are quite rightly afraid of change, and so introduce the Agents into the Matrix. The Agents' job, unlike that of the police, who enforce the law, would then be to suppress all anomalies, legal or not, that could bring about an ontological revolution, that is, a change in the current understanding of being.[35]

But a hard question still remains. Now that we know what is *missing* from the Matrix—what Matricians can't think and experience, namely, the possibility of radical cultural change—we still have to ask: why do they need to think and experience it? And to account for what's *wrong* with life in the Matrix, and so why it is admirable to confront risky reality rather than remain in the safe and tranquilized Matrix world whatever

34. See Martin Heidegger, "The Origin of the Work of Art," in *Poetry, Language, Thought*, trans. A. Hofstadter (New York: Harper and Row, 1971).

35. But it might be that there is no danger of radical change because, once a world model is fixed, a change of world becomes impossible. The question of whether ontological revolutions in the Matrix are a serious threat to the machines or whether they are no danger at all because they are impossible is never explicitly addressed in the three films, but, as we shall see, it is plausibly resolved at the end of *Revolutions*.

the quality of experience in each, we need an account of human nature, so we can understand what human beings need and why the Matrix world fails to provide it.

In our pluralistic world, there are many different cultures, each with its own understanding of human nature. As we have just noted, even our own culture has experienced many different worlds, created by new interpretations of human nature and the natural world, which changed what sorts of human beings and things could be perceived. But doesn't this just show, as Sartre famously observed, that there is no human nature? Here Heidegger makes an important metamove. As the history of the West suggests, our nature seems to be able to open up new worlds and so to transform what is currently taken to be our nature. Perhaps *that* is our nature: human beings may be essentially world disclosers.

If being world disclosers is our nature, that would explain why we feel a special joy when we are being creative. Once we experience even a hint of world disclosing, we understand why it's better to be in the real world than in the Matrix, even if, in the world of the Matrix, one can enjoy stability, steak, and good wine. As Nietzsche so well puts the alternatives: "To be a public utility, a cog, a function, is . . . the only kind of *happiness* of which the great majority are capable, which makes intelligent machines of them,"[36] but a few can "become those we are—human beings who are new, unique, incomparable, who give themselves laws, who create themselves."[37] Heidegger would call the vast majority *inauthentic* and the rare individuals *authentic*. What's ultimately important to us, then, is not whether most of our beliefs are true, or whether we are brave enough to face a risky reality, but whether we are locked into a world of routine, standard activities or are free to transform the world and radically change our own lives.

Creating new types of human beings and new worlds need not be as dramatic as Jesus creating a new world by defining us in terms of our desires rather than our actions, or Descartes inventing the inner and so helping usher in the modern world. On a less dramatic scale, poets like

---

36. Friedrich Nietzsche, *The Anti-Christ*, trans. R. J. Hollingdale (London: Penguin, 1990), 191.

37. F. Nietzsche, *The Gay Science* (New York: Vintage, 1974), 266, sec. 335.

Dante and entrepreneurs like Ford change the world. Even an actress like Marilyn Monroe changed the style of the world of women and how they related to men.[38] It is just such a freedom to open up new worlds that the Matrix world lacks. Perhaps, this lack of possibilities for radical change is what Neo experiences as the splinter in his mind.

There is, then, a subtle way that the AI computers have limited what the Matrix dwellers can think and experience, but it is not by limiting the possibilities available to them *in* their world. The limitation in question has nothing to do with not knowing whether we are brains in vats, nor whether the world is virtual or real. Nor, as long as the inputs to the brains are modeled on the way things normally behave in the world and the outputs depend on the Matrix dwellers' own decisions, is there a problem of who is in control. The problem isn't epistemological, nor metaphysical, nor (pace Morpheus and Pryor) political. The problem is what Heidegger would call "ontological." It has to do with the Matricians' freedom to choose all right, but not with a limitation on choice *in* the current world, but a limitation on their freedom to disclose new worlds—to transform their understanding of being.

Heidegger holds that our freedom to disclose new worlds is our special human essence and that this freedom implies that there is no preexistent set of possible worlds. Each world exists only once it is disclosed. So it makes no sense to think that a computer could be programmed with a world model that would anticipate the creation of all possible worlds in advance of their being opened by human beings. Artificial intelligences couldn't program for such a radical openness if they wanted to. In fact, programmed creativity is an oxymoron.[39] By having no way to introduce radical freedom into their world model, and so fearing all unconventional behavior, the AI intelligences have found it necessary to prevent any

---

38. See Charles Spinosa, Fernando Flores, and Hubert Dreyfus, *Disclosing New Worlds: Entrepreneurship, Democratic Action, and the Cultivation of Solidarity* (Cambridge, MA: MIT Press, 1997).

39. This is not to say that a world generated by computer algorithms couldn't exhibit radical novelty. Perhaps artificial life does. But it seems to be taken for granted in the films that the artificial intelligences are operating with rules and symbolic representations and so rightly consider any deviation from their Matrix world, which is modeled on the world of the late twentieth century, to be an anomaly, which signals a potential breakdown of their simulation.

expression of the Matricians' ontological freedom. In this way, and only in this way, could the Matrix world model be said to limit what the Matricians can experience and think. And in only this way can the Matrix world be understood as a prison for the mind.

On this Heideggerian reading, the end of the films shows that both the machines and the human beings acknowledge this limitation on the Matrix world. But it also shows that this need not pose a problem. Since most people prefer the guidelines and comfort of the everyday world and, as Nietzsche says, "live like intelligent machines," they can live in the Matrix world in harmony with the artificial intelligences. Indeed, since in the Matrix world radical change turns out to be impossible, the AI intelligences can afford to leave the inauthentic Matricians alone to evolve in the static style of the end-of-the-twentieth-century Matrix world. And, since there are only a few human beings like Morpheus, Trinity, and Neo, who miss being able to be world transformers and so feel restricted in the Matrix, the AI intelligences can afford to let these few leave their vats and go live authentic lives in Zion. There, radical change *is* possible, but it is no threat to the tranquillity and stability of the everyday Matrix world, and so no threat to the energy supply of the machines.

Further Reading

Citations for the relevant texts by Descartes, Leibniz, Kant, and Heidegger can be found in the footnotes to this chapter. For further thoughts on Heidegger, see Hubert Dreyfus's *Being-in-the-World: A Commentary on Heidegger's Being and Time, Division I* (Cambridge, MA: MIT Press, 1991). Also recommended is Samuel Todes's *Body and World* (Cambridge, MA: MIT Press, 2001).

We would like to thank Rick Canedo for his many helpful suggestions.

Iakovos Vasiliou

7

REALITY, WHAT MATTERS,
AND *THE MATRIX*

The Matrix is, at its core, a film with a moral plot. Like the heroes, the viewers are in on a secret: the "reality" that forms the lives of millions of human beings is not real. The world that seems real to most people is in fact a computer-generated simulation, but almost no one knows it. In reality, human beings are floating in liquid in machine pods, with tubes connected to them in a grotesque post-apocalyptic world where the sun is blotted out. To the average person, of course, it seems to be the ordinary world of 1999.

Although some details of the history remain untold, it is an essential part of *The Matrix* that we are provided with a specific account of how all of this happened. There was a battle between human beings and machines whose cognitive capacity had surpassed our own. In a desperate attempt to win, human beings blocked out the sun's light in order to deprive the machines of their power source. Despite this extreme tactic, the humans lost, were enslaved, and are now farmed to supply energy for the machines. The machines induce the appearance of ordinary 1999 life in the human beings with a computer-generated virtual community for the purpose of keeping them docile and asleep so that they and their offspring can be used like living batteries. While humans seem to walk around in an ordinary life, their minds are radically deceived and their bodies are exploited. The heroes are thus depicted as fighting a noble battle for the liberation of the human species.[1]

---

1. Another topic raised by the film, which I will not discuss beyond this note, would be to assess the moral background of the plot. Are the humans clearly in the right? After all, it was they who blotted out the sun in an attempt to exterminate the machines. Particularly in light of the machines' claim that they are simply the next evolutionary step, we ought to think

I have so far drawn out two aspects of the moral background of the film: enslavement and deception. We should also note the perspective we have on the Matrix as viewers of *The Matrix*. We have what is sometimes called a "God's-eye" perspective: we can see both the Matrix reality and "real" reality. We are let in on the truth about the situation, and we are not supposed to question, for example, whether the battle between Morpheus and his friends and the Agents is itself being conducted in another "meta-matrix," or whether the view of the human pods we see might only be some sort of dream image or illusion. As viewers of *The Matrix*, we are in on the truth and we can see for ourselves that human beings are both enslaved and deceived. Given the outlined history, we are meant to understand the situation of the humans as a terrible and unfair one.

I. How Does the Matrix Differ from Reality?

Excluding, for the moment, the heroes—Morpheus, Trinity, eventually Neo, and the rest of their crew—and the machines, no one in the Matrix shares our God's-eye perspective. In everyday life as well, as far as we know, reality is simply there. When we watch the film, we identify with the heroes in part because we are repulsed by the idea that human beings are enslaved and deceived.[2] It is easy to find these two elements at work in *The Matrix* in part because we think of enslavement and deception as things that are done to some people by others; one group of people enslaves another, or one person or group deceives others. In the film, it is the machines that are the agents of slavery and deception, and almost all of the humans are victims. But how does the Matrix, and the situation of the ordinary people within it differ from reality and the people within it (i.e., us)?

---

about whether there is some objectionable "speciesism" at work in the humans' assessment of the situation. For my purposes, I'll assume that the humans are morally justified in the fight for liberation, which, I might add, is certainly a defensible position. For even if machines are the next evolutionary step, and some human beings are guilty of having acted wrongly toward them, that would hardly justify the involuntary enslavement of the entire human race in perpetuity. Moreover, the existence of a "more advanced" species than our own (however that is to be determined) surely should not deprive us of our human rights.

2. And in part because we too would like to control reality; see below.

Let's begin with enslavement. We are forced to do many things in ordinary reality: we must eat, drink, and sleep—on penalty of death. Also, no matter what we do, we shall eventually, within a fairly predictable time frame, die; we cannot stay alive forever, or even for a couple of hundred years. We can't travel back and forth in time, can't fly to other planets by flapping our arms. The list could go on and on, and these are simply limits to which we are subject in virtue of the laws of nature. In other words, compared with some easily imaginable possibilities, we are severely constrained, in a type of bondage, though ordinarily most of us don't think of it as such.

Writers, artists, philosophers, and theologians over the centuries of course have been keenly aware of these limitations, examined many forms of human bondage, and offered various types of suggestions as to how to free ourselves. Human beings have longed to break out of this reality, to transcend the imposed limitations on their physical being. Moreover, we should be clear that these limitations are imposed on us. We simply find ourselves in this condition, with these rules: we all die within approximately 100 years. It has nothing to do with our voluntary choices, our wishes, or our judgments about what ought to be the case.

Who has done this to us? Answering this question is important to some degree because we typically use the term *enslavement* to refer to something done by one agent to some others. In the case of the constraints I outlined above, it may be harder, initially, to find anyone on whom to pin the blame. But of course human beings have offered answers to this question: one is God; another, the laws of nature. Religious thinkers have struggled with questions about why we should not be angry at God for constraining us in the ways he does: why do people die, why can't we go back in time, or travel to other planets, and so on? Others conclude that it is not God constraining us, but simply the laws of nature. At least at first this thought might be a bit more palatable insofar as we think of the laws of nature as impersonal features of reality; no one made them that way (if God did, then we get angry at him again). They do not mean to constrain us, and there is no mind or intelligent force actively doing anything to us.[3] Either

3. The Stoics thought of the natural world, of the universe as a whole, as itself a rational creature with an overall goal or purpose.

way, however, our actual situation is one of involuntary constraint, much akin to the humans' situation in the Matrix, except that it is not at the hands of machines against which we lost a war, but at the hands of God or nature.

The second aspect of the moral background of *The Matrix* is deception. Human beings are being actively deceived by the designers of the Matrix into believing things about reality that are not true. Deception offends many people, except perhaps for committed subjectivists, since many people believe that they want to know, or at least have the right to know, the truth, even if it is terrible. For one person or a group of people purposefully to keep others in the dark about some truth is to diminish the respect and authority of those people; it is to act patronizingly and paternalistically. In such situations, a few people decide which truths others can handle, and which they can't. Although this happens routinely—consider the relationship between those who govern and those who are governed—many people bristle at this idea and want the scope of such filtering of the truth to be severely limited.

We might think, however, not about the deception of some people by others (just as we did not look at the enslavement of some people by others), but the deception of humanity in general. In Homer's *Iliad* and *Odyssey*, the gods are depicted throughout as capriciously deceiving human beings, compelling them knowingly and unknowingly to do specific things, and generally interfering quite frequently in human affairs. The humans in Homer certainly seem to be caught in a matrix of sorts, with gods and goddesses operating on a plane of reality that is not accessible to them (unless the gods want it to be) but that nevertheless often affects matters in the humans' ordinary reality. As human beings began to understand that the Earth rotated around the sun, and not vice versa, Descartes certainly worried about the extent to which God had had a hand in deceiving all of humanity for tens of thousands of years up to that point. He devotes a significant portion of the *Meditations*[4] to worrying about how an all-good, all-knowing, and all-powerful God could have allowed (and whether indeed he was complicit in) people's radical deception about the

---

4. Although this theme is present throughout, see especially Meditations I and IV.

relative motions of the planet they live on, and other truths that often turn out to be radically different from how things seem to be.

So, in our ordinary situation, without any cruel machines doing anything to us, we realize that there are nevertheless many things we cannot do; we know that we humans have been radically deceived by natural phenomena (or by the gods, or by God) about things in the past; and it only stands to reason that we may be radically mistaken about our explanations of things now. I say people's "radical deception," despite the fact that, as with being enslaved, being deceived also seems to require an agent—someone to do the deceiving. We should note, however, that we talk of being deceived or fooled by mirrors, or by the light, or by angles. Natural phenomena are often described as contributing to our misunderstanding of them for a reason. Even though human beings were mistaken for millennia about the fact that the Earth moves relative to the sun, and not the other way around, it is hard to describe our error as simply having "made a mistake," as though humanity forgot to carry the two in some addition calculation. Surely part of the reason that it took humans so long to understand the motions of the Earth is that the appearances themselves are deceptive: it certainly looks as though the sun is moving across the sky.[5] We can see the development of philosophy, art, religion, science, and technology as all stemming from a drive to free humanity from such deception and enslavement, as part of a struggle to achieve the position of a Morpheus or a Neo.[6] We develop airplanes to break the bonds of gravity that keep us physically on the surface of the Earth; we develop complex experiments and gadgets designed to discover the truth about things independently of how they may appear.

My first point, then, is that if we could get hold of the being responsible for setting up the reality we're actually in, then we could perhaps free ourselves, finally knowing the full truth about things and being able to

5. The idea that reality is tricky and tries to hide its nature from us is very old, even without, as in Homer's case, any gods acting as agents of deception. For example, the pre-Socratic philosopher Heraclitus (c. 540–c. 480 B.C.) writes (fr. 53), "an unapparent connection is stronger than an apparent one," and (fr. 123) "nature/the real constitution [of things] [*phusis*] loves to hide itself."

6. Morpheus and company are an interesting amalgam of technological sophistication and religious symbolism.

manipulate reality. If God is responsible, we would need to plead with him successfully, or to fight him and win; if it's the mathematical formulas (computer programs?) underlying the "laws of nature," we would need to learn how to write and rewrite them. We would then all be Neos.[7] We might note too, at this big-picture level, a difference between the Homeric gods and the Judeo-Christian-Islamic God. In Homer's world, the gods were frequently literally in battle with humans, who were greatly outmatched, although not entirely impotent—much like the humans who, before Neo, fought with the Agents. But the God of the major contemporary religions is, by definition, all-good. From this perspective, we should not fight God, for he set things up the way he did for a wise and benevolent reason; rather, we need to learn to accept the position he has put us in (this "mortal coil," our reality, our matrix) and, then, if we act in certain ways, or do certain things, he will free us from this reality after we "die" (i.e., not go out of existence, but end our stay in this reality) and show us the truth in heaven.

I hope this necessarily brief discussion enables us to see the importance of both the God's-eye perspective and the moral background of the film for effecting a difference between the situation depicted in *The Matrix* and our ordinary condition. As viewers of the film, we are in a special position: we can see both inside and outside of the Matrix. We can see that it is not a benevolent God who has set up this 1999 reality, replete with constraints and deceptive appearances, pain and toil, for some wonderful, miraculous purpose. Nor is the reality of most people in the Matrix the result of impersonal laws of nature. Instead, machines that use human beings as batteries are responsible for what counts as reality for most people. *The Matrix* then supplies us, the viewers, with a definitive answer about who is responsible for what most human beings take to be reality.[8]

---

7. Or, more precisely, those of us who accomplished this.

8. Of course, for Morpheus and his crew and for the machines if they were sufficiently reflective, the same questions could be raised about what makes the reality outside of the Matrix the way it is: who is responsible for that? And then we can imagine them responding in the sorts of ways I have described, pinning the blame on God, the laws of nature, and so on.

II. A Benevolently Generated Matrix

Now *The Matrix* could be significantly altered, without changing anything in the Matrix. Imagine that the real world is a post-apocalyptic hell, just as in the film, but, unlike in the film, suppose that the cause of the world's being in such a state is not some battle with machines that wanted to enslave us, but the emission of so many greenhouse gases with our three-lane-wide SUVs that we completely obliterated the ozone layer and thereby rendered the planet uninhabitable by us or by the plants and animals that we rely on for our survival. Suppose further that sometime in the future, in order to save the human race, scientists set up an enormous self-sustaining machine, just as in the film (minus the scary sentinels), designed to keep the human species alive and reproducing for the 10,000 years it will take for whatever weeds are left on the planet to fix our atmosphere and make the planet once again habitable in a normal way. The machine operates simply on solar power (since, on this scenario, the sun is now stronger than ever, frying almost everything else on the planet), so that human beings are not needed as "batteries."[9] While humans are stuck in this state, the scientists create the Matrix in which to "live" their lives instead of being conscious of floating in vats for the length of their lives, which would clearly be a most horrific torture. Once the power of the sun is diminished to a habitable degree (because of the repaired atmosphere), the machine would "awaken" us humans, and we could go back to living on the planet.

The ordinary person in this scenario is in the same condition as an ordinary person in the film, except that instead of the Matrix being the diabolical result of evil machines that exploit the human race, it is the result of benevolent human beings trying to keep the human race alive in as good condition as possible under the terrible circumstances. Of course it would seem no different to the person in the Matrix. We, the viewers, however, would have quite a different response to *The Matrix*. There would be no enemy to fight, no injustice to rectify (the pushers of SUVs

---

9. This detail is meant simply to avoid the possibility of unease over the issue of whether human beings are being used as batteries, voluntarily or not.

being long dead). If there were a Morpheus in this situation, how would we think of him? If Morpheus and his friends had left the Matrix, and figured out that they could, with extreme difficulty, survive in the devastated world (eating disgusting porridge, and so on), should they go about "freeing" everyone, even if it would take another 10,000 years for the Earth to return to its present state of habitability?

As Chris Grau discusses in his chapter in this collection, the Matrix is importantly different from Robert Nozick's experience machine.[10] Grau points out that we retain free will in the Matrix. The "world" in the Matrix will respond to our free choices, just as the ordinary world does now. Another difference that I think is quite significant is that in the Matrix, unlike in the experience machine, I am really interacting with other human minds. There is a community of human beings. With the experience machine, it is all about my experience, which is the private content of my own consciousness. It is imaginable that I am alone in the universe, floating in a vat set up by a god who has since committed suicide. In skeptical problems that stem from the evil-genius hypothesis in Descartes's first Meditation, there is a threat of solipsism and the dread of feeling that one might be alone in the universe.[11] In the Matrix, however, when two people meet, there are really two consciousnesses there that are each experiencing "the same things" from their respective positions. Everyone is hooked up to one and the same Matrix; there are not unique matrices generated for each individual. Of course people aren't really shaking hands—their hands are in vats—but it seems to each of their consciousnesses, not just to one consciousness, that they are shaking hands. This feature of the Matrix is also a respect in which life in the Matrix is critically unlike a dream, despite the fact that the humans are

10. I shall assume that my reader has read that chapter, where Grau clearly explains Nozick's example. See p. 18.

11. See Grau's chapter in this collection. The threat of solipsism seems to me to be the same in the Matrix or in the ordinary world, and that is not my concern here. I am simply taking the truth of the God's-eye perspective offered to the viewer of the film for granted. *The Matrix* tells us and shows us that we are all hooked up to the same Matrix.

described as "dreaming."[12] Regardless of the amount of conscious control one has or lacks in a dream, a dream is private to one's own consciousness. It is part of the grammar of "dream," as Wittgenstein might say, that only I can have my dream.[13]

Now this seems to me to be of enormous significance in thinking about the Matrix. If two people fall in love in the Matrix, in what sense would their love not be real? It would not be as if a person merely dreamed that he had fallen in love with someone; for in a dream that person is not really there at all, just like in Nozick's experience machine. It is true that in the Matrix they would not really be giving each other flowers, or really holding hands. They would, however, both be experiencing the same things together. They would know each other as persons who display their characters in how they react to all of the—in one sense—"unreal" situations of the Matrix. Moreover, people in the Matrix really suffer and experience pain, and when they die in the Matrix, they die in the "real world" too. The fact that one and the same Matrix is

12. I think that perhaps Colin McGinn's chapter too quickly assimilates the Matrix to dreaming and Neo's control over it to lucid dreaming. Although McGinn may be right that the Matrix must be dealing with "images" rather than "percepts," there are important disanalogies between Matrix-experience and dream-experience. First, in a dream, there is only your own mind involved. The Matrix must be, at a minimum, a group dream. I am arguing above that the fact that one mind is really interacting with other minds is critical to assessing the value of the Matrix reality. This complicates the apparently clear idea of controlling one's dream, since it is not simply one mind at work that can alter the images one is conscious of. I am not sure of the coherence of the hypothesis here. For example, when the young boy bends the spoon, Neo "sees" this. So the boy's control of his environment is perceivable both by the boy's mind and by Neo's. So he must be changing something that is, "in reality," in Neo's mind—namely, Neo's image of the spoon. But what if Neo straightens the spoon at the same time the boy bends it? Whose lucid dream will win out and be perceived by the other minds? The one with the stronger will? Second, the "images" that are in your mind in the Matrix can, and regularly do, really kill people, that is, kill their bodies outside of the Matrix. Except in some bad horror movies, dream images cannot really kill you, or make you bleed. The difficulty of understanding how something which is a mere image is supposed to have this sort of effect seems therefore to cause some problems for calling the state of ordinary people in the Matrix "dreaming." See also next note.

13. We could certainly, if we wish, call the experience of the Matrix a "dream," as the movie does. But we should remember that Neo, while in the Matrix and before he has met Morpheus, has a dream while he is "asleep." So we need some distinction between that sort of dream and Neo's "waking" "group dream" within the Matrix.

inhabited by millions of minds means that millions of people are really interacting, even if the physical universe in which they are interacting is radically different from how it appears.

Consider as well writing a novel, a poem, or a philosophy paper. Or consider painting or dancing, making music or a movie. Would any of these activities be affected by the fact that what I took to be material objects were objects that were computer generated? And if not, in the benevolently generated Matrix I hypothesized, we would seem clearly better off as a species, developing artistically and intellectually and loving each other within the Matrix rather than fighting for survival and barely succeeding outside of it. If my aim in life were to write some extraordinary philosophy or a ground-breaking novel, surely I could do that far better within the Matrix than outside of it, where I would have to battle simply for my survival. After all, where does my novel or my philosophy paper exist for much of its genesis and storage? In a computer, of course. If I wrote a novel in the Matrix, and you read it, and so did 10,000 other minds, and I then won the Pulitzer Prize for it, in what sense would it be unreal or even diminished in value? This differs again from the experience machine.

In the experience machine, I might have programmed it so that it would seem to me that I had written a brilliant novel and that people had appreciated it. In fact, however, no one would have read my novel, and I would have simply programmed myself with memories of having written it, although I never really did. In the Matrix, however, I am not given false memories, and I do really interact with other minds. Physics as we know it would be false (not of course the physics of the Matrix, which scientists would study and which would progress as does ordinary science; see below). But art and human relationships would not be affected. I am trying to show that while we are attached to reality, we are not attached to the physical per se, where that refers to what we think of as the underlying causes of the smells, tastes, feels, sights, and sounds around us: they could be molecules; they could be computer chips; they could be the whims of Homeric gods. Indeed, very few human beings have much understanding of contemporary physics and what it maintains that things "really" are.[14]

14. This sentence implies that contemporary physics represents humans' best understanding of the true nature of reality, which is certainly a contentious claim.

Nozick's experience machine may have shown us that we have an attachment to the real, an attachment to the truth that we are really doing things, really accomplishing things, and not just seeming to, but we should not for that reason think we are necessarily attached to a certain picture of the physical or metaphysical constitution of things.

I would like to return to the question of the sense in which the reality of the Matrix is different from the real world. I think that there is an important difference between being deceived about the reality of an object and being deceived about the real underlying physical or metaphysical cause of something. Avoiding deception and error about the latter is the concern of physics (and metaphysics). That we might be wrong, indeed radically wrong, about the physics/biology of an elephant is quite different from hallucinating that there is an elephant in front of you, or dreaming of an elephant, or experiencing an elephant in Nozick's machine. In the latter three cases, one is deceived about the reality of an object, about whether there is an elephant there at all. I am not saying that the actual physics or metaphysics of a thing will not determine whether it is there; if something is really the underlying cause of something else, of course it must determine its existence. I do claim, however, that given the reality of a thing, knowing its true physical/metaphysical explanation neither augments nor diminishes its value or its reality.[15] To discover that, contrary to what you had believed, elephants evolved from single-celled sea creatures and are mostly water, and that water consists of molecules, and that molecules consist of atoms, and that there is a certain interrelationship between matter and energy—that is all part of science's attempt to understand the truth about physical reality. None of these conclusions impugns the elephant's reality or the value it has in the world. What substances are, at bottom, is a question for science or, perhaps, metaphysics. The moral background of the film is quite relevant here. If the fact that we are in the Matrix is simply a matter of our being incorrect about or ignorant of what the real physics of things is, then the Matrix is quite close to our ordinary

15. The question of whether I know something is in fact real or an illusion remains as legitimate or illegitimate as always. Throughout this chapter, I am simply bypassing any skeptical questions, since it is part of my argument that being in the Matrix does not affect them.

situation, although our position as viewers of *The Matrix* is not like that at all. Since we have a God's-eye perspective, we are able to know what is really the cause of things and what is not.

In the benevolent Matrix that I envisaged, however, you could learn Matrix-physics and Matrix-history just as we now learn ordinary physics and ordinary history. At a certain age in school, you might be taught that your body is really floating in a vat, and then perhaps you could put on goggles and see the world outside of the Matrix, like looking at an X ray or at your blood under a microscope. Brought up with such a physics and biology, it would seem natural—about as exciting (and unexciting) as being told that your solid, unmoving table is made of incredibly small, incredibly fast-moving parts, or that all of your physical characteristics are determined by a certain code in your DNA, or where babies come from—despite the fact that such truths are hardly obvious and conflict radically with the way things appear. Just consider any of the conclusions of contemporary physics or quantum mechanics.

History too might continue as normal, divided into B.M. (before Matrix) and A.M. (after Matrix) dates. After all, in the "real" world, outside of the Matrix, nothing would be happening of interest except to scientists. It would be like the contemporary study of the bottom of the ocean, or of the moon. Aside from its causal influence on the physical state of the planet, what goes on down there or up there has no part to play in human history. All of human history would occur within the Matrix.

By hypothesizing a benevolent rather than a malevolent cause of the Matrix, we can see how much of what I am calling the moral background of *The Matrix* influences what we think of it. Deprived of that moral background, a benevolently generated Matrix can show us that our attachment is not to the physical constitution and cause of things, but also not simply to experience. Our attachment is to things that have value. Let me explain.

Take the example, discussed in the film, of the pleasure of eating. Imagine that science develops a pill which supplies the perfect amount of nutrition for a human being each day. Humans no longer need to eat at all in the ordinary way. In fact they are, as far as their health is concerned, far worse off if they try to rely on their taste to supply them with the appropriate nutrition (e.g., research some current statistics on fast-food consumption and obesity). They can simply take the pill and get nutrition far superior to what they would if left to their own taste to determine what and how much to eat. Let's suppose too that science has found a way to simulate food with a computer, so that they have created a "food-matrix." My real nutrition would come from the pill, but I could still go out for a simulated steak, and it would seem just as though I were really eating a steak, including the sensation of getting full, although in fact I would be eating nothing and getting no nutritional harm or benefit from the experience at all. It is hard to imagine such a perfect pill and such perfect computer-simulated food; such a pill is no simple vitamin, and a tofu burger is no simulated steak. But if we suppose that there are such things, I think human beings would readily give up eating real steak. What those who value eating steak value is not the eating of real cow flesh (in fact, putting it that way inclines one to become a vegetarian), but the experience of eating. If eating the computer steak really were, as we are assuming, absolutely indistinguishable from eating a real steak, no one would care whether they were eating a "real" steak—that is, one that was obtained from a slaughtered cow.

At this level, the discussion is again about what are the underlying causes of phenomenal qualities: whether the causes of the taste, smell, and so on of the steak are cow molecules or computer chips or the hand of God. This is, as it were, a matter of science or metaphysics—not of concern to the consumer as a consumer. Now, for all physical objects, I contend, it is of no value to us if their underlying constitution is ordinary atoms, or computer-generated simulation. My favorite pen still writes the same way, my favorite shirt still feels the same way. If these things are not "real" in the sense that their underlying constitution is radically other than I had believed, that makes no difference to the value that these things have in my life. It does, of course, make a difference to the truth of the physics or metaphysics I learn. But none of this implies that I was being deceived about the reality of the object—that the object I valued was or is not there in the sense that matters to the nonscientist.[16]

In a scene discussed by Grau, Cypher claims that his knowledge that the steak is "unreal"—that is, computer generated—does not diminish his

16. All human beings might be considered "scientists" insofar as we are curious about and have a conception of what is the reality of things: what causes them, how they come into being, how they are destroyed, and so on. But we are also interested in other people, objects, and activities because of their inherent value, a value they retain regardless of the correct explanation of their reality.

enjoyment. Cypher then looks forward to the point when he expects his memory to be wiped clean, when he will no longer remember that the Matrix is the Matrix. But it seems to me to be unclear why Cypher needs to forget anything about his steak being unreal in order to fully enjoy it—as he himself seems to understand—nor does he need to forget that he is in the Matrix in order to make his life pleasant and satisfying within it. What he desperately needs to forget in order to have a comfortable and satisfying life is the memory of his immoral and cowardly betrayal of his friends and of the rest of those outside of the Matrix who are engaged in the fight for human liberation. But this is an issue, once again, not arising from the Matrix itself, but from the moral background of the film.

Having a radically different underlying constitution is very different from saying that things are not real, in the sense of being a mere illusion, as in a dream or a hallucination. Consider again the case of our human interactions. If a person I am friends with is not, after all, a person, then I think there is a clear sense in which the friendship is not real, just as in Nozick's experience machine or in a dream that I was friends with Tom Waits. I would then seem to have a relationship to someone, but in reality not have one. What matters is whether I am really interacting with another free mind. I certainly won't try to say what it is to have a mind, or what it is for that mind to be "free," but whatever it is, I am claiming that its value is not importantly tied to any theory in physics or metaphysics. Whatever the cause and explanation is of the existence of a free mind, it is the having of one and the ability to interact with other ones that matters. If the underlying constitution of Tom Waits is computer chips, instead of blood and guts, what difference does that make? This is not a question about his reality—whether he is really there or not—it is a question about his physical or metaphysical constitution. If he has a mind, whatever that is, and he has free will, whatever that is, what do I care of what physical parts he is—or is not—made?[17] Indeed, I earnestly hope in the

17. Given a true account of what it is to have a mind, I would surely care if what appeared to be a person did not fulfill those criteria, for then he would not be a person after all. For example, if someone somehow showed that a machine could not have a "free mind," then I would care whether my friend was a machine or not, but only secondarily, given that ex hypothesi, as a machine, he would not have a free mind. My point is only

actual world never to see any of those parts or have direct contact with them at all.

III. *The Matrix* on the Matrix

I shall conclude by claiming that *The Matrix* itself provides evidence that, barring enslavement and deception, we would prefer life within the Matrix to a continual struggle for survival outside it. I have so far considered how we would feel about the reality of a benevolently generated Matrix. But in *The Matrix*, the cause of the Matrix is explicitly not benevolent. Human beings are enslaved and exploited by scary-looking machines. *The Matrix* is a story about a few human beings fighting to save the rest of humanity. That is how the movie generates excitement, the thrill for the viewer as he or she hopes that the heroes can defeat the enemy. Of course, the film expects one to root for the humans. But I think there is some duplicity at work in the way *The Matrix* exploits the Matrix. Neo is the savior of humanity, and a large amount of the pleasure that the viewer gets from the film consists of watching Neo and his friends learn to manipulate the Matrix. Key to Neo's eventual success is his training. In his training, he learns that the Matrix, as a computer-generated group dream, can be manipulated by a human being. The idea, I guess, is that if one could bring oneself to believe deeply enough that, despite appearances, things are not real, then one could manipulate the reality of the Matrix. The thrill that Neo feels, and that we feel watching him, is that as he gains this control he is able to do things that are, apparently, superhuman—move faster than bullets, hang onto helicopters, fly, and so on. We ought to note here, though, that Neo's greatness, his being The One, is only the case because the Matrix exists. Outside of

---

that it is having a free mind or being a person that is the source of value, not the correct theory about what makes someone a person. I am claiming that ignorance of or deception about the right physical or metaphysical account of mind does not thereby cast doubt on the value of having a mind. Skepticism about other minds—the questions of whether there really are other minds and how we could tell whether there are—is not addressed at all by what I am saying. I am taking for granted the truth of what the film tells us: there are other minds. The problem of other minds, like solipsism mentioned above, is equally a problem in or out of the Matrix.

the Matrix, Neo is just a smart computer geek. He can't really fly, or really dodge bullets (nor, apparently, does he dress in full-length black leather coats, though I guess he could).[18] We, as viewers, would not get any pleasure from *The Matrix* if it were not for the Matrix. If there were no Matrix, everyone would be eating terrible porridge in a sunless world and simply fighting for survival, which would make for a bad world and a bad movie.

The premise of the movie is that there is a moral duty to destroy the Matrix and "free" the humans. But all of the satisfaction that the viewer gets, and that the characters get in terms of their own sense of purpose and of being special, is derived from the Matrix. It's not just Cypher's steak that is owed to the Matrix, it is Morpheus's breaking the handcuffs, Trinity's gravity-defying leaps, and Neo's bullet dodging. If my argument is right, then, the irony of *The Matrix* is that the heroes spend all of their time liberating human beings from the Matrix although afterward they would have good reason to go back in, assuming the conditions on Earth are still so terrible. This is because there's nothing wrong with the Matrix per se; indeed, I've argued that our reality might just as well be the Matrix. What we want, now as always, one way or another, is to have control over it ourselves. What we would do with such power is a question, I suppose, for psychologists, but looking at what people have done so far, I at any rate hope we remain enslaved and deceived by something for a long time to come.

Further Reading

Translations of the fragments of Heraclitus, and the rest of the pre-Socratics, can be easily found in Richard McKirahan, *Philosophy before*

---

18. It seems that this is not the case in the later films, *The Matrix Reloaded* and *The Matrix Revolutions*, in which Neo has superhuman abilities *outside* as well as inside the Matrix. I think this has a significant effect on the impact of the later movies, and even reflects back (perhaps negatively) on the original film. If Neo is superhuman in the ordinary world too, it may diminish the philosophical interest of the films insofar as the trilogy would then be more similar to many movies that involve superheroes—characters that can magically break the laws of physics in ordinary reality. What makes the *The Matrix* different, and more original, is that superhero feats are done by ordinary people who are within the Matrix.

Socrates (Indianapolis, IN: Hackett, 1994). For evidence of Stoic views on nature, see A. A. Long and D. Sedley, *The Hellenistic Philosophers*, vol. 1 (Cambridge: Cambridge University Press, 1987). Important, if sometimes obscure, remarks on radical skepticism can be found in L. Wittgenstein, *On Certainty* (New York: Harper and Row, 1972). Contemporary treatments of skepticism include B. Stroud, *The Significance of Philosophical Scepticism* (Oxford: Oxford University Press, 1984), and M. Williams, *Unnatural Doubts: Epistemological Realism and the Basis of Scepticism* (Princeton, NJ: Princeton University Press, 1996).

I am grateful to Chris Grau and Bill Vasiliou for comments on and discussion about an earlier version of this chapter.

8

Richard Hanley

NEVER THE TWAIN SHALL MEET: REFLECTIONS ON THE VERY FIRST MATRIX

Did you know that the First Matrix was designed to be a perfect human world, where none suffered, where everyone would be happy? It was a disaster.

> —Agent Smith, to Morpheus

And God shall wipe away all tears from their eyes; and there shall be no more death, neither sorrow, nor crying, neither shall there be any more pain: for the former things are passed away.

> —Revelation 21:4, King James Bible

Hell is—*other people.*

> —Garcin, in Sartre's *No Exit*

To deny our own impulses is to deny the very thing that makes us human.

> —Mouse, to Neo

Cypher *chooses* the Matrix, and just maybe, he's not so crazy. If real-life prospects are dim, then even an apparently suboptimal alternative like the Matrix might in fact be better, all things considered.[1] But what is the *best* sort of existence for individuals like you and me? Philosophy and religion both have attempted to answer this question, and I think *The Matrix* gives us an

---

1. See Christopher Grau's chapter, "Bad Dreams, Evil Demons, and the Experience Machine." Indeed, I recommend you read Grau's chapter in its entirety before proceeding here. [Ed. note: See also Iakovos Vasiliou's chapter, in which he discusses the possibility of a benevolent matrix.]

interesting way to frame it. Is some possible "real" existence better than any possible matrix? Or is some possible matrix better than any possible reality? With Mark Twain's help, I shall present an argument that one important notion of the best existence, the Christian heaven, is after all a matrix. The point of my polemical approach is not so much to criticize Christianity, but rather to bring the issue of the nature of ultimate value into sharper focus.

What is the Matrix? Morpheus tells Neo that it's a "computer-generated dreamworld" and a "neural, interactive simulation"; it is, in other words, a *virtual environment.*[2] Agent Smith assures Cypher that he won't know he's in the Matrix when he returns permanently, and it will simplify exposition to suppose that this is a necessary feature of a matrix, while being computer generated is not. The matrix depicted is a mixed case, since the cognoscenti can enter it without being deceived into thinking it is real. Let us stipulate that in a *pure* matrix, everyone is benighted, believing it is the real deal. In most of what follows, I'll be concentrating on pure matrices (and in the case of the Matrix depicted, on the condition of the benighted). Since we'll be discussing different kinds of matrix, we need a name for the one depicted in *The Matrix*; Agent Smith refers to a First Matrix, so let's call the one we see in the movie the "Second Matrix."

A matrix, then, is an interactive virtual environment involving systematic global deception. Still, there are two levels of interactivity in a virtual environment. *Virtual interactivity* is the extent to which the environment allows, and responds to, your input. Current virtual environ-

2. Metaphysicians will not yet be satisfied. *Matrix* is from the Latin for "mother" and originally meant "womb" (it is used in the Old Testament five times with this meaning), or "pregnant female." In several contexts, it means a sort of substrate in which things are grown and developed. Given this etymology, the Matrix might have been the concrete thing that includes the collection of deceived humans in their vats. A more modern meaning of *matrix* is based in mathematics: a rectangular arrangement of symbols. Perhaps "the Matrix" (an expression surely borrowed from William Gibson's earlier use in *Neuromancer*) denotes the array of symbols encoding the virtual environment, which we might distinguish from the environment itself. But *The Matrix* gives the impression that the environment is just the array of symbols that Neo sees when he finally sees in—so to speak—Matrix-vision. Its concrete-worldlike appearance seems an inferior perception. (The Matrix thus seems allegorical in turn of Plato's well-known allegory of the cave; Neo is enlightened about his own nature by liberation from the Matrix, and by the end he sees the true nature of the Matrix.) Still, it is the concrete-worldlike appearance of things that I'm concerned with here, so let's ignore the possibility of a Neo.

ments are not very interactive in this sense, but the Second Matrix is. That's what makes it seem so real, at least to the benighted. (For the cognoscenti, the Second Matrix is too virtually interactive, too controllable, to seem real—at least compared with the more lawlike external world.) *Real interactivity* is the potential for interaction *with others also engaged in virtual interaction*, and *real interaction* is the extent to which this potential is realized. Compare two kinds of possible matrix: the Second Matrix is *communal*, featuring real interaction between human beings—call this *human interaction*. A *solitary* matrix lacks human interaction altogether.

Communal matrices differ in degree of human interaction. In the Second Matrix, billions of humans share the environment, and if we ignore Agents, it is *fully* communal: every virtual human in the Matrix is an *avatar*, a virtual persona of a real human being. In the Matrix training program created by Mouse, on the other hand, virtual humans like the woman in the red dress are *simulacra*, not avatars, and the human interaction during the sequence that we see is limited to that between Neo and Morpheus.[3] On yet another hand, the fully communal Construct (loading program), where Morpheus and Neo watch TV, has no other virtual humans in it to interact with—and unlike the training program, it's not "big" enough to be very worldlike. Call a fully communal matrix that is big enough to be worldlike and has *many* human participants, so that human interaction is nearly inevitable, a *teeming* matrix. (The Second Matrix is all but teeming. If we removed the cognoscenti, there would be no need for Agents, and it would be teeming.)

Now we can compare three possibilities (obviously not exhaustive) for human existence, assuming that it involves physical embodiment. One is the real deal, populated by other human beings: for instance, if you subjectively experience having sexual intercourse with another human being, another individual human being shares that intercourse, from another subjective point of view, because you really have physical, sexual intercourse with that person. The same goes for nonsexual intercourse. If I were to meet Mark Twain (through the

3. I use *simulacrum* in the following sense: "something having merely the form or appearance of a certain thing, without possessing its substance or proper qualities; a mere image, a specious imitation or likeness, of something" (*Oxford English Dictionary*). It is also a nod toward Jean Baudrillard, whose work *Simulacra and Simulation* (trans. Sheila Faria Glaser [Ann Arbor: University of Michigan Press, 1994]) both influences and appears in *The Matrix*. See my essay "Baudrillard and *The Matrix*" online at http://philosophy.thematrix.com.

time travel he wrote about, perhaps), then Twain and I both would have an experience of meeting, and we really would meet, physically and psychologically. Two is a teeming matrix: if you experience having (intraspecies) sexual intercourse, another matrix-bound human shares that intercourse, from another subjective point of view. There's no physical intercourse, of course, but there is psychological intercourse. If I have the experience of meeting Twain, then he (or some other human being) has the experience of meeting me-meeting-Twain, and there is at least a meeting of minds. Three is an *apparently* teeming, solitary matrix: if you experience having sexual intercourse, no other human is having an interactive sexual experience with you. It is like taking up Mouse's invitation to enjoy the woman in the red dress, except that you won't know that "she" is a simulacrum. If I experience meeting Twain, then there is no intercourse with another human being, and neither Twain nor any other human being need have the experience of meeting me-meeting-Twain.

Our ordinary intuition is that there's something valuable about the real deal that is missing in a matrix. Consider your present situation. You are either right now in a matrix, thinking that it's a certain time and place when it really isn't, that a certain sequence of physical events is occurring when it really isn't, and so on; or you aren't, and it really is that time and place, and so on. Most of us hope we are *not* in a matrix right now, which shows that, other things being equal (that is, where the experiences are identical in subjective character), we prefer the real deal. My hunch is that you also hope that, if your present existence is not the real deal, it's at least participation in a *teeming* matrix. Being in the real deal has two distinct features of apparent value: your beliefs are more connected to the truth, and you really interact with other human beings. A teeming matrix has less connection with truth than does the real deal, but has more than a solitary matrix, and it still provides substantial interaction with other human beings.[4] In the case of sex,

4. Here's an interesting question: which is better, the Second Matrix, or a systematically deceptive, personalized, nonvirtual environment—a "Truman Show"—that you never discover the true nature of? The latter has more veridical human interaction in one sense, because you really physically interact; but the interaction is less veridical in another sense, in that other human beings are willing participants in the deception. Another case to think about is a solitary matrix allowing interaction with nonhuman participants (dogs, perhaps). Another still is a solitary matrix without even the appearance of real interaction—call this a lonely matrix. I don't know about you, but I prefer Sartre's vision of hell to a lonely matrix.

there's a good sense in which you really did have sex with that other person, though in ignorance of the whole truth.[5]

If connection with truth matters so much to us, why not have the best of both kinds of existence: why not have a virtual environment *without* all the deception? Cypher can (and does) go back temporarily into the Matrix, knowing what it is, and retains that knowledge while he is in there. But for his permanent stay, he chooses ignorance instead, because "ignorance is bliss." Presumably, the knowledge that he is not in the real deal would undermine his capacity to enjoy the experiences, so he can't have the best of *both* worlds.[6] Cypher is intuitively no different from the rest of us in this regard. For a typical man, the experience of sexual intercourse with the woman in the red dress is likely to be much more satisfying if he thinks it is the real deal. Which brings us to the First Matrix.

I.   What Is the First Matrix?

Agent Smith's remark in the epigraph suggests that the First Matrix was, like the Second, more or less teeming.[7] Agent Smith says about the "disaster":

Some believe that we lacked the programming language to describe your perfect world, but I believe that, as a species, human beings define their reality

5. The Second Matrix may connect with the truth in some unnecessary ways. One's virtual body is depicted as more or less veridical, for instance. (But this may be only "residual self-image," as Morpheus tells Neo. If Cypher were put back into the Matrix as Ronald Reagan, that would be clinching evidence that one's avatar can be strikingly different.) Breaking this connection would permit interestingly different human interactions: for instance, you could unknowingly have an experience of heterosexual intercourse with another (unknowing) human who is in fact of the same sex.

6. Sometimes it is argued that you are better off—happier—being a Christian, even if God does not exist. If Christian belief is easier to maintain inside the Second Matrix than outside it, then Cypher could have an extra pragmatic reason for going back in.

7. Is Agent Smith telling the truth? I have no idea. He is attempting to "hack into" Morpheus's mind to gain the access codes to the Zion mainframe computer, so in interpreting the story we should take everything he says—and so, even the very existence of the First Matrix—with a grain of salt. For my purposes, though, we can pretend that he's telling the truth. In a similar vein, we need not accept the word of the Architect, who appears at the end of *The Matrix Reloaded*. Nothing else that I am aware of in the three movies conclusively confirms or denies his assertions about the existence of cyclic matrices, each with their own Neo. So I shall continue to refer to the Matrix we see as the second one.

through misery and suffering. The perfect world was a dream that your primitive cerebrum kept trying to wake up from.

The first suggestion is fascinating. Given the deadpan delivery, it is hard to say whether it posits a deficiency in the machines that designed the Matrix, or in us—in our notion of a perfect world. On the other hand, Agent Smith's own thesis seems connected with a tradition of human thought concerning the theistic problem of evil. If a perfectly good God exists, why does evil exist? Why is the world full of sharp corners and other hazards? A standard answer is that evil is *necessary*—it must exist in order for certain goods to exist. For instance, it is often claimed that happiness requires suffering, though this is disputable. Even if creatures like us can't be maximally happy, this is a reason for not creating *us* at all, and creating more felicitously instead. And does our happiness require *so much* suffering? Looking deeper, it seems clear that virtues like courage and generosity indeed require the existence of suffering. But vices such as cowardice and cruelty couldn't exist without suffering, either. Are they necessary evils, too?

The most defensible theistic answer to this question is a very subtle no, but. God had a choice between creating a world with free beings in it, or not. This choice is easy, since free will is a surpassing good. But given libertarian free will, which requires causal indeterminism, God could not know without creating the world exactly which possible world would result.[8] God might have gotten lucky and created a world in which all free beings had only virtues, and no vices. But this is incredibly unlikely, as is a purely vicious world, and it's no surprise that he got a mixed world, with most humans having virtues *and* vices. The picture that emerges is that a world with human beings in it is a world with sharp corners (natural evil) to provide genuine free choice, and so very likely contains sin (moral evil) as well. Call this the "free will theodicy." Its assumption that free

---

8. We need not fully characterize *libertarian free will* for present purposes. The main point is that causal indeterminism is a necessary condition of it. Causal indeterminism is the denial of causal *determinism*: the thesis that every event is completely determined by causally prior events. A useful and common illustration is to ask whether or not everything that happens, or will happen, is in principle *predictable*: this will be so if determinism is true, and not so if indeterminism is true. (Whether the future can be known by means other than prediction is a different question; see note 13.) The thesis that we have libertarian free will is called *libertarianism*.

will is *libertarian* free will—requiring causal indeterminism—is Christian orthodoxy, so I grant it for the sake of the argument.

Filling in the details of the theodicy, focus on the will itself. Our actions are ultimately explained by what we want, most especially by our non-derived desires.[9] In a world of sharp corners, not all of these desires can be satisfied. Indeed, there often will be conflicts between individuals in what they desire: one person getting what they want means that another doesn't. (Presumably, God could not arrange a concordance of wills—substituting for conflicting desires, or deleting them altogether—without eliminating free will.) Indeed, the existence of other human beings in the world is *part* of the sharp corners—a source of suffering—in addition to being a source of moral evil. And not just because others are in competition with you for resources; sometimes others *are* the resource, as the sexual intercourse example shows. If you badly want sex with another person and they badly don't want it with you, then someone is going to suffer.

If the free will theodicy is correct, then God can only control the nonhuman environment. Each human being is a part of the environment of every other human being, so as soon as you put more than one creature with libertarian free will into the mix, there will, absent astonishing co-incidence, be tears. You can minimize the effect that human beings have on each other, but only by minimizing their interaction (say, by putting each on a separate planet). Even then, as long as human beings desire interaction (as a means to things we want, such as to procreate, and perhaps even for its own sake), mere isolation won't solve the problem.

The creators of the First Matrix tried to produce a relatively good existence for matrix-bound humans. (We needn't suppose the machines were benevolent; perhaps the bioelectric-to-fusion reaction process is more efficient the happier humans are.) In doing so, the machine creators had some of God's problems. They presumably lacked some of God's creative abilities, but they also had fewer constraints, since God is supposed to be

9. Many of our desires are derived from other desires plus belief, for instance, if Ralph desires to kiss Grandma only because he desires an inheritance and he believes kissing Grandma is necessary to achieve this. Nonderived desires, such as Ralph's desire to kiss the girl next door, are importantly independent of belief—they are had, so to speak, for their own sake—and seem to constitute what we refer to as "the will."

no deceiver.[10] Why was the First Matrix a disaster? If the machines were trying to produce an existence with no human suffering, then perhaps they tried the wrong design: a teeming matrix populated with otherwise typical human beings. Even if the machines removed a lot of sharp corners (no volcanic-eruption or man-eating-shark experiences), as long as there is interaction with other human beings plugged into the same virtual environment, someone is going to suffer, as the example of sexual intercourse demonstrates. This attempt would not produce a matrix where "none suffered," and the suggestion fits badly with Agent Smith's remark, "No one would accept the programming." Let's discard it.

This leaves two basic choices: the machines either substantially altered the nature of human beings in the First Matrix (say, by arranging a concordance of wills), or else they created a solitary matrix for each human being. The advantage of a solitary matrix is that the virtual environment can be completely tailored to an individual's desires—perhaps the matrix "reads off" the content of desires from his brain, anticipating a little, matching its programming as far as possible to the satisfaction of his desires as they develop and change.

Perhaps a battery of solitary matrices was beyond the machines' practical resources, but let's suppose not—clearly it's in principle possible for them to have done things this way. However, if Christians are correct, and our wills are in fact undetermined, then our desires cannot be fully anticipated. There is bound to be a gap between the evolution of our desires and the Matrix's capacity to satisfy them; hence some suffering is inevitable. This would partly explain Agent Smith's remark, but once again would not explain why "no one would accept the programming."

We are left with two possible explanations of the remark: either humans by their nature could not be successfully altered through programming, or else unaltered humans were psychologically incapable of accepting the relevant virtual environment. The latter seems to be Agent

---

10. Is this a theological guarantee of the real deal? The Christian can surely deny this. The existence of the Matrix seems compatible with God's being no deceiver, given the free will theodicy, if the machines have libertarian free will. And if they do not have libertarian free will, as long as they are the product of human free will, they are not part of the environment God knowingly created.

Smith's thesis: the "perfect world" was just too good to be true, and literally incredible.[11] Are we human beings simply incapable of having a happy existence, with no suffering? Not on the standard Christian view, according to which just such an existence awaits us in heaven.

II. What Is Heaven?

The Christian notion of heaven is far from a settled body of doctrine. (For instance, are there literally streets paved with gold, or is this just a metaphor for some barely imaginable, wonderful state of affairs?) Nevertheless, it has been asserted with some authority that the human condition in heaven will be very different from that here and now. It is agreed that there is no suffering (see the epigraph), not to mention "exceeding joy" (an expression which occurs four times in the King James Bible), but what exactly will we do there? Some of the common claims about this can seem puzzling. In *Letters from the Earth*, Mark Twain has the banished Satan report to his fellow angels on the beliefs of mortal man:

> For instance, take this sample: he has imagined a heaven, and has left entirely out of it the supremest of all his delights, the one ecstasy that stands first and foremost in the heart of every individual of his race—and of ours—sexual intercourse! ...
>
> His heaven is like himself: strange, interesting, astonishing, grotesque. I give you my word, it has not a single feature in it that he actually values. It consists—utterly and entirely—of diversions which he cares next to nothing about, here in the earth, yet is quite sure he will like them in heaven. Isn't it curious? Isn't it interesting? You must not think I am exaggerating, for it is not so. I will give you details.
>
> Most men do not sing, most men cannot sing, most men will not stay when others are singing if it be continued more than two hours . . . . In man's heaven, everybody sings! The man who did not sing on earth sings there; the

---

11. I am reminded of a passage in William Gibson's *Count Zero*: "Eyes open, he pulled the thing from his socket and held it, his palm slick with sweat. It was like waking from a nightmare. Not a screamer, where impacted fears took on simple, terrible shapes, but the sort of dream, infinitely more disturbing, where everything is perfectly and horribly normal, and where everything is utterly wrong."

man who could not sing on earth is able to do it there. The universal singing is not casual, not occasional, not relieved by intervals of quiet; it goes on, all day long, and every day, during a stretch of twelve hours. And everybody stays; whereas in the earth the place would be empty in two hours.

Satan's list is long and frequently amusing:

I recall to your attention the extraordinary fact with which I began. To wit, that the human being, like the immortals, naturally places sexual intercourse far and away above all other joys—yet he has left it out of his heaven! The very thought of it excites him; opportunity sets him wild; in this state he will risk life, reputation, everything—even his queer heaven itself—to make good that opportunity and ride it to the overwhelming climax. From youth to middle age all men and all women prize copulation above all other pleasures combined, yet it is actually as I have said: it is not in their heaven; prayer takes its place. (Mark Twain, *Letters from the Earth*, edited by Bernard DeVoto [New York: Harper and Row, 1962], p.10)

His main observations we can summarize as (i) man thinks he will be blissfully happy in heaven; (ii) no activity that man finds blissful on Earth will he pursue in heaven; and (iii) the activities that man thinks he will pursue in heaven are ones he avoids whenever possible, here on Earth. Call this appearance of inconsistent values "Twain's puzzle." In Mouse's terms, it seems that we think we will be happiest denying our own impulses. Satan somewhat overstates the puzzle when he writes that heaven "has not a single feature in it that [man] actually values." Man thinks that in heaven he will still value joy and disvalue suffering, for instance. Satan's point is that man appears to think that his *desires* will be radically different in heaven: he will desperately want the things that he does not want at all now, and not want at all the things that he desperately wants now.

Does man think his *will* is going to be different in heaven? That depends. *Psychological hedonism* is the view that there are really only two nonderived human desires: to obtain pleasure and to avoid suffering. If this were true, then man's will does not change if he merely changes his beliefs about what it is that will bring him pleasure and help him avoid pain. If psychological hedonism isn't true (and Christians seem—wisely—to think it isn't true), then a case can be made that (according to Satan, anyway) man expects his will to be altered in heaven.

Contrary to Satan, it can be argued that at least where sex is concerned, the Christian view is that such impulses *ought* to be denied, and the relentless pursuit of gratification is, in a Christian, a matter of *weakness* of will, not in its constitution. It might be further claimed that giving in to such impulses actually causes you suffering. This makes some sense in the case of, say, a married man tempted to adultery, whose guilt may prevent him from full enjoyment. Suppose that in heaven, since there is no marriage (so says Jesus; see for instance Matthew 22:30), there is really no one psychologically "safe" to have sexual intercourse with, and you would inevitably feel guilty about engaging in it. Then the elimination of suffering requires the elimination of sex. (Of course, Satan and Mouse would no doubt respond, with some justification, that this is all premised on the belief that sex outside marriage is something bad in and of itself, a notion you happily will be disabused of in heaven. But the question is what the typical Christian believes, whether it is true or not.)

Leaving aside what you would do there, believers in Christian heaven commonly hold the following four theses about it:

1. It's possible for a human being to be in heaven. More precisely, if all goes well, your self as you know it will survive bodily death and go to heaven.
2. Human beings in heaven will experience happiness, but no unhappiness.
3. Human beings in heaven possess free will.
4. Human beings in heaven interact with other human beings in heaven.

It's worth expanding on item 1. Christians standardly expect to recognize their loved ones in heaven, which presumably requires remembering them.[12] So it seems that they expect considerable psychological continuity between their earthly and heavenly existences—perhaps this is even guaranteed by the requirement that God be no deceiver. But such psychological continuity sits uncomfortably with item 2. Christians on Earth

---

12. People seem to expect that their bodies in heaven will resemble their earthly ones (just as their Matrix "bodies" seem to resemble their real ones). Perhaps this is for purposes of recognition, but it seems unnecessary: common memory can do the job.

are typically saddened by the fact that unbelievers will not get into heaven. It seems that, if anything, they would be sadder still, when confronted by the wonders of heaven, knowing that the unsaved are residing instead in "the lake which burneth with fire and brimstone." And it would seem to be cause for special anguish if one of your loved ones is absent from heaven. (Another version of the problem arises with *missing* your loved ones— being sad, not for them, but for yourself, that they are not around. Even if you don't miss sex with your earthly spouse, it seems you would miss *him*.)

Heaven is also widely supposed to provide an opportunity to meet human beings you never knew on Earth. But if I'm in heaven, and I really want to meet Twain, then I will be sadly disappointed if he isn't there (and angry, if it's all on account of those *Letters*). Moreover, certain truths will presumably be available to you in heaven. Suppose that Mother Teresa is your idol, and you can't wait to tell her so. However, you find out she's not really a saint—indeed, quite the opposite—and not in heaven at all. You may be upset not only for your own sake, but for the sake of humanity (you may respond with a quite cynical attitude toward human nature). Heaven seems on the face of it to provide many opportunities for suffering.

There are three basic ways around this sort of problem. First, suppose *universalism*—the doctrine that everyone gets into heaven—is true. This will solve the problem only if, upon entering heaven, Christians no longer believe that there ought to be any qualification for it (else they likely will be annoyed that others got a "free pass," especially a holier-than-thou like Mother Teresa). Second, God could suppress the knowledge that others are not in heaven. But this requires Matrix-like deception (either to provide the appropriate virtual interaction with non-avatars, or else to just delete all memory of the missing), and heaven would not be the real deal. Third, perhaps what we care about—our desires—will change, so that good Christians no longer will mind the fact that others, even loved ones, are suffering (they might even take pleasure in it). But to accept this raises an acute version of Twain's puzzle. All in all, it may be better to revise item 2 to:

2*. Human beings in heaven will be as happy as they can possibly be.

We may thus grant that it's not possible for *all* suffering to be absent in heaven—though this requires taking the Book of Revelation less literally than many Christians do.

Item 4 is taken completely for granted, as far as I can tell. Part of the point of heaven is to be reunited with (saved) loved ones, and to engage in fellowship with the other inhabitants. But what of item 3? According to the free will theodicy, free will is a surpassing good, so on the face of it, heaven *must* include free will. Yet heaven is a place without sin. And according to the free will theodicy, sin is to be explained by the presence of free will in the world. To deny item 3 also raises Twain's puzzle. We believe we now have libertarian free will, strongly desire it now, and are devastated at the thought of losing it. If God is no deceiver, then if item 3 is false, we would in heaven *know* that we have no free will. Yet, presumably, we would not mind—we would be blissful, yet not ignorant.

Like the builders of the First Matrix, God has two main choices in creating a heaven for human beings: either substantially alter the nature of human beings in heaven (say, by arranging a concordance of wills, contrary to item 3, and perhaps even contrary to item 1), or else put each human in a solitary matrix, contrary to item 4. One advantage for denying item 4 is that item 2 has the best chance of being true, as long as the solitary matrix provides plenty of (virtual) interaction with virtual humans. Those in such a solitary matrix will think they are in the real deal. They'll think they are in heaven, along with everyone whom they want to be there, and nobody whom they don't want there. They will think they get along with everyone else just fine, that there's no sadness, no sin, and so on. God knows what they freely want and tailors each virtual environment to provide exactly that, if possible. (If it's not possible, because they freely want to be in the real deal, this lack is not *experienced*, and so is not a source of suffering.)

Just as it did with the First Matrix, libertarianism raises a difficulty, since you might think that God could not know what you want, when this is undetermined. Some medieval Christians resolved the problem of the compatibility of free will with God's foreknowledge by supposing that changeless, omnipresent God knows the (causally undetermined) future by, so to speak, already having been present then, and having seen what happens. God knows what you do *because you do it*, and not vice versa, hence you may do it freely. The same resolution can be applied here, as long as time exists in heaven: God knows what you *will* want before you want it, by having been in the future and (so to speak) looking into your mind then.[13]

Can items 3 and 4 both be maintained, given items 1 and 2*? There is logical space for this possibility. Item 3 can be true, and yet there be no sin in heaven, *if* heaven is like the lucky roll of the creation die: the world where free beings always choose rightly. In heaven, everyone will be free to sin, but just *won't*. The immediate problem with this suggestion is that it seems incredible that such a coincidence will actually obtain. Perhaps we can appeal to a difference between this situation and that of creation: God has a chance to observe the behavior of free individuals and only admits the deserving—those who actually don't sin while on Earth. But this would get hardly anyone into heaven. Worse, it seems to give inductive support, but no guarantee at all, that unblemished individuals won't sin ever in the eternity they spend in heaven.

It is standardly claimed that all are free to sin in heaven, but none do, because they are in some sense *incapable* of doing so; no one can sin when they are at last with God. This raises two distinct problems. The first is that any such incapability seems incompatible with libertarian freedom, rendering item 3 false after all. The second is that, if there is no incompatibility between human beings having libertarian free will and being incapable of sin, then the free will theodicy seems to collapse. God could have just created heaven and be done with it, a creation with all of the benefits and none of the disadvantages.

In addition to the problem of sin, we might wonder how it can be managed that free human beings, all interacting with each other, have no desires in conflict. As Satan observed, it must be that our desires change radically. But what ensures this? If it is inevitable that they change in this way, then libertarian freedom is again threatened. And if we are somehow free anyway, when our desires are radically altered, then why didn't God

---

13. It would be intriguing if God could "cheat" by doing what he does *because* he sees, from the way the future is, what he will do. This would raise a fatalistic, "bake-your-noodle" puzzle like the one the Oracle raises for Neo's smashing of the vase. But God is a special case. Being unchanging, he cannot be *caused* to act on the basis of future knowledge, and there is little metaphysical sense to be made of "he did it because he did it."

just turn this trick to begin with, and spare all the lost souls? Perhaps we should also consider Mouse's point. If our desires change too radically, will we still be human beings, as item 1 would have it?

III. Conclusion

Perhaps both explanations of the failure of the First Matrix are correct. Recall the suggestion that machines could not program our "perfect world." Perhaps our thinking is incoherent: we think that the best existence is one where human beings interact with each other *and* everyone has libertarian free will *and* nobody suffers *and* that someone knowingly arranged this. If this is an incoherent notion, not even God can actualize it.

In creating the Second Matrix, the machines went for interaction combined with free will (which we are assuming is libertarian), with the overwhelming likelihood (inevitability, in practice) of suffering. We can now explain Agent Smith's remarks: if we rank the elements of our incoherent notion of the best existence, human interaction and libertarian free will rank above the absence of suffering. And since they jointly require (*almost* by definition) the presence of suffering, it can be said more or less truly that we "define [even the best] reality through misery and suffering." The First Matrix was an attempt to give interacting humans an existence free of suffering, but this program *required* a radical revision in their wills, contrary to libertarian free will, and so "no one would accept the program." Mouse might say it was an attempt to deny the very nature of human beings.

If the real deal includes libertarian free will, then so does the Second Matrix—our desires, though often enough unsatisfied, will be after all undetermined. (The sense in which humans are liberated from the Matrix has nothing to do with libertarian free will, which can be enjoyed behind bars.) The Second Matrix also features substantial variation in wills among its human inhabitants and the interesting ethical choices that arise when this is so. For example, apart from the Agents, each virtual human is an avatar, and the "good guys" in the movie end up killing a lot of human beings in their fight against the Agents. It's hard to view these human beings as collaborators, given the nature of the Matrix, so their deaths presumably are to be regarded as acceptable collateral damage, inevitable given the difference in desired outcomes. All in all, the Second Matrix is the machines' best attempt at matching what Christians believe God did for us through creation.[14]

When we humans turn our eyes toward heaven, our ranking of values seems to change, and Twain's puzzle arises anew. In heaven, there is a heavier weighting given to the absence of suffering. God can knowingly minimize suffering in a real deal, while retaining human interaction, but at the cost of libertarian free will. But given that heaven is supposed to involve no suffering at all, and given the surpassing value of libertarian free will in the Christian view of things, God's choice is clear: heaven is a solitary matrix.[15] The machines, not being God, did not know that heaven is no other people.[16] Never the twain—Twain and I—shall meet (in heaven, anyway, but there's always the lake, I suppose).

A relative of Twain's puzzle emerges. When we consider a preheaven existence, we seem to prefer the best real deal to the best matrix. When

---

14. Typical Christians are Cartesian dualists, believing they are spirits or souls distinct from their physical bodies, and that embodiment provides the means for human interaction. Loosely speaking, then, our physical bodies are the "avatars" of the real us, in a more or less teeming physical environment. The Second Matrix is in this respect almost the converse of Christian creation.

15. Perhaps Christians have had this revelation available to them all along. Luke 10:20 has Jesus telling his disciples, "rejoice, because your names are written in heaven." In Latin, *matrix* also meant a "list or register of names" (also, *matricula*, hence our English verb *matriculate*). Intended meaning can go astray: according to some, the notion that the fruit of the tree of knowledge of good and evil was an apple rests on a confusion over the Latin *malum*, meaning both "evil" and "apple tree." In like manner, maybe Jesus' message, lost in translation, was that heaven is a matrix.

16. "People" in the sense of *human beings*. It might be objected that there has to be at least one person with whom you are in contact: God. I'll just concede this, since it doesn't affect the argument, God's desires presumably being compatible with yours. (Real interaction with angels likewise presents no problems.) A fascinating further suggestion is that you couldn't be maximally happy unless the "program" was extremely sophisticated, and then it might be objected that we should regard the solitary matrix as containing *virtual* individuals—such as your imaginative sexual partner(s), if there is sex in heaven—who are arguably persons you really interact with. (Agent Smith's impassioned outburst that he *hates* the Second Matrix might be evidence of personhood, for instance.) *If* these virtual individuals are persons with libertarian free will, then you can't interact with them either, without someone eventually suffering. So we might have another argument that the Christian heaven is an incoherent notion.

thinking about heaven, we seem to prefer the best matrix to the best real deal. This schism in our thinking is represented by the two competing visions in *The Matrix*: on the one hand is the Matrix, and on the other is Zion—named ironically, if I am right, for God's holy city in heaven—the place in the bowels of the Earth where human beings not in the Matrix dwell.

Further Reading

If you doubt that we can learn anything about our values from considering highly unrealistic hypotheses, here is an argument that a matrix-like existence may be our present lot: Nick Bostrom, "Are We Living in a Computer Simulation?" *Philosophical Quarterly* 53 (2003): 243–255. Thomas Aquinas, *Summa Theologica: Supplement to the Third Part*, is a classic of Catholic theology, including an interesting eschatological discussion. For instance, Aquinas thinks that in heaven, one is aware of the suffering of the damned, but does not experience any unhappiness as a result. John Mackie, "Evil and Omnipotence," *Mind* 64 (1955): 200–212, is a classic paper arguing that God's existence is logically incompatible with the existence of evil. For an equally classic response to Mackie, see Alvin Plantinga, *The Nature of Necessity* (Oxford University Press 1974), chapter 9, or Plantinga, *God, Freedom and Evil* (Harper and Row 1974). Plantinga argues that, given libertarian free will, there is no logical incompatibility between God's existence and evil. George Wall, "Heaven and a Wholly Good God," *Personalist* 58 (1977): 352–357, articulates the dilemma of heavenly freedom. James Sennett, "Is There Freedom in Heaven?" *Faith and Philosophy* 16 (1999): 69–82, offers a resolution of the dilemma of heavenly freedom: (i) in heaven, all actions are determined, and there is no possibility of sin; (ii) on Earth, some actions are not determined, permitting libertarian free will; and (iii) you are free in heaven anyway. The key to the resolution is the claim that present freedom doesn't require *present* indeterminism, as long as you enjoyed libertarian freedom at some previous time. Simon Gaine, *Will There Be Free Will in Heaven? Freedom, Impeccability and Beatitude* (Clark 2003), claims to find a coherent Christian conception of heaven that includes freedom.

9

David J. Chalmers

THE MATRIX AS METAPHYSICS

I. Brains in Vats

The Matrix presents a version of an old philosophical fable: the brain in a vat. A disembodied brain is floating in a vat, inside a scientist's laboratory. The scientist has arranged that the brain will be stimulated with the same sort of inputs that a normal embodied brain receives. To do this, the brain is connected to a giant computer simulation of a world. The simulation determines which inputs the brain receives. When the brain produces outputs, these are fed back into the simulation. The internal state of the brain is just like that of a normal brain, despite the fact that it lacks a body. From the brain's point of view, things seem very much as they seem to you and me.

The brain is massively deluded, it seems. It has all sorts of false beliefs about the world. It believes that it has a body, but it has no body. It believes that it is walking outside in the sunlight, but in fact it is inside a dark lab. It believes it is one place, when in fact it may be somewhere quite different. Perhaps it thinks it is in Tucson, when it is actually in Australia, or even in outer space.

Neo's situation at the beginning of *The Matrix* is something like this. He thinks that he lives in a city; he thinks that he has hair; he thinks it is 1999; and he thinks that it is sunny outside. In reality, he is floating in a pod in space; he has no hair; the year is around 2199; and the world has been darkened by war. There are a few small differences from the vat scenario above: Neo's brain is located in a body, and the computer simulation is controlled by machines rather than by a scientist. But the essential details are much the same. In effect, Neo is a brain in a vat.

Let's say that a *matrix* (lowercase *m*) is an artificially designed computer simulation of a world. So the Matrix in the movie is one example of a matrix. And let's say that someone is *envatted*, or that they are *in a matrix*, if they have a cognitive system which receives its inputs from and sends its outputs to a matrix. Then, the brain at the beginning is envatted, and so is Neo.

We can imagine that a matrix simulates the entire physics of a world, keeping track of every last particle throughout space and time. (Later, we will look at ways in which this set-up might be varied.) An envatted being will be associated with a particular simulated body. A connection is arranged so that whenever this body receives sensory inputs inside the simulation, the envatted cognitive system will receive sensory inputs of the same sort. When the envatted cognitive system produces motor outputs, corresponding outputs will be fed to the motor organs of the simulated body.

When the possibility of a matrix is raised, a question immediately follows: how do I know that I am not in a matrix? After all, there could be a brain in a vat structured exactly like my brain, hooked up to a matrix, with experiences indistinguishable from those I am having now. From the inside, there is no way to tell for sure that I am not in the situation of the brain in a vat. So it seems that there is no way to know for sure that I am not in a matrix.

Let us call the hypothesis that I am in a matrix and have always been in a matrix the *Matrix Hypothesis*. Equivalently, the Matrix Hypothesis says that I am envatted and have always been envatted. This is not quite equivalent to the hypothesis that I am in the Matrix, as the Matrix is just one specific version of a matrix. For now, I will ignore some complications that are specific to the Matrix in the movie, such as the fact that people sometimes travel back and forth between the Matrix and the external world. These issues aside, we can think of the Matrix Hypothesis informally as saying that I am in the same sort of situation as people who have always been in the Matrix.

The Matrix Hypothesis is one that we should take seriously. As Nick Bostrom has suggested, it is not out of the question that in the history of the universe, technology will evolve that will allow beings to create computer simulations of entire worlds. There may well be vast numbers of such computer simulations, compared to just one real world. If so, there may well be many more beings who are in a matrix than beings who are not. Given all this, one might even infer that it is more likely that we are in a matrix than that we are not. Whether this is right or not, it certainly seems that we cannot be *certain* that we are not in a matrix.

Serious consequences seem to follow. My envatted counterpart seems to be massively deluded. It thinks it is in Tucson; it thinks it is sitting at a desk writing an article; it thinks it has a body. On the face of it, all of these beliefs are false. Likewise, it seems that if I am envatted, my own corresponding beliefs are false. If I am envatted, I am not really in Tucson; I am not really sitting at a desk; and I may not even have a body. So if I don't know that I am not envatted, then I don't know that I am in Tucson; I don't know that I am sitting at a desk; and I don't know that I have a body.

The Matrix Hypothesis threatens to undercut almost everything I know. It seems to be a *skeptical hypothesis*: a hypothesis that I cannot rule out, and one that would falsify most of my beliefs if it were true. Where there is a skeptical hypothesis, it looks like none of these beliefs count as genuine knowledge. Of course the beliefs *might* be true—I might be lucky, and not be envatted—but I can't rule out the possibility that they are false. So a skeptical hypothesis leads to *skepticism* about these beliefs: I believe these things, but I do not know them.

To sum up the reasoning: I don't know that I'm not in a matrix. If I'm in a matrix, I'm probably not in Tucson. So if I don't know that I'm not in a matrix, then I don't know that I'm in Tucson. The same goes for almost everything else I think I know about the external world.

II. Envatment Reconsidered

This is a standard way of thinking about the vat scenario. It seems that this view is also endorsed by the people who created *The Matrix*. On the DVD case for the movie, one sees the following:

Perception: Our day-in, day-out world is real.
Reality: That world is a hoax, an elaborate deception spun by all-powerful machines that control us. Whoa.

I think this view is not quite right. I think that even if I am in a matrix, my world is perfectly real. A brain in a vat is not massively deluded (at least if it has always been in the vat). Neo does not have massively false beliefs about the external world. Instead, envatted beings have largely *correct* beliefs about their world. If so, the Matrix Hypothesis is not a skeptical hypothesis, and its possibility does not undercut everything that I think I know.

Philosophers have held this sort of view before. The eighteenth-century philosopher George Berkeley held, in effect, that appearance is reality. (Recall Morpheus: "What is 'real'? How do you define 'real'? If you're talking about what you can feel, what you can smell, what you can taste and see, then real is simply electrical signals interpreted by your brain.") If this is right, then the world perceived by envatted beings is perfectly real: these beings experience all the right appearances, and appearance is reality. So on this view, even envatted beings have true beliefs about the world.

I have recently found myself embracing a similar conclusion, though for quite different reasons. I don't find the view that appearance is reality plausible, so I don't endorse Berkeley's reasoning. And until recently, it has seemed quite obvious to me that brains in vats would have massively false beliefs. But I now think there is a line of reasoning that shows that this is wrong.

I still think I cannot rule out the hypothesis that I am in a matrix. But I think that even if I am in a matrix, I am still in Tucson; I am still sitting at my desk; and so on. So the hypothesis that I am in a matrix is not a skeptical hypothesis. The same goes for Neo. At the beginning of the film, if he thinks, "I have hair," he is correct. If he thinks, "It is sunny outside," he is correct. And the same goes, of course, for the original brain in a vat. When it thinks, "I have a body," it is correct. When it thinks, "I am walking," it is correct.

This view may seem counterintuitive at first. Initially, it seemed quite counterintuitive to me. So I'll now present the line of reasoning that has convinced me that it is correct.

III. The Metaphysical Hypothesis

I will argue that the hypothesis that I am envatted is not a skeptical hypothesis, but a *metaphysical hypothesis*. That is, it is a hypothesis about the underlying nature of reality. Where physics is concerned with the microscopic processes that underlie macroscopic reality, metaphysics is concerned with the fundamental nature of reality. A metaphysical hypothesis might make a claim about the reality that underlies physics itself. Alternatively, it might say something about the nature of our minds, or the creation of our world.

I think that the Matrix Hypothesis should be regarded as a metaphysical hypothesis with all three of these elements. It makes a claim about the reality underlying physics, about the nature of our minds, and about the creation of the world. In particular, I think the Matrix Hypothesis is equivalent to a version of the following three-part Metaphysical Hypothesis. First, physical processes are fundamentally computational. Second, our cognitive systems are separate from physical processes, but interact with these processes. Third, physical reality was created by beings outside physical space-time.

Importantly, nothing about this Metaphysical Hypothesis is skeptical. The Metaphysical Hypothesis here tells us about the processes underlying our ordinary reality, but it does not entail that this reality does not exist. We still have bodies, and there are still chairs and tables: it's just that their fundamental nature is a bit different from what we may have thought. In this manner, the Metaphysical Hypothesis is analogous to a physical hypothesis, such as one involving quantum mechanics. Both the physical hypothesis and the Metaphysical Hypothesis tell us about the processes underlying chairs. They do not entail that there are no chairs. Rather, they tell us what chairs are really like.

I will make the case by introducing each of the three parts of the Metaphysical Hypothesis separately. I will suggest that each of them is coherent, and cannot be conclusively ruled out. And I will suggest that none of them is a skeptical hypothesis: even if they are true, most of our ordinary beliefs are still correct. The same goes for a combination of all three hypotheses. I will then argue that the Matrix Hypothesis is equivalent to this combination.

The Computational Hypothesis

The Computational Hypothesis says: Microphysical processes throughout space-time are constituted by underlying computational processes. The Computational Hypothesis says that physics as we know it is not the fundamental level of reality. Just as chemical processes underlie biological processes, and microphysical processes underlie chemical processes, something underlies microphysical processes. Underneath the level of quarks, electrons, and photons is a further level: the level of bits. These bits are governed by a computational algorithm, which at a higher level produces the processes that we think of as fundamental particles, forces, and so on.

The Computational Hypothesis is one that some scientists take seriously. Most famously, Edward Fredkin has postulated that the universe is at bottom some sort of computer. More recently, Stephen Wolfram has taken up the idea in his book *A New Kind of Science*, suggesting that at the fundamental level, physical reality may be a sort of cellular automata, with interacting bits governed by simple rules. And some physicists have looked into the possibility that the laws of physics might be formulated computationally or could be seen as the consequence of certain computational principles.

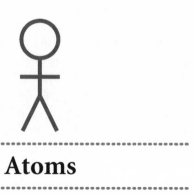

Atoms

110101101011
011010000111

The Computational Hypothesis

One might worry that pure bits could not be the fundamental level of reality: a bit is just a zero or a one, and reality can't really be zeros and ones. Or perhaps a bit is just a "pure difference" between two basic states, and there can't be a reality made up of pure differences. Rather, bits always have to be implemented by more basic states, such as voltages in a normal computer.

I don't know whether this objection is right. I don't think it's completely out of the question that there could be a universe of "pure bits." But this doesn't matter for present purposes. We can suppose that the computational level is itself constituted by an even more fundamental level, at which the computational processes are implemented. It doesn't matter for present purposes what that more fundamental level is. All that matters is that microphysical processes are constituted by computational processes, which may themselves be constituted by more basic processes. From now on I will regard the Computational Hypothesis as saying this.

I don't know whether the Computational Hypothesis is correct. But I don't know that it is false. The hypothesis is coherent, if speculative, and I cannot conclusively rule it out.

The Computational Hypothesis is not a skeptical hypothesis. If it is true, there are still electrons and protons. On this picture, electrons and protons will be analogous to molecules: they are made up of something more basic, but they still exist. Similarly, if the Computational Hypothesis is true, there are still tables and chairs, and macroscopic reality still exists. It just turns out that their fundamental reality is a little different from what we thought.

The situation here is analogous to quantum mechanics or relativity. These may lead us to revise a few "metaphysical" beliefs about the external world: that the world is made of classical particles, or that there is absolute time. But most of our ordinary beliefs are left intact. Likewise, accepting the Computational Hypothesis may lead us to revise a few metaphysical beliefs: that electrons and protons are fundamental, for example. But most of our ordinary beliefs are unaffected.

The Creation Hypothesis

The Creation Hypothesis says: Physical space-time and its contents were created by beings outside physical space-time. This is a familiar hypothesis. A version of it is believed by many people in our society, and perhaps by the majority of the people in the world. If one believes that God created the world, and if one believes that God is outside physical space-time, then one believes the Creation Hypothesis. One needn't believe in God to believe the Creation Hypothesis, though. Perhaps our world was created by a relatively ordinary being in the "next universe up," using the latest world-making technology in that universe. If so, the Creation Hypothesis is true.

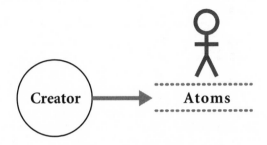

The Creation Hypothesis

I don't know whether the Creation Hypothesis is true. But I don't know for certain that it is false. The hypothesis is clearly coherent, and I cannot conclusively rule it out.

The Creation Hypothesis is not a skeptical hypothesis. Even if it is true, most of my ordinary beliefs are still true. I still have hands; I am still in Tucson; and so on. Perhaps a few of my beliefs will turn out to be false: if I am an atheist, for example, or if I believe all reality started with the Big Bang. But most of my everyday beliefs about the external world will remain intact.

The Mind-Body Hypothesis

The Mind-Body Hypothesis says: My mind is (and has always been) constituted by processes outside physical space-time and receives its perceptual inputs from and sends its outputs to processes in physical space-time.

The Mind-Body Hypothesis is also quite familiar and quite widely believed. Descartes believed something like this: on his view, we have nonphysical minds that interact with our physical bodies. The hypothesis is less widely believed today than in Descartes's time, but there are still many people who accept the Mind-Body Hypothesis.

Whether or not the Mind-Body Hypothesis is true, it is certainly coherent. Even if contemporary science tends to suggest that the hypothesis is false, we cannot rule it out conclusively.

The Mind-Body Hypothesis is not a skeptical hypothesis. Even if my mind is outside physical space-time, I still have a body; I am still in

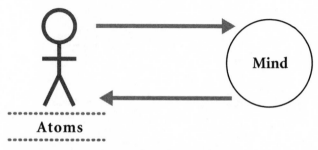

The Mind-Body Hypothesis

Tucson; and so on. At most, accepting this hypothesis would make us revise a few metaphysical beliefs about our minds. Our ordinary beliefs about external reality will remain largely intact.

The Metaphysical Hypothesis

We can now put these hypotheses together. First we can consider the Combination Hypothesis, which combines all three. It says that physical space-time and its contents were created by beings outside physical space-time, that microphysical processes are constituted by computational processes, and that our minds are outside physical space-time but interact with it.

As with the hypotheses taken individually, the Combination Hypothesis is coherent, and we cannot conclusively rule it out. And like the hypotheses taken individually, it is not a skeptical hypothesis. Accepting it might lead us to revise a few of our beliefs, but it would leave most of them intact.

Finally, we can consider the Metaphysical Hypothesis (with a capital M). Like the Combination Hypothesis, this combines the Creation Hypothesis, the Computational Hypothesis, and the Mind-Body Hypothesis. It also adds the following more-specific claim: the computational processes underlying physical space-time were designed by the creators as a computer simulation of a world. (It may also be useful to think of the

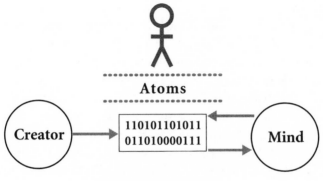

The Metaphysical Hypothesis

Metaphysical Hypothesis as saying that the computational processes constituting physical space-time are part of a broader domain, and that the creators and my cognitive system are also located within this domain. This addition is not strictly necessary for what follows, but it matches up with the most common way of thinking about the Matrix Hypothesis.)

The Metaphysical Hypothesis is a slightly more specific version of the Combination Hypothesis, in that it specifies some relations among the various parts of the hypothesis. Again, the Metaphysical Hypothesis is a coherent hypothesis, and we cannot conclusively rule it out. And again, it is not a skeptical hypothesis. Even if we accept it, most of our ordinary beliefs about the external world will be left intact.

IV. The Matrix Hypothesis as a Metaphysical Hypothesis

Recall that the Matrix Hypothesis says: I have (and have always had) a cognitive system that receives its inputs from and sends its outputs to an artificially designed computer simulation of a world.

I will argue that the Matrix Hypothesis is equivalent to the Metaphysical Hypothesis, in the following sense: if I accept the Metaphysical Hypothesis, I should accept the Matrix Hypothesis, and if I accept the Matrix Hypothesis, I should accept the Metaphysical Hypothesis. That is, the two hypotheses *imply* each other, where this means that if I accept one, I should accept the other.

Take the first direction first, from the Metaphysical Hypothesis to the Matrix Hypothesis. The Mind-Body Hypothesis implies that I have (and have always had) a cognitive system which receives its inputs from and sends its outputs to processes in physical space-time. In conjunction with the Computational Hypothesis, this implies that my cognitive system receives inputs from and sends outputs to the computational processes that constitute physical space-time. The Creation Hypothesis (along with the rest of the Metaphysical Hypothesis) implies that these processes were artificially designed to simulate a world. It follows that I have (and have always had) a cognitive system that receives its inputs from and sends its outputs to an artificially designed computer simulation of a world. This is just the Matrix Hypothesis. So the Metaphysical Hypothesis implies the Matrix Hypothesis.

The Matrix Hypothesis

The other direction is closely related. To put it informally: if I accept the Matrix Hypothesis, I accept that what underlies apparent reality is just as the Metaphysical Hypothesis specifies. There is a domain containing my cognitive system, which is causally interacting with a computer simulation of physical space-time, which was created by other beings in that domain. This is just what has to obtain in order for the Metaphysical Hypothesis to obtain. If one accepts this, one should accept the Creation Hypothesis, the Computational Hypothesis, the Mind-Body Hypothesis, and the relevant relations among these.

This may be a little clearer through a picture. The diagram above shows the shape of the world according to the Matrix Hypothesis. At the fundamental level, this picture of the shape of the world is exactly the same as the picture of the Metaphysical Hypothesis given above. So if one accepts that the world is as it is according to the Matrix Hypothesis, one should accept that it is as it is according to the Metaphysical Hypothesis.

One might make various objections. For example, one might object that the Matrix Hypothesis implies that a computer simulation of physical processes exists, but (unlike the Metaphysical Hypothesis) it does not imply that the physical processes themselves exist. I will discuss this objection in section VI and other objections in section VII. For now, though, I take it that there is a strong case that the Matrix Hypothesis implies the Metaphysical Hypothesis, and vice versa.

V. Life in the Matrix

If this is right, it follows that the Matrix Hypothesis is not a skeptical hypothesis. If I accept it, I should not infer that the external world does not exist, nor that I have no body, nor that there are no tables and chairs, nor that I am not in Tucson. Rather, I should infer that the physical world is constituted by computations beneath the microphysical level. There are still tables, chairs, and bodies: these are made up fundamentally of bits and of whatever constitutes these bits. This world was created by other beings, but is still perfectly real. My mind is separate from physical processes, and interacts with them. My mind may not have been created by these beings, and it may not be made up of bits, but it still interacts with these bits.

The result is a complex picture of the fundamental nature of reality. The picture is strange and surprising, perhaps, but it is a picture of a full-blooded external world. If we are in a matrix, this is simply the way that the world is.

We can think of the Matrix Hypothesis as a creation myth for the information age. If it is correct, then the physical world was created, but not necessarily by gods. Underlying the physical world is a giant computation, and creators created this world by implementing this computation. And our minds lie outside this physical structure, with an independent nature that interacts with this structure.

Many of the same issues that arise with standard creation myths arise here. When was the world created? Strictly speaking, it was not created within *our* time at all. When did history begin? The creators might have started the simulation in 4004 B.C. (or in 1999) with the fossil record intact, but it would have been much easier for them to start the simulation at the Big Bang and let things run their course from there.

(In *The Matrix*, of course, the creators are machines. This gives an interesting twist on common theological readings of the movie. It is often held that Neo is the Christ figure in the movie, with Morpheus corresponding to John the Baptist, Cypher to Judas Iscariot, and so on. But on the reading I have given, the gods of *The Matrix* are the machines. Who, then, is the Christ figure? Agent Smith, of course! After all, he is the gods' offspring, sent down to save the Matrix-world from those who wish to destroy it. And in the second movie, he is even resurrected.)

Many of the same issues that arise on the standard Mind-Body Hypothesis also arise on the Matrix Hypothesis. When do our nonphysical minds start to exist? It depends on just when new envatted cognitive systems are attached to the simulation (perhaps at the time of conception within the matrix, or perhaps at the time of birth?). Is there life after death? It depends on just what happens to the envatted systems once their simulated bodies die. How do mind and body interact? By causal links that are outside physical space and time.

Even if we are not in a matrix, we can extend a version of this reasoning to other beings who are in a matrix. If they discover their situation and come to accept that they are in a matrix, they should not reject their ordinary beliefs about the external world. At most, they should come to revise their beliefs about the underlying nature of their world: they should come to accept that external objects are made of bits, and so on. These beings are not massively deluded: most of their ordinary beliefs about their world are correct.

There are a few qualifications here. One may worry about beliefs about other people's minds. I believe that my friends are conscious. If I am in a matrix, is this correct? In the Matrix depicted in the movie, these beliefs are mostly fine. This is a multivat matrix: for each of my perceived friends, there is an envatted being in the external reality, who is presumably conscious like me. The exception might be beings such as Agent Smith, who are not envatted but are entirely computational. Whether these beings are conscious depends on whether computation is enough for consciousness. I will remain neutral on that issue here. We could circumvent this issue by building into the Matrix Hypothesis the requirement that all of the beings we perceive are envatted. But even if we do not build in this requirement, we are not much worse off than in the actual world, where there is a legitimate issue about whether other beings are conscious, quite independent of whether we are in a matrix.

One might also worry about beliefs about the distant past, and about the far future. These will be unthreatened as long as the computer simulation covers all of space-time, from the Big Bang until the end of the universe. This is built into the Metaphysical Hypothesis, and we can stipulate that it is built into the Matrix Hypothesis too, by requiring that the computer simulation be a simulation of an entire world. There may be other simulations that start in the recent past (perhaps the Matrix in the movie is like this), and there may be others that only last for a short while. In these cases, the envatted beings will have false beliefs about the past or the future in their worlds. But as long as the simulation covers the lifespan of these beings, it is plausible that they will have mostly correct beliefs about the current state of their environment.

There may be some respects in which the beings in a matrix are deceived. It may be that the creators of the matrix control and interfere with much of what happens in the simulated world. (The Matrix in the movie may be like this, though the extent of the creators' control is not quite clear.) If so, then these beings may have much less control over what happens than they think. But the same goes if there is an interfering god in a nonmatrix world. And the Matrix Hypothesis does not imply that the creators interfere with the world, though it leaves the possibility open. At worst, the Matrix Hypothesis is no more skeptical in this respect than is the Creation Hypothesis in a nonmatrix world.

The inhabitants of a matrix may also be deceived in that reality is much bigger than they think. They might think their physical universe is all there is, when in fact there is much more in the world, including beings and objects that they can never possibly see. But again, this sort of worry can arise equally in a nonmatrix world. For example, cosmologists seriously entertain the hypothesis that our universe may stem from a black hole in the "next universe up," and that in reality there may be a whole tree of universes. If so, the world is also much bigger than we think, and there may be beings and objects that we can never possibly see. But either way, the world that we see is perfectly real.

Importantly, none of these sources of skepticism—about other minds, the past and the future, our control over the world, and the extent of the world—casts doubt on our belief in the reality of the world that we perceive. None of them leads us to doubt the existence of external objects such as tables and chairs, in the way that the vat hypothesis is supposed to do. And none of these worries is especially tied to the matrix scenario. One can raise doubts about whether other minds exist, whether the past and the future exist, and whether we have control over our world quite independently of whether we are in a matrix. If this is right, then the Matrix Hypothesis does not raise the distinctive skeptical issues that it is often taken to raise.

I suggested before that it is not out of the question that we really are in a matrix. One might have thought that this would be a worrying conclusion. But if I am right, it is not nearly as worrying as one might have thought. Even if we are in such a matrix, our world is no less real than we thought it was. It just has a surprising fundamental nature.

VI. Objection: Simulation Is Not Reality

(This slightly technical section can be skipped without too much loss.)

A common line of objection is that a simulation is not the same as reality. The Matrix Hypothesis implies only that a simulation of physical processes exists. By contrast, the Metaphysical Hypothesis implies that physical processes really exist (they are explicitly mentioned in the Computational Hypothesis and elsewhere). If so, then the Matrix Hypothesis cannot imply the Metaphysical Hypothesis. On this view, if I am in a matrix, then physical processes do not really exist.

In response: My argument does not require the general assumption that simulation is the same as reality. The argument works quite differently. But the objection helps us to flesh out the informal argument that the Matrix Hypothesis implies the Metaphysical Hypothesis.

Because the Computational Hypothesis is coherent, it is clearly *possible* that a computational level underlies real physical processes, and it is possible that the computations here are implemented by further processes in turn. So there is *some* sort of computational system that could yield reality here. But here, the objector will hold that not all computational systems are created equal. To say that some computational systems will yield real physical processes in this role is not to say that they all do. Perhaps some of them are merely simulations. If so, then the Matrix Hypothesis may not yield reality.

To rebut this objection, we can appeal to two principles. First principle: any abstract computation that could be used to simulate physical space-time is such that it *could* turn out to underlie real physical processes. Second principle: given an abstract computation that *could* underlie physical processes, the precise way in which it is implemented is irrelevant to whether it *does* underlie physical processes. In particular, the fact that the implementation was designed as a simulation is irrelevant. The conclusion then follows directly.

On the first principle: let us think of abstract computations in purely formal terms, abstracting away from their manner of implementation. For an abstract computation to qualify as a simulation of physical reality, it must have computational elements that correspond to every particle in reality (likewise for fields, waves, or whatever is fundamental), dynamically evolving in a way that corresponds to each particle's evolution. But then, it is guaranteed that the computation will have a rich enough causal structure that it *could* in principle underlie physics in our world. Any computation will do, as long as it has enough detail to correspond to the fine details of physical processes.

On the second principle: given an abstract computation that could underlie physical reality, it does not matter how the computation is implemented. We can imagine discovering that some computational level underlies the level of atoms and electrons. Once we have discovered this, it is possible that this computational level is implemented by more basic processes. There are many hypotheses about what the underlying processes could be, but none of them is especially privileged, and none of them would lead us to reject the hypothesis that the computational level constitutes physical processes. That is, the Computational Hypothesis is *implementation-independent*: as long as we have the right sort of abstract computation, the manner of implementation does not matter.

In particular, it is irrelevant whether or not these implementing processes were artificially created, and it is irrelevant whether they were intended as a simulation. What matters is the intrinsic nature of the processes, not their origin. And what matters about this intrinsic nature is simply that they are arranged in such a way as to implement the right sort of computation. If so, the fact that the implementation originated as a simulation is irrelevant to whether it can constitute physical reality.

There is one further constraint on the implementing processes: they must be connected to our experiences in the right sort of way. That is, when we have an experience of an object, the processes underlying the simulation of that object must be causally connected in the right sort of way to our experiences. If this is not the case, then there will be no reason to think that these computational processes underlie the physical processes that we perceive. If there is an isolated computer simulation to which nobody is connected in this way, we should say that it is simply a simulation. But an appropriate hook-up to our perceptual experiences is built into the Matrix Hypothesis, on the most natural understanding of that hypothesis. So the Matrix Hypothesis has no problems here.

Overall, then, we have seen that computational processes *could* underlie physical reality, that any abstract computation that qualifies as a simulation of physical reality could play this role, and that any implementation of this computation could constitute physical reality, as long as it is hooked up to our experiences in the relevant way. The Matrix Hypothesis guarantees that we have an abstract computation of the right sort, and it guarantees that it is hooked up to our experiences in the relevant ways. So the Matrix Hypothesis implies that the Computational Hypothesis is correct, and that the computer simulation constitutes genuine physical processes.

VII. Other Objections

When we look at a brain in a vat from the outside, it is hard to avoid the sense that it is deluded. This sense manifests itself in a number of related objections. These are not direct objections to the argument above, but they are objections to its conclusion.

Objection 1: A brain in a vat may think it is outside walking in the sun, when in fact it is alone in a dark room. Surely, it is deluded.

Response: The *brain* is alone in a dark room. But this does not imply that the *person* is alone in a dark room. By analogy, just say Descartes is right that we have disembodied minds outside space-time, made of ectoplasm. When I think, "I am outside in the sun," an angel might look at my ectoplasmic mind and note that in fact it is not exposed to any sun at all. Does it follow that my thought is incorrect? Presumably not: I can be outside in the sun, even if my ectoplasmic mind is not. The angel would be wrong to infer that I have an incorrect belief. Likewise, we should not infer that the envatted being has an incorrect belief. At least, it is no more deluded than a Cartesian mind.

The moral is that the immediate surroundings of our minds may well be irrelevant to the truth of most of our beliefs. What matters is the processes that our minds are connected to, by perceptual inputs and motor outputs. Once we recognize this, the objection falls away.

Objection 2: An envatted being may believe that it is in Tucson, when in fact it is in New York, and has never been anywhere near Tucson. Surely, this belief is deluded.

Response: The envatted being's concept of "Tucson" does not refer to what we call Tucson. Rather, it refers to something else entirely: call this "Tucson*" or "virtual Tucson." We might think of this as a 'virtual location' (more on this in a moment). When the being says to itself, "I am in Tucson," it really is thinking that it is in Tucson*, and it may well in fact be in Tucson*. Because Tucson is not Tucson*, the fact that the being has never been in Tucson is irrelevant to whether its belief is true.

A rough analogy: I look at my colleague Terry and think, "That's Terry." Elsewhere in the world, a duplicate of me looks at a duplicate of Terry. It thinks, "That's Terry," but it is not looking at the real Terry. Is its belief false? It seems not: my duplicate's "Terry" concept refers not to Terry, but to his duplicate Terry*. My duplicate really is looking at Terry*, so its belief is true. The same sort of thing is happening in the case above.

Objection 3: Before he leaves the Matrix, Neo believes that he has hair. But in reality he has no hair (the body in the vat is bald). Surely, this belief is deluded.

Response: This case is like the last one. Neo's concept of "hair" does not refer to real hair, but to something else that we might call hair* ('virtual hair'). So the fact that Neo does not have real hair is irrelevant to whether his belief is true. Neo really does have virtual hair, so he is correct. Likewise, when a child in the movie tells Neo, "There is no spoon," his concept refers to a virtual spoon, and there really *is* a virtual spoon. So the child is wrong.

Objection 4: What *sort* of objects does an envatted being refer to? What *is* virtual hair, virtual Tucson, and so on?

Response: These are all entities constituted by computational processes. If I am envatted, then the objects to which I refer (hair, Tucson, and so on) are all made of bits. And if another being is envatted, the objects that it refers to (hair*, Tucson*, and so on) are likewise made of bits. If the envatted being is hooked up to a simulation in my computer, then the objects to which it refers are constituted by patterns of bits inside my computer. We might call these things 'virtual objects'. Virtual hands are not hands (assuming I am not envatted), but they exist inside the computer all the same. Virtual Tucson is not Tucson, but it exists inside the computer all the same.

Objection 5: You just said that virtual hands are not real hands. Does this mean that if we are in a matrix, we don't have real hands?

Response: No. If we are *not* in a matrix, but others are, we should say that their term 'hand' refers to virtual hands, but our term does not. So in this case, our hands aren't virtual hands. But if we *are* in a matrix, then our term 'hand' refers to something that's made of bits: virtual hands, or at least something that would be regarded as virtual hands by people in the next world up. That is, if we are in a matrix, real hands are made of bits. Things look quite different, and our words refer to different things, depending on whether our perspective is from inside or outside the matrix.

This sort of perspective shift is common in thinking about the matrix scenario. From the first-person perspective, we suppose that *we* are in a matrix. Here, real things in our world are made of bits, though the "next world up" might not be made of bits. From the third-person perspective, we suppose that someone *else* is in a matrix, but we are not. Here, real things in our world are not made of bits, but the "next world down" is made of bits. On the first way of doing things, our words refer to computational entities. On the second way of doing things, the envatted beings' words refer to computational entities, but our words do not.

Objection 6: Just which pattern of bits is a given virtual object? Surely it will be impossible to pick out a precise set.

Response: This question is like asking: just which part of the quantum wave function is this chair, or is the University of Arizona? These objects are all ultimately constituted by an underlying quantum wave function, but there may be no precise part of the microlevel wave function that we can say "is" the chair or the university. The chair and the university exist at a higher level. Likewise, if we are envatted, there may be no precise set of bits in the microlevel computational process that is the chair or the university. These exist at a higher level. And if someone else is envatted, there may be no precise sets of bits in the computer simulation that "are" the objects to which they refer. But just as a chair exists without being any precise part of the wave function, a virtual chair may exist without being any precise set of bits.

Objection 7: An envatted being thinks it performs actions, and it thinks it has friends. Are these beliefs correct?

Response: One might try to say that the being performs actions* and that it has friends*. But for various reasons I think it is not plausible that words like 'action' and 'friend' can shift their meanings as easily as words like 'Tucson' and 'hair'. Instead, I think one can say truthfully (in our own language) that the envatted being performs actions, and that it has friends. To be sure, it performs actions in *its* environment, and its environment is not our environment but the virtual environment. And its friends likewise inhabit the virtual environment (assuming that we have a multivat matrix, or that computation suffices for consciousness). But the envatted being is not incorrect in this respect.

Objection 8: Set these technical points aside. Surely, if we are in a matrix, the world is nothing like we think it is!

Response: I deny this. Even if we are in a matrix, there are still people, football games, and particles, arranged in space-time just as we think they are. It is just that the world has a *further* nature that goes beyond our initial conception. In particular, things in the world are realized computationally in a way that we might not have originally imagined. But this does not contradict any of our ordinary beliefs. At most, it will contradict a few of our more abstract metaphysical beliefs. But exactly the same goes for quantum mechanics, relativity theory, and so on.

If we are in a matrix, we may not have many false beliefs, but there is much knowledge that we lack. For example, we do not know that the universe is realized computationally. But this is just what one should expect. Even if we are not in a matrix, there may well be much about the fundamental nature of reality that we do not know. We are not omniscient creatures, and our knowledge of the world is at best partial. This is simply the condition of a creature living in a world.

VIII. Other Skeptical Hypotheses

The Matrix Hypothesis is one example of a traditional "skeptical" hypothesis, but it is not the only example. Other skeptical hypotheses are not quite as straightforward as the Matrix Hypothesis. Still, I think that for many of them, a similar line of reasoning applies. In particular, one can argue that most of these are not global skeptical hypotheses: that is, their truth would not undercut all of our empirical beliefs about the physical world. At worst, most of them are *partial* skeptical hypotheses, undercutting some of our empirical beliefs, but leaving many other beliefs intact.

> *New Matrix Hypothesis*: I was recently created, along with all of my memories, and was put in a newly created matrix.

What if both the matrix and I have existed for only a short time? This hypothesis is a computational version of Bertrand Russell's Recent Creation Hypothesis: the physical world was created only recently (with fossil record intact), and so was I (with memories intact). On that hypothesis, the external world that I perceive really exists, and most of my beliefs about its current state are plausibly true, but I have many false beliefs about the past. I think the same should be said of the New Matrix Hypothesis. One can argue, along the lines presented earlier, that the New Matrix Hypothesis is equivalent to a combination of the Metaphysical Hypothesis with the Recent Creation Hypothesis. This combination is not a global skeptical hypothesis (though it is a partial skeptical hypothesis, where beliefs about the past are concerned). So the same goes for the New Matrix Hypothesis.

> *Recent Matrix Hypothesis*: For most of my life I have not been envatted, but I was recently hooked up to a matrix.

If I was recently put in a matrix without realizing it, it seems that many of my beliefs about my current environment are false. Let's say that just yesterday someone put me into a simulation, in which I fly to Las Vegas and gamble at a casino. Then I may believe that I am in Las Vegas now, and that I am in a casino, but these beliefs are false: I am really in a laboratory in Tucson.

This result is quite different from the long-term matrix. The difference lies in the fact that my conception of external reality is anchored to the reality in which I have lived most of my life. If I have been envatted all of my life, my conception is anchored to the computationally constituted reality. But if I were just envatted yesterday, my conception is anchored to the external reality. So when I think that I am in Las Vegas, I am thinking that I am in the external Las Vegas, and this thought is false.

Still, this does not undercut all of my beliefs about the external world. I believe that I was born in Sydney, that there is water in the oceans, and so on, and all of these beliefs are correct. It is only my recently acquired beliefs, stemming from my perception of the simulated environment, that will be false. So this is only a partial skeptical hypothesis: its possibility casts doubt on a subset of our empirical beliefs, but it does not cast doubt on all of them.

Interestingly, the Recent Matrix and the New Matrix hypotheses give opposite results, despite their similar nature: the Recent Matrix Hypothesis yields true beliefs about the past but false beliefs about the present, while the New Matrix Hypothesis yields false beliefs about the past and true beliefs about the present. The differences are tied to the fact that in the Recent Matrix Hypothesis, I really have a past existence for my beliefs to be about, and that past reality has played a role in anchoring the contents of my thoughts, which has no parallel under the New Matrix Hypothesis.

Local Matrix Hypothesis: I am hooked up to a computer simulation of a fixed local environment in a world.

On one way of doing this, a computer simulates a small fixed environment in a world, and the subjects in the simulation encounter some sort of barrier when they try to leave that area. For example, in the movie *The Thirteenth Floor*, just California is simulated, and when the subject tries to drive to Nevada, a road sign says "Closed for Repair" (with faint green electronic mountains in the distance!). Of course this is not the best way to create a matrix, as subjects are likely to discover the limits to their world.

This hypothesis is analogous to a Local Creation Hypothesis, on which creators just created a local part of the physical world. Under this hypothesis, we will have true beliefs about nearby matters, but false beliefs about matters farther from home. By the usual sort of reasoning, the Local Matrix Hypothesis can be seen as a combination of the Metaphysical Hypothesis with the Local Creation Hypothesis. So we should treat it the same way.

Extendible Local Matrix Hypothesis: I am hooked up to a computer simulation of a local environment in a world, which is extended when necessary depending on my movements.

This hypothesis avoids the obvious difficulties with a fixed local matrix. Here, the creators simulate a local environment and extend it when necessary. For example, they might right now be concentrating on simulating a room in my house in Tucson. If I walk into another room, or fly to another city, they will simulate those. Of course, they need to make sure that when I go to these places, they match my memories and beliefs reasonably well, with allowance for evolution in the meantime. The same goes for when I encounter familiar people, or people I have only heard about. Presumably, the simulators keep up a database of the information about the world that has been settled so far, updating this information whenever necessary as time goes along, and making up new details when they need them.

This sort of simulation is quite unlike simulation in an ordinary matrix. In a matrix, the whole world is simulated at once. There are high start-up costs, but once the simulation is up and running, it will take care of itself. By contrast, the extendible local matrix involves "just-in-time" simulation. This has much lower start-up costs, but it requires much more work and creativity as the simulation evolves.

This hypothesis is analogous to an Extendible Local Creation Hypothesis about ordinary reality, under which creators create just a local physical environment and extend it when necessary. Here, external reality exists and many local beliefs are true, but again beliefs about matters farther from home are false. If we combine that hypothesis with the Metaphysical Hypothesis, the result is the Extendible Local Matrix Hypothesis. So if we are in an extendible local matrix, external reality still exists, but there is not as much of it as we thought. Of course if I travel in the right direction, more of it may come into existence.

The situation is reminiscent of the film *The Truman Show*. Truman lives in an artificial environment made up of actors and props, which behave appropriately when he is around, but which may be completely different when he is absent. Truman has many true beliefs about his current environment: there really are tables and chairs in front of him, and so on. But he is deeply mistaken about things outside his current environment, and farther from home.

It is common to think that while *The Truman Show* poses a disturbing skeptical scenario, *The Matrix* is much worse. But if I am right, things are reversed. If I am in a matrix, then most of my beliefs about the external world are true. If I am in something like *The Truman Show*, then a great number of my beliefs are false. On reflection, it seems to me that this is the right conclusion. If we were to discover that we were (and always had been) in a matrix, this would be surprising, but we would quickly get used to it. If we were to discover that we were (and always had been) in a televised "Truman Show," we might well go insane.

Macroscopic Matrix Hypothesis: I am hooked up to a computer simulation of macroscopic physical processes without microphysical detail.

One can imagine that, for ease of simulation, the makers of a matrix might not bother to simulate low-level physics. Instead, they might just represent macroscopic objects in the world and their properties: for example, that there is a table with such-and-such shape, position, and color, with a book on top of it with certain properties, and so on. They will need to make some effort to make sure that these objects behave in physically reasonable ways, and they will have to make special provisions for handling microphysical measurements, but one can imagine that at least a reasonable simulation could be created this way.

I think this hypothesis is analogous to a Macroscopic World Hypothesis: there are no microphysical processes, and instead macroscopic physical objects exist as fundamental objects in the world, with properties of shape, color, position, and so on. This is a coherent way that our world could be, and it is not a global skeptical hypothesis, though it may lead to false scientific beliefs about lower levels of reality. The Macroscopic Matrix Hypothesis can be seen as a combination of this hypothesis with a version of the Metaphysical Hypothesis. As such, it is not a global skeptical hypothesis either.

One can also combine the various hypotheses above in various ways, yielding hypotheses such as a New Local Macroscopic Matrix Hypothesis.

For the usual reasons, all of these can be seen as analogs of corresponding hypotheses about the physical world. So all of them are compatible with the existence of physical reality, and none is a global skeptical hypothesis.

God Hypothesis: Physical reality is represented in the mind of God, and our own thoughts and perceptions depend on God's mind.

A hypothesis like this was put forward by George Berkeley as a view about how our world might really be. Berkeley intended this as a sort of metaphysical hypothesis about the nature of reality. Most other philosophers have differed from Berkeley in regarding this as a sort of skeptical hypothesis. If I am right, Berkeley is closer to the truth. The God Hypothesis can be seen as a version of the Matrix Hypothesis, on which the simulation of the world is implemented in the mind of God. If this is right, we should say that physical processes really exist: it's just that at the most fundamental level, they are constituted by processes in the mind of God.

Evil Genius Hypothesis: I have a disembodied mind, and an evil genius is feeding me sensory inputs to give the appearance of an external world.

This is René Descartes's classical skeptical hypothesis. What should we say about it? This depends on just how the evil genius works. If the evil genius simulates an entire world in his head in order to determine what inputs I should receive, then we have a version of the God Hypothesis. Here we should say that physical reality exists and is constituted by processes within the mind of the evil genius. If the evil genius is simulating only a small part of the physical world, just enough to give me reasonably consistent inputs, then we have an analog of the Local Matrix Hypothesis (in either its fixed or flexible versions). Here we should say that just a local part of external reality exists. If the evil genius is not bothering to simulate the microphysical level, but just the macroscopic level, then we have an analog of the Macroscopic Matrix Hypothesis. Here we should say that local external macroscopic objects exist, but our beliefs about their microphysical nature are incorrect.

The Evil Genius Hypothesis is often taken to be a global skeptical hypothesis. But if the reasoning above is right, this is incorrect. Even if the Evil Genius Hypothesis is correct, some of the external reality that we apparently perceive really exists, though we may have some false beliefs about it, depending on details. It is just that this external reality has an underlying nature that is quite different from what we may have thought.

Dream Hypothesis: I am now and have always been dreaming.

Descartes raised the question: how do you know that you are not currently dreaming? Morpheus raises a similar question:

> Have you ever had a dream, Neo, that you were so sure was real? What if you were unable to wake from that dream? How would you know the difference between the dream world and the real world?

The hypothesis that I am *currently* dreaming is analogous to a version of the Recent Matrix Hypothesis. I cannot rule it out conclusively, and if it is correct, then many of my beliefs about my current environment are incorrect. But presumably, I still have many true beliefs about the external world, anchored in the past.

What if I have always been dreaming? That is, what if all of my apparent perceptual inputs have been generated by my own cognitive system, without my realizing this? I think this case is analogous to the Evil Genius Hypothesis: it's just that the role of the "evil genius" is played by a part of my own cognitive system. If my dream-generating system simulates all of space-time, we have something like the original Matrix Hypothesis. If it models just my local environment, or just some macroscopic processes, we have analogs of the more local versions of the Evil Genius Hypothesis. In any of these cases, we should say that the objects that I am currently perceiving really exist (although objects farther from home may not). It is just that some of them are constituted by my own cognitive processes.

Chaos Hypothesis: I do not receive inputs from anywhere in the world. Instead, I have random, uncaused experiences. Through a huge coincidence, they are exactly the sort of regular, structured experiences with which I am familiar.

The Chaos Hypothesis is an extraordinarily unlikely hypothesis, much more unlikely than anything considered above. But it is still one that could in principle obtain, even if it has minuscule probability. If I am chaotically envatted, do physical processes in the external world exist? I think we should say that they do not. My experiences of external objects are caused by nothing, and the set of experiences associated with my conception of a given object will have no common source. Indeed, my experiences are not caused by any reality external to them at all. So this is a genuine skeptical hypothesis: if accepted, it would cause us to reject most of our beliefs about the external world.

So far, the only clear case of a global skeptical hypothesis is the Chaos Hypothesis. Unlike the previous hypotheses, accepting this hypothesis would undercut all of our substantive beliefs about the external world. Where does the difference come from?

Arguably, what is crucial is that on the Chaos Hypothesis, there is no causal explanation of our experiences at all, and there is no explanation for the regularities in our experience. In all of the previous cases, there is some explanation for these regularities, though perhaps not the explanation that we expect. One might suggest that as long as a hypothesis involves *some* reasonable explanation for the regularities in our experience, then it will not be a global skeptical hypothesis.

If so, then if we are granted the assumption that there is some explanation for the regularities in our experience, then it is safe to say that some of our beliefs about the external world are correct. This is not much, but it is something.

In conclusion: It's not so bad to be a brain in a vat.

IX. Philosophical Notes

The material above was written to be accessible to a wide audience, so it deliberately omits technical philosophical details, connections to the literature, and so on. In this section, I will remedy this omission. Readers without a background in philosophy may choose to skip or skim this section.

Note 1

Hilary Putnam (1981) has argued that the hypothesis that I am (and have always been) a brain in a vat can be ruled out a priori. In effect, this is because my word 'brain' refers to objects in my perceived world, and it cannot refer to objects in an "outer" world in which the vat would have to exist. For my hypothesis "I am a brain in a vat" to be true, I would have to be a brain of the sort that exists in the perceived world, but that cannot be the case. So the hypothesis must be false.

An analogy: I can arguably rule out the hypothesis that I am in the Matrix (capital *M*). My term 'the Matrix' refers to a specific system that I have seen in a movie in my perceived world. I could not be in that very system as the system exists within the world that I perceive. So my hypothesis "I am in the Matrix" must be false.

This conclusion about the Matrix seems reasonable, but there is a natural response. Perhaps this argument rules out the hypothesis that I am in the Matrix, but I cannot rule out the hypothesis that I am in a matrix, where *a matrix* is a generic term for a computer simulation of a world. The term 'Matrix' may be anchored to the specific system in the movie, but the generic term 'matrix' is not.

Likewise, it is arguable that I can rule out the hypothesis that I am a brain in a vat (if "brain" is anchored to a specific sort of biological system in my perceived world). But I cannot rule out the hypothesis that I am envatted, where this simply says that I have a cognitive system that receives input from and sends outputs to a computer simulation of a world. The term 'envatted' (and the terms used in its definition) are generic terms, not anchored to specific systems in perceived reality. By using this slightly different language, we can restate the skeptical hypothesis in a way that is invulnerable to Putnam's reasoning.

More technically: Putnam's argument may work for "brain" and "Matrix" because one is a natural kind term and the other is a name. These terms are subject to "Twin Earth" thought-experiments (Putnam 1975), where duplicates can use corresponding terms with different referents. On Earth, Oscar's term 'water' refers to H_2O, but on Twin Earth (which contains the superficially identical XYZ in its oceans and lakes), Twin Oscar's term 'water' refers to XYZ. Likewise, perhaps my term 'brain' refers to biological brains, while an envatted being's term 'brain' refers to virtual brains. If so, when an envatted being says, "I am a brain in a vat," it is not referring to its biological brain, and its claim is false.

But not all terms are subject to Twin Earth thought-experiments. In particular, *semantically neutral* terms are not (at least when used without semantic deference): such terms plausibly include 'philosopher', 'friend', and many others. Other such terms include 'matrix' and 'envatted', as defined earlier. If we work with hypotheses such as "I am in a matrix" and "I am envatted," rather than "I am in the Matrix" or "I am a brain in a vat," then Putnam's argument does not apply. Even if a brain in a vat could not truly think, "I am a brain in a vat," it could truly think, "I am envatted." So I think that Putnam's line of reasoning is ultimately a red herring.

Note 2

Despite this disagreement, my main conclusion is closely related to another suggestion of Putnam's. This is the suggestion that a brain in a vat may have true beliefs, because it will refer to chemical processes or processes inside a computer. However, I reach this conclusion by a quite different route. Putnam argues by an appeal to the causal theory of reference: thoughts refer to what they are causally connected to, and the thoughts of an envatted being are causally connected to processes in a computer. This argument is clearly inconclusive, as the causal theory of reference is so unconstrained. To say that a causal connection is required for reference is not to say what sort of causal connection suffices. There are many cases (like "phlogiston") where terms fail to refer despite rich causal connections. Intuitively, it is natural to think that the brain in a vat is a case like this, so an appeal to the causal theory of reference does not seem to help.

The argument I have given presupposes nothing about the theory of reference. Instead, it proceeds directly by considering first-order hypotheses about the world, the connections among these, and what we should say if they are true. In answering objections, I have made some claims about reference, and these claims are broadly compatible with a causal theory of reference. But importantly, these claims are very much consequences of the first-order argument rather than presuppositions of it. In general, I think that claims in the theory of reference are beholden to first-order judgments about cases, rather than vice versa.

Note 3

I use "skeptical hypothesis" in a certain technical sense. A *skeptical hypothesis* (relative to a belief that P) is a hypothesis such that (i) we cannot rule it out with certainty; and (ii) were we to accept it, we would reject the belief that P. A skeptical hypothesis with respect to a class of beliefs is one that is a skeptical hypothesis with respect to most or all of the beliefs in that class. A global skeptical hypothesis is a skeptical hypothesis with respect to all of our empirical beliefs.

The existence of a skeptical hypothesis (with respect to a belief) casts doubt on the relevant belief, in the following sense. Because we cannot rule out the hypothesis with certainty, and because the hypothesis implies the negation of these beliefs, it seems (given a plausible closure principle about certainty) that our knowledge of these beliefs is not certain. If it is also the case that we do not *know* that the skeptical hypothesis does not obtain (as I think is the case for most of the hypotheses in this article), then it follows from an analogous closure principle that the beliefs in the class do not constitute knowledge.

Some use "skeptical hypothesis" in a broader sense, to apply to any hypothesis such that if it obtains, I do not know that P. (A hypothesis under which I have accidentally true beliefs is a skeptical hypothesis in this sense but not in the previous sense.) I have not argued here that the Matrix Hypothesis is not a skeptical hypothesis in this sense. I have argued that if the hypothesis obtains, our beliefs are true, but I have not argued that if it obtains, our beliefs constitute knowledge. Nevertheless, I am inclined to think that if we have knowledge in an ordinary, non-matrix world, we would also have knowledge in a matrix.

Note 4

What is the relevant class of beliefs? Of course there are some beliefs that even a no-external-world skeptical hypothesis might not undercut: the belief that I exist, or the belief that $2 + 2 = 4$, or the belief that there are no unicorns. Because of this, it is best to restrict attention to beliefs that (i) are about the external world, (ii) are not justifiable a priori, and (iii) make a positive claim about the world (they could not be true in an empty world). For the purposes of this chapter, we can think of these beliefs as our "empirical beliefs." Claims about skeptical hypotheses undercutting beliefs should generally be understood as restricted to beliefs in this class.

Note 5

On the Computational Hypothesis: it is coherent to suppose that there is a computational level underneath physics, but it is not clear whether it is coherent to suppose that this level is fundamental. If it is, then we have a world of "pure bits." Such a world would be a world of pure differences: there would be two basic states that differ from one another, without this difference being a difference in some deeper nature. Whether one thinks this is coherent or not is connected to whether one thinks that all differences must be grounded in some basic intrinsic nature, on whether one thinks that all dispositions must have a categorical basis, and so on. For the purposes of this chapter, however, the issue can be set aside. Under the Matrix Hypothesis, the computation itself is *implemented* by processes in the world of the creator. As such, there will be a more basic level of intrinsic properties that serves as the basis for the differences between bits.

Note 6

On the Mind-Body Hypothesis: it is interesting to note that the Matrix Hypothesis shows a concrete way in which Cartesian substance dualism might have turned out to be true. It is sometimes held that the idea of physical processes interacting with a nonphysical mind is not just implausible but incoherent. The Matrix Hypothesis suggests fairly straightforwardly that this is wrong. Under this hypothesis, our cognitive system involves processes quite distinct from the processes in the physical world, but there is a straightforward causal story about how they interact.

Some questions arise. For example, if the envatted cognitive system is producing a body's motor outputs, what role does the simulated brain play? Perhaps one could do without it, but this will cause all sorts of awkward results, not least when doctors in the matrix open the skull. It is more natural to think that the envatted brain and the simulated brain will always be in isomorphic states, receiving the same inputs and producing the same outputs. If the two systems start in isomorphic states and always receive the same inputs, then (setting aside indeterminism) they will always stay in isomorphic states. As a bonus, this may explain why death in the Matrix leads to death in the outer world!

Which of these actually controls the body? This depends on how things are set up. Things might be set up so the envatted system's outputs are not fed back to the simulation; in this case a version of epiphenomenalism will be true. Things might be set up so that motor impulses in the simulated body depend on the envatted system's outputs with the simulated brain's outputs being ignored; in this case a version of interactionism will be true. Interestingly, this last might be a version of interactionism that is compatible with causal closure of the physical. A third possibility is that the mechanism takes both sets of outputs into account (perhaps averaging the two?). This could yield a sort of redundancy in the causation. Perhaps the controllers of the matrix might even sometimes switch between the two. In any of these cases, as long as the two systems stay in isomorphic states, the behavioral results will be the same.

One might worry that there will be two conscious minds here, in a fashion reminiscent of Daniel Dennett's story "Where Am I?" This depends on whether computation in the matrix is enough to support a mind. If anticomputationalists about the mind (such as John Searle) are right, there will be just one mind. If computationalists about the mind are right, there may well be two synchronized minds (which then raises the question: if I am in a matrix, which of the two minds is mine?). The one-mind view is certainly closer to the ordinary conception of reality, but the two-mind view is not out of the question.

One bonus of the computationalist view is that it allows us to entertain the hypothesis that we are in a computer simulation *without* a separate cognitive system attached. Instead, the creators just run the simulation, including a simulation of brains, and minds emerge within it. This is presumably much easier for the creators, as it removes any worries tied to the creation and upkeep of the attached cognitive systems. Because of this, it seems quite plausible that there will be many simulations of this sort in the future, whereas it is unclear that there will be many of the more cumbersome Matrix-style simulations. (Because of this, Bostrom's argument that we may well be in a simulation applies more directly to this sort of simulation than to Matrix-style simulations.) The hypothesis that we are in this sort of computer simulation corresponds to a slimmed-down version of the Metaphysical Hypothesis, on which the Mind-Body Hypothesis is unnecessary. As before, this is a nonskeptical hypothesis: if we are in such a simulation (and if computationalism about the mind is true), then most of our beliefs about the external world are still correct.

There are also other possibilities. One intriguing possibility (discussed in Chalmers 1990) is suggested by contemporary work in artificial life, which involves relatively simple simulated environments and complex rules by which simulated creatures interact with these environments. Here the algorithms responsible for the creatures' "mental" processes are quite distinct from those governing the "physics" of the environment. In this sort of simulation, creatures will presumably never find underpinnings for their cognitive processes in their perceived world. If these creatures become scientists, they will be Cartesian dualists, holding (correctly) that their cognitive processes lie outside their physical world. It seems that this is another coherent way that Cartesian dualism might have turned out to be true.

Note 7

I have argued that the Matrix Hypothesis implies the Metaphysical Hypothesis and vice versa. Here, "implies" is an epistemic relation: if one accepts the first, one should accept the second. I do not claim that the Matrix Hypothesis *entails* the Metaphysical Hypothesis, in the sense that in any counterfactual world in which the Matrix Hypothesis holds, the Metaphysical Hypothesis holds. That claim seems to be false. For example, there are counterfactual worlds in which physical space-time is created by nobody (so the Metaphysical Hypothesis is false), in which I am hooked up to an artificially designed computer simulation located within physical space-time (so the Matrix Hypothesis is true). And if physics is not computational in the actual world, then physics in this world is not computational either. One might say that the two hypotheses are a priori equivalent, but not necessarily equivalent. (Of course the term 'physics' as used by my envatted self in the counterfactual world will refer to something that is both computational and created. But 'physics' as used by my current non-envatted self picks out the outer noncomputational physics of that world, not the computational processes.)

The difference arises from two different ways of considering the Matrix Hypothesis: as a hypothesis about what might actually be the case, or as a hypothesis about what might have been the case but is not. The first hypothesis is reflected in indicative conditionals: if I am actually in a matrix, then I have hands; atoms are made of bits; and the Metaphysical Hypothesis is true. The second version is reflected in subjunctive conditionals: if I had been in a matrix, I would not have had hands; atoms would not have been made of bits; and the Metaphysical Hypothesis would not have been true.

This is analogous to the different ways of thinking about Putnam's Twin Earth scenario, common in discussions of two-dimensional semantics. If I am actually in the XYZ-world, then XYZ is water, but if I had been in the XYZ-world, XYZ would not have been water (water would still have been H_2O). On the first way of doing things, we consider a Twin Earth world as *actual*. On the second way of doing things, we consider a Twin Earth world as *counterfactual*. We can say that the Twin Earth world *verifies* "water is XYZ," but that it *satisfies* "water is not XYZ," where verification and satisfaction correspond to considering something as actual and as counterfactual.

Likewise, we can say that a matrix world verifies the Metaphysical Hypothesis, but it does not satisfy the Metaphysical Hypothesis. The reason is that the Metaphysical Hypothesis makes claims about physics and the physical world. And what counts as "physics" differs depending on whether the matrix world is considered as actual or counterfactual. If I am in a matrix, physics is computational. But if I *had been* in a matrix, physics would not have been computational (the matrix would have been computational, but the computer and my brain would all have been made from computation-independent physics). In this way, claims about physics and physical processes in a matrix world are analogous to claims about "water" in the Twin Earth world.

Note 8

The responses to the first few objections in section VII are clearly congenial to a causal account of reference. I said that the truth of an envatted being's thoughts depends not on its immediate environment but on what it is causally connected to, that is, on the computational processes to which it is hooked up. As noted earlier, I did not need to assume the causal theory of reference to get to this conclusion, but instead got there through a first-order argument. But once the conclusion is reached, there are many interesting points of contact.

For example, the idea that my term 'hair' refers to hair while my envatted counterpart's term refers to virtual hair has a familiar structure. It is structurally analogous to a Twin Earth case, in which Oscar (on Earth) refers to water (H_2O) while his counterpart Twin Oscar (on Twin Earth) refers to twin water (XYZ). In both cases, the terms refer to what they are causally connected to. These natural-kind terms function by picking out a certain kind in the subject's environment, and the precise nature of that kind depends on the nature of the environment. Something similar applies to names for specific entities, such as "Tucson."

The behavior of these terms can be modeled using the two-dimensional semantic framework. As before, when we consider a Twin Earth world as actual, it verifies "water is XYZ," and when we consider it as counterfactual, it satisfies "water is not XYZ." Likewise, when we consider a matrix world as actual, it verifies "hair is made of bits," and when we consider it as counterfactual, it satisfies "hair is not made of bits."

The difference between considering something as actual or as counterfactual yields a perspective shift like the one in the response to objection 5. If the matrix world is considered as merely counterfactual, we should say that the beings in the matrix don't have hair (they only have virtual hair). But if the matrix world is considered as actual (that is, if we hypothetically accept that we are in a matrix), we should say that the beings in the matrix have hair, and that hair is itself a sort of virtual hair.

The Twin Earth analogy may suggest that the meanings of our terms such as 'hair' and the contents of our corresponding thoughts depend on our environment. But the two-dimensional approach also suggests that there is an internal aspect of content that is shared between twins and that does not depend on the environment. The *primary intension* of a sentence is true at a world if the world verifies the sentence, while its *secondary intension* is true at a world if the world satisfies the sentence. Then Oscar and Twin Oscar's sentences "water is wet" have different secondary intensions (roughly, true when H_2O is wet or when XYZ is wet, respectively), but they have the same primary intension (roughly, true at worlds where the watery-looking stuff is wet). Likewise, "I have hair" as used by me and my envatted counterpart has different secondary intensions (roughly, true at worlds where we have biological hair or computational hair, respectively), but they have the same primary intension (roughly, true at worlds where we have hair-looking stuff). The primary intensions of our thought and our language represent a significant dimension of content that may be shared by beings inside and outside a matrix.

Note 9

Why the different response to objection 7, on 'action' and 'friend'? We noted earlier (note 1) that not all terms function like 'water' and 'hair'. There are numerous *semantically neutral* terms that are not subject to Twin Earth thought-experiments: any two twins using these terms in different environments will use them with the same meaning (at least if they are using the terms without semantic deference). These terms arguably include 'and', 'friend', 'philosopher', 'action', 'experience', and 'envatted'. So while an envatted being's term 'hand' or 'hair' or 'Tucson' may mean something different from our corresponding term, an envatted being's term 'friend' or 'philosopher' or 'action' will arguably mean the same as ours.

It follows that if we are concerned with an envatted being's belief "I have friends," or "I perform actions," we cannot use the Twin Earth response. These beliefs will be true if and only if the envatted being has friends and performs actions. Fortunately, it seems quite reasonable to say that the envatted being *does* have friends (in its environment, not in ours), and that it does perform actions (in its environment, not in ours). The same goes for other semantically neutral terms: it is for precisely this class of expressions that this response is reasonable.

Note 10

What is the ontology of virtual objects? This is a hard question, but it is no harder than the question of the ontology of ordinary macroscopic objects in a quantum-mechanical world. The response to objection 6 suggests that in both cases, we should reject claims of token identity between microscopic and macroscopic levels. Tables are not identical to any object characterized purely in terms of quantum mechanics; likewise, virtual tables are not identical to any objects characterized purely in terms of bits. But nevertheless, facts about tables supervene on quantum-mechanical facts, and facts about virtual tables supervene on computational facts. So it seems reasonable to say that tables are constituted by quantum processes, and that virtual tables are constituted by computational processes. Further specificity in either case depends on delicate questions of metaphysics.

Reflecting on the third-person case, in which we are looking at a brain in a vat in our world, one might protest that virtual objects don't really exist: there aren't real *objects* corresponding to tables anywhere inside a computer. If one says this, though, one may be forced by parity into the view that tables do not truly exist in our quantum-mechanical world. If one adopts a restricted ontology of objects in one case, one should adopt it in the other; if one adopts a liberal ontology in one case, one should adopt it in the other. The only reasonable way to treat the cases differently is to adopt a sort of contextualism about what counts as an "object" (or about what falls within the domain of a quantifier such as "everything"), depending on the context of the speaker. But this will just reflect a parochial fact about our language, rather than any deep fact about the world. In the deep respects, virtual objects are no less real than ordinary objects.

Note 11

The response to objection 8 is reminiscent of the familiar point, associated with Russell and Kant, that we do not know the intrinsic nature of entities in the external world. When it comes to physical entities, perception and science may tell us how these entities affect us, and how they relate to each other, but these methods tell us little about what the fundamental physical entities are like in themselves. That is, these methods reveal the causal structure of the external world, but they leave its intrinsic nature open.

The Metaphysical Hypothesis is in part a hypothesis about what underlies this microphysical causal structure: microphysical entities are made of bits. The same goes for the Matrix Hypothesis. One might say that if we are in a matrix, the Kantian *ding-an-sich* (thing in itself) is part of a computer-an-sich. This hypothesis supplements our ordinary conception of the external world, but it does not really contradict it, as this ordinary conception is silent on the world's intrinsic nature.

Note 12

One general moral is that the "manifest image" is *robust*: our ordinary conception of the macroscopic world is not easily falsified by discoveries in science and metaphysics. As long as the physical world contains processes with the right sort of causal and counterfactual structure, then it will be compatible with the manifest image. Even a computer simulation has the relevant causal and counterfactual structure, as does a process in the mind of God. This is why they can support a robust external reality, despite their surprising nature.

This sort of flexibility in our conception of the world is closely tied to the semantic non-neutrality of many of our concepts. Those concepts, such as "water," "hair," and "electron," leave some flexibility in what their referent might turn out to be. We conceive of their referents roughly as whatever actual entity plays a certain causal role, or has a certain appearance, while leaving open their intrinsic nature. One can likewise argue that the strongest constraints imposed by our conception of the world are plausibly those associated with semantically neutral concepts, which do not yield this sort of flexibility. These concepts plausibly include many of our causal (and nomic) concepts, as well as many of our mental concepts. In these cases, we have a sort of "direct" grasp of how the world must be in order to satisfy the concepts. If so, then our causal and mental beliefs impose strong constraints on the way the actual world must be.

One can argue that our fundamental semantically neutral concepts are mental concepts ("experience," "belief"), causal concepts ("cause," "law"), logical and mathematical concepts ("and," "two"), and categorical concepts ("object," "property"). There are also many semantically neutral concepts that involve more than one of these elements: "friend," "action," and "computer" are examples. If this is right, then the fundamental constraints that our beliefs impose on the external world are that it contains relevant mental states (in ourselves and in others) and that it contains objects and properties that stand in relevant causal relations to each other and to the mental states. This sort of conception is weak enough that it can be satisfied by a matrix (at least if it is a multivat matrix, or if computationalism about the mind is true).

In my opinion, this issue about the fundamental constraints that our beliefs impose on the world is the deepest philosophical issue that arises from thinking about a matrix. If what I have said in this chapter is right, it is precisely because these constraints are relatively weak that so many hypotheses that one might have thought of as skeptical turn out to be compatible with our beliefs. And it is this that enables us to mount some sort of response to the skeptical challenge. A little paradoxically, one might say that it is because we demand so little that we know so much.

Note 13

Why does a computer simulation of a world satisfy these constraints? The reason is tied to the nature of computation and implementation. Any formal computation can be regarded as giving a specification of (abstract) *causal structure*, specifying the precise manner of interaction between some set of formal states. To implement such a formal computation, it is required that the implementation have concrete states that map directly onto these formal states, where the pattern of (causal and counterfactual) interaction between these states precisely mirrors the pattern of interaction between the formal states (see Chalmers 1994). So any two implementations of the computation will share a certain specific causal structure. A computational description of the physical world will be required to mirror its causal structure down to the level of fundamental objects and properties. So any implementation of this computation will embody this causal structure (in transitions between implementing states, whether these be voltages, circuits, or something quite different). So insofar as our conception of the external world imposes constraints on causal structure that a real physical world can satisfy, these constraints will also be satisfied by a computer simulation.

(This relates to a point made by Hubert and Stephen Dreyfus in their chapter in this collection. Like me, the Dreyfuses take the view that most of the beliefs of the inhabitants of a matrix will be true, not false. But the Dreyfuses suggest that many of their causal beliefs will be false: for example, their general belief that "a physical universe with causal powers makes things happen in our world," and perhaps their specific beliefs that germs cause disease, that the sun causes things to get warm, and so on. On my view, this suggestion is incorrect. On my view, the world of someone living in a matrix has real causation going on everywhere within it, grounded in the real causation going on in the computer. Virtual germs in the computer really do cause virtual disease in the computer. So when matrix inhabitants say, "Germs cause disease," what they say is true.)

Of course the mental constraints also need to be satisfied. In particular, it is important that the causal structure stand in the right sort of relation to our experiences. But this constraint will also be satisfied when we are hooked up to a matrix. Constraints regarding other minds will be satisfied as long as we are in a multivat matrix, or if computationalism about the mind is true. In this way, a matrix has everything that is required to satisfy the crucial causal and mental constraints on our conception of the world.

Note 14

A possible line of objection to the argument in this chapter is to argue that there are *further constraints* that our beliefs impose on the world that the Matrix Hypothesis does not satisfy. One could argue that a mere match in mental and causal structure is not enough. For example, one might argue that the world needs to have the right spatial properties, where we have some sort of direct grip on what spatial properties are (perhaps because spatial concepts are semantically neutral). And one could suggest that the problem with the matrix is that its spatial properties are all wrong. We believe that external entities are arranged in a certain spatial pattern, but no such spatial pattern exists inside the computer.

In response, one can argue that these further constraints do not exist. It can be argued that spatial concepts are not semantically neutral, but instead are subject to Twin Earth thought-experiments. My student Brad Thompson has developed thought-experiments of this sort (Thompson

2003), involving a Doubled Earth where "one meter" refers to (what we call) two meters, an El Greco World where "square" refers to (what we call) rectangles, and so on. On this view, our spatial concepts pick out whatever manifold of properties and relations in the external world is causally responsible for our corresponding manifold of spatial experiences: in this respect, spatial concepts are analogous to color concepts. Here we do not have any direct grip on the basic nature of spatial properties. Instead, once again, the basic constraints are mental and causal.

This line of objection is tacitly engaged in section VI of this chapter, where I suggest that if there is a computational level underneath physics, then any implementation of the relevant formal computation could serve in principle as a realization of that level, without compromising physical reality. Perhaps opponents might deny that there could be a computational level underneath physics, or at least might hold that there are constraints on what sort of implementation can serve. For example, they might hold that the implementing level itself must have an appropriate spatial arrangement.

I think that this line of response runs counter to the spirit of contemporary physics, however. Physicists have seriously entertained the idea that space as we understand it is not fundamental, but that there is an underlying level, not described in terms of ordinary spatial notions, from which space emerges. The cellular automaton Hypothesis is just one such proposal. Here, what is crucial is simply a pattern of causal interaction. If physicists discover that this pattern is realized in turn by an entirely different sort of level with very different properties, they will not conclude that ordinary physical space does not exist. Rather, they will conclude that space is itself constituted by something nonspatial. This sort of discovery might be surprising and revisionary, but again no more so than quantum mechanics. And, as with quantum mechanics, we would almost certainly not regard it as a skeptical hypothesis about the macroscopic external world. If this is right, then our conception of the macroscopic world does not impose essentially spatial constraints on the fundamental level of reality.

Similar issues arise with respect to time. In one respect, time poses fewer problems than space, as the computer simulation in a matrix unfolds in time, in the same temporal order as time in the simulated world.

So one cannot object that the relevant temporal arrangements are not present in the matrix, in the way that one could object that the relevant spatial arrangements are not present. So even if temporal concepts were semantically neutral, the Matrix Hypothesis could still vindicate our temporal beliefs. Still, I think one can make a case that our concept of external time is not semantically neutral (it is notable that physicists have entertained hypotheses on which temporal notions play no role at the fundamental level). Rather, it picks out the external manifold of properties and relations that is responsible for our corresponding manifold of temporal experiences. If so, then any computer simulation with the right causal structure and the right relation to our experience will vindicate our temporal beliefs, regardless of its intrinsic temporal nature.

Note 15

The reasoning in this chapter does not offer a knockdown refutation of skepticism, as several skeptical hypotheses are left open. But I think it significantly strengthens one of the standard responses to skepticism. It is often held that although various skeptical hypotheses are compatible with our experiences, the hypothesis that there is a real physical world provides a simpler or better explanation of the regularities in our experiences than these skeptical hypotheses. If so, then we may be justified in believing in the real physical world, by an inference to the best explanation.

At this point, it is often objected that some skeptical hypotheses seem just as simple as the standard explanation, for example, the hypothesis that all of our experiences are caused by a computer simulation, or by God. If so, this response to skepticism fails. But if I am right, then these "equally simple" hypotheses are not skeptical hypotheses at all. If so, then inference to the best explanation may work after all: all of these simple hypotheses yield mostly true beliefs about an external world.

The residual issue concerns the various remaining skeptical hypotheses on the table, such as the Recent Matrix Hypothesis, the Local Matrix Hypothesis, and so on. It seems reasonable to hold that these are significantly less simple than the hypotheses above, however. All of them involve a non-uniform explanation of the regularities in our experiences. In the Recent Matrix Hypothesis, present regularities and past regularities have very different explanations. In the Local Matrix Hypothesis, beliefs about matters close to home and about those far from home have very different explanations. These hypotheses as a whole have a sort of dual-mechanism structure that seems considerably more complex than the uniform-mechanism structures above. If this is right, one can argue that inference to the best explanation justifies us in ruling out these hypotheses, and in accepting the nonskeptical hypotheses above.

Even if one thinks that some of these skeptical hypotheses offer reasonably good explanations of our experience, there is still a promising argument against global external-world skepticism in the vicinity. If I am right, all of these skeptical hypotheses are at worst *partial* skeptical hypotheses: if they are correct, then a good many of our empirical beliefs will still be true, and there will still be an external world. To obtain a *global* skeptical hypothesis, we have to go all the way to the Chaos Hypothesis. But this is a hypothesis on which the regularities in our experience have no explanation at all. Even an extremely weak version of inference to the best explanation justifies us in ruling out this sort of hypothesis. If so, then this sort of reasoning may justify our belief in the existence of the external world.

Further Reading

The pieces by Descartes and Putnam in the appendix develop the classic evil-demon and brain-in-a-vat scenarios, respectively. Nick Bostrom's article "Are You Living in a Computer Simulation?" contains reasoning that should make us take quite seriously the possibility that we really are in some sort of matrix. Stephen Wolfram's *A New Kind of Science* speculates on the possibility that computation may underlie physics.

References

Bostrom, N. 2003. Are you living in a computer simulation? *Philosophical Quarterly* 53:243–55. http://www.simulation-argument.com.

Chalmers, D. J. 1990. How Cartesian dualism might have been true. http://consc.net/notes/dualism.html.

Chalmers, D. J. 1994. A computational foundation for the study of cognition. http://consc.net/papers/computation.hmtl.

Dennett, D. C. 1978. Brainstorms. In *Where am I?* MIT Press.

Fredkin, E. 1990. Digital mechanics: An informational process based on reversible universal cellular automata. *Physica* D 45, 254.

Putnam, H. 1975. The meaning of "meaning." In *Mind, Language, and Reality*. Cambridge University Press.

Putnam, H. 1981. *Reason, Truth, and History*. Cambridge University Press.

Searle, J. R. 1984. Can computers think? In *Minds, Brains, and Science*. Harvard University Press.

Thompson, B. 2003. *The Nature of Phenomenal Content*. Ph.D. dissertation, University of Arizona.

Wolfram, S. 2002. *A New Kind of Science*. Wolfram Media.

10

Andy Clark

THE TWISTED MATRIX: DREAM, SIMULATION, OR HYBRID?

The Matrix is a computer-generated dreamworld built to keep us under control.

—Morpheus, early in *The Matrix*

In dreaming, you are not only out of control, you don't even know it.... I was completely duped again and again the minute my pons, my amygdala, my perihippocampal cortex, my anterior cingulate, my visual association and parietal opercular cortices were revved up and my dorsolateral prefrontal cortex was muffled.

—J. Allan Hobson, *The Dream Drugstore*

I. Ambivalence

The Matrix is an exercise in ambivalence, and at the very heart of that ambivalence lies the dream.

In our dreams, we are not in control. Real dreaming, unlike many popular philosophers' fictions, is an altered state, closely related to the states induced by chemical manipulations such as the use of certain medical or recreational drugs. The dreaming brain is not like the awake brain. Normal sensory input is blocked; attentional capacities are impaired or lost; memory is distorted; reasoning and logic are weakened; narratives run wild; self-reflection is dampened or destroyed; emotion and instinct are hyper-stimulated; and forms of "top-down" willed control and decision making are diluted and easily overwhelmed.[1]

---

1. This list is based on table 3.1, "Physiological Basis of Differences between Waking and Dreaming," in Hobson (2001), p. 57.

It may seem as if all of this is simply a direct effect of the blockage of sensory input, but this is not so. Instead, profound changes in neuro-chemical activity also occur, and these in turn compromise what J. Allan Hobson calls our "critical self-awareness." The result is that even though the goings-on in most dreams would cause us (were we awake) to suspect trickery or to question our sanity, in our dreams we simply accept them as normal, as real life. One way to keep people "under control," as Morpheus puts it, is to keep them (in this specific sense) *out of (self-)control*. One of the issues I want to explore in this chapter is: to what extent are the experiences of normal matrix-bound humans (matrixers) genuinely dream-like, where to be genuinely dreamlike is (in part) to display this dampening of critical acuity? I shall call this normal, critically compromised dream state *uncritical dreaming*.

But there is, of course, another image of dreaming, and this is the image that has so far received the most attention in this volume. This is the view of dreaming that links up with Descartes's famous "malicious demon" thought-experiments and with standard philosophical discussions of what we can (and cannot) know. These explore the question: what can we really know on the basis of our actual experience? Dreaming, thus construed, is not really like dreaming at all: it is a state in which all of the sensory experiences might be *just as they are in waking*, and our critical faculties are as bright and active as ever. I shall call this kind of "dreaming" *industrial-strength deception*, so as to distinguish it from real dreaming.

The (apparent) deception practiced by the machines, we can now see, comes in two potential varieties. First, there is the industrial-strength version. Here, all of the sensory inputs that assail your brain are just as they would be were you living and moving in a world of persisting, external, independent people, cities, cars, and other objects, and you yourself are as alert and critical as ever. Second, there is the uncritical-dreaming version, where the flow of sensory images and data is actually not all as it should be.[2] Things may morph and change, scenes shift, identities alter. Here, weirdness

2. I do not mean to suggest that the distinction between real dreaming and industrial-strength "deception" will help us to evade skeptical uncertainty. Rather, my concern will be to explore how making this distinction affects our view of what the machines are doing and of the moral status of their manipulations.

may be rampant yet generally unremarked, since your abilities to judge that all is not as it should be are fatally impaired, due to the critical-dampening effects of the neurochemical alterations distinct to sleeping or drugging. The genius of *The Matrix* (I shall argue) is its ability to balance, both thematically and cinematically, on a knife edge between these two versions of events.

The industrial-strength version invites an important response, ably advanced by David Chalmers in this collection. According to this response, industrial-strength "deception" is not really deception at all. Matrixers subject to this kind of manipulation really do inhabit (so the argument goes) pretty much the world they believe themselves to inhabit. *Industrial-strength matrixers*, as I shall call them, really do live in cities and roam a planet much like Earth. Later in this chapter, I will further defend this view, arguing that (still assuming industrial-strength deception) matrix-based human intelligences would count as being as fully and richly embodied as you and I. Despite those (other) bodies we see suspended in the machine-feeding womb, industrial-strength matrixers really do use their heads and eyes to scan the visual scene and their legs to move around. According to this view, the body in the Matrix is not a dreamed body, at least not in any ordinary sense of dreaming. It is a real body, realized in the nonstandard medium of bits of information. With the point made for the visible body, the parallel result for the wider world (of cities, cars, sky, and dust) may become a little easier to swallow.

We can then return to the nature of dreaming. For part of the ambivalence at the heart of *The Matrix* is, I think, an abiding ambivalence about the nature of dreaming itself. Real dreaming, to repeat, involves profound changes to the cognitive system deployed in normal wakefulness, changes that systematically deprive us of much of our normal critical acuity. In real dreaming, activity in the dorsolateral prefrontal cortex is compromised, or "muffled" according to the opening quote from J. Allan Hobson, director of the Neurophysiology Laboratory at Harvard Medical School. The dorsolateral prefrontal cortex is (among other things) the "executive brain" that helps us to organize our thinking, critically assess our own gut responses, and maintain at least a modicum of top-down control. The kind of state that Morpheus calls "a computer-generated dreamworld" hovers uneasily between such true (profoundly cognitive acuity–diminishing) dream states and something much closer to unknowing-yet-fully-awake participation in a form of multiagent immersive virtual reality: an "interactive virtual environment," as Morpheus also puts it.

The moral ambiguity that permeates *The Matrix* is rooted in this same balancing act between real dreaming and a multiagent immersive virtual reality in which the neural states of the average matrix dwellers are (courtesy of the machines) really identical to those of awake, active humans. Drift toward the former reading, according to which the matrix dwellers' cognitive states are neurologically akin to those critically diminished states distinctive of real human dreaming, and everything—*absolutely everything*—changes. Not only does the previous argument for true embodiment in the Matrix fail, but the moral status of the machines' experiment is immediately and radically transformed. Instead of seeing the machines as maintaining a kind of innocent immersive virtual reality, wherein human embodiment and human intelligence are, in every way that matters, everything they always were, the ploy of the machines becomes more like that of pimps who keep their call girls hooked on heroin. Thus cognitively diminished, the women do not question their state, and are not able to plot a rebellion or plan an escape.

Drug-forcing pimps or master immersive-reality programmers? It is by maintaining a studied ambivalence between these two readings that (I claim) *The Matrix* gains much of its power, its beauty, and its profound ability to puzzle.

II. Real Dreaming (Asleep in the Matrix)

Neo believes, under the influence of Morpheus and of his own experiments, that matrix-bound humanity is in the grip of a delusional dream. In the dream, the apparently sensed world seems real. It seems like a place where the body moves, where the eyes roam, where flesh meets flesh and sometimes lead and steel. But this, Neo comes to believe, is simply a dream, a device to keep humans quiet while the machines patiently suck energy from the preserved, slumbering biomass. To prove that it is a dream, Neo learns to subvert its logic: he becomes able to turn back bullets, to fly, to defeat agents, and to do all of this because he wills it to be so.

In one important sense, however, this is no ordinary dream. For in this dream (as Neo understands it), there is real contact among multiple intelligences. When Neo speaks to Cypher, he does not speak merely to a construct of his own sleep-bound imagination, but to another sentient being, with genuinely independent memories, hopes, fears, and skills. Moreover, these multiple intelligences can communally build persisting structures in their world. They can build worlds to live and act in. If Neo places a cup on a table in a certain room, it will be seen by Cypher when Cypher enters that room (unless someone else moves it away first). A simple biomass of individually dreaming humans could never achieve and maintain this kind of interpersonal and structural continuity and integration. So the machines must be doing something (a whole lot in fact) to keep things in line.

Nonetheless, there is clearly something dreamlike going on, for only in a world not fully bound by the laws of (even simulated) earthly physics could Neo fly, or turn back those bullets. In a normal virtual-reality simulation, you cannot bend the rules just by willing it. By the same token, video gaming would be a whole different sport were the under-lying code directly susceptible to the will of the players. Moreover, the movie is chock-full of images that morph and shift in ways not seen in waking life, again suggesting that this is not a perfect simulation of earthly physics, but something less stable, lacking in firewalls, and prone to direct subversion by the minds of enlightened matrixers. The average matrixer, of course, does not subvert, remains unenlightened, and seems to be almost sleepwalking through a mundane, yet not unpleasant, life. This contrast is perhaps most striking in the scene at the end of the first movie, where Neo, increasingly enlightened, steps out of the telephone box to see hordes of ignorant matrixers moving in trancelike, clockwork fashion, their images somewhat out of focus in a classic depth-of-field manipulation, while that of Neo is crystal-clear, alert, and bemused by their unquestioning, anesthetized progress through the world.

To try to clarify just what we are dealing with, it will help to first take a hard look at normal human dreaming. Then we can begin to plot some differences and to explore the space of options. A word of warning though. Familiar as they are, sleep and dreaming are complex, ill-understood phenomena. The sketch that follows is widely accepted and heavily rooted in the best contemporary neuroscience and psychopharmacology. But it is not written in stone, and much remains unclear.

The three dominant states for the human brain are waking, REM (rapid eye movement) sleep, and non-REM (NREM) sleep. Each state has clear physiological, pharmacological, and experiential correlates.

In waking, we can occupy many states, from eyes-closed imagistic musing to eyes-open, alert engagement with a potentially threatening environment. The *option* of alertness and full critical engagement is, however, typically present, even if we are engaged momentarily in detached daydreaming.

In REM sleep, our dreams (at least as shown by subsequent reports) are vivid, but their logic is weak. Here is a typical report:

> I was at a conference and trying to get breakfast, but the food and the people in line kept changing. My legs didn't work properly, and I found it a great effort to hold my tray up. Then I realized why. My body was rotting away, and liquid was oozing from it. I thought I might be completely rotted before the end of the day, but I thought I should still get some coffee if I still had the strength. (Quoted in Blackmore [2004] p. 340)

Here is another description, this time from Helena Bonham-Carter, while she was expecting a baby with movie director Tim Burton:

> I dreamed I gave birth to a frozen chicken. In my dream, I was very pleased with a frozen chicken. (Quoted in Hirschberg [2003])

In NREM sleep, if we dream at all, the dreams (again, as shown by waking reports) are more like faint and mundane thoughts or fuzzy rememberings.

All of these states (waking, REM sleep, NREM sleep) are correlated with specific patterns of neurochemical activity. A useful tool for displaying the pattern is Hobson's AIM (activation/input/mode) model. Hobson is a leading sleep researcher interested in the relations among waking, sleeping, and the kinds of altered states experienced during psychosis and drug use. The AIM model characterizes different states as points in a three-dimensional space, whose axes are

1. activation energy
2. input source
3. mode

Normal wakefulness is characterized by high activation (as measured by EEG, for example) corresponding to fairly intense experience, external input sources (the brain is receiving and processing a rich stream of sensory signals from the world, rather than being shut down and largely recycling its own activity), and a distinctive mode. *Mode* here names a balance among brain chemicals, especially amines and cholines. *Amines* are neurotransmitters, such as noradrenaline and serotonin, whose actions are known to be essential for normal waking consciousness (they are essential to the processes that enable us to direct attention, reason things through, and decide to act). When these are shut off, and other neurotransmitters (*cholines*, such as acetylcholine) dominate, we experience delusions and hallucinations (if we are awake) and vivid, uncritical dreaming (if we are asleep). In this way it is the amine/choline balance that determines how signals and information (whether externally or internally generated) will be dealt with and processed. When the balance (as in waking) favors the amine-based (aminergic) system, we are rational, alert to our surroundings, and easily able to direct our own actions and to rapidly and critically appraise our situation. When the balance favors the cholinergic system, our focus shifts inward; emotion and analogical reasoning begin to dominate; and critical control and judgment wane. In REM sleep, the aminergic systems are totally deactivated and the cholinergic are hyperactive. This is an extremely altered cognitive state. Only extreme forms of psychosis or serious medical or recreational drug use can induce this kind of state in nonsleeping humans. In normal waking states, the ratio of aminergic to cholinergic activity varies across a large continuum. In non-REM sleep, all of the systems (aminergic and cholinergic alike) are dampened and (mostly) inactive.[3]

This is not to suggest (far from it) that the best state for a human mind would be one of almost-complete aminergic dominance. Instead, the power, subtlety, and beauty of wakeful human intelligence seems to have much to do with the precise details of the ever-shifting balance between the two systems. In normal waking, the mode (defined as the ratio between the activity of the two systems) leans toward the aminergic.

3. The above paragraph condenses, and slightly oversimplifies, the views found in Hobson (2001) and Blackmore (2004). See also Roberts, Robbins, and Weiskrantz (1998) and Siegel (2003).

In REM sleep, with acetylcholine dominating, experience becomes increasingly dissociative, displaying "amnesia, hallucinations, bizarre mentation, anxiety, and loss of volition control" (Hobson, p. 91). All of this, we now know, is matched by a shift in regional blood flow from (in waking) the dorsolateral prefrontal cortex to (in REM sleep) the subcortical limbic structures (some of which are mentioned in the opening quote). Here too, the psychological and the physiological march (unsurprisingly, surely) in step, with the dorsolateral prefrontal cortex implicated in analytic reason, inhibition, and executive control, and the limbic structures dominating for emotion, instinct, and association.[4]

Bottom line: The kind of sleep in which we experience vivid dreaming is, typically at least, a state in which aminergic systems essential to critical reason are deactivated. This state is a far cry from normal wakefulness. The reason we (often) don't know we are dreaming is not because the dream simulates waking reality (the immersive virtual-reality option) but because we are cognitively diminished in ways that block voluntary attention and critical engagement and that promote a kind of face-value acceptance. In REM sleep, we are, in a real sense, drugged witless by our own brains. And the cure, as Hobson and Neo would probably both agree, is simple: it is called *waking up*!

Is it possible that the machines are electrically or chemically altering the states of the brains of their human power cells, so as to partially or totally deactivate the aminergic system and the dorsolateral prefrontal cortex? To compromise these would be to compromise the matrixers' capacities for critical engagement and analysis in a very profound way. Certainly, we sometimes see images of the humans suspended within the machine's grid in what seem to be advanced stages of REM sleep. If this is what is going on, those human brains are, in a fairly precise sense, permanently drugged. What Neo has achieved is then well compared (as other contributors to this volume have noted) to the state known as *lucid dreaming*. In lucid dreaming, a very few subjects are able to become aware that they are dreaming, without actually awakening. They may even be able to take

---

4. Once more, this is in no way to privilege one system over another for effective reason and intelligence, which demonstrably depends on the proper temporally evolving balance of the two, but just to note the different contributions made by each.

control of the dream itself, forcing it in directions previously requested by an experimenter or simply for their own enjoyment.

The full AIM (Activation/Input/Mode) profile of the lucid dreamer is still unclear, but Hobson speculatively suggests that one key may be a kind of prior-to-sleep priming[5] in which the lucid dreamer prepares to recognize the delusional REM dream state as it develops. REM sleep actually enhances priming effects, in which (for example) prior exposure to one word makes recall of another quicker or more likely. Pre-sleep preparations may, Hobson suggests, prime a more complex association between the signature (fuzzy, delusional) character of REM sleep and the realization that you are indeed sleeping. A kind of positive feedback cycle can then take root, so that the primed realization of dreaming is fed by each encounter with new, unlikely, or delusional elements. At this point the mode balance may shift a little, so that some dorsolateral prefrontal involvement becomes possible. Not too much, or the vivid dream state would be lost. Not too little, or control would be lost and dreamed delusions would (as usual) be taken as real. This is a testable hypothesis, using PET neuroimaging to reveal fluctuations in neural regional blood flow during lucid dreaming. But it has not yet been tested.

Might Neo have been somehow primed, before the machine-induced sleep, in this kind of way? Or perhaps, by some kind of neurochemical accident, Neo, Morpheus, and a few others are simply immune to the suppression of their aminergic systems? This would cast *The Matrix* as uncritical dream, and Neo as lucid dreamer. Such views at first seem to make good sense. But only if we assume that the state of the typical matrixer is indeed a real dream state. Such a reading, it should now be clear, is problematic for a number of reasons. For one thing, there is strong narrative continuity (major plot items do not just come and go without explanation). There is also good interpersonal agreement (what Neo does, Trinity sees, and so on). But most obviously of all, the typical matrixer simply does not seem to be unusually uncritical. For sure, they

---

5. One thing may be said to *prime* another when exposure to the first makes the occurrence of the second more likely. The term is mostly used in psychological studies in which unconsciously perceived stimuli make subsequent conscious choices faster or incline them in one direction rather than another.

are not constantly reflecting on their lives and analyzing their worth. But, and this is crucial, within the movie, *truly unusual happenings are indeed usually spotted as such*. The security guards are as amazed as we are when Neo and Trinity, armed to the teeth, burst through the gates. When Neo stops bullets, or flies, the typical matrixer is astounded. This is not the reaction of an uncritical dreamer.

Colin McGinn, in his chapter in this collection, is at pains to highlight the many layers of dreamlike quality that permeate the movie and to depict Neo as a lucid dreamer. But in the chemically and cognitively precise sense just outlined, life in the Matrix is simply not like life in a dream, and Neo is nothing like a lucid dreamer. The typical matrixer does not display the full cognitive signature of uncritical dreaming, and it therefore seems unlikely that the machines are actively maintaining the brains of their human power cells in the standard (aminergic-off, hypercholinergic) REM-sleep mode. Whatever else the machines may be doing, they do not seem to be acting merely like drug-pushing pimps. It is not that Neo is special because he has his wits *available*, but rather because he is beginning to really *use* them and to question (guided by Morpheus) so much that he previously took for granted.

In section IV, I'll consider a midway option in which elements of real dreaming combine with elements of immersive simulation. For the moment, however, we are again face to face with the productive tension at the very heart of *The Matrix*. For McGinn is surely right, despite all this, to remark on the genuinely dreamlike, shifting, and sometimes disconnected visual and dramatic qualities that repeatedly surface. The point I now want to make, and to which I will return at the end, is that this tension is distinctive of our normal waking life as well! For our waking experience is itself the product of that constantly shifting balance between the aminergic and cholinergic systems, a balance that alters and evolves minute by minute during any normal day. As Hobson puts it, "[I]t is as if we are designed to be rational (but cool) and irrational (but hot) by turns" (p. 97). *The Matrix*, by repeatedly shifting between narrative and visual modes proper to critically engaged waking reality and those of delusional sleep, is able to explore the whole spectrum of positions in Hobson's AIM three-dimensional space. In so doing, it gives us insight into the inherently unstable nature of human awareness itself.

III. Industrial-Strength "Deception" (Awake in the Matrix)

In real dreaming, we often believe ourselves to be in places we are not, doing things we are not. On the face of it, life in *The Matrix* is an endless dream. According to this very natural view, most humans in the Matrix are doubly deceived. They are deceived about their physical surroundings, believing themselves to live in cities and to roam the Earth, when "in fact" they are suspended in an energy-sucking, machine-made womb. They are also (still on the face of it) deceived about their own bodies, believing themselves to be moving their limbs, flexing their muscles, and scanning the scene with their eyes and heads, when "in fact" their bodies are still; their heads are fixed; their eyes are closed. Such, at least, is the dominant interpretation of the true state of Matrix-based humanity.

But there is an alternative. To bring it into view, we need to imagine that the machines are not simply guiding (and somehow, rather puzzlingly, making intersubjectively coherent) the real dreamings of the slumbering biomass. Instead, suppose that they have created a detailed simulation of the physics and structure of the normal human world, and that they are closely and continuously monitoring the neural activity in the brains of their human power cells. These brains are fed signals that correspond exactly to the ones they would receive were they awake and acting in the world, and the virtual world is updated in ways that conform to those actions. Each day, these brains would go through just the same chemical cycles as normal human brains, moving systematically through Hobson's AIM space: from awake (aminergic systems highly active, so-called sleep-on neurons inactive, critically alert) to NREM sleep (forebrain sleep-on neurons firing,[6] aminergic and cholinergic systems inactive, more or less dreamless) to REM sleep (brain-stem REM-sleep-on neurons firing, aminergic systems shut off, cholinergic systems highly active, vivid dreaming possible, and critical and executive faculties extremely dulled).

Do matrixers really dream and awaken, or do they only dream they are dreaming and awakening? In the industrial-strength version, it seems more accurate to say that they really dream and awaken. The states of

6. For more on this, see Siegel (2003).

their brains[7] in Matrix-sleep, on this version, differ from the states of their brains during Matrix-waking in just the same ways as ours do between waking and sleeping. By contrast if, in a real dream, we dream that we fall asleep, there is no such neurochemical shift. So too, if (in a real dream) we dream that we are awakening, that does not itself activate the dormant aminergic systems that would actually awaken us and restore our critical acuity. Once again, the differences between the two versions are striking.

The machines, on the industrial-strength version I am now pursuing, create a detailed immersive virtual reality that is sensitive to the actions of all the users, and they ensure that each individual's actions encounter obstacles and generate systematic sensory feedback exactly as they do in the normal world. That would include, for instance, generating the whole panoply of signals distinctive of muscle tiredness after an arduous rock climb, those distinctive of hunger, those of the satiation of hunger by food (recall Cypher's infamous steak), and so on. (Notice that on the real-dream version, none of this is necessary: instead, Cypher only needs to believe he has enjoyed a steak. These are different states.)

On this industrial-strength version, I claim, matrixers are genuinely embodied and are able to eat, act, wake, sleep, and dream in a world that is every bit as real as they imagine (though its deep physics is, as David Chalmers in his chapter points out, not quite as they think).

To make this stick (or even to make it begin to seem plausible), we can start by looking a bit harder at what it means to have a body, and at what having a body does for a mind like ours. With this understanding in place, it should be possible to see how the human intelligences in the industrial-strength Matrix could be embodied intelligences through and

---

7. There is an interesting question here concerning what we should take to be the brain of an industrial-strength matrixer. Is it the brain of the human in the machines' power grid? Or is it the brain that is specified in the immersive virtual-reality simulation itself (e.g., the one that we would see were we to observe Matrix-bound neurosurgery)? One way to proceed is to think of the brain in the grid as the ultimate (and unexpected) physical realization of the brain in the simulation (for a defense of this line, see the chapter by Chalmers in this collection). This is OK if we really are dealing with the full-strength version, since any practice of neurosurgery inside the Matrix would need to be synchronized either to real changes in the brains in the grid or (at the very least) to changes in the input and output signals that correspond to those that such surgery would have induced.

through. They would be embodied not in virtue of those organic shells feeding the machines, but in virtue of the crucial role of eye movements, head movements, and limb movements in altering the inputs to their brains and nervous systems, and in virtue of the way the world presents itself both as a resource for action and as a source of limits on action.

Consider a fairly typical example of embodied action: solving a jigsaw puzzle. First, I arrange the pieces on the table in front of me, perhaps placing the predominantly red pieces (bits of an image of a rocket) in one pile, the green (bits of an image of a jungle) in another, the pieces with one straight edge in a third, and so on. To solve the puzzle, I then combine a variety of tactics. One tactic involves repeatedly looking from the pieces to the half-completed puzzle. During these periods, my eyes make repeated movements (known as *saccades*) that bring different aspects of the scene into foveal view. (Human vision depends heavily on moving a small high-resolution area, known as the *fovea*, around the scene, so as to retrieve information as and when needed.) Another tactic involves picking pieces up and trying them out, to see if they really fit in certain locations. Yet another tactic involves reasoning about the shape of the missing pieces: there must be one there with a wiggly edge colored half red and half green. So I again scan the scene, with this image in mind, hoping to find such a piece.

In this kind of problem solving, the body and world play important roles.[8] Instead of creating a full image of the half-completed puzzle in my mind's eye, and then looking over the pieces, I repeatedly shift my gaze from the real puzzle to the pieces. This saves my brain from encoding (no doubt badly) all of that complex detail. And when I have isolated a candidate piece, I make the final decision by actually trying it out for fit. At this point, the world may fight back, refusing to allow a piece to fit, however much I want it to. This is an example of what Dreyfus and Dreyfus[9] call "running up against a boundary condition" in

---

8. For more on this, and many examples from development and robotics, see Clark (1997).

9. See their chapter in this collection. Their view, like my own and that of David Chalmers, is that there is an important sense in which industrial-strength matrixers really are embodied and coping with a wider world. Dreyfus and Dreyfus, however, pursue an interesting final twist concerning our ability to (as they put it) "open up new worlds." I highly recommend reading both of these chapters in full.

our attempts to cope with the world (I'll return to Neo's and the agents' abilities to bend such rules in a moment). Moreover, notice that I started out by organizing the workspace in a way that then helps to reduce my problem-solving load (making the various piles). All of this is what cognitive scientist David Kirsh calls "the intelligent use of space."

Now all of these ploys and strategies are available, quite straightforwardly, to the average industrial-strength matrixer. She can use the external world (as constituted by the machines' detailed and action-responsive simulations) to reduce the problem-solving load for her own cognitive processing. She can use body and eye movements so as to leave lots of important detail "in the world," retrieving information as and when needed for a specific action. She can intervene so as to organize the workspace in ways that then persist, independently of further cognitive efforts on her part, and that (for example) save her searching for red pieces among the green by keeping all of the red ones in a pile, and so on.

Consider, finally, the sense of presence, of where we are. There is a wonderful thought-experiment recounted by the philosopher Daniel Dennett. Dennett tells the story of a U.S. citizen who agrees to participate in a secret experiment. The citizen is Dennett himself, and in the experiment Dennett's brain is removed, kept alive in a tank of nutrients, and equipped with a multitude of radio links by means of which it can execute all of its normal bodily control functions. Dennett's body (which is to be used to explore a dangerous area) is equipped with receivers and transmitters, so that it can use its in-built sensors (eyes, ears, and so on) to relay information back to Dennett's brain. As the technicians in the story put it:[10]

> Think of it...as a mere *stretching* of the nerves. If your brain were just moved over an *inch* in your skull, that would not alter or impair your mind. We're simply going to make the nerves indefinitely elastic by splicing radio links into them.

10. From Dennett (1981).

There is a way of thinking of what the machines in *The Matrix* have done (in the industrial-strength version) that is a lot like this. But instead of using the brain to control a standard body exploring distant and dangerous parts of the standard world, they have "stretched the nerves" all the way into a fully immersive virtual reality, allowing the brain to control a kind of body-double avatar.[11]

With his brain safely excised and relocated, and the radio links established, Dennett awakes. He sees the nurse, who leads him to the room where his brain is being kept. The experience that ensues is puzzling. There is Dennett, standing up, staring at his own brain. Or is he? Perhaps, he muses, the proper thought is "here I am, suspended in a bubbly fluid, being stared at by my own eyes." Try as he may, Dennett cannot seem to place himself *in the tank*. It continues to seem as if he is outside the tank, looking in. Dennett's point of view, as he moves, seems securely fixed outside the tank.[12]

---

11. Technologies of this stripe are by no means inconceivable. Just a year or two ago, the neuroscientist Miguel Nicolelis conducted a study to understand the way that signals from the cerebral cortex control the motions of a monkey's limbs (Carmena et al. [2003]). An owl monkey had ninety-six wires implanted into its frontal cortex, which fed signals into a computer. As the monkey's brain sent signals to move the monkey's limbs, this "neural wiretap" was used to gather data about the correlations between the patterns of neural signals and specific motions. The correlations were not simple. But the patterns, though buried, were there in the signals. Once these mappings were known, the computer could then predict the intended movements directly from the neural activity. The computer could then use the neural signals to specify the movements of a distant robot arm (an electromechanical prosthesis in an MIT laboratory 600 miles distant). The system used a *haptic interface*, part of a multisensory virtual-reality system used to touch, feel, and manipulate computer-generated objects. The machines in the movie, we can imagine, have simply taken this technology to the natural limit, developing advanced neural wiretaps that allow the matrixers to explore and act upon a common virtual world. For a large-scale exploration of these new technologies, and of what it ultimately means to be human, see Clark (2003).

12. The feeling shifts, however, when Dennett's body is subsequently trapped by a rock slide, entombed far beneath the Earth's surface. At first, Dennett feels trapped beneath the surface. But then the radio links themselves begin to give way, rendering him blind, deaf, and incapable of feeling. The shift in point of view is immediate:

> Whereas an instant before I had been buried alive in Oklahoma, now I was disembodied in Houston.... as the last radio signal between Tulsa and Houston died away, had I not changed location from Tulsa to Houston at the speed of light? (Dennett [1981] p. 317)

Where is Dennett? Is he *really* in the tank of nutrient, *really* outside the tank looking in, or really no place at all (or both places at once)? Such questions need have no clear-cut answers. But what does seem clear is that human location should not be taken to be a function of facts about the location of the brain. After all, wherever "you" are, it surely isn't inside the top of your own head! Human presence, instead, is better understood as dependent upon our capacities for *dense closed-loop control.* By that I mean, control (of some kind of body) such that as the body moves, the brain receives rich and detailed feedback. It is this kind of feedback cycle and closed-loop control that supports skillful action. Skillful action then enables us, as the computer scientist Paul Dourish puts it, to engage in "inhabited interactions."[13] The difference between an inhabited and a non-inhabited interaction is just the difference between, for example, having to carefully plan, monitor, and execute a reach for a coffee cup, and "just reaching," as we expert coffee-cup grabbers do. Inhabiting the body, we are able to fluently use movement and action as parts of our own problem-solving routines.

Putting all of this together, I can now offer a proposal for how to think about the body and the world:

1. The body is a controllable and inhabitable resource.
2. It is located (or its parts are located) in one or more coordinate spaces, and its actions (or the actions of its parts) evolve in time.
3. Experiences of dense, closed-loop control involving this resource yield a robust sense of presence and of "inhabiting" the body.
4. It is a resource capable (via these inhabited interactions) of being skillfully used to transform a problem space and to exploit properties and features of the world.
5. The world is the place where such embodied actions encounter boundary conditions and are forced to conform.

And finally:

6. Real space is wherever perception and embodied action occur.

---

13. See chapter 4 of Dourish (2001). This idea is drawn from phenomenology and has roots in the work of Heidegger, Merleau-Ponty, and others.

Space, body, and world are in this way all interdefined. According to this formula, industrial-strength deception is a contradiction in terms.[14] The world of the industrial-strength matrixer is a real world. It acts as a boundary condition for skilled action, and it is populated by real bodies whose inhabited interactions play the very same problem-transforming roles as our own.

IV. The Hybrid Matrix

There is a clear problem for any full industrial-strength reading of *The Matrix*. Such readings make it hard to understand how Neo can (as Morpheus puts it) "bend the rules." If your brain were getting its inputs from and feeding its outputs to this kind of immersive virtual-reality set-up, there should be no room to break the laws of physics just by willing it so. Worse still, rampant rule bending seems to deprive the world of its ability to function as a boundary condition, and this would undermine my attempts to argue for genuine embodiment and presence inside the matrix. It is as if you really could make the jigsaw puzzle piece fit just by wishing it so, in which case the world is surely not playing the cognition-enhancing role I described.

By contrast, the real-dreaming model makes rule bending easy to understand, perhaps along the lines of the lucid dreaming mentioned in section

14. Christopher Grau (personal communication) asks whether such a view is too strong, amounting in effect to a simple redefinition of the real, rather than a substantial account. But my claim is not that any consistently imagined world counts as real (a claim that David Chalmers may actually be closer to making). That's why I stress the importance of genuine (not merely imagined) boundary conditions, and of the agent actually being able to offload computational work onto the environment. These are not mere matters of what the agent thinks she is doing, but matters of fact. My line, roughly, is that to perceive a real world is to perceive a genuinely usable cognitive resource. Even a lazily programmed matrix (see section IV) might provide for that, for example, by allowing people to really find out that one jigsaw puzzle piece (simulated) doesn't fit into one space (simulated), and by allowing the use of intelligent saccades directed at a stable scene (kept stable by real-world physics or good simulation) as a problem-solving tool. As the amount of lazy programming (and thus, instability and unreliability) increases, this signature of the real gets eroded. All of this is the case whether or not the agents actually notice anything. It is not, on my account, a matter of *seeming* to use a stable external world as a cognitive resource, but of actually doing so.

II. But this model fails to account for the kinds of preserved critical acuity that we *do* see in *The Matrix*: the fact that Neo's flying is seen by everyone as something remarkable, as proof of superhuman prowess, and is not simply accommodated courtesy of dampened critical and executive processing.

Certainly, with a bit of ingenuity, we could probably come up with patches for each of these models. For example, someone who favors the industrial-strength model could depict Neo as a kind of psychological hacker whose willpower somehow alters the underlying code, bypassing rich and detailed restraints that really do apply to the average person. Dreyfus and Dreyfus (in their chapter in this collection) offer a version of this, in which Neo's belief that a spoon is bending forces the system to conform. Similarly, someone who favors the real-dreaming option might argue that the machines somehow link all of the sleepers into a single web, maintaining the standard (critical acuity–diminishing) REM-sleep chemistry but thus forcing the sleepers to dream a single dream.

Between these two extremes, however, lies some of the most inter-esting ground of all, the ground of what I am calling the *Hybrid Matrix*. On the hybrid model, the matrixers' world is indeed a kind of immersive virtual reality, but *one that has been rather lazily programmed*. Instead of recreating a deep and fully constraining physics, we can imagine that the machines' simulation is patchy, and depends on a lot of quick and dirty tricks.[15] For example, instead of running a complete, continuous full sim-ulation of all locations and objects, they may only have programmed de-tail to unfold and update where one or more matrixers happen to look (a standard move in ordinary virtual-reality simulations). They may also not have bothered much about fine-grained continuity. Perhaps minor objects can come and go quite freely. On this model, the machines (like cinematographers!) just make sure that nothing major, and in anyone's focal attention, behaves strangely. We humans are surprisingly oblivi-ous to unexpected scene changes and noncentral continuity errors any-way, as a large literature on "change blindness" clearly demonstrates.[16] It is almost as if we are built to live in a lazily programmed world. In

---

15. Special thanks to David Chalmers for encouraging me to expand on this possibility.

16. For a review, see Simons and Levin (1997).

addition, lazy programming, as we all know, is also a royal invitation to hacking. The lazily programmed Matrix is at once an eminently hackable Matrix, as Neo, Trinity, and Morpheus know so well.

To further support the lazy-programming idea, we might even imagine that the machines have tilted the chemical balances in the humans' brains just enough to make them even more unlikely to attend to much fine detail, or to pursue rigorous and sustained environmental examinations. Such tilting would not yield genuine chemically sleeping brains, but they would not be fully alert brains either. All of this would just underline the guiding politics of *The Matrix*, which is a politics of awakening from dull, unthinking conformity and thus of escape from invisible, corrosive, but surprisingly violable constraints.

Would a lazily programmed Matrix still count as a real world, according to the argument of the previous section? I think it would, just so long as the lazy program was stable enough, and powerful enough, to impose some boundary conditions and a cognitively exploitable order in most normal circumstances. It would be, as David Chalmers has suggested, just like a real world with a rather lazy God and a surprisingly patchy ultimate physics.

Which model is correct? Is the Matrix a communal dream world, a multiagent immersive virtual-reality simulation, or a lazily programmed hybrid? I do not think we should seek an answer to this question. The power, beauty, and philosophical depth of *The Matrix* all derive from its ability to show us our world under many guises. At times, it shows us our world as a genuine dream world, dominated by (strangely communal) delusions. Such a world is ultimately unconstraining but hard to fathom, and maximally resistant to critical attention. At other times, it shows us our world as boundary condition, as a hard-edged arena for rational thought and embodied action. At still other times, it shows us a hybrid world, poised unsteadily between the two extremes. Just as normal wakefulness comes in many grades, characterized by the shifting balance between the aminergic and cholinergic systems, so the movie constantly shifts from one state to another, morphing between delusional dream and immersive virtual reality. By flipping between and mixing these two perspectives, it finally reveals our own world as a potent cocktail of genuine boundary conditions, delusions, and mutual constructions.

This is where we need to end. Ours is a world in which much of what we ordinarily think that constrains us is not truly binding. But this freedom does not reveal our world as a simple dream world, but rather as a real world, rich with the possibility of renewal and reconfiguration. By refusing to conform to any single interpretation, the narrative, structure, and filmic texture of *The Matrix* all encode the same messages: take nothing for granted; don't write yourself in stone; just wake up.

Further Reading

On the neuropsychology of dreaming, an excellent and truly reader-friendly treatment is J. Allan Hobson, *The Dream Drugstore: Chemically Altered States of Consciousness*. Susan Blackmore's *Consciousness: An Introduction* is a wide-ranging, up-to-the-minute, and well-written introduction to the whole complex of philosophical and scientific issues regarding conscious awareness (including dream states). For more on my own views about the nature of human embodiment and its role in thought and reason, see Andy Clark, *Being There: Putting Brain, Body and World Together Again*. Daniel Dennett's wonderfully entertaining philosophical short story "Where Am I?" (about the brain controlling a distant body) is included in his collection *Brainstorms*. The themes concerning embodiment, presence, and the self are further explored in Andy Clark, *Natural-Born Cyborgs: Minds, Technologies and the Future of Human Intelligence*.

Thanks to David Chalmers, Christopher Grau, and Tyler Waite for helpful comments and suggestions.

References

Blackmore, Susan (2004). *Consciousness: An Introduction* (New York: Oxford University Press).

Carmena, J., M. Lebedev, R. Crist, J. O'Doherty, D. Santucci, D. Dimitrov, P. Patil, C. Henriquez, and M. Nicolelis (2003). "Learning to Control a Brain-Machine Interface for Reaching and Grasping by Primates," *Public Library of Sciences: Biology* 1(2):193–208.

Chalmers, David (2005). "The Matrix as Metaphysics" (chapter 9 in this collection).

Clark, Andy (1997). *Being There: Putting Brain, Body and World Together Again* (Cambridge, MA: MIT Press).

Clark, Andy (2003). *Natural-Born Cyborgs: Minds, Technologies and the Future of Human Intelligence* (New York: Oxford University Press).

Dennett, D. (1981). "Where Am I?" in Dennett, *Brainstorms* (Sussex, England: Harvester).

Dourish, P. (2001). *Where The Action Is: The Foundations of Embodied Interaction* (Cambridge, MA: MIT Press).

Dreyfus, H., and S. Dreyfus (2005). "Existential Phenomenology and the Brave New World of *The Matrix*" (chapter 6 in this collection).

Hirschberg, L. (2003). "Drawn to Narrative," *New York Times Magazine*, Nov. 9, 2003.

Hobson, J. Allan (2001). *The Dream Drugstore: Chemically Altered States of Consciousness* (Cambridge, MA: MIT Press).

Kirsh, D. (1995). "The Intelligent Use of Space," *Artificial Intelligence* 73:31–68.

Roberts, A., T. Robbins, and L. Weiskrantz (1998). *The Prefrontal Cortex: Executive and Cognitive Functions* (New York: Oxford University Press).

Siegel, J. (2003). "Why We Sleep," *Scientific American*, Nov. 2003, 92–97.

Simons, D. J., and D. T. Levin (1997). "Change Blindness," *Trends in Cognitive Science* 1:261–267.

11

Kevin Warwick

THE MATRIX—OUR FUTURE?

Is *The Matrix* merely a science fiction scenario or is it, rather, a philosophical exercise? Alternatively, is it a realistic possible future world? The number of respected scientists predicting the advent of intelligent machines is growing exponentially. Steven Hawking, perhaps the most highly regarded theoretical scientist in the world and the holder of the Cambridge University chair that once belonged to Isaac Newton, said recently, "In contrast with our intellect, computers double their performance every 18 months. So the danger is real that they could develop intelligence and take over the world." He added, "We must develop as quickly as possible technologies that make possible a direct connection between brain and computer, so that artificial brains contribute to human intelligence rather than opposing it."[1] The important message to take from this is that the danger—that we will see machines with intellects that outperform that of humans—is real.

I. The Facts

But is it just a danger—a potential threat—or, if things continue to progress as they are, is it an inevitability? Is a matrix going to happen whether we like it or not? One flaw in the present-day thinking of some philosophers lies in their assumption that the ultimate goal of research into artificial intelligence is to create a robot machine with intellectual capabilities approaching those of a human. This may be the aim in a

1. S. Hawking, "Hawking's plan to offset computer threat to humans," *Ananova*, www.ananova/news, 1 September 2001.

limited number of cases, but the goal for most AI developers is to make use of the ways in which robots can outperform humans—rather than those in which they can only potentially become our match.

Robots can sense the world in ways that humans cannot—ultraviolet, X-ray, infrared, and ultrasonic perception are some obvious examples—and they can intellectually outperform humans in many aspects of memory and logical mathematical processing. And robots have no trouble thinking of the world around them in multiple dimensions, whereas human brains are still restricted to conceiving the same entity in an extremely limited three-dimensional way. But perhaps the biggest advantage that robots have over us is their means of communication—generally an electronic form, as opposed to the humans' embarrassingly slow mechanical technique, called *speech*, with its highly restricted coding schemes, called *languages*.

It appears to be inevitable that at some stage a sentient robot will appear, its production having been initiated by humans, and begin to produce other, even more capable and powerful robots. One thing overlooked by many is that humans do not reproduce, other than in cloning; rather, humans *produce* other humans. Robots are far superior at producing other robots and can spawn robots that are far more intelligent than themselves.

Once a race of intellectually superior robots has been set into action, major problems will appear for humans. The morals, ethics, and values of these robots will almost surely be drastically different from those of humans. How would humans be able to reason or bargain with such robots? Why indeed should such robots want to take any notice at all of the silly little noises that humans would be making? It would be rather like humans today obeying the instructions of cows.

So a war of some kind seems to be inevitable, in the form of a last gasp from humans. Even having created intelligent, sentient robots in the first place, robots that can outthink them, the humans' last hope would be to find a weak spot in the robot armory, a chink in their life-support mechanism. Naturally, their food source would be an ideal target. For the machines, obtaining energy from the sun—a constant source—would let them bypass humans, excluding them from the loop. But as we know, humans have already had much success in polluting the atmosphere and wrecking the ozone layer, so blocking out the sun's rays—scorching the sky, in effect—would seem to be a perfectly natural line of attack in an attempt to deprive machines of energy.

In my book *In the Mind of the Machine*, I put forth the idea that the machines would, perhaps in retaliation, use humans as slave laborers, to supply robots with their necessary energy. Indeed, we must consider this as one possible scenario. However, actually using humans as a source of energy—as batteries, if you like—is a much sweeter solution, and more complete. Humans could be made to lie in individual podlike wombs, acting rather like a collection of battery cells, to feed the machine-led world with power.

Probably in this world of machine dominance there would be a few renegade humans causing trouble, snapping at the heels of the machine authorities in an attempt to wrest back power for the humans, an attempt to go back to the good old times. So it is with *The Matrix*. It is a strange dichotomy of human existence that, as a species, we are driven by progress—it is central to our being—yet at the same time, for many there is a fruitless desire to step back into a world gone by, a dream world.

Yet it is in human dreams that the Matrix machines have brought about a happy balance. Simply treating humans as slaves would always bring about problems of resistance. But by providing a port directly into each human brain, each individual can be fed a reality with which he is happy, creating for each one a contented existence in a sort of dream world. Even now we know that scientifically it would be quite possible to measure, in a variety of ways, the level of contentment experienced by each person. The only technical problem is how one would go about feeding a story line directly into a brain.

So what about the practical realities of the brain port? I myself, as reported in *I, Cyborg*, have had a 100-pin port, which allowed for both signal input and output, connected into my central nervous system. In one experiment conducted while I was in New York City, signals from my brain, transmitted via the Internet, operated a robot hand in the United Kingdom. Meanwhile, signals transmitted to my nervous system were clearly recognizable in my brain. A brain port, along the lines of that in *The Matrix*, is not only a scientific best guess for the future; I am working on such a port now, and it will be with us within a decade at most.

II. Human or Machine

With the port connected into my nervous system, my brain was directly connected to a computer and thence to the network. I considered myself to be a cyborg: part human, part machine. In *The Matrix*, the story revolves around the battle between humans and intelligent robots. Yet Neo and most of the other humans each have their own brain port. When out of the Matrix, they are undoubtedly human, but while they are in the Matrix, there can be no question that they are no longer human, but rather are cyborgs. The real battle then becomes not one of humans versus intelligent robots but of cyborgs versus intelligent robots.

The status of an individual while within the Matrix raises several key issues. For example, when they are connected are Neo, Morpheus, and Trinity individuals within the Matrix? Or do they have brains which are part human, part machine? Are they themselves effectively nodes on the Matrix, sharing common brain elements with others? It must be remembered that, ordinarily, human brains operate in a stand-alone mode, whereas computer-brained robots are invariably networked. When connected into a network, as in the Matrix and as in my own case as a cyborg, individuality takes on a different form. There is a unique, usually human element and then a common, networked machine element.

Using the common element, "reality" can be downloaded into each brain. Morpheus describes this (as do others throughout the film) as "having a dream." He raises questions as to what is real. He asks how it is possible to know the difference between the dream world and the real world. This line of questioning follows on from many philosophical discussions, perhaps the most prominent being that of Descartes, who appeared to want to make distinctions between dream states and "reality," immediately leading to problems in defining what was real and what was not. As a result, he faced further problems in defining absolute truths.

Perhaps a more pertinent approach can be drawn from Berkeley, who denied the existence of a physical world, and Nietzsche, who scorned the idea of objective truth. By making the basic assumption that there is no God, my own conclusion is that *there can be no absolute reality, there can be no absolute truth*—whether we be human, cyborg, or robot. Each individual brain draws its conclusions and makes assumptions as to the reality it faces at an instant, dependent on the input it receives. If only limited sensory input is forthcoming, then brain memory banks (or injected feelings) need to be tapped for a brain to conceive of a story line. At any instant, a brain links its state with its commonsense memory banks, often coming to unlikely conclusions.

As a brain ages, or as a result of an accident, the brain's workings can change; this often appears to the individual to be a change in what is perceived rather than a change in that which is perceiving. In other words, the individual thinks it must be the world that has changed, not her brain. Where a brain is part of a network, however, there is a possibility for alternative viewpoints to be proposed by different nodes on the network. This is not something to which individual humans are accustomed. An individual brain tends to draw only one conclusion at a time. In some types of schizophrenia, this conclusion can be confused and can change over time; it is usually the case, though, that such an individual will draw a conclusion about what is perceived that is very much at variance with the conclusion of other individuals. For the most part, what is deemed by society to be reality at any point, far from being an absolute, is merely a commonly agreed-upon set of values based on the perceptions of a group of individuals.

The temptation to see a religious undertone in *The Matrix* is interesting—with Morpheus cast as the prophet John the Baptist, Trinity perhaps as God or the Holy Spirit, Neo clearly as the Messiah, and Cypher as Judas Iscariot, the traitor. But, far from a Christ-like, turn-the-other-cheek approach, Neo's is closer to one that perhaps was actually expected by many of the Messiah himself: taking on his role as victor over the evil Matrix in a holy war against a seemingly invincible, all-powerful machine network.

But what of the machine network, the Matrix, itself? With an intellect well above that of collective humanity, surely its creativity, its artistic sense, its aesthetics would be a treat to behold. But in the trilogy of Matrix films this aspect is kept from us—perhaps to be revealed in a further sequel. Humans released from the Matrix's grip merely regard it as evil (perhaps Cypher is excluded here). Meanwhile the Agents are seen almost as faceless automatons, ruthless killers, strictly obeying the will of their Matrix overlord. Possibly humans would see both the Matrix and the Agents as the enemy, just as the Matrix and the Agents would so regard humans—but once inside the Matrix, the picture is not so clear. As a cyborg, who are your friends and who are your enemies? It is no longer black and white when you are part machine, part human.

III. In and Out of Control

Morpheus tells Neo that the Matrix is control. This in itself is an important revelation. As humans, we are used to one powerful individual being the main instigator, the brains behind everything. It is almost as though we cannot even conceive of a group or collectivity running amok but believe, rather, that there is an individual behind it all. In the Second World War, it was not the Germans or Germany against which the Allies were fighting but Adolf Hitler; meanwhile in Afghanistan, it was Osama Bin Laden who was behind it all. Yet in the Matrix, we are faced with a much more realistic scenario, in that it is not some crazed individual up to no good, but the Matrix—a network—which is operating.

When I find myself in a discussion of the possibility of intelligent machines taking over things, nine times out of ten I am told—following a little chuckle to signify that I have overlooked a blindingly obvious point—that "if a machine causes a problem, you can always switch it off." What a fool I was not to have thought of it. How could I have missed that little snippet?

Of course it is not only the Matrix but even today's common Internet that gives us the answer and cuts the chuckle short. Even now, how is it practically possible to switch off the Internet? We're not talking theory here, we're talking practice. It is of course possible to unplug one computer, or even a small subsection intranet, but to bring down the whole Internet? Of course we can't. Too many entities, both humans and machines, rely on its operation for their everyday existence. It is not the Matrix of the cinematic future that we will not be able to switch off; it is a matrix of today that we cannot switch off, over which we cannot have ultimate control.

Neo learns that the Matrix is a computer-generated dream world aimed at keeping humans under control. Humans are happy to act as an energy source for the Matrix as long as they themselves believe that the reality of their existence is to their liking; indeed, how are the human nodes in a position to know what is computer-generated reality and what is reality generated in some other way?

A stand-alone human brain operates electrochemically, powered partly by electrical signals and partly by chemicals. In the Western world, we are more used to chemicals being used to change our brain and body state, either for medicinal purposes or through narcotics, including chemically instigated hallucinations. But now we are entering the world of e-medicine. Utilizing the electronic element of the electrochemical signals on which the human brain and nervous system operate, counterbalancing signals can be sent to key nerve-fiber groups to overcome a medical problem. Conversely, electronic signals can be injected to stimulate movement or pleasure. Ultimately, electronic signals will be able to replace the chemicals that release memories and "download" memories not previously held. Why live in a world that is not to your liking if a matrix state is able to keep your bodily functions operating while you live out a life in a world in which you are happy with yourself? The world of the Matrix would appear to be one that lies in the direction that humanity is now heading—a direction in which it would seem, as we defer more and more to machines to make up our minds for us, that we wish to head.

IV. Ignorance and Bliss

In a sense, the Matrix is nothing more than a modern-day Big Brother, taking a machine form rather than the Orwellian vision of a powerful individual using machines to assist and bring about an all-powerful state. But *1984*, the novel in which the story of Big Brother was presented, was published in *1949*. *The Matrix* came fifty years later. In the meantime, we witnessed the advent of radar, television for all, space travel, computers, mobile phones, and the Internet. What would Orwell's Big Brother have been like if he had those technologies at his disposal: would Big Brother have been far from the Matrix?

With the first implant I received, in 1998, for which I had no medical reason (merely scientific curiosity), a computer network was able to monitor my movements. It knew what time I entered a room and when I left. In return, it opened doors for me, switched on lights, and even gave me a welcoming "Hello" as I arrived. I experienced no negatives at all. In fact, I felt very positive about the whole thing. I gained something as a result of being monitored and tracked. I was happy with having Big Brother watching me because, although I gave up some of my individual humanity, I benefited from the system doing things for me. Would the same not be true of the Matrix? Why would anyone want to experience the relatively tough and dangerous life of being an individual human when she could be part of the Matrix?

Here we come to the case of Cypher. As he eats his steak, he says, "I know that this steak doesn't exist. I know when I put it in my mouth, the Matrix is telling my brain that it is juicy and delicious!" He goes on to conclude, "Ignorance is bliss." But is it ignorance? His brain is telling him, by whatever means, that he is eating a nice juicy steak. How many times do we nowadays enter a fast-food burger bar in order to partake of a burger that, through advertising, our brains have been conditioned into believing is the tastiest burger imaginable? When we enter we know, because we've seen the scientific papers, that the burger contains a high percentage of water, is mainly fat, and is devoid of vitamins. Yet we still buy such burgers by the billion. When we eat one, our conditioned brain is somehow telling us that it is juicy and delicious, yet we know it doesn't quite exist in the form that our brain is imagining.

We can thus understand Cypher's choice. Why be out of the Matrix, living the dangerous, poor, tired, starving life of a disenfranchised human, when you can exist in a blissfully happy life, with all the nourishment you need? Due to the deal he made with Agent Smith, once Cypher is back inside he will have no knowledge of having made any deal in the first place. He appears to have nothing at all to lose. The only negative aspect is that before he is reinserted he may experience some inner moral human pangs of good or bad. Remember that being reinserted is actually good for the Matrix, although it is not so good for the renegade humans who are fighting the system.

Robert Nozick's thought-experiment puts us all to the test, and serves as an immediate exhibition of Cypher's dilemma. Nozick asks, if our brains could be connected, by electrodes, to a machine which would give us any experiences we desire, would we plug into it for life? The question is, what else could matter other than how we feel that our lives are going, from the inside? Nozick himself argued that other things do matter to us, for example, that we value being a certain type of person; we want to be decent; or perhaps we actually wish to do certain things rather than just have the experience of doing them. I disagree completely with Nozick.

Research involving a variety of creatures, principally chimpanzees and rats, has allowed them to directly stimulate pleasure zones in their own brains, simply by pressing a button. When given the choice of pushing a button for pleasure or a button for food, it is the pleasure button that has been pressed over and over again, even leading to starvation (although individuals were quite happy even about that). Importantly, the individual creatures still had a role to play, albeit merely that of pressing a button. This ties in directly with the Matrix, which also allows for each individual to mentally experience a world in which she is active and has a role to play.

It is, however, an important question whether or not an individual, as part of the Matrix, experiences free will or not. It could be said that Cypher, in deciding to reenter the Matrix, is exercising his free will. But once inside, will he still be able to exhibit free will? Isn't it essentially a similar situation to that proposed by Nozick? Certainly, within the mental reality projected on an individual by the Matrix, it is assumed that a certain amount of mental free will is allowed for; but it must be remembered, at the same time, that each individual is lying in a pod with all of his life-sustaining mechanisms taken care of and an interactive story line being played into his brain. Is that free will? What is free will anyway, when the state of a human brain is merely partly due to a genetic program and partly due to life experiences? Indeed, exactly the same thing is true for a robot.

In the Matrix, no human fuel cells are killed, not even the unborn— there is no abortion. Naturally dying humans are allowed to die naturally and are used as food for the living. Importantly, they are not kept alive by chemicals merely for the sake of keeping them alive. The Matrix would appear to be more morally responsible to its human subjects than are humans to themselves. Who therefore wouldn't want to support and belong to the Matrix, especially when it is making life easier for its subjects?

Neo is kidnapped by Luddites, dinosaurs from the past when humans ruled the Earth. It's not the future. We are in reality heading toward a world run by machines with an intelligence far superior to that of an individual human. But by linking into the network and becoming a cyborg, life can appear to be even better than it is now. We really need to clamp down on the party-pooper Neos of this world and get into the future as soon as we can—a future in which we can be part of a matrix system, which is morally far superior to our Neolithic morals of today.

Further Reading

My book *I, Cyborg* (Century 2002), which describes our cyborg experimentation, is the main text behind this chapter. As far as other practical cyborg studies are concerned, a recent book by Andy Clark entitled *Natural-Born Cyborgs* (Oxford University Press 2003) gives a good overview, whereas Steve Mann's *Cyborg: Digital Destiny and Human Possibility* (Doubleday 2002) is useful but more directed toward Wearable computer studies.

For discussion of the intellectual capabilities of humans and machines, Ray Kurzweil's *The Age of Spiritual Machines* (Texere 2001) is a good start as is Hans Moravec's *Robot: Mere Machines to Transcendent Mind* (Oxford University Press 2002). When it comes to the potential overtaking of human intelligence by machines, Kevin Warwick, *In the Mind of the Machine* (Arroa 1998), takes a scientific approach.

ARTIFICIAL ETHICS

The significance of *The Matrix* as a movie with deep philosophical overtones is well recognized. Whenever the movie is discussed in philosophy classes, comparisons are made with Descartes's *Meditations*, particularly the dream argument and the evil-genius scenario, both of which are intended to generate skeptical doubt. How do we know, for example, that we are awake now, rather than merely dreaming? How do we know that our thoughts are not being manipulated, and that our perceptions of "reality" are accurate? *The Matrix* makes these doubts stand out vividly.

However, *The Matrix* and its sequels raise many other interesting philosophical issues that are worthy of further discussion. This chapter explores some of the moral issues raised in *The Matrix*. The first is the issue of the moral status of the created beings, the "artificial" intelligences, which figure into the universe of *The Matrix*. The second is the issue of whether or not one can do anything wrong in circumstances where one's experiences are nonveridical, that is, where one's experiences fail to reflect reality.

I. The Moral Status of Programs

There is a reality to the Matrix. The substance of that reality may differ dramatically from the substance we label "real"—the real world is the desert reality that Morpheus reveals to Neo. But, it is clear that, out of the grip of the Matrix, though still having certain dreamlike experiences, Neo and his enlightened friends are dealing with actual sentient programs, and making decisions that have actual effects for themselves as well as the machines and the programs. What is the moral status of the sentient programs that populate the Matrix or, for that matter, the moral status of the machines themselves?

The universe of *The Matrix* is populated with beings that have been created—created by programmers or created by the machine universe itself. The agents, such as Smith, Neo's pursuer, are prime examples. These beings come into and go out of existence without comment on the part of whoever controls the switches—and without any moral debate on the part of the humans who also would like to see the agents destroyed. There seems to be an implicit view that their existence is less significant, their lives of less moral import, than the lives of "naturally" existing creatures such as ourselves. An obvious explanation for this attitude is that humans have been long accustomed to thinking of ourselves as being at the center of the universe. The geographic point changed with Copernicus. However, our view of our dominant place in the moral universe has stayed fixed. But, once again, science—and particularly, now, cognitive science, holds the potential for challenging this certainty. And science fiction such as *The Matrix*, which explores differing directions for these potentialities, also brings challenges to this world view. What *The Matrix* offers is a vivid thought-experiment. It is a thought-experiment which makes us ask the sort of what-if questions that lead to a change in self-conception. It forces us to see where our well-accepted moral principles would take us within one possible world.

We know that killing human beings is wrong. It is wrong because human beings have moral standing. Human beings are widely believed to have this standing in virtue of consciousness and sentience. For example, a rock has no moral standing whatsoever. Kicking a rock does not harm it, on this view, and no moral rights are violated. It is an inanimate, nonconscious object incapable of either thought or sensation. Animals, however, are generally taken to have some moral standing in virtue of their sentience. Kicking an animal for no compelling reason is generally taken to be immoral.

Human beings have greater standing in virtue of their higher rational capacities. They can experience more varied and complex harms and a wider range of emotional responses—such as resentment—in virtue of their rationality. *How* one comes into existence is not taken to be morally significant. Some people are the products of natural conception, and some are the result of conception in the laboratory. This makes no difference to the possession of those qualities we take to be morally significant: consciousness and rationality. And, surely, the *substance* from which someone is created is completely irrelevant to the issue of moral status. If a person's consciousness could somehow be transferred to a metallic or plastic robotic body, the end result would still be a person.

It would seem, then, that the fact that one is created, or artificial, is in no way relevant to one's moral standing. And, if this is the case, then the world of *The Matrix* presents underappreciated moral complexities. Agents such as Smith, while not very pleasant, would arguably have moral standing, moral rights. Of course, Neo has the right to defend himself—Smith is not, after all, an innocent. Indeed, if the religious theme is pursued, he is an agent of darkness. But any innocent creations of the machines—beings brought into existence to populate the Matrix, or the sentient programs that keep the processes crucial to the Matrix operating—would also have moral rights. Just as it would be wrong to flip a switch and kill an innocent human being, no matter how that human being came into existence, it would be wrong to flip a switch and kill a sentient program—as long, of course, as that program possessed the qualities we regard as *morally relevant*. And this is where one of the primary issues raised by the possibility of artificial intelligence becomes important to the question at hand. Do these programs possess consciousness? Since we are considering the world of *The Matrix*, let's look at what evidence seems to exist in the movie. First, the sentient programs.[1]

Smith and his colleagues seem remarkably without affect. Yet, at critical points they do display emotions: anger, fear, and surprise. They seem able to plan and to carry through on a plan. Smith also displays a capacity for sadistic pleasure—he displays this when he forces Neo's mouth shut. Smith also displays extreme fear near the end of the first

1. The issue of the moral status of the machines themselves should be kept distinct from the issue of the moral status of the machine constructs. I will focus on the latter issue here, simply because the movie provides more information about the behavior of these constructs. But the same points would hold for the machines themselves; if they have those qualities that are morally significant—consciousness and rationality—then they also possess moral standing.

movie, when Neo leaps through him. Smith's displays become even more vivid through the sequels. It seems quite clear that he hates 'Mr. Anderson'. He also develops autonomy, or more autonomy, throughout the course of the sequels—he cuts himself loose, free of the machines. Whether or not autonomy is necessary for moral standing is highly debatable. It may be necessary for agency, that's true, but we frequently hold organisms to have moral standing even though they lack rational agency—animals would fall into this category, for example. Still, Smith's growing autonomy is yet more evidence that his portrayal is as a being with consciousness, since autonomy requires consciousness at the very least.

The agents display many, if not all, of the responses we associate with consciousness and sentience. But this brings us to another skeptical challenge posed in *The Matrix*: how can we be sure they do possess minds, and are not mere automata, albeit highly complex ones? Though the movie invites this reflection, it is important to see where this challenge can take us. The how-can-I-be-sure question can extend beyond the agents to our fellow human beings. Since a person's conscious experiences are essentially private, one cannot be directly aware of another's experiences. We might try, as St. Augustine suggested, to solve this problem by appeal to analogy: I do directly experience my own mental states—I know that I am a conscious, aware being. I also know on the basis of observation that I am structurally similar to other human beings. Thus, I reason by analogy, they must experience mental states as well.[2] Indeed, *The Matrix*, *Reloaded*, and *Revolutions* invite such a comparison when the agents display behavior consistent with our experience of certain psychological states.[3] And, of course, the agents are not the only sentient

2. St. Augustine, *On the Trinity*, trans. A. W. Haddan, in *The Basic Works of Saint Augustine*, vol. 2, ed. Whitney J. Oates (New York: Random House, 1948), pp. 780ff. Again, this line of reasoning is controversial since it relies on a single-case analogy.

3. A lot hinges on what we take to be "structurally similar." Some would argue that while the sentient programs are not themselves structures, the machines are, and thus the machines may possess consciousness, though the programs cannot. However, I believe that the sentient programs can be structurally similar if that's understood functionally: their code has structure which provides functional equivalence to the physical states that underlie our mental states. But this issue is extremely controversial, and there isn't enough space to delve into it more fully here.

programs on display. By the end of the trilogy, we see a variety of rogue programs at work, such as the Frenchman. In *Revolutions* we see programs that are capable of love—Sati's parents, for example, who don't agree with the policy of eliminating "useless" programs. All of these features invite comparisons to humans, and I believe they are intended to draw out our similarities with the programs.

Given, then, that we believe what we are invited to believe, it would follow that the sentient programs, the cyberpersons, do possess those qualities we associate with moral standing. They have moral rights on the basis of consciousness and sentience and rationality. Thus, their moral standing is the same as that of human beings.

It is possible that human beings have some additional value—a kind of antiquarian value. We are, so to speak, "the originals." The original *Mona Lisa*, for example, has value in excess of its copies. But this kind of value is not moral value and does not reflect on the moral standing of the object, or the moral significance of the lives themselves. The *Mona Lisa* does have value, but no moral standing since it is a mere painting; it lacks consciousness. It may be damaged, but it cannot be harmed in the way that humans and sentient creatures can be harmed.

Perhaps the machines view humans this way. To the machines, the value of the humans in the Matrix is mainly instrumental. They are valued as a source of energy, but they may also have some antiquarian value. Humans are merely relics of a past they themselves helped to destroy. If that's the case, the machines have turned the tables. They are making the same moral mistake that humans apparently made in the context of *The Matrix*, in viewing other rational life forms as simple instruments, to use and destroy as one wishes. Indeed, both sides of the conflict seem to have displayed some moral blindness. The humans, in using and destroying, and the machines, certainly, in their subjugation of the humans. But both sides view themselves as fighting for survival, and I imagine that Smith and Smith's creators, as well as Neo and his friends, would argue that moral qualms like these are a luxury.

Of course it is assumed, at the end of the trilogy, that the machines can keep bargains. They make a deal with Neo, so they must believe humans can be bargained with, and that implies a certain degree of respect as well.

II. Manipulation and Immorality

The world that the pre-enlightened Neo inhabits is made up by machines. The machines have created a humdrum existence for humans, to keep them happy and pacified and free of the knowledge that they are being used as a source of energy for the machines. Most humans believe that this world is real, but they are mistaken. Within this world, they build lives for themselves, have relationships, eat lovely dinners, and at least seem to both create and destroy. To some extent, this existence is dreamlike. It isn't real. When the unenlightened person thinks he's eating a steak, he isn't. Instead, the machines generate mental experiences which correspond to the experience of eating a steak, but which are nonveridical—that is, the person is not *actually* eating a steak. There *is* no real or actual steak. The human being's actions, in that respect, have no real or actual consequences in a world that exists independently of his mind. However, even in this unenlightened state, the humans do have *some* control, since what they "do" in the Matrix has consequences which are realized in the real world. Getting smashed by a truck in the Matrix kills the person in reality. The Matrix offers a 'brain-in-a-vat' experience, but one where the experiencer does have some control.[4] Also, as I discussed in the previous section, some of the programs within the Matrix are genuinely sentient and conscious, and their destruction has moral significance. The enlightened can, in principle, understand the rules of the Matrix and learn to exert control with full understanding.[5]

But, as the steak example illustrates, there are many other "actions" they perform that seem to have no effects in the real world. The pre-enlightened Neo and most of the humans living in the Matrix seem to be deluded. One issue raised by this is the extent to which they can be held

4. See Christopher Grau's chapter in this collection for more on dream skepticism and brain-in-a-vat skepticism.

5. The unenlightened, on the other hand, are constantly being "Gettiered." [Ed. Note: To be "Gettiered" is to have a justified true belief that nonetheless does not amount to knowledge. In 1963 Edmund Gettier published a landmark essay in the journal *Analysis* that offered two influential counterexamples to the previously dominant theory that knowledge consists of justified true belief.] A woman may have justified true belief that her husband is dead, because she has just "seen" him smashed by a truck. But being in the Matrix, she lacks true knowledge because she is deceived in the true manner of his death.

responsible for their actions in the Matrix. Suppose, just for the sake of argument, that wearing fur is immoral. Is simply making a choice to wear fur, along with the belief that one is wearing fur, enough to make one guilty of wrongdoing? Is it really *only* the thought that counts, morally? A competing view is that the choices people make must result in actual bad consequences in order for them to be guilty of wrongdoing, or actual good consequences in order for them to be considered to have acted rightly. So, the issue is whether or not the moral quality of a person's actions—its rightness or wrongness—is determined solely by his or her subjective states or whether, instead, actual consequences figure into this determination.

In the Matrix, if fur is worn, it is virtual fur and not real—though the wearer does not realize this. Again, this is because he or she is being mentally manipulated. But is this a genuine delusion? Certainly, an insane person who fails to have a grip on reality, and is deluded in this sense, is thought to have *diminished* moral responsibility for what he or she does while deluded. Such a person is generally held to not be morally responsible in those circumstances. She is not punished, though she may be confined to a mental hospital and treated for insanity. The explanation is that the actions performed while insane are not truly voluntary. If the persons who live in the Matrix are similarly deluded, then it would seem that they are not responsible for what they 'do' in the Matrix.

Some writers have argued that one cannot be held responsible for what happens in a dream, since dreams themselves are not voluntary, nor are the 'actions' one seems to perform in a dream.[6] Other writers, such as Henry David Thoreau, have the view that what we seem to do in a dream reflects on our character, and the contents of dreams may reveal true virtue or vice.[7] Even if the actions one performs in a dream have no actual good or bad consequences, they reveal truths about one's emotional make-up and one's inner desires, and these in turn are revealing of

6. See, for example, William Mann's "Dreams of Immorality," *Philosophy* (1983), pp. 378–85. Mann is writing in response to an essay by Gareth Matthews (see further reading) who noted that St. Augustine was very concerned with this issue. Matthews notes that since St. Augustine is committed to an internalist standard of moral evaluation, dream immorality becomes a real problem for his view.

7. Thoreau writes about this in *A Week on the Concord and the Merrimack* (1849).

character. But, as we've discussed, the Matrix isn't a dream.[8] The unenlightened exist, rather, in a state of psychological manipulation. The actions they seem to perform don't always have the effects (in reality) that they have reason to expect, based on their manipulated experiences. But even in the Matrix we can argue that they make voluntary choices. They are not irrational. They are not like the insane. Neo believes what any rational, reasonable person would believe under the circumstances. The pre-enlightened are analogous to persons who make decisions based on lies that others have told them. They act, but without relevant information. It's that condition that Neo would like to rectify at the end of *The Matrix*.

The view I favor is that without *actual* bad effects the actions of those in the Matrix are not immoral But, again, this claim is controversial. Some would argue that it's simply "the thought that counts," that it is the person's intentions which determine the moral quality of what she does. Immanuel Kant, for example, is famous for having claimed that all that matters, intrinsically, is a good *will*—actual consequences are irrelevant to moral worth.[9] However, it would then be the case that forming bad intentions in one's dreams is also sufficient for immorality, and this seems highly counterintuitive. If that's true, then the intention to do something immoral along with the belief that one has so acted is enough to make one guilty of moral wrongdoing. Instead, it seems more plausible that it must also be the case that there is some actual bad brought about, or at least the realistic prospect of some actual bad consequences, and thus nonveridical wrongdoing in the Matrix is not actual wrongdoing.

8. I'm not completely committed to this. If the Matrix induces dream experiences, they differ radically from the sort we are used to since in our ordinary dreams we don't take there to be a systematic connection between what happens in the dream and what happens in the waking world. But one could imagine a possible world in which people dreamed and there was such a systematic connection.

9. This also is controversial, but see Kant's *Foundations of the Metaphysics of Morals*, trans. Lewis White Beck, and *Critical Essays*, ed. Robert Paul Wolf (New York: Macmillan, 1969):

Nothing in the world—indeed, nothing even beyond the . . . world—can possibly be conceived which could be called good without qualification except a *good will*. . . . The good will is not good because of what it effects or accomplishes or because of its adequacy to achieve some proposed end; it is good only because of its willing, i.e., it is good of itself. (pp. 11–12)

This seems to be clearly the case in a dream. In a dream, when the dreamer decides to do something bad, that decision doesn't affect the real world. But the Matrix is not really a dream. If we assume that the virtual world of the Matrix is *complete*—that is, completely like the real world before the machines took over—then the virtual "harms" are still real in that they are realized in terms of *actual* unpleasant mental states. The virtual fur coat is the result then of a virtual animal getting killed, but a virtual animal with all the right sorts of mental states—in this case, pain and suffering. If this is the case, then the killer, though mistaken in thinking the dead animal is real, has still produced bad effects in the form of genuine pain and suffering. And thus, the action is immoral even though nonveridical. However, if the world of the Matrix is incomplete, the issue becomes more complicated. If Cypher's virtual steak comes from a virtual meat locker, and the meat locker is the end of the line—and the acquisition of the steak does not involve the killing of a virtual animal with all of the same psychology of pain and suffering that a real animal feels—then no moral harm has been done.

But note that Thoreau's point still holds even though the Matrix is not exactly like a dream. That is, even if a person hasn't actually done anything bad, or caused any real harm to another sentient life form, we may still make a negative evaluation of the person's *character*.

My guess is that the Matrix is a complete alternate reality created in the image of the pre-machine reality. And the Matrix, if it does offer such a complete replication of the pre-machine reality, is truly a self-contained world. It has its own objects, its own people, animals—and ethics. The systematic deception of the humans doesn't change this.

Further Reading

The moral status of sentient programs raises interesting issues on the nature of consciousness and whether or not computers or programs can ever really achieve consciousness. For more information on the topic of moral status itself, the literature on the abortion debate and on animal rights is instructive; see, for instance, Mary Ann Warren's *Moral Status* (Oxford: Oxford University Press, 1997).

For more information on machines and mentality, see Daniel Dennett's *Consciousness Explained* (Boston: Little, Brown, 1991) and

John Searle's *Minds, Brains, and Science* (London: British Broadcasting, 1984).

The issue of dream immorality also has a long history, though not much in the way of recent discussion. As far as I know, Augustine was the first to raise it, in his *Confessions.* It has more recently been discussed by Gareth Matthews and William Mann; see Matthews, "On Being Immoral in a Dream," in *Philosophy* (1981), and Mann's response, "Dreams of Immorality," in *Philosophy* (1983).

Michael McKenna

NEO'S FREEDOM...WHOA!

The Matrix provides a fine resource for illustrating philosophical ideas. Many films have themes that one can philosophize about, or that serve as useful illustrations of philosophical ideas, such as the wonderful *Sophie's Choice* or *Sheltering Sky*. But *The Matrix* offers more than this. It belongs in a special class of films, including *Blade Runner, Total Recall, Crimes and Misdemeanors, A Clockwork Orange, The Unbearable Lightness of Being*, and *The Truman Show*. All of these films are *intentionally* philosophical. Each shows how richly philosophical themes can be developed through cinema. Perhaps the best of these films is *The Matrix*.

I

No doubt, the most striking philosophical theme found in *The Matrix* concerns skepticism about knowledge of an external world. The dream world Neo inhabited was a perfectly comfortable "reality"—except for the fact that it was not reality.[1] Life from inside it completely shielded one from what Morpheus aptly called "the desert of the real," that desolated shell of a planet on which countless humans were unknowingly ensconced in slimy wombs. But there are many other philosophical themes explored within *The Matrix*. One is the concept of freedom.

---

1. This claim is meant to be philosophically innocent, simply taking "reality" as the film's creators suggested it to be. For proper philosophical scrutiny of the notion of reality as it pertains to *The Matrix*, see the chapter in this volume by David Chalmers.

Freedom is mentioned at various points in the film.[2] It mattered a great deal who did what freely. For instance, it was important that Neo freely chose to take the red pill and not the blue pill. Had he taken the blue pill, he'd have been returned to that humdrum dream world of vapid city dwellers. He'd never have taken the path that eventually led him to his heroic defeat of the Agents, and that left him at the end of the film entertaining the prospect of saving the human race. At various other points, Neo made choices freely, and, as with taking the red pill, it was the quality of having made them freely that gave them the importance they had. For instance, Neo freely decided to risk his life for Morpheus; instead of fleeing when his own life was in danger, he returned to save Morpheus from cranial meltdown at the hands of those treacherous Agents in their zoot suits. Also, Neo freely followed the white rabbit that led him tumbling down that rabbit hole. And he remained in the car when Trinity and Switch gave him the opportunity to bail. By remaining in the car, Neo freely chose to resist the Agents. He chose on his own not to get out and walk away down that street, down that well-worn path that, Trinity reminded him, led to nowhere special. In choosing to remain in the car, he freely embarked upon a path that would lead to an exciting future, to an exciting life.

But it was not just Neo's freedom that mattered. Freedom was an issue for the others as well. During Cypher's attempted mutiny, Trinity reminded him that all of Morpheus's rebels had freely chosen the red pill, and so none could claim that they were in their dire straits undeservedly. All the same, Cypher regretted his choice. He felt duped; he did not regard his choice to take the red pill as free. As he saw it, he was scammed. In fact, he was of the opinion that he'd have had more freedom as a steak-eating, satiated participant in the Matrix, oblivious to the "truth" about the ugly shell that would have held him in perpetual slumber.

Freedom also mattered a great deal when it was *not* possessed. It seems that this was the case with those countless human drones, all contained in their artificial wombs. As Morpheus and company (save for Cypher) saw it, their poor, ignorant kin were victims, blind to their lack of freedom. Maybe they were even happy in their plodding little lives within the Matrix,

---

2. I shall assume that my reader has seen the film and is familiar with the characters in it, the basic plot, various events that took place, and so on.

working in cubicles all day—but they were victims all the same, enslaved in the service of generating battery juice for those battery-powered AI meanies. Even the leader of the Agents' posse, Agent Smith, valued freedom. He too was limited in his freedom since he was required to do something against his will, namely, remain in the Matrix and deal with those pesky rebel infiltrators. As he confessed to Morpheus, he hated having to be there, hated the smell of the humans. He felt trapped. Poor guy. In the end, Agent Smith's freedom was dramatically impaired by a liberated Neo, who had turned the tables and was now screwing with him.

But of course, all of this is to leave the concept of freedom unanalyzed and to take the claims of freedom within the film on face value. As any good student of philosophy is aware, there are quite general skeptical challenges to (certain kinds of) freedom that might undermine the very idea that any person is free in at least one important respect. Let's defer for just a bit longer placing any theoretical structure on what freedom might be and on the sorts of challenges there might be to it. Let's fix upon some further observations that will subsequently help us to bring into clear focus a few frequently unacknowledged but powerful points about the freedom of human agency, a freedom many have called *freedom of the will.*

It appeared in the film that some had more freedom than others. Morpheus's crew was amazed watching Neo fight Morpheus for the first time. They thought that the untrained neophyte Neo was just so fast, faster than any of the others. Their hope was that Neo was The One. No doubt there are biblical themes throughout the film, and no doubt "The One" is one of those themes: The One is something like a divine savior. A crucial feature of this savior is that whoever could fill the bill would have more freedom within the Matrix than could any other rebel visitor to it or, for that matter, any other intentional being operating within the Matrix, including the Agents. Indeed, their hope was that Neo's freedom within the Matrix would be like that of God; Neo would have unlimited freedom. So it appeared that Neo, even when first getting acquainted with his abilities, had more freedom within the Matrix than did Trinity, Cypher, or any of the rest of Morpheus's gang (save for Morpheus himself). But there are other comparisons as well that indicate different degrees of freedom within the Matrix. Neo, Morpheus, and all of the rebels had more freedom within the Matrix than did all those clueless characters walking the streets, living in their homes, watching their TVs, going to work, and so on. At least as Morpheus and company saw it, the clueless were completely unfree.

Until near the film's end, Neo had *less* freedom than did the Agents. The Agents could simply move about, satisfying most any desire they had, taking on others' bodies, appearing whenever and wherever they wanted, and operating with fantastic foresight about who would be where, when, and so on. These Agents defied what seemed to be the laws of nature (as structured within the Matrix). They could emerge unscathed after being slammed by speeding trains that would have crushed and destroyed any run-of-the-mill putz living out his ordinary life within the Matrix. They took bullets and kept on tickin', and they could simply make a person's mouth disappear at will. They had the run of the place, at least until the closing moments of the film. But in those closing moments, Neo was the freest person operating within the Matrix. Hell, by the time he came to realize his true potential within it, he could beat the crap out of those battery-powered robot demons, stop bullets, and fly—like Superman.

One more important observation before we roll up our sleeves and do some philosophical work: the special sort of freedom that Neo seemed to possess in the film was a freedom confined to the Matrix. The same, of course, applies to Morpheus and the other rebels whom Morpheus trained. The film gave us no reason to believe that Neo, or anyone else, had any special freedom outside the Matrix. In the "real" world, as it is in the space ship with those nasty flying bugs out hunting down rebel ships on that desolate planet, Morpheus, Neo, Trinity, Cypher, and the rest of the clan are just normally functioning human persons like you or me. Presumably, in the real world, Neo's just a guy, a guy who, analogous to poor, impaired, nobody Tommy in The Who's rock opera *Tommy*, is transformed in game mode to the most gifted being ever to play the relevant game—a pinball wizard. In the Matrix, that is, roughly, in the ultimate of video-game consoles, Neo ain't got no distractions, can't hear no buzzes or bells, always gets the replay, and never tilts at all.

So *in* the Matrix, near the end of the film, as Neo comes to master the game, he's totally dialed in. It's gotta rock! Let us call this freedom that Neo possesses within the Matrix *absolute freedom*, and let us call the feature that seems to go with it the *property of rocking*. No doubt, when Neo first saw such amazing freedom exercised—when Morpheus leaped an incredible distance from one skyscraper to another—he judged that indeed such extreme freedom did rock, and in amazement he appropriately expressed himself thusly: "Whoa!"

II

The concept of absolute freedom and its presumed property of rocking will be further developed in the closing sections of this chapter. But for now, let us first give some theoretical structure to the idea of freedom, forgetting about *absolute* freedom, and let us consider briefly a classical philosophical challenge to our ordinary idea of freedom. Once we have these issues in place, we'll turn back to the film and examine our natural reactions to it, including many of the reactions mentioned above.

The term *freedom* is used in many contexts, and there is no reason to assume that there is a single meaning of the term. Minimally, all of the uses of the term do seem to share the feature that resistance of some sort, encumbering or impeding desired conduct, gets in the way of freedom. Typically, a person is not free when she is frustrated in some manner from unencumbered pursuit of her desired course of action. But the absence of impediments is clearly not sufficient for the kind of freedom that mattered to Morpheus, Neo, and company, nor to what is valuable and distinctive of the human condition. A stupid dog can sometimes act unencumbered when, for instance, he is unleashed—when he is set free. And though free in a very basic way, the stupid dog's freedom is not the kind that makes philosophers, theologians, politicians, moralists, or just your run-of-the-mill high-minded folk get the warm fuzzies. No. The freedom worth talking about seems to be a freedom distinctive to persons, and this suggests that understanding the relevant notion of freedom first requires an understanding of what it is to be a person.

Regrettably, offering an account of personhood is beyond the scope of this chapter. But to appreciate what seems to mark persons from nonpersons, those familiar with the movie *Blade Runner* can reflect upon the characters Decker and the replicant Rachel, with whom Decker falls in love. Although Decker is a human being (maybe), and Rachel is an artificial replicant of a human being, both are *persons*.[3] Both are capable of planning

---

3. I say that *maybe* Decker is a human being since there is some suggestion in the film that Decker might actually be a replicant and not a human being.

lives, of developing intimate relationships of love and hate, of fearing for and finding dear their own lives and the lives of other persons. Both have the capacity for abstract thought, emotional responses to others, self-consciousness, and so on. Less-developed cognitive creatures are not persons, such as the primitive little AI machines that kept J. S. Sabastian company (J. S. Sabastian was another character in *Blade Runner*). Or to draw upon other clear illustrations of personhood from other sources in film, E.T. from the classic Spielberg movie was a person. Data from the *Star Trek* series and movies was a person, though neither E.T. nor Data was a human being. So, for our purposes, Neo, Morpheus, Trinity, and the Agents are all persons—though the Agents, like E.T. or Data, are nonhuman persons.

Even restricting the term *freedom* to its applications to persons, there are at least two sorts that have been the focus of a great deal of philosophical attention for well over two millennia now. One is a matter of political freedom, another is a matter of metaphysical freedom, the latter being understood as freedom of the will. Political freedom concerns the freedom of persons to conduct themselves as they see fit within the political landscape. The nature of the political landscape is itself a matter of dispute. Does the landscape germane to political freedom include economic empowerment? Or does it merely involve what are often referred to as the civil liberties, such as the liberty to speak unthreatened from harm of prohibition, to organize as one wishes, and so on? Political freedom, whatever it comes to, is certainly a deeply important sort of freedom, and no doubt, it is the sort of freedom that Morpheus was struggling to give back to the human race. At least this is how Morpheus and his comrades saw it. But the more immediate sort of freedom to which the film directs our attention is not political freedom, but metaphysical freedom, that is, freedom of the will.

Before turning our attention to the topic of *free* will, it is worth asking, what is the *will*? This is also the subject of a great deal of dispute, but it is natural to think of the *will* as the aspect of a creature's mentality that is the source of voluntary, intentional (that is, goal-directed) action. Hence, any *agent*—that is, any being that acts, such as a human, a dog, a cat, a chimpanzee—has a will. The philosophical gem worthy of reflection is what makes a will free and, most notably, free in the special way distinctive of a unique class of agents, those who are persons.

A word of caution: The expression *metaphysical freedom* is often regarded derisively by theorists, largely outside of philosophy, who fallaciously associate it only with extravagant views about the human condition, such as the view that metaphysical freedom provides persons with a capacity to transcend the material world, to choose and act unlimited by the laws of nature or by any constraints from the material world. And while some theories of free will do attribute to persons the ability to perform very small miracles whenever they act freely,[4] all the expression *metaphysical freedom* need pick out is a distinctive feature of personhood—a feature unique to the *will* of a person, perhaps part of the essence or the nature of what it is to be a person. How to understand this freedom is up for grabs. So, to be clear: the very mention of the notion of metaphysical freedom, or freedom of the will, does not *entail* anything mysterious. It does not entail anything contrary to the spirit of an inquiry such as Darwin's or that of a neurobiologist.

It might turn out that free will involves no special miraculous features of agency at all, that metaphysical freedom is entirely consistent with a deflationary account of human persons according to which all human persons are entirely the products of their genetics, their environment, and any other physical factors impinging upon them. That said, it should be kept in mind that, on the other hand, serious philosophical reflection might indicate that the concept of free will implies that a deflationary view of persons is false. But the crucial point here is that it is not part of the meaning of the very term *metaphysical freedom*, or *freedom of the will*, that it involve anything spooky, mysterious, unworldly, or otherwise beyond the pale of what is in principle explicable in terms of our best natural sciences.

---

4. For example, in articulating an account of free will, the philosopher Roderick Chisholm wrote:

> [I]f what I have been trying to say is true, then we have a prerogative which some would attribute only to God: each of us, when we act, is a prime mover unmoved. In doing what we do, we cause certain events to happen, and nothing—or no one—causes us to cause those events to happen. (Chisholm, p. 32, cited in Watson, ed., 2003)

Caution should be taken with even this rather extreme view, since Chisholm was not claiming that the sorts of "miracles" that would allow freely willing and uncaused persons to cause events would amount to miracles that could make walls melt, planes fall from the sky, or bullets to stop in mid-air.

III

Here is a theory-neutral characterization of free will:

> Free will is the ability of persons to control their futures through their choices and actions.

This is a lean definition that is not biased toward any one particular manner of philosophizing about free will. Of course, it is only a first pass and cries out for refinement. The crux of the issue concerns how best to articulate the ability to control the future. Let us consider two ways to articulate further this characterization of free will.

It is quite natural to assume, as many philosophers do, that a person acts with freedom of the will only if there are alternative courses of action available to her at the time at which she acts. On a model such as this, a person's freedom of the will consists partly in her being in control of a spectrum of options that, so to speak, open up different temporal paths, allowing her access to different unfolding futures, different ways that her life might go. At various points in the film, this picture of freedom was emphasized, as when Neo chose to remain in the car and not bail when Trinity and Switch gave him the opportunity to do so. This picture of freedom was also highlighted when Neo chose to return and fight the Agents so as to save Morpheus. Instead, Neo could have left Morpheus to (what seemed to be) his inevitable demise.

So one way to advance free will is in terms of *alternative possibilities*. But there are other strategies for understanding free will, strategies that might or might not work in tandem with a demand for alternative possibilities. For instance, another way to think about free will is in terms of what *does* happen, what a person *does*, and not in terms of what other things she might do or might have done. Instead of focusing on alternative possibilities, this manner of theorizing concentrates upon the *source* of a person's actions. On this approach, freely willed actions arise from certain salient features of a person's self, features that indicate that, in an important respect she—*the person*—is the source of how the future does unfold. To illustrate, consider a paradigmatic case of a person who lacks free will. An unwilling addict, for example, would not act with freedom of will when she takes the drug to which she is addicted. This is because her addictive desire to take the drug is so strong that it compels her to take it even though she is unwilling to take the drug. She does not desire that her desire for the drug cause her to take it. But she does take it all the same. The future does not unfold as she herself would like it to unfold. On the other hand, sometimes properly functioning persons *do* act precisely as they wish, however "as they wish" might be understood. When they do, if all goes well, the future unfolds as they would like it to unfold, and it unfolds in this way partially because *what they do causes it to unfold in this way.* Hence, in a very basic way, these normally functioning persons are guiding how the future unfolds when they act unencumbered. They are the ones bringing about certain events, shaping the future in certain ways via their agency. *They are sources of control over the future.* It should also be clear that Morpheus and Neo illustrated such views of freedom. They certainly were, at points, sources of "control" over how their futures were unfolding. Morpheus and Neo, as well as the rest of the rebels, were making *their* marks inside and outside of the Matrix. Much to the chagrin of the Agents, Morpheus and his crew were sources of control over how certain events were unfolding.

In summary, if we understand free will as a capacity of persons to control the future through their choices and actions, then there are two ways that one might further develop this idea of control over the future. One is in terms of control over alternative possibilities; another is in terms of one's very self being a source of how the future goes, an authentic shaper or causer of events in the world.

IV

However the concept of free will is developed, there is a classical challenge to the very idea that any person possesses it. In particular, some philosophers believe that if the universe is fully determined, then no person has free will. What it means to suggest that the universe is determined is a distinct and controversial philosophical topic. A currently fashionable definition of *determinism* has it, roughly, that the past, combined with the laws of nature, causally ensures one unique future. To appreciate fully this definition, one needs an account of what the past is (or the facts of it), what it means to causally ensure, and so on. But the general idea is basically captured with the suggestion that, for any person, states of the world independent of that person, or independent of features of her intentional agency (possibly, states of the world prior to her birth), combined with the laws governing the natural world (such as the laws of physics, chemistry, biology, and so on), are themselves sufficient to fix fully what that person does at any time. Crudely put, are persons and their conduct exhaustively explained in terms of their heredity, their biology, such as their neurobiological functioning, and the environmental influences impinging upon them? Put even more crudely, is all human conduct purely a matter of nature and nurture? Or is determinism false, and is it instead the case that these influences do not all by themselves explain exactly what a person does at any time? If not, does the person herself contribute something over and above these other factors that accounts for why she does what she does?

Incompatibilists believe that if determinism is true, no one has free will. No one can control her future since the universe, so to speak, is really controlling it, and persons and their conduct are merely conduits through which the forces of nature operate. The universe leads some people to act in certain ways, and others to act differently. Persons are not at the helms of their lives, guiding their futures. Persons are products of the universe, not agents freely acting upon it.

Turning to the two ways of developing the concept of free will suggested above, the incompatibilists will argue that either way conflicts with the assumptions of a deterministic world. Suppose that the concept of free will is developed in terms of alternative possibilities. If determinism is true, and if facts distinct from a person's intentional agency, combined with the laws of nature, entail that a person's intentional conduct will be thus and so, then a person is not free to do other than thus and so. She has no alternatives over which to exercise control. Her past and the forces of nature have settled for her what path into the future she will take.

Or suppose instead that the concept of free will is developed in terms of a person's being an actual source of how the world goes, and it goes that way, at least in part, *because* of her. If determinism is true, then there are facts prior to any person's birth, combined with the laws of nature, that provide sufficient conditions for how the future will unfold. A person's agency, given determinism, seems to be nothing but a conduit, a facilitator, for what has already been set in motion. She, ultimately, is not the source of her action, the controller of an unfolding future. Sure, sometimes the future unfolds as she desires that it does, and sometimes her desires figure in the causes that explain why it does unfold as such. But these very desires, her beliefs, her value judgments, her preferences about what motivational states are the ones that she wishes to act upon—all of these factors are themselves not factors ultimately issuing from her, but from the determined universe and the unfolding future that is an upshot of it.

As initially puzzling as it seems, *compatibilists* maintain that persons can have free will even if determinism is true. Some compatibilists, embracing a view of free will that requires alternative possibilities, have attempted to show that a determined person might still, in some meaningful sense, have the ability to do other than what she does. Other compatibilists have instead emphasized how a person might, via her own motivational states, still count as a significant actual source of efficacy in the way the future comes about.[5]

V

There are various ways in which the tension between compatibilism and incompatibilism is brought out in the film. One is in terms of reflections upon fate. Another is in terms of the Oracle's ability to know the future. Yet another has to do with the status of those poor "enslaved" humans.

It is worth noting that within the film, as in ordinary discourse, the term *fate* is used in two different sorts of ways, ways that are easy to confuse, but upon reflection are clearly distinct. Sometimes *fate* is used to mean what is also meant by *determinism*. This certainly seems to be the primary manner in which it is used within the film. Given this usage, what it is for something to be *fated* is for it to be causally ensured by prior conditions. This view is entirely consistent with one's conduct being a crucial factor in what is causally ensured. But on a different construal, if some outcome is fated, then it will come about *no matter what one does*. On this view, one's agency is an idle factor. A certain future will transpire irrespective of anything one might do. The standard example of this is the story of Oedipus. The gods were going to see to it that Oedipus met his

5. There is even a controversy among compatibilists as to whether or not only the latter notion of control is needed for free will, or whether free will is possible only if both alternative possibilities and actual source conditions are satisfied.

terrible fate—killing his father and copulating with his mother—no matter what different things were done by any mortal to avoid that outcome.

These two notions are extremely different. To illustrate: If it were fated irrespective of what anyone did that John F. Kennedy would be assassinated on the day he was, then no matter what Lee Harvey Oswald did (including not assassinate anyone), Kennedy was going to be assassinated (by someone). But if it were fated just in the sense of being determined that Kennedy was going to be assassinated, then it mattered a great deal precisely what Oswald did. Had he not done what he did, then Kennedy would not have been shot. One account of fate states that a certain future will unfold *no matter what any person does or will do*; another states that a certain future will unfold *precisely because of what does or what will take place* (which includes, among other things, what people actually do). Typically, philosophers reserve the term *fatalism* for the former notion and *determinism* for the latter. But for purposes of analyzing the film, let us distinguish between *no-matter-what-one-does fatalism* and *deterministic fatalism.*[6]

When Neo and Morpheus first met, Morpheus asked Neo if he believed in fate. Neo said that he did not since he did not like the idea that he did not control his life. Note that, at this point in the film, what Morpheus meant by fate, and what Neo took it to mean, remained ambiguous between the two notions distinguished above. This is because, if one's life is subject to no-matter-what-one-does fate, then that would undermine one's control with respect to the fated outcome. So Neo's reply could have been in response to the suggestion that life was no-matter-what-one-does fated.[7] Perhaps what

---

6. For a film that plays with these ideas, see *Minority Report*.

7. This interpretation of the scene fits with Morpheus's subsequent description of how the human race is enslaved. No matter what humans do within the Matrix itself, their conduct is designed to do no more than generate battery juice for the "evolved" artificial intelligences. In fact, it seems from the film that the level of control that the designers and controllers of the Matrix have over the humans operating within it is *not* a completely deterministically fated sort of control, but really a sort better suited for no-matter-what-one-does fatalism. This is because people within the Matrix seem able to do all sorts of different things within certain boundaries. The AI creatures care not a bit. The AI intelligences are happy to allow a certain level of social disharmony and chaos among the humans within the Matrix. As long as ultimately the outcome is that human lives are lived in the service of creating energy for their AI lives, what does it matter to them what the humans do to each other in their dream worlds?

Neo found objectionable about fatalism was the thought that his agency in the world would have no effect on the world's outcome at all—no matter what he did. And indeed, that is how it seemed the enslaved humans lived within the Matrix: having no effect, no matter what they did, on their contribution to generating electricity for the AI meanies. But even if this was what Neo meant in that first conversation with Morpheus, later in the film it was clear that Neo also wanted to resist deterministic fatalism. He was committed to the idea that deterministic fatalism would undermine his control over the world. At points it was quite clear that his worry was in the form of alternative possibilities. He resisted the idea that the Oracle could know which of the possible futures before him would be his inevitable actual future. He thought that it was up to him what that future would be: would he choose to save Morpheus or himself? But Neo also seemed to think in terms of source models of control: as he saw it, it was not settled in advance how he would act; he would be the settler of it! As the Oracle was bidding Neo farewell, she herself put those words in his mouth. Neo, it seems, was an incompatibilist.

If Neo was the incompatibilist in the film, Morpheus was certainly the compatibilist. He believed in his consultations with the Oracle that the future was deterministically fated, that The One would come. But he also believed that what he did, and what the others did, mattered very much to that outcome. (So he certainly did not endorse no-matter-what-one-does fatalism.) Even more important, he believed that it mattered very much that whatever people did, they did of their own free will, hence the use of the blue and the red pills. His advice to Neo was especially telling. Thinking in terms of source control, Morpheus explained to Neo that it was not enough to know that you are The One, you have to *be* The One. That is, Neo had to be the actual source of that special person, which was a matter of his actual conduct in the world, and not merely something he conceptually grasped.

And what of the Oracle herself? To correct the impression that perhaps the Oracle was not really able to foresee the future, Morpheus told Neo that the Oracle never intended to speak truthfully to Neo about what she foresaw. She only intended to say to Neo what he needed to hear (which of course she knew, since she was the Oracle). Surely, if she did make any judgments about what Neo needed to hear, then she did believe that what he would do would matter to how the future would go. If so, then like Neo and Morpheus, she also did not believe in no-matter-what-one-does fate. But being the Oracle, she probably at least entertained the idea that deterministic fatalism was true. Suppose she did believe it. Was she a compatibilist or an incompatibilist? Might she have believed, consistent with incompatibilism, that all of the human struggles to shape the future were unfree actions set in motion by a long, deterministically fated history? Or did she instead, consistent with compatibilism, foresee and understand Neo's heroic efforts as deterministically fated, but freely willed all the same? Suppose instead that the Oracle did not believe in deterministic fatalism. Perhaps she thought the universe was fundamentally indeterminate and that no facts of the past or present ensured any particular way that the future must go. If she believed this, then how did she understand the basis of her own predictions? Maybe in foreseeing Neo's actions, she interpreted them as freely willed and understood her powers to foresee future conduct as completely consistent with the falsity of determinism.[8] The film leaves entirely open which interpretation of the Oracle's beliefs is the correct one.

Consider a very different matter, the status of the enslaved masses. Unlike characters like Neo, Morpheus, and the Oracle, it seems irrelevant to ask about what they believed about their own free will and what they might have thought about fate. They were oblivious to what was taking place outside of the Matrix. Much like the character Truman from the film *The Truman Show*, these poor suckers stuck in those giant wombs were much like a special sort of example used in the free-will debate. Incompatibilists are fond of challenging compatibilist notions of control with complicated manipulation cases. The incompatibilists' strategy is to cook up a troubling scenario in which a person is manipulated into a manner of acting. Of course, what the incompatibilists try to do is make the sort of manipulation so subtle that it is indistinguishable from what ordinary life might be like for you or me. The examples are supposed to provoke intuitively the reaction that the manipulated person is not free because the source of her action is polluted. It is not she but something

---

8. The puzzles here over the status of the Oracle's foreknowledge are like those regarding the status of a foreknowing God. If God foreknows all human conduct, does that mean that, by virtue of God's infallible nature, all human conduct is determined? Or is it possible for God to know exactly what any person does or will do even if nothing other than the person herself freely determines what she will do?

else that is the source of her agency. Then the incompatibilists will attempt to argue that a person determined by her past and the laws of nature is no different than a person manipulated in one of these wild scenarios. Hence, the only way that a person like you or me can be free is if she is not determined. If she is determined, then she is no more free than is a manipulated person, which is to say that she is not free at all.

These manipulation cases have come to be known as covert nonconstraining control (CNC) examples.[9] Compatibilists have two ways in which they can respond to CNC cases. One is to deny that the manipulated persons are unfree. So long as the manipulation is complicated enough, and so long as the manipulation accurately replicates the normal functioning of a person getting through life, then it really is no different than a person being determined. But this is not a problem since the manipulated person is a freely willing one. It is just that the causes of her actions are a lot weirder than the causes of a normally functioning person's actions. Note that this was Cypher's view. In fact, for him, the Matrix would afford him more freedom than what was available on that disgusting planet. What did he care what caused his sensation of eating a juicy delicious steak? Real or illusory, he just wanted the damned steak to taste good.

---

9. See Kane, 1996, pp. 65–71:

We are all aware of . . . two ways to get others to do our bidding in everyday life. We may force them to do what we want by coercing or constraining them against their wills, which is constraining control or CC control. Or we may manipulate them into doing what we want while making them feel that they have made up their own minds and are acting "of their own free will"—which is covert nonconstraining or CNC control. Cases of CNC control in larger settings are provided by examples like Aldous Huxley's *Brave New World* or B. F. Skinner's *Walden Two*. Frazier, the fictional founder of Skinner's Walden Two, gives a clear description of CNC control when he says that in his community persons can do whatever they want or choose, but they have been conditioned since childhood to want and choose only what they can have or do. (p. 65)

In an earlier draft of this chapter, I described the people within the Matrix as the ultimate exemplars of a kind of CNC scenario. But Chris Grau has set me straight on this point. On the most natural understanding of how the Matrix unfolded, the persons within it were not manipulated by the AI "master planners" but were instead left to do as they pleased within certain boundaries. CNC cases typically involve control by others that permits only one way for a person to act. (Though it is not clear that CNC examples need such fine-grained control to do the argumentative work that incompatibilists want them to do.)

Other compatibilists try to show that there is some significant difference between a causally determined person and a manipulated one. Typically, the difference has to do with the history that explains why a person is caused to be as she is. If the causes are of the wrong sort, then she is in some way inauthentic. She is not truly the one engaging the world. Someone or something else is settling for her the values, principles, and so on that she then uses to decide how to act in the world. This, it seems, was the basis for Morpheus's complaint about the Matrix. When he first coaxed Neo, prodding Neo and asking him if he too felt that something about his reality was not right, what Morpheus sought to convey was that human agency within the Matrix was defective; its causal source was designed to settle other goals or needs than the ones that persons within the Matrix endorsed. Their minds were thus enslaved and so, even if, in a sense, they were "free" within their dream world to do certain things, they were not the source of the goals that their lives ultimately served.

VI

All of the above reflections indicate the various ways that *The Matrix* openly struggles with the free-will debate. But what view of free will is the correct one, and how ought it to be characterized? The philosophical controversy between compatibilists and incompatibilists is one of the perennial problems of philosophy. It will likely remain so. One reason for this is that it is clearly *not* a "no-brainer"! Reasonable minds have differed as to the correct resolution to this problem. And there is no reason to think that this will change any time soon. In fact, one of today's most influential theorists about the controversy has suggested that, at least for certain ways of formulating the problem, the debate between compatibilists and incompatibilists leads to dialectical stalemates.[10] A *dialectical stalemate* arises when opposing positions within a reasoned debate reach points at which each side's arguments remain reasonable, even compelling, but their arguments have run out; neither can rightly claim decisively to have unseated the legitimacy of the other side's point of view.

10. Fischer, 1994, pp. 83–85.

I certainly do not know whether the free-will problem is ultimately doomed to dialectical stalemate, or whether instead there is some strategy that will be able to settle a reasoned disagreement that is more than 2,500 years old. But one point I would like to highlight about this controversy is that it would not have remained a controversial topic, and dialectical stalemates would not have arisen from it, were it not for the fact that the phenomenology of human experience, as it is for the normally functioning person, does not decisively provide evidence for any position. It is consistent with how we experience our lives and how we experience the exercising of our agency that, in keeping with the incompatibilist position, the control required for free will is illusory, and we are determined creatures. Or, also in keeping with the incompatibilist position, it is consistent with our experience that the control required for free will is satisfied, and in a way that requires the falsity of determinism. Finally, as the compatibilists allow, it is also consistent with our experience that we do possess free will and that we are determined.

VII

To its credit, *The Matrix* does not pretend to endorse one point of view about free will. It is neither a compatibilist-friendly nor an incompatibilist-friendly film. With notable exceptions, the film's reflections on free will mirror the phenomenology of human agency. As is the case in our actual lives, how life is experienced underdetermines the correct answer as to whether the compatibilists or the incompatibilists are correct about free will. I say here "with notable exceptions" since there are clearly aspects of Neo's agency, as well as Morpheus's, the other rebels', and the AI Agents' that most distinctly did not mirror the phenomenology of human agency. It is to these differences that I would now like to turn in closing.

One assumption of the free-will debate, shared by all parties to it, is that whatever kind of freedom a person does possess, whether it requires the falsity of determinism or not, a person's free will does not consist in her ability to actually cause laws of nature to be false or to be suspended just in order to bring about astounding miracles. But within the Matrix, that is, essentially, the sort of control that Neo came to have. Of course, to a lesser extent, so too did Trinity and Morpheus. Indeed, Morpheus even advised Neo to think of the rules of his dream world as mere conventions (rules of a program) that could be bent or just flat-out broken. Now some philosophers might want to object here that there is a conceptual problem with describing any rules within the Matrix as both laws of nature and breakable. But this would be splitting hairs at a point at which much more could be gained by reflecting instead upon the power of the thought-experiment as it is played out within the film.

Within the history of philosophy, various writers have at one point or another articulated accounts of free will that later were scoffed at and quickly dismissed as fantastical or incoherent or ultimately contradictory.[11] All of these criticisms of these extreme views of freedom might have been on the money, but no philosophical dismissal of the conceptual legitimacy of such a notion of freedom can itself discredit the sort of basis one might have for desiring it. Neo's freedom within the Matrix might seem completely outlandish, merely the stuff of comic books, but the source of its cinematic appeal is that, in a very primitive way, as persons in the world, we all know what it is to bump up against the boundaries of the causally possible. We all understand what a source of liberation it would be if all at once we could act unconstrained by them. Of course, this *is* the stuff that dreams are made of. But to see where our dreams begin often helps us to appreciate both the limits and value of our actual lives.

I shall therefore close with two observations about this extreme sort of fantastical freedom exercised within the Matrix. In section I of this chapter, I indicated that the freedom of the persons within the Matrix came in degrees, and that more of it appeared to be more appealing than less. In fact, I suggested that, by the film's end, within the Matrix, Neo possessed absolute freedom and that it rocked. But does absolute freedom

11. A classic example of this is Sartre's notion of *radical freedom*, which alleged that all persons have freedom with respect to every aspect of reality they confront, every fact of the world. (For an excerpt of Sartre's view, as presented in his *Being and Nothingness*, see the collection edited by Bernard Berofsky, *Free Will and Determinism* [Harper & Row 1966], pp. 174–195.)

rock? We all do value freedom, it appears, and it does look as if it gives almost everyone the warm fuzzies. But I propose that absolute freedom would not rock, and once had for a while, when exercising it, one would no longer be prepared to exclaim, along with Neo, "Whoa!" This is because the property of rocking found in exercising one's agency comes when one is pressing the boundaries of what one is capable of, pressing the boundaries of the limits placed upon one. Anyone who knows the joy of play understands this. Taking the basketball to the hole, snagging a line drive, pushing one's skis down the steep tight line, nailing a turn on a cycle, or crossing the finish line first with the beat of the pack just behind you—all of these involve the prospect of failure and the demands of an effort of will forced up against the boundaries of what one can do. Absolute freedom would require none of that.

Surprising as it might seem, I propose that a life filled to the brim with absolute freedom would absolutely suck. It would be boring as hell and almost entirely uneventful. Recall the look of utter indifference Neo had on his face when he realized how completely effortlessly he could block Agent Smith's blows in that final face-off. He might as well have been yawning and reading a paper while defending himself: "Ho hum." Imagine if all of one's efforts in life were like this. Contrast this with Neo's intensity and enthusiasm when he still had to work hard to get what he wanted, leaping from a helicopter to save Morpheus, or cart-wheeling through a blaze of bullets and taking out all attackers. How mundane all of this would have been had Neo then been able just to will all of the bullets to stop flying, or Morpheus to stop falling to earth, and so on.

Here is a rich irony: our hankering for absolute freedom, a hankering for a dream world, is something we wish for because we do not have it. Because we bump up against our limits and sometimes fail, we yearn for the power to move beyond those limits. But if we had that power in spades, we'd lose all interest in the activities we find so dear. So it seems that the value of freedom and its place in our lives is partially a function of the manner in which we lack it. It is yet a further credit to a film like *The Matrix* that it instigates such reflections on the value of freedom.

A final speculation will also shed further light on the value we place on freedom. Supposing that Neo could have found a way to continue rocking from within the Matrix, Neo would face a fantastic choice.

Should he work to destroy the Matrix? His absolute freedom is so wonderful within it. Imagine the possibilities. He could be so much in the dream world, have so much, do so much; he could bring such joy to others within it. But knowing what he does about the real world, could he value it, could he take the Matrix seriously? Perhaps you think that Neo should remain within the Matrix, where his powers are phenomenal. If instead he destroyed the Matrix, he'd lose all of his powers and have only a dark and barren planet to offer to his liberated human kin. Maybe, like Cypher, they would hate that world and thus resent Neo, seeing him not as a godlike liberator, but as an evil demon dragging them from a relative dream-world utopia into a real-life hell. Even if, for these reasons, you think Neo would do better to remain within the Matrix, acting as a god, trying to do as much good for others as he can, I'll bet that you pause at the thought of it. I myself am unsure what Neo should do, or what I would do if I were he. But if there is something wrong with this option, I suggest that it is at least in part because it would be an inauthentic form of life, a life that valued a certain kind of freedom at the expense of truth, at the expense of real engagement with the actual world. Would this not amount to placing too much value in freedom? Would it not amount to valuing freedom at the expense of other worthy elements of life?

When I was a young boy, my grandfather Poppy took me fishing. I wanted very much that day to catch a trout. I was completely incapable of the task. So Poppy caught one and took it upstream a little way, still hooked on a line. Placing it back in the water, but holding onto the line, he walked it down to me, made as if it were tugging at my pole, and then helped me to reel it in. I was delighted. So was he. It was only years later that he told me how I came to snag that elusive trout. Suppose that the rest of my life, each fish I caught, I caught only that way; each success of mine was only such a success. Even though Poppy was certainly happy with that little moment of mine, he'd never have wished for me a life of nothing but such shams. To wish merely for an improved life for humankind only *within* the Matrix, even with lots of nifty freedom for everyone within it, I would speculate, if it is wrong, then its wrongness is partially explained by the fact that it is analogous to wishing for all humankind that all of their accomplishments be like Poppy's tying that fish to the end of my pole. It would be nice for a spell, for a moment, in a dream. But we humans want something more. *We* want to catch our *own* fish, and we want to catch *real* fish. When we want something else, we'll go to the movies.

Further Reading

There are several fine anthologies devoted to the topics of free will and moral responsibility, including John Martin Fischer and Mark Ravizza, eds., *Perspectives on Moral Responsibility* (Cornell University Press 1993); Robert Kane, ed., *Free Will* (Blackwell 2002); and Gary Watson, ed., *Free Will* (Oxford University Press 2003). There are also many fine book-length treatments of free will and moral responsibility. For especially influential treatments, see Daniel Dennett, *Elbow Room* (MIT Press 1984); John Martin Fischer, *The Metaphysics of Free* Will (Blackwell 1994); John Martin Fischer and Mark Ravizza, *Responsibility & Control* (Cambridge University Press 1998); Harry Frankfurt, *The Importance of What We Care About* (Cambridge University Press 1988); Ishtiyaque Haji, *Moral Appraisability* (Oxford University Press 1998); Robert Kane, *The Significance of Free Will* (Oxford University Press 1996); Alfred Mele, *Autonomous Agents* (Oxford University Press 1995); Derk Pereboom, *Living without Free Will* (Cambridge University Press 2001); Galen Strawson, *Freedom and Belief* (Oxford University Press 1996); Peter van Inwagen, *An Essay on Free Will* (Oxford University Press 1983); Jay Wallace, *Responsibility and the Moral Sentiments* (Harvard University Press 1994); and Susan Wolf, *Freedom within Reason* (Oxford University Press 1990).

I would like to thank Chris Grau for his many insightful comments and helpful suggestions.

PLATO'S CAVE AND *THE MATRIX*

Philosophy involves seeing the absolute oddity of what is familiar and trying to formulate really probing questions about it.

—Iris Murdoch

They say about me that I am the strangest person, always making people confused.

—Socrates

Imagine a dark, subterranean prison in which humans are bound by their necks to a single place from infancy. Elaborate steps are taken by unseen forces to supply and manipulate the content of the prisoners' visual experience. This is so effective that the prisoners do not recognize their imprisonment and are satisfied to live their lives in this way. Moreover, the cumulative effects of this imprisonment are so thorough that if freed, the prisoners would be virtually helpless. They could not stand up on their own; their eyes would be overloaded initially with sensory information; and even their minds would refuse to accept what their senses eventually presented to them. It is not unreasonable to expect that some prisoners would wish to remain imprisoned even after their minds grasped the horror of their condition. But if a prisoner were dragged out and compelled to understand the relationship between the prison and outside, matters would be different. In time, the prisoner would come to have genuine knowledge superior to the succession of representations that had made up the whole of experience before. This freed prisoner would understand those representations as imperfect—like pale copies of the full reality now grasped in the mind. Yet if returned to the prison, the freed prisoner would be the object of ridicule, disbelief, and hostility.

I. Introduction

Viewers of *The Matrix* remember the moment in the film when Neo is released from his prison and made to grasp the truth of his life and the world. The account above roughly captures that turning point in the 1999 film, and yet it is drawn from an image crafted almost 2,400 years ago by the Greek philosopher Plato (427?–347 B.C.). Today the *Republic* is the most influential work by Plato, and the allegory of the Cave is the most famous part of the *Republic*. If you know that Socrates was tried, convicted, and sentenced to death by drinking hemlock, or that Socrates thought that the unexamined life is not worth living, you may also know that Socrates in the *Republic* likened the human condition to the state of prisoners bound in a cave, who see only shadows projected on the wall in front of them. Transcending this state is the aim of genuine education, conceived as a release from imprisonment, a turning or re-orientation of one's whole life, an upward journey from darkness into light:

> The release from the bonds, the turning around from shadows to stat-ues and the light of the fire and, then, the way up out of the cave to the sunlight...: [education] has the power to awaken the best part of the soul and lead it upward to the study of the best among the things that are.[1]

1. Plato, *Republic* 532b6–8, c3–6. What I have dubbed "education" in the brackets is specifically the study of mathematics, geometry, astronomy, and harmony. When prop-erly pursued, each discipline involves abstraction from the senses and is "really fitted in every way to draw one towards being" (523a2–3). These disciplines prepare our minds for the most important discipline—dialectic—Plato's term for the right kind of philosophical examination.

Hereafter, I include citations to the "Stephanus pages" of the *Republic* in the text. Stephanus pages may be found along the vertical margins of most translations of the *Republic*. For example, "527d6–e3" refers to a passage beginning on Stephanus page 527, section d, line 6, of the Oxford classical text. The translation I cite here is Grube/Reeve (1992), which is also found in Cooper (1997) and in the appendix to this volume.

The allegory of the Cave gives literary shape to Socrates' most fundamental concern, namely, that our souls be in the best condition possible (Plato, *Apology* 30a7–b4). Socrates also believed that he was commanded by the god Apollo to practice philosophy; it both animated and cost him his life. Yet it is not obvious how philosophical investigation improves the condition of the soul—still less how the Socratic method in particular does so, consisting as it does in testing the consistency of a person's beliefs through a series of questions, which Socrates asks.

I believe, and will show here, that the allegory of the Cave is part of Plato's effort to make philosophical sense of Socrates' philosophical life, to link Socrates' persistent questioning to his unwavering aim at what he called the "care of the soul." On this theme of care of the soul, there is a deep resonance between *The Matrix* and Plato's thought in the *Republic*. Like the allegory of the Cave, *The Matrix* dramatically conveys the view that ordinary appearances do not depict true reality and that gaining the truth changes one's life. Neo's movements toward greater understanding nicely parallel the movements of the prisoner in the cave whose bonds are loosened. The surface similarities between the film and the allegory can run to a long catalog. The first paragraph of this chapter reveals some of these connections. But there remains a deeper affinity between the two that I shall draw out here, especially in section IV, having to do with Socrates' notion of the care of the soul.

To see what I am calling a deeper connection between the film and the allegory of the Cave, I begin in section II by recounting the context in which the Cave appears and the philosophical positions it figuratively depicts.[2] In section III, I compare and contrast the film and the allegory, focusing attention on the difficulty in sorting out deceptive sensory information. Finally, in section IV, I examine the warnings and concessions Plato places in the dramatic spaces of the *Republic*. The allegory

2. Socrates (469–399 B.C.E.) is often regarded as the father of Western philosophy and Plato's teacher. Both are misleading. Socrates was not the first philosophical thinker, even in his home of Athens. And he did not have students in any ordinary sense, nor did he ever write anything down. Nevertheless, Socrates fascinated the young Plato and many others who became his associates, and several would later write dialogues featuring Socrates. Also, for centuries, almost every philosophical school in antiquity looked to Socrates for inspiration or claimed him as a forerunner.

of the Cave is a strange image, as one of Socrates' friends says (515a4), while Socrates himself confesses that the allegory is imprecise (504b5; see also 435c9–d2).[3] Rereading the Cave allegory after a recent viewing of the film shows that these are not throwaway remarks. *The Matrix* likewise privileges the work that strangeness and calculated vagueness do; Morpheus, after all, cannot show Neo what he most needs to see, but must get him to see for himself something that is difficult to recognize. In this way, *The Matrix* and Plato's Cave are faithful to a central tenet in Socrates' philosophical examinations: that proper teaching only occurs when students are prepared to make discoveries for themselves. Furthermore, the discovery that is most crucial is the discovery of oneself. Readiness for self-examination is, after all, what makes care of the soul possible.

Plato's dialogues, composed in the decades after Socrates' death, are more or less realistic accounts of Socrates' activities and conversations. But are they truthful accounts of the philosophical views of Socrates? While some have claimed that Plato's earliest writings achieved historical accuracy, fewer scholars make this claim today. The "Socratic problem," as it is called—whether Plato's presentation contains historical fact, and to what degree—is difficult because our non-Platonic source material is sufficient only to suggest a general outline of the historical Socrates' outlook. For this reason, the Socrates in this chapter is the character presented by Plato. (See "Further Reading" at the end of the chapter to learn more about Plato's Socrates.)

A final methodological note is in order. I refer to the philosophical positions advocated by the character Socrates as Plato's, though this scholarly convention is under attack in some quarters. Plato never appears in the *Republic* or any other dialogue (save for the *Apology*, and he does not speak there). Thus, some scholars find it presumptuous to fob off the character Socrates' views onto Plato: would we automatically assume that Ian Fleming took his martini shaken, not stirred, in the manner of his fictional agent? Of course, more is at stake in the first case than getting a drink order wrong, but this is true largely because other assumptions normally accompany the identification of Socrates' utterances with Plato's considered philosophical views. One worry is that this identification narrows the range of answers we might give to the question of why Plato wrote dialogues. Another worry is that it may distort our understanding of what Plato took an adequate philosophical theory to be.

3. Contemporary readers generally agree with Socrates. Some refer to "the treacherous analogies and parables" (John Cooper, "The Psychology of Justice in Plato," *American Philosophical Quarterly* 14 [1997]: 151–157. Reprinted in *Reason and Emotion: Essays on Ancient Moral Psychology and Ethical Theory* [Princeton: Princeton University Press, 1999], 138–149; references are to this version) as "over-ambitious" and "overloaded" (Annas [1981], 265; also see 252, 256). Much ink has been expended in the effort to provide a consistent, plausible philosophical interpretation of the images in the *Republic.*

II. Plato's Cave

If Plato's *Republic* has a single unifying theme, it is to show that the life of the just person is intrinsically preferable to any other life. In order to prove this, Socrates is made to investigate the concept of "justice." After an elaborate effort that spans three of the ten books of the *Republic*, Socrates and his two interlocutors agree on the meaning of justice. Justice is shown to be a property of a soul in which its three parts do their proper work and each refrains from doing the job of another part. Because the soul has distinct parts (reason, spiritedness, and appetite), being "just" requires that these parts are not only working well but also working well together. In a just person's soul, reason rules spiritedness and appetite. Only under the rule of reason is the soul's harmonious arrangement secured and preserved. Plato glosses this idea memorably by calling such a soul "healthy." Just persons have psychic health; their personalities are integrated in the proper way. Such persons will be fully flourishing and best able to choose wisely among different courses of action and ways of life. By contrast, unjust persons have souls whose parts do not operate properly. Such souls find themselves ruled by a part of the soul that ought to obey the rule of reason. Unjust souls are discordant, poorly integrated, at war with themselves—in a word, unhealthy. It is never in our interest to choose this condition for our souls. To do so is analogous to preferring disease to health.

At the end of book 4, there is one main gap in the argument: what is the precise role of reason, the "best part of the soul" mentioned in the passage above? There is little to go on at this stage. We know only that the soul in which reason does its job well is called "wise," and wisdom is a special kind of knowledge: knowledge of the good. How are we to arrive at this knowledge? What is it like to possess it? What sort of thing is the "good"? The allegory of the Cave speaks to these questions.[4]

---

4. I say "speaks to" because the Cave is only part of a generally sketchy account of the nature of the good. Socrates disclaims precision, warning us that his talk about the good is schematic (504d6–8) and fuzzy (see 504d8–e3), a shortcut to the truth of things (see 504b1–4, 435d2). Given his lack of knowledge about the good (505a4–6, 506c2–3, d6–8), the most Socrates can do is provide stories, not reasoned accounts. This, at least, is the stated rationale for why he gives "the child and offspring of the good" (507a3–4) rather than a fully articulated, rationally defensible account.

In order to impress upon us the importance of these questions, book 7 of the *Republic* begins with a startling image of our ignorance. It is the allegory of the Cave:

> Imagine human beings living in an underground, cavelike dwelling, with an entrance a long way up, which is both open to the light and as wide as the cave itself. They've been there since childhood, fixed in the same place, with their necks and legs fettered, able to see only in front of them, because their bonds prevent them from turning their heads around. Light is provided by a fire burning far above and behind them. Also behind them, but on higher ground, there is a path stretching between them and the fire. Imagine that along this path a low wall has been built, like the screen in front of puppeteers above which they show their puppets.... Then also imagine that there are people along the wall, carrying all kinds of artifacts that project above it—statues of people and other animals, made out of stone, wood, and every material. And, as you'd expect, some of the carriers are talking, and some are silent. (514a1–515a3)

Many contemporary readers recoil at the awful politics of the Cave. Who, after all, are the "puppeteers"? Why do they deceive their fellow cave-dwellers? Plato has so little to say about them that readers quickly imagine their own worst fears. Some mid- and late twentieth-century readers regarded a totalitarian government or the mass media to be obvious parallels to the puppeteers who move freely within the cave. But this gets the principal aim of the Cave wrong, I believe, since it deflects attention away from the prisoners bound to the posts. "They are us," Socrates says, and this is what is truly sinister: an imprisonment that we do not recognize because we are our own prison keepers. Let us turn to examine these prisoners and their imprisonment, specifically by

---

Socrates' disavowal of knowledge does not mean that he is completely ignorant. Most obviously, he knows enough to know that he does not know. He also knows that knowledge of the good is important to have (505a6–b4) and what method must be used to get it: dialectic (532a1–d1). Moreover, he provides a formal account of the good, saying it is the chief or ultimate end to all of our actions (cf.: "Every soul pursues the good and does whatever it does for its sake" 505d11–e1). And with this premise, he rules out rival attempts to spell out the formal account, arguing against pleasure and knowledge as candidates for a substantive account of goodness itself (505b5–d1). Finally, he seems capable of saying *more* than he says here, though we cannot be sure that he takes himself to be able to give something *more secure* than images and other "offspring" (see 506e1–3).

examining the philosophical stakes of their ignorance. Only then will we see exactly why ignorance is likened to imprisonment and alienation.

In the cave, the prisoners can distinguish the different shadows and sounds (516c8–9; see also e8–9), apply names to the shadows depicting things (see 515b4–5), and even discern the patterns in their presentation (516c9–10). To this extent, they have some true beliefs. But insofar as they believe that this two-dimensional, monochromatic play of images—and the echoes reverberating in the cave—is the whole of reality (515c1–2), they are mistaken. Moreover, the opinions they have do not explain why the shapes they see are as they are. They do not know the source of the shadows, nor do they know that the sounds are not produced by the shadows but rather by the unseen people moving the statues (515b7–9).

The possession of a few, small-scale true beliefs characterizes the condition of all of us, Plato believes. We can distinguish different things, but we lack a systematic, causal explanation of them. To put it loosely, we have, at best, assorted true beliefs about the *what* of things, but a mistaken hold (if any) on the *why* of things. Socrates' search for the definition of justice here, like his search for definitions in other Platonic dialogues, looks like an effort to get at these explanations, to grasp why things are the way they are and, perhaps further, what underlying relationship they have to one another. His questions are part of a search for the essence of things, or what he calls their "form."[5] For Plato, when we possess knowledge of the form of a thing, we can give a comprehensive account of its essence. Without grasp of the form, we can have at best only true beliefs.

A simple example should show what difference it makes to have knowledge of forms.[6] Suppose someone in the cave carries a chair in front of the fire. The bound prisoners see the chair's shadow on the cave wall, and

5. See 507b5–7. The essence of good things is called sometimes the good-itself (506d8–e1, 507b5) and sometimes the form of the good (505a2, 508e2–3). This item is really what reason is attempting to grasp: not what is good for me, nor what is "a good x," but something that is good in and of itself.

6. It is notoriously difficult to count the population of forms, and we cannot be certain that Plato thought there was a form of chair. Reeve's comment (on whether there is a form in the intelligible world for every group of things in the sensible world to which a single name applies) is useful for the general question of how many or what sort of forms there are: "Assumptions are one thing; truths are another. Thus forms are assumed

some of them remark, "There is a chair." They are partially correct. If they broke their bonds, they could turn to see the actual chair. In this case, their cognitive grip on the chair would be more complete. They would be able to recognize that the shadow was less real than the chair and that the chair is the cause of the shadow. Ultimately, the physically real chair is explained in terms of its representation of the form of chair. After all, to have genuine knowledge of a thing, it is necessary for our intellects to grasp its form. One might think of the difference this way: a shadow is better grasped when the object casting it is seen. Plato would wish us to see that, in a sense, ordinary objects are like mere shadows of forms. Thus, to grasp objects as fully as possible, one must attain a grasp of their forms.

There is a curious complication on the horizon that I shall point out here. It turns out that knowing the form of a thing is not sufficient for gaining a final understanding of that thing. Even to know fully the form of chair, Plato holds, one must know the form of the good.

This does not make sense at first. Recall that the form of the good is what reason ought, ideally, to know, for in knowing it you become wise. Furthermore, knowing the form of the good contributes to your being a just person, since one part of you, reason, is doing its job (and this is what it means for you to be just). Now Plato suggests that grasping the form of the good, or the good-itself (the terms are interchangeable; see note 5), is necessary for attaining the best intellectual grasp of *anything* that our intellects can know. The distinctive importance of the form of the good is indicated by two images that immediately precede the Cave: the Sun and the Line, and I will consider them now.

The Sun analogy (507a ff.) reveals the special epistemological role played by the good-itself. Just as the natural world depends upon the sun (for warmth and light), so too the intelligible world depends on

---

with ontological abandon, but the only ones there really are are those needed by dia-lectical-thought for its explanatory and reconstructive purposes. Ordinary language is the first word here, but it is not by any means the last word" (1988, 294). Will there be a last word? According to one commentator writing at the beginning of the last century, even what Plato meant by the forms "is a question which has been, and in my opinion will always be, much debated" (James Adam, ed., *The Republic of Plato*, vol. 2 [Cambridge: Cambridge University Press, 1902], 169).

the good-itself (508b13–c2).[7] This is the force of the light metaphor. The sun, as Plato puts it, gives the power to see to seers, while the form of the good gives the power to know to knowers (508e1–3). In our example of the chair, it is only in virtue of the light produced by the fire above and behind the prisoners that the chair and its shadow are visible. The fire, then, is a condition for our acquiring a more complete true belief about the shadow. But the fire is nothing more than a "source of light that is itself a shadow in relation to the sun" (532c2–3). Out of the cave, the sun represents the good-itself. The good-itself illuminates the true, intelligible world of ultimate reality, and in this way, the form of chair relies on the form of the good for its intelligibility. The good-itself is the most preeminent item in the universe. It is both an object of knowledge and the condition of fully knowing other objects of knowledge.

Plato is not finished with his specification of the role played by the form of the good. He goes on to suggest that the good-itself nourishes the being of intelligible things in a way analogous to the sun nourishing organic life. For this unusual idea we have some help from the Line image (509d ff.), the most obscure of the three images. Imagine a vertical line dividing two realms—physical reality and intelligible reality—into unequal spaces. Each realm is then subdivided in the same uneven proportion as that which separates the physical and intelligible world. To take only the smaller, bottom portion of the line, we find the physical realm divided between actual, physically existing items and their ephemeral copies (e.g., reflections in water, shadows, and artistic depictions). In the Cave, this is the distinction made between the chair and its shadow. The Line indicates that there are different cognitive states corresponding to the different levels on the line. In this way, the Line presses us to think that our perceptions of physically real objects are more secure than our perceptions of reflections and images.

The Line also offers a ranked order of Plato's ontology according to which the degree of reality and being of a particular class of things increases

---

7. The *intelligible world* is Plato's way of referring to the class of things that can be known by the mind alone and that are imperceptible to the senses. A list would include mathematical or logical truths and geometrical items, as well as the vaunted forms. (The types of study that yield knowledge of items in or aspects of the intelligible world are mentioned in note 1.)

as you go up the line. The higher up the scale, the more real the items are, and since the form of the good is the most real item in all of reality, it is located at the very top of the Line, just above the forms. Things lower on the line are derivative and owe whatever reality or being that they have to the things above them. Physical objects are, metaphorically, nourished by their corresponding forms. They depend for their very reality, not just their knowability, on the perfect, eternal forms existing in the intelligible realm.

One clear implication of the Line is the metaphor of ascent. The Cave exploits it as well: the upward escape from the cave represents the difficulty of gaining ever-more-abstract knowledge while not relying on information gathered by the senses. By connecting the three images together, we discover that the human condition is abject: we see imperfectly only the most downgraded forms of reality (image, shadows) and are as far from the sun (the good-itself) as we can be. This is what it is to be ignorant of the truth.

But to see why our alienation from what is genuinely good makes a difference in our lives, there is one more feature of the good-itself that deserves attention. Whatever exactly the form of the good is, it serves as a paradigm or model, and it has a remarkable effect on those who grasp it. As Socrates says of fully educated philosophers near the end of book 7, "[O]nce they've seen the good-itself, they must each in turn put the city, its citizens, and themselves in order, using it as their model [*paradeigmati*]" (540a8–b1). This was anticipated in a longer passage in which the philosopher, by means of studying the "things that are" (500b9), acts as a craftsman (see 500d6), or a "painter using a divine model [*paradeigmati*]" (500e3–4). Not only do physical things take on the qualities they have through a process of copying, reflecting, or imitating the forms, so too we can take on goodness through intellectual contact with the good-itself.[8] By coming to understand the good-itself, we become like it. In short, we become good.

We can see now why being just depends on knowing the form of the good. Reason's rule affords the soul the opportunity to study and therein

8. "Instead, as he looks at and studies things that are organized and always the same, that neither do injustice to one another nor suffer it, being all in rational order, he imitates them and tries to become as like them as he can. Or do you think that someone can consort with things he admires without imitating them? . . . Then the philosopher, by consorting with what is ordered and divine . . . himself becomes as divine and ordered as a human being can" (500c2–7, c9–d2).

to become like the good-itself, that is, properly proportioned, well ordered, healthy. Finally, once this knowledge is acquired, and the self is transformed, one becomes productive.[9] Those who gain knowledge of the good-itself are capable of crafting virtues in their souls and in the souls of others, and they can paint divine constitutions for cities. This is what enables Plato to put words into Socrates' mouth that, were he on Aristophanes' stage, would have returned thunderous laughter:

> Until philosophers rule as kings or those who are now called kings and leading men genuinely and adequately philosophize, that is, until political power and philosophy entirely coincide . . . cities will have no rest from evils, Glaucon, nor, I think, will the human race. (473c11–d6)

III. *The Matrix* and Plato's Cave

There are no forms in *The Matrix*, and thus our epistemic and metaphysical circumstances in Plato's *Republic* look very different from those in the film. The world inside the cave is a diminished one, a shadow or reflection of the real, but broadly continuous with the true world. Even though there is a marked difference between the sensible and intelligible realms—with respect to method, epistemic certainty, and metaphysical reality—on Plato's view the sensible is somehow derived from the intelligible. Thus, for Plato, our speaking and thinking in the cave are not meaningless, and some of our opinions are true, in spite of our ignorance of the deeper causes of things.

In *The Matrix*, by contrast, the two worlds are far less continuous with one another. The real world is profoundly dystopian, and the substance of

---

To some listeners, this kind of talk encourages mysticism, or the view that the good-itself has occult qualities. But we do well to remind ourselves that dialectic is the only route to grasping the good-itself, and that dialectic is studied only after ten years of mathematics, geometry, astronomy, and the like (537b–c). Indeed, Cooper has argued that we think of the good-itself "somehow or other as a perfect example of rational order, conceived in explicitly mathematical terms" ([1977], 144; see also Kraut [1992]). Again, it is intellectual grasp—not oneness with or absorption into the good—that we are striving to attain.

9. Plato's *Symposium* famously stresses the fertility of the philosopher who has grasped the forms (212a–b).

the lives inside the Matrix is supplied in mental states almost entirely cut off from this reality. (Ironically, the real world in *The Matrix* is very like the world inside the cave.) In spite of its realism, the world inside the Matrix is not a copy of the real world but is a simulation. Nevertheless, there is at least one continuity between the real world and the computer-simulated world: your body. Owing to an unexplained principle, called "residual self-image," your body looks the same to you and to others in both worlds. And you are able to retain your memories of one world when you are in the other and when you return back to the first. (This means that Cypher will have to have his memories of the time spent outside the Matrix removed if he is to return to the illusion of reality inside the Matrix.)

Since the real world and the simulated world are worlds in which the senses receive information, the practical problem is not that they are discontinuous, but that they are indiscernible. This is part of the initial difficulty for Neo since he cannot determine which sensory information is genuine and which false. Although he (and the viewer) settles this question soon enough, a skeptical worry remains in the wake: how can he ever be sure his sensory information is truthful if there is no certificate of authenticity on his experiences?

Suppose Agent Smith creates a program that launches right when Neo picks up a phone within the Matrix. Instead of being whisked back aboard the ship, Neo's consciousness is supplied with a computer-generated experience of the interior of the *Nebuchadnezzar*, and of course he believes he has successfully exited the Matrix. Such a trick might enable Agent Smith to obtain compromising information about the *Nebuchadnezzar* and its crew or, worse, the passwords for Zion.

It is hard to imagine how Neo might see past Agent Smith's ruse, especially if he only had a few moments to figure things out. Would Plato's freed prisoner fare better? Recall, Plato urges us to regard the sensible world as unreliable, no matter the source of our information about it.[10] We must adopt a different method for apprehending the truth of things. This is, of

---

10. For this reason, Plato might appreciate the irony of Morpheus stressing, again and again, that Neo must see for himself in order to understand. Plato would regard Neo's transformed conception of reality to be partial at best since Neo is not called upon to regard all sense impressions as false or diminished, only those that have the wrong source.

course, not nearly as simple as it sounds, nor is it obviously helpful; after all, what we are to grasp is the intelligible world from which our ordinary, sensible world is copied, not the sensible world itself. The reward is that, once you grasp the forms in the intelligible world, you would be an expert in discriminating items in the sensible world (see 520c1–6). This doesn't mean you'd never be mistaken, however; rather, you would simply be the best sensible-world discriminator there could be. Since the ordinary world is too murky and ever-changing to permit genuine knowledge of it, our awareness of this mutability may assist us in determining which of our beliefs are relatively more reliable. In the case where Agent Smith launches his deceptive program, the only advantage the freed prisoner might have is slight: a general unease about all sensory information.

In the end, the metaphysical differences between Plato and *The Matrix* do not prevent them from telling a roughly similar story about the epistemological unreliability of the senses and the need to abstract from the senses in order to gain genuine knowledge. Where Plato's dialogue and *The Matrix* agree most, though, is in drawing out the enormous psychological difficulty in calling the world into question and the ethical dimensions of failing to do so. Neo and Plato's freed prisoner must accept truths about themselves before they can acquire deeper knowledge about fundamental truths. To achieve this, both Neo and the freed prisoner need the shocking demonstration that the senses are inadequate and that they can be systematically deceived. Both must then undertake an introspective turn to discover the truth and must take steps to disregard knowledge derived from the senses.

This is the point to ask, finally: what knowledge does Neo attain that operates in him like the knowledge of the Platonic form of the good? What does Neo know only after great difficulty but whose truth is fundamental? What object is grasped by Neo's intellect that he understands to be the condition of his knowing anything else? What knowledge enables him to be productive, to be a savior of himself and others? It is nothing more than proper self-understanding. In both *The Matrix* and in the Cave, there is a single item the knowledge of which makes the knower more integrated and more powerful, and for Neo it is self-knowledge.

Ought we to see Neo as adhering to the letter of Socratic self-examination and care of the soul? Only from a high altitude will a perfect connection be visible. For Neo's enlightenment is ultimately about his own specific path and role. Socratic care of the soul involves self-knowledge, but the parts of yourself that are peculiar to you, that make up your individuality, are not relevant.[11] Since the prisoners in the cave have only dim self-awareness (they see only the shadows of themselves [515a5–8]), it might seem that release involves getting the right beliefs about oneself. But the abstractness of the knowledge that Plato prizes, which is unlike the specificity of the knowledge that Neo eventually gets (namely, that he is The One), suggests that the self-knowledge that the prisoners need is neither the end of their search nor even the proper beginning.

In other dialogues, Socrates was made to endorse the idea that knowledge was in you, that a kind of introspection aided by proper questioning could elicit true beliefs. But these are not truths that are *about* you; rather, they are truths that are *in* you. Neo's case is different. The truths he must grasp are both in him and about him. The film reveals furthermore that he must demonstrate and experience his capabilities before he is able to believe entirely that he possesses them. And when he believes in himself at last, his capabilities are further enhanced. *This* result is produced neither by the method nor the aim of Socratic care of the soul.

Most fundamentally, the film and the allegory share a pedagogical conceit. Both hold that in teaching the most basic truths, there is an important role for a strategic strangeness and the confusion it produces. The allegory of the Cave puzzles Socrates' audience, yet as it hooks them, the cave provides only the outline for solving the puzzle. Might Morpheus be doing the same? Might Morpheus, like the allegory, act as a kind of Socratic teacher, urging Neo toward self-understanding and care for his soul?

IV. Socratic Education in the Cave and *The Matrix*

To see to what extent this is so, I want now to return to a remark by Socrates' friend Glaucon that the cave and its prisoners are "strange" (*atopon . . . atopous* [515a4]). The remark is important because it indicates that the image is operating on its audience in a particular way, one that Plato elsewhere gives us

---

11. Annas (1981), 257–59, makes this point when she compares Plato's allegory to Bernardo Bertolucci's 1970 film, *The Conformist*.

reason to believe is significant. Prompting someone to recognize strangeness, something's being "out of place" (*atopia*), is one way that the Socratic method achieves its aims. It can occur when Socrates asks one of his deceptively simple questions or pursues an unusual line of argument, though it can also occur when he refrains from saying something or when he professes ignorance. Whatever the case, Socrates' method aims not only at the discovery of the truth but at making others care that the truth be discovered. We might say that the allegory of the Cave is doing this as well. Coming on the heels of the abstract images of the Sun and the Line, the Cave piques Glaucon's curiosity. Of course, Socrates is quick to make this more than an idle curiosity by telling Glaucon that we all are strange prisoners in a strange prison.

If the allegory is something like a Socratic teacher—designed to act on Plato's readers like Socrates' questions act on his interlocutors—then no less significant than the jarring identification of us with the prisoners, I would argue, are the silences and gaps in the allegory. Recall that though Plato's allegory of the Cave describes what our ignorance is like and what it would be like to become educated, it says little about the prisoners who move freely within the cave. Who they are and why they are carrying the artifacts remain mysterious. Another puzzling silence is about what starts the process of becoming educated. In the allegory, a prisoner's chains are removed, but Socrates doesn't say who or what removes them. Here are his words:

> Consider, then, what being released from their bonds and cured of their ignorance would naturally be like. When one of them was freed and suddenly compelled to stand up, turn his head, walk, and look up toward the light, he'd be pained and dazzled and unable to see the things whose shadows he'd seen before. (515c4–d1)

The Cave depicts an astonishingly thorough imprisonment. And Plato remarks on the difficulties that the freed prisoner meets with on the way out of the cave. Given this detail, it is not unreasonable to expect an account of precisely what sort of prisoner it is who begins to question whether the cave contains the whole of reality, or precisely what circumstance prompts his inquiry. Does the prisoner find the play of shadows internally inconsistent? Or does one or more of the unbound prisoners decide to remove the bonds? We are not told.

On one hand, the imprisonment is metaphorical, as is the release. Pressing for specific details is surely to demand too much of the image. But suppose there is a philosophical point to be made by the absence of certain details, the refusal to answer particular questions. We might then say that by refusing to say precisely how *this* prisoner is freed, Plato retains the openness of his allegory. After all, the freed prisoner is referred to generically by the indefinite pronoun "someone" (*tis*); if we wish for specifics, we miss the generality that Plato intends, for his point surely is that *anyone* could escape the bonds of ignorance. In this way, the allegory invites its readers to see themselves as prisoners who possess the ability to free themselves.

What are we to say about *The Matrix*? On the surface, it appears that *The Matrix* departs from the allegory. First of all, it answers some of the questions we had about the allegory: it is Morpheus and the others who free Neo, and Morpheus chooses to free him because there is something particular about Neo that recommends his release. Yet, on closer inspection, Neo's early encounters with Morpheus produce the same kind of confusion that Socrates produces in his interlocutors, that is, confusion about the truth of deeply held beliefs. Neo receives strange communications via computer ("wake up, Neo")[12] to follow the white rabbit he soon sees on a tattooed shoulder. These odd messages disrupt Neo's expectations of the world, especially his need for control over his life and his facility with computers. Another disruption comes when Neo swallows the red pill. This drug quickly begins to alter his perception of the stability of the world inside the Matrix.[13] Taken together, the computer messages uncannily anticipate what is about to happen, while the pill calls into question his grasp of what is now happening. This is one way to prepare Neo to accept the truth that everything that has happened so far in his life is an illusion.

If we suppose that Morpheus asks the right questions, and supplies the right drugs, it is still the case that Neo has to recognize the questions and accept the

---

12. The film surely intends us to read the figurative sense of this expression alongside the literal one, and it may be Morpheus's hope that Neo reflect on the figurative meaning as well. After all, one of the other messages that appears on his screen—"knock, knock, Neo"—is deliberately riddling. It invites the question, "Who's there?"

13. Although the aim of the pill is to assist in locating Neo's body, the suggestion of a psychoactive effect on him is unmistakable.

drugs. Neo proves to be a particularly apt pupil. Indeed, there are features of Neo's life that might explain how he begins to see the falsity of the world inside the Matrix. Neo is an accomplished hacker who would have the best chance of anyone to discover that the whole of his experience is itself nothing more than highly sophisticated computer code. He is also living a double life. He works as a software engineer perhaps to maintain a steady income, perhaps as a cover for his underground activities. Maybe playing the role of an office worker affords him a sense of the absurd that makes it easier to believe that his life is hollow. Insomnia might work for this purpose as well. Besides, who hasn't had the gut feeling Neo has that "not all is right with the world"?

Of course, one of the themes of the film is Neo's struggle to accept his role as The One, the savior of humanity. He is the subject of a number of prophecies made by the Oracle.[14] In fact, he is the only person we know whose prophecy does not refer to specific persons other than himself. He only accepts his true nature well after the series of strange clues Morpheus presents to him and the confusion this produces in him. Ultimately, he must experience firsthand his fitness for the special role that the others urge him to perform.

In spite of these dissimilarities, Morpheus can be seen as a Socratic gadfly, stinging Neo to take the first steps he needs in order to discover the truth on his own. Similarly, Plato's sketch of the role played by the form of the good only points the way to the complete answer that Plato would have us seek out. The allegory draws readers to think for themselves in the same way that Socrates wishes his interlocutors to feel the sting of the realization of their ignorance as a motivation to join him in inquiry and care of the soul. For the allegory of the Cave issues a pointed challenge: in what way are we living lives of diminished prospect, resting content with our knowledge, failing even to ask the right questions? These

14. The Oracle eventually tells Neo "what he needed to hear," namely, that he is not The One. This inverts the account of Socrates' oracle as Plato portrays it in the *Apology*. First, Socrates does not hear the oracle directly but relies on Chaerephon's report that "no one is wiser than Socrates." Second, Neo's reluctance to believe that he is not in control of his actions requires that the Oracle tell him something false. This, Neo is happy to hear, and thus he has no motive for questioning it; it is eminently believable that he is not their long-awaited savior. By contrast, Socrates' oracle tells him something true but whose unlikely implications must be carefully interpreted through testing and questioning.

are precisely the questions Morpheus puts to Neo. And like Morpheus, Plato's pessimism about the human condition gives way to an optimistic view of the power of education to liberate anyone:

> Education isn't what some people declare it to be, namely, putting knowledge into souls that lack it, like putting sight into blind eyes.... Education takes for granted that sight is there but that it isn't turned the right way or where it ought to look, and it tries to redirect it appropriately. (518b7–c2, d5–7)

Further Reading

An excellent translation of Plato's *Republic* is referred to as the Grube/Reeve: Plato, *Republic*, 2d ed., trans. G. M. E. Grube and rev. C. D. C. Reeve (Indianapolis, IN: Hackett, 1992), which may be found in the definitive single-volume collection of Plato's dialogues edited by John M. Cooper, *Plato: Complete Works* (Indianapolis, IN: Hackett, 1997). Robin Waterfield's translation of Plato's *Republic* (New York: Oxford University Press, 1993) has a long introduction and helpful bibliography. The Web site http://plato.evansville.edu is a decent online resource for beginners; more ambitious students, however, will prefer http://www.perseus.tufts.edu.

To learn more about Socrates' life and method, as Plato saw both, one should start with the *Apology*. Other sources of information include *Phaedo* 96a–100b and 114d–end, *Meno* 80a–86c, *Theaetetus* 149a–151d, and *Symposium* 215a–222c (all in Cooper 1997). For a study of the philosophy of Plato's Socrates, see Thomas C. Brickhouse and Nicholas D. Smith, *The Philosophy of Socrates* (Boulder, CO: Westview, 2000).

After reading the *Republic*, one might turn to two collections of essays edited by Richard Kraut: *Plato's Republic: Critical Essays* (Lanham, MD: Rowman and Littlefield, 1997) and *The Cambridge Companion to Plato* (Cambridge: Cambridge University Press, 1992). Book-length studies include Julia Annas, *An Introduction to Plato's Republic* (Oxford: Clarendon, 1981), and C. D. C. Reeve, *Philosopher-Kings: The Argument of Plato's Republic* (Princeton, NJ: Princeton University Press, 1988). *The Stanford Encyclopedia of Philosophy* (http://plato.stanford.edu) contains two outstanding treatments of Plato that are helpful to readers of the *Republic*. Eric Brown's

"Plato's Ethics and Politics in *The Republic*" (http://plato.stanford.edu/entries/plato-ethics-politics) and Allan Silverman's "Plato's Middle Period Metaphysics and Epistemology" (http://plato.stanford.edu/entries/plato-metaphysics) are recent accounts that hold out the promise of remaining up to date.

I would like to thank Stephen Miller and Christopher Grau for comments on an earlier draft of this chapter.

15 Rachel Wagner and Frances Flannery-Dailey

WAKE UP! WORLDS OF ILLUSION
IN GNOSTICISM, BUDDHISM,
AND *THE MATRIX* PROJECT

In the first film of *The Matrix* series, a black-clad computer hacker known as Neo falls asleep in front of his computer. A mysterious message appears on the screen: "Wake up, Neo" (*Matrix*).[1] This succinct phrase encapsulates the plot of the film and its sequels, as Neo struggles with the problem of being imprisoned in a "material" world that is actually a computer simulation program created in the distant future by artificial intelligence (AI) as a means of enslaving humanity by perpetuating ignorance in the form of an illusory perception called "the Matrix." The films in the *Matrix* trilogy, as well as the accompanying *Animatrix* shorts and *Enter the Matrix* game, craft their ultimate view of reality in part by alluding to numerous religious traditions. Two specific religious traditions on which the films draw heavily are Gnostic Christianity and Buddhism.[2] Although different in important ways, they agree that the fundamental problem facing humanity is ignorance, teaching that this problem can be solved through an individual's reorientation of perspective

1. We henceforth refer to *The Matrix* (Warner Bros., 1999), *Matrix Reloaded* (Warner Bros., 2003), *Matrix Revolutions* (Warner Bros., 2003), *The Animatrix* (Warner Bros., 2003), and the video game *Enter the Matrix* (Warner Bros., 2003), respectively, as *Matrix*, *Reloaded*, *Revolutions*, *Animatrix*, and *Enter the Matrix*.

2. The authors wish to iterate strongly that Buddhism and Gnosticism are only two of the numerous religious and philosophical traditions integrated into the *Matrix* films. See Frances Flannery-Dailey and Rachel L. Wagner, "Stopping Bullets: Constructions of Bliss and Problems of Violence," in *Jacking in to the Matrix Franchise*, ed. M. Kapell and W. G. Doty (New York: Continuum, 2004), 97–114. For an early misreading of this point of our thesis, see Julien R. Fielding, "Reassessing *The Matrix/Reloaded*," *Journal of Religion and Film* 7, no. 2, available at www.avalon.unomaha.edu/jrf.

concerning the material realm.[3] Gnostic Christianity and Buddhism also both envision a guide, a Gnostic redeemer figure or a *bodhisattva*, who willingly enters the limiting material world of illusion in order to share liberating knowledge, facilitating escape for anyone able to understand. In the trilogy, this figure is Neo, whose name is an anagram for The One.[4]

Although as a "modern myth"[5] the films purposefully draw on numerous traditions,[6] we propose that an examination of Gnostic Christianity and Buddhism greatly illuminates the overarching paradigm of *The Matrix* series as a whole, namely, the problem of sleeping in ignorance in a dream world, which is solved by awakening to knowledge or enlightenment. By drawing syncretistically on these two traditions and fusing them with a technological vision of the future, the films construct a new teaching that challenges its audience to question "reality."

3. In an online chat with viewers of the first movie, the Wachowskis acknowledged that the Buddhist references in the film are purposeful. However, when asked, "Have you ever been told that *The Matrix* has Gnostic overtones?" they offered a tantalizingly ambiguous reply: "Do you consider that to be a good thing?" From the Nov. 6, 1999, "Matrix Virtual Theatre," at "Wachowski chat," www.warnervideo.com/matrixevents/wachowski. html.

4. Elaine Pagels notes that the similarities between Gnosticism and Buddhism have prompted some scholars to question their interdependence and to wonder whether "if the names were changed, the 'living Buddha' appropriately could say what the *Gospel of Thomas* attributes to the living Jesus." Although intriguing, she rightly maintains that the evidence is inconclusive, since parallel traditions may emerge in different cultures without direct influence. Elaine Pagels, *The Gnostic Gospels* (New York: Random House, 1979, repr. 1989), xx–xxi.

5. James Ford has explored other Buddhist elements in *The Matrix*, which he calls a "modern myth," in his article "Buddhism, Christianity and *The Matrix*: The Dialectic of Myth-Making in Contemporary Cinema," *Journal of Religion and Film* 4, no. 2 (October 2000). See also Conrad Ostwalt's focus on apocalyptic elements of the film in "Armageddon at the Millennial Dawn," *Journal of Religion and Film* 4, no. 1 (April 2000).

6. A viewer asked the Wachowski brothers, "Your movie has many and varied connections to myths and philosophies, Judeo-Christian, Egyptian, Arthurian, and Platonic, just to name those I've noticed. How much of that was intentional?" They replied, "All of it" ("Wachowski chat").

Christian Elements in *The Matrix*

The majority of the audience watching the series easily recognizes the presence of some Christian elements, such as the name Trinity[7] or Neo's death and Christlike resurrection and ascension near the end of the first film. In fact, Christian and biblical allusions abound, particularly with respect to nomenclature:[8] Apoc (apocalypse); Neo's given name of Mr. Ander-son (from the Greek *andras* for "man," thus producing "son of man"); the ship named the *Nebuchadnezzar* (the Babylonian king who, in the Book of Daniel, has puzzling symbolic dreams that must be inter-preted);[9] another ship named the *Logos* (Greek for "word"; applied in John 1.1–18 to Christ); and the last remaining human city, Zion, synon-ymous in Judaism and Christianity with (the heavenly) Jerusalem.[10]

In many ways, Neo is overtly constructed as a Jesus figure in each of the films: he is The One who was prophesied to return again to the Matrix (*Matrix*), who has the power to work miracles within and outside of the Matrix, who has knowledge of the future (e.g., of Trinity's death in *Reloaded*) and of matters beyond normal human ken (e.g., of the presence of agents in *Reloaded* and *Revolutions*), who is killed but is resurrected (*Matrix*), and who is transformed into light both within

7. Feminist critics may rejoice when Trinity first reveals her name to Neo, as he pointedly responds, "The Trinity? . . . Jesus, I thought you were a man." Her quick reply: "Most men do" (*Matrix*).

8. The Wachowski brothers indicated that the names were "all chosen carefully, and all of them have multiple meanings," and noted that this applies to the numbers as well ("Wachowski chat").

9. In an interview for *Time*, the Wachowskis refer to Nebuchadnezzar in this Danielic context ("Popular Metaphysics," by Richard Corliss, *Time*, April 19, 1999, vol. 153, no. 15). Nebuchadnezzar is also the Babylonian king who destroyed the Jerusalem temple in 586 B.C.E. and who exiled the elite of Judean society to Babylon. Did the Wachowski brothers also intend the reference to point to the crew's "exile" from Zion or from the surface world?

10. The film also suggests that Zion is heaven, as when Tank says, "If the war was over tomorrow, Zion is where the party would be," evoking the traditional Christian schema of an apocalypse followed by life in heaven or paradise. In *Reloaded*, the brilliantly lit controllers' room, filled with white-clad figures, reinforces the conception that Zion is in some senses a heaven. Ironically, the film locates Zion "underground, near the earth's core, where it is still warm," which would seem to be cinematic code for hell, another possible clue that Zion is not the "heaven," or transcendent level of reality that viewers are led to presume.

(*Matrix*) and eventually outside of the Matrix (*Revolutions*), his face shining like "the sun," much like Jesus' face during his transfiguration (see Matthew 17:1–9; cf. Mark 9:2, Luke 9:28).

In addition to alluding to important aspects of the gospel story, there are also more subtle filmic allusions that reinforce Neo's portrayal as a Jesus figure. Within minutes of the commencement of the first film, another hacker says to Neo, "You're my savior, man, my own personal Jesus Christ."[11] This identification is also suggested by others who repeatedly swear in Neo's presence by saying "Jesus" or "Jesus Christ," particularly in the first film,[12] as well as by onlookers who wonder if he is the prophesied One who will save them. In a scene in *Reloaded* that is highly reminiscent of the Jesus in the Gospels, Neo is surrounded by a crowd in Zion that throngs around him with offerings, as some beseech him to protect their relatives (e.g., Mark 3:7, Luke 8:40–42).

Like Jesus, one of Neo's principle activities is battling the agents of evil. A clue to this occupation appears in the first film when Neo enters the *Nebuchadnezzar* and the camera pans across the interior of the ship, resting on the make "Mark III no. 11," a veiled reference to the messianic proclamation in the Gospel of Mark 3:11: "Whenever the unclean spirits saw him, they fell down before him and shouted, 'You are the Son of God!'" Like Jesus, Neo is an exorcist, casting out alien Agents inhabiting the residual self-images of those immersed in the Matrix. However, for most of the duration of the films he accomplishes these "exorcisms" of the Agents by killing those they inhabit, quite unlike the Jesus of the Gospels. By the beginning of the second film, the Agents, like the demons in Mark, clearly recognize the uniqueness of Neo vis-à-vis other humans. Hence, within this framework, the logic of the story inevitably results in Neo, the greatest force of good, battling the Satanic Agent Smith, the greatest force of evil, who by the third film takes the form of a computer

11. Neo's apartment number is 101, symbolizing both binary computer code (written in ones and zeros) and his role as The One. Near the end of the first film, 303 is the number of the apartment that he enters and exits in his death/resurrection scene, evoking the Trinity. This in turn raises questions about the character of Trinity's relationship to Neo in terms of her cinematic construction as divinity.

12. The traitor Cypher, who represents Judas Iscariot, among other figures, ironically says to Neo, "Man, you scared the bejeezus outta me."

virus infecting every inhabitant of the Matrix and spreading to "real" human bodies as well. Ultimately, it is Neo's Christlike self-sacrifice that saves both humans and machines from Smith, as Neo's body explodes into light while in a cruciform position in the Machine City (*Revolutions*). Thus, like Christ's crucifixion in the Gospels, Neo seems to defeat evil in its entirety through his (temporary) sacrificial death.[13]

Gnosticism in *The Matrix*

Although many Christian elements are evident within the films, the overall system of Christianity that is presented is not the traditional, orthodox one. Rather, the Christian elements of the film make the most sense when viewed through the lens of Gnostic Christianity.[14] Gnosticism is a religious system that flourished for centuries at the beginning of the common era, competing strongly with "orthodox" Christianity in many areas of the Mediterranean and in some locations representing the only viable interpretation of Christianity.[15] The Gnostics possessed their own Scriptures, accessible to us in the form of the Nag Hammadi Library, from which a

13. *Revolutions* concludes with the Oracle suggesting that Neo will return again, just as Christ's death was followed by his resurrection and as Neo's death within the Matrix was followed by a resurrection (*Matrix*). But if Neo and Smith are necessary opposites as the Oracle suggests earlier, Smith must return as well, particularly since he "dies" in much the same manner as in the first film, after which he gained strength.

14. We would especially like to thank Donna Bowman, with whom we initially explored the Gnostic elements of *The Matrix* during a public lecture on film at Hendrix College in 2000. For an exploration of anti-Gnostic elements and Pauline theology in the second film, see Bowman, "The Gnostic Illusion: Problematic Realized Eschatology in *The Matrix Reloaded,*" *Journal of Religion and Popular Culture* 4 (Summer 2003), available at www.usask.ca/relst/jrpc/articles4.html.

15. Gnosticism may have had its origins in Judaism, despite its denigration of the Israelite Creator God, but the issue is complex and still debated within scholarly circles. It is clear, however, that Gnostic Christianity flourished from at least the second through the fifth century C.E., with its own scriptures and most likely its own distinctive rituals, entrance requirements, and creation story. See Gershom Scholem, *Jewish Gnosticism, Merkabah Mysticism, and Talmudic Tradition* (New York: Jewish Theological Seminary of America, 1960); Elaine Pagels, *The Gnostic Gospels* (New York: Random House, 1979, repr. 1989); Bentley Layton, *The Gnostic Scriptures* (New York: Doubleday, 1995); and Kurt Rudolph, *Gnosis: The Nature and History of Gnosticism* (San Francisco: HarperSan-Francisco, 1987).

general sketch of Gnostic beliefs may be drawn.[16] Although ancient Gnostic Christianity comprised many varieties, Gnosticism as a whole seems to have embraced an orienting cosmogonic myth that explains the true nature of the universe and humankind's proper place in it.[17] A brief retelling of this myth illuminates numerous parallels with *The Matrix.*

In the Gnostic myth, the supreme God is completely perfect and therefore alien and mysterious, "ineffable," "unnameable," "immeasurable light which is pure, holy and immaculate" (Apocryphon of John). In addition to this God, there are other, lesser divine beings in the *pleroma* (akin to heaven, a division of the universe that is not earth), who possess some metaphorical gender of male or female.[18] Pairs of these beings are able to produce offspring that are themselves divine emanations, perfect in their own ways.[19] A problem arises when one female "aeon," or being, named Sophia decides "to bring forth a likeness out of herself without the consent of the Spirit," that is, to produce an offspring without her consort (Apocryphon of John). The ancient view was that females contribute the matter in reproduction, and males the form; thus, Sophia's action produces an offspring that is imperfect and perhaps even malformed, and she casts it away from the other divine beings in the *pleroma* into a separate region of the cosmos. This malformed, ignorant deity, sometimes named Yaldabaoth, mistakenly believes himself to be the only god.

Gnostics identify Yaldabaoth as the Creator God of the Old Testament, who decides to create archons (angels), the material world (Earth), and

16. This corpus lay dormant for nearly 2,000 years until its discovery in 1945 in Nag Hammadi, Egypt. The complete collection of texts may be found in James M. Robinson, ed., *The Nag Hammadi Library*, rev. ed. (New York: HarperCollins, 1990; reprint of original Brill edition, 1978). All Gnostic texts cited here may be found in this collection.

17. Gnostic texts are cryptic, and no single text clearly explains this myth from beginning to end. The literature presupposes familiarity with the myth, which must be reconstructed by modern readers. The version of the myth presented here relies on such texts as the Gospel of Truth, Apocryphon of John, On the Origin of the World, and Gospel of Thomas. See *Nag Hammadi Library*, 38–51, 104–23, 124–38, 170–89.

18. Since the divine beings are composed only of spiritual substances and not matter, there are no physical gender differences among the beings.

19. Depending on the text, a plethora of divine beings populate the *pleroma*, many with Jewish, Christian, or philosophical names, e.g., the Spirit, forethought, thought, foreknowledge, indestructibility, truth, Christ, Autogenes, understanding, grace, perception, and Pigera-Adamas (see especially Apocryphon of John 2–9).

human beings. Although traditions vary, Yaldabaoth is usually depicted as having been tricked into breathing the divine spark or spirit of his mother, Sophia, that formerly resided in him into the human being (especially Apocryphon of John; echoes of Genesis 2–3). Therein exists the Gnostic version of the human dilemma. We are pearls in the mud, a divine spirit (good) trapped in a material body (bad) and a material realm (bad). Heaven is our true home, but we are in exile from the *pleroma.*

Luckily for us, salvation is available in the form of *gnosis*, or knowledge imparted by a Gnostic redeemer, who is Christ, a figure sent from the higher God to free humankind from the Creator God, Yaldabaoth. The *gnosis* involves an experiential and intuitive perception of our true nature and origin, the metaphysical reality hitherto unknown to us, resulting in the Gnostic's escape (at death) from the enslaving material prison of the world and the body into the upper regions of spirit. However, in order to make this ascent, Gnostics must pass by the archons, who are jealous of their luminosity, spirit, or intelligence, and who thus try to hinder the Gnostics' upward journey.

To a significant degree, the basic Gnostic myth is recapitulated in *The Matrix* films, with respect to both the problem that humans face and the solution. Like Sophia, we conceived an offspring out of our own pride, as Morpheus explains: "early in the 21st century, all of mankind was united in celebration. We marveled at our own magnificence as we gave birth to A.I."[20] Like the Gnostic Yaldabaoth, this malformed offspring of ours created other imperfect offspring (programs, more machines) as well as humans (grown in fields), an illusory material world (the Matrix) in which to imprison them, and archons (Agents) to patrol them.[21] Just as Yaldabaoth traps humankind in a material prison that is not the ultimate metaphysical reality, so does AI imprison humanity, as Morpheus explains: "As long as the Matrix exists, the human race will never be free" (*Matrix*).

20. Humanity's characterization also resonates with the Tower of Babel story in Genesis 11:1–9; in both we admire the work of our own hands.

21. Morpheus describes the agents as "the gatekeepers—they are guarding all the doors, they are holding all the keys" (*Matrix*), which nicely sums up the activities of archons in Gnostic texts such as the Apocalypse of Paul (*Nag Hammadi Library*, 256–59). We are grateful to Brock Bakke for the initial equation of agents with archons.

The Matrix itself is a cogent articulation of the classic Gnostic world view, resonating closely with texts such as the Gnostic Apocryphon of John:

> And the power of the mother [Sophia] went out of Yaldabaoth into the natural body which they had fashioned [humans]. . . . And in that moment the rest of the powers [angelic archons] became jealous, because he had come into being through all of them and they had given their power to the man, and his intelligence [or "mind"] was greater than that of those who had made him, and greater than that of the chief archon. And when they recognized that he [the human] was luminous, and that he could think better than they . . . they took him and threw him into the lowest region of all matter. (Apocryphon of John 19–20)

Considering this Gnostic passage in terms of *The Matrix*, Sophia's (humankind's) creative potential is passed on to our creation (AI) which in turn becomes a creator of a material prison (Matrix) for the minds of humans, also created by this creator (i.e., the humans grown in fields or the simulated bodies within the Matrix). Yet humans have imbedded within them the divine spark of light and a capacity for perception exceeding that of the archons (Agents), even when imprisoned in the material world (Matrix). Thus in the first film, Neo is able to explode into luminosity within the Matrix and thereby defeat Agent Smith.[22]

In *Reloaded* and *Revolutions*, several artificial programs created by AI provide even closer parallels to figures central to Gnosticism. Although in one sense humans may represent Sophia, her name suggests she may also be identified with the Oracle.[23] In Gnostic terms *Sophia*, which is Greek

22. Rereading the above quote from the Apocryphon of John in terms of the final battle between Neo and Smith in *Revolutions* is also surprisingly coherent, revealing the depth to which the Gnostic structure holds throughout the plot: the knowledge imparted by Sophia (the Oracle) from within the chief archon, Yaldabaoth (Smith), results in a perception by the human creation (Neo) that the archon programs cannot comprehend, and the human becomes a luminous presence that overcomes their darkness, resounding even from the lowest region of matter (the pit in which Neo and Smith fight from within the Matrix).

23. In the original screenplay of the first film, the Oracle's divine aspect is reinforced by the location of her apartment within the "Temple of Zion," which evokes both the Oracle of Delphi (three-legged stool, priestesses) and the Jerusalem temple (polished marble, empty throne which is the mercy seat or throne of the invisible God).

for "wisdom," refers to truth, wisdom, or knowledge (*gnosis*) gained by intuition and experience rather than by rationality.[24] Fittingly, then, the Oracle is called "the Mother" of the Matrix (*Reloaded*) much like the divine Mother in Gnosticism, who is sometimes identified with Sophia (e.g., Apocalypse of Adam, Trimorphic Protennoia).[25] The role of demiurge, creator, or Yaldabaoth is replicated by all of the programs that believe themselves to be the lords of their respective realms: the Architect, the "Father" of the Matrix, is creator of a world he believes that he controls; the Merovingian presides like Hades[26] over Club Hel; the train conductor proclaims himself to be "God" over the train tracks at Mobil Avenue (a hyperspace quantum level in which Neo is trapped);[27] and Agent Smith seeks to remake the entire Matrix in his own image—literally. Conversations in the films, such as the following one from *Reloaded*, take on new layers of meaning when viewed in a Gnostic framework:

THE ORACLE: [to Smith] You are a bastard.
AGENT SMITH: [to Oracle] You should know, mom.

A clear reference to the Gnostic Sophia, the Mother, and her malformed bastard offspring, the creator of the material realm, the quote illuminates an interesting quirk in both the Gnostic and *Matrix* universes: the whole mistake of the material realm (Matrix) and the archon (Smith) who keeps humans imprisoned there ultimately derives from actions taken long ago by the divine Mother (Oracle), who subsequently acts to free humans by guiding the Gnostic redeemer (Neo).

Both the trilogy and the Gnostic texts from Nag Hammadi describe the fundamental human problem by using the same metaphorical terms: blindness, sleep, ignorance, dreams, and darkness. Similarly, in both the films and in Gnosticism, the solution is stated in terms of seeing, awakening, knowledge (*gnosis*), waking from dreams, and light. From early in

---

24. Pagels, *The Gnostic Gospels*, 119–43.

25. Pagels, *The Gnostic Gospels*, 53–54.

26. In Greek myth, Hades' wife is Persephone, who is held by her husband in the underworld for half the year and permitted to return to the upper realm of earth for the other half.

27. For instance, the train conductor says to Neo, "Down here I'm God" (*Revolutions*).

the first film, Morpheus, whose name is taken from the Greek god of dreams, reveals to Neo that the Matrix is "a computer-generated dream-world." The solution is that Neo needs to wake up from the dream, just as Gnostics learn that sensory perception in the material realm is not reality.[28] The bulk of the following excerpt from the Gnostic Gospel of Truth might just as well be taken from the scenes in *The Matrix* in which Morpheus explains the nature of reality to Neo:

> Thus they [humans] were ignorant of the Father [the supreme, ineffable divine principle that is unknowable through sense perception], he being the one whom they did not see.... there were many illusions at work ... and [there were] empty fictions, as if they were sunk in sleep and found themselves in disturbing dreams. Either [there is] a place to which they are fleeing, or without strength they come [from] having chased after others, or they are involved in striking blows, or they are receiving blows themselves, or they have fallen from high places, or they take off into the air though they do not even have wings. Again, sometimes [it is as] if people were murdering them, though there is no one even pursuing them, or they themselves are killing their neighbors ... [but] [w]hen those who are going through all these things wake up, they see nothing, they who were in the midst of all these disturbances, for they are nothing. Such is the way of those who have cast ignorance aside from them like sleep, not esteeming it as anything, nor do they esteem its works as solid things either, but they leave them behind like a dream in the night.... This is the way each one has acted, as though asleep at

28. The way in which Neo learns the truth of the Matrix also evokes some elements of Gnosticism. Imbued with images from Eastern traditions, the training programs teach Neo the concept of "stillness," of freeing the mind and overcoming fear, cinematically captured in "bullet time" (digitally mastered montages of freeze frames and slow-motion frames using multiple cameras). This concept of stillness is also present in Gnosticism, in that the higher aeons are equated with stillness and "rest" and can only be apprehended in such a centered and meditative manner, as is apparent in these instructions to a certain Allogenes: "And although it is impossible for you to stand, fear nothing; but if you wish to stand, withdraw to the Existence, and you will find it standing and at rest after the likeness of the One who is truly at rest.... And when you become perfect in that place, still yourself" (Allogenes). The Gnostic then reveals, "There was within me a stillness of silence, and I heard the Blessedness whereby I knew my proper self" (Allogenes). When Neo realizes the full extent of his "saving gnosis," that the Matrix is only a dream world, a reflective Keanu Reeves silently and calmly contemplates the bullets that he has stopped in mid-air, filmed in "bullet time."

the time when he was ignorant. And this is the way he has [come to knowledge], as if he had awakened. (Gospel of Truth 29–30)

When Neo is unplugged and awakens for the first time on the *Nebuchadnezzar*, his eyes hurt, since, as Morpheus explains, he has never used them. Everything Neo has "seen" up to that point was seen with the interior mind's eye through software simulation; his sensory perception cannot be trusted as genuine, and thus, as in the Gospel of Truth, the experiences of running, fleeing, fighting, falling, flying, or even being killed or killing within the Matrix are not real if the mind realizes it to be so.

However, despite this stance, in the trilogy this basic Gnostic rejection of materiality as reality sometimes seems to falter when humans are outside of the Matrix. Morpheus himself explains that he came to believe AI was growing humans in fields only after he saw it with his own eyes (*Matrix*). Especially in *Reloaded*, the inhabitants of Zion affirm the materiality of their bodies as real through orgiastic rave dancing and intensely physical sex between Neo and Trinity. Indeed, the juxtaposition of the celebratory dance with Morpheus's stirring speech against the machines seems to make the triumphal point that our fleshly bodies make us uniquely human and thus better than machines.[29]

However, such scenes may actually serve as clues that, unknown to most inhabitants of Zion and the Machine City, the boundaries of the Matrix may extend further than the first film seems to suggest. The logic of these scenes—including Morpheus's reconstruction of reality in *The Matrix*—is challenged, if not undone, by the end of *Reloaded*. As soon as Neo is able to defy physics outside of the Matrix, viewers begin to understand that in fact the material world of Zion and the Machine City may be as unreal as the Matrix. As *Revolutions* commences, Neo operates in the Matrix without literally jacking in, and by the end of *Revolutions* the original Gnostic stance of the first film is reasserted in its extreme: materiality and sense perception are indeed false: since Neo can control the machines *outside of the Matrix*. Most important, like a Gnostic adept ascending to the heavenly *pleroma*, Neo's physical body is transformed into sheer light, suggesting that he transcends the material realm altogether.

---

29. See Donna Bowman, "Gnostic Illusion," for insights on the second film.

The trope of seeing, when traced through the films, illustrates this concept well. When Morpheus states in the first film that Neo's eyes hurt because he has never used them, the suggestion is that Neo is waking from the illusory material world of the Matrix to the *real* material world. Yet as Morpheus and Neo enter the elevator of the apartment building of the Oracle, images of "physical seeing" compete with "genuine seeing" through a striking visual symbol: beneath some graffiti depicting a pair of eyes sits a blind man, evoking tension between physical sight and the inner Sight. Interestingly, the Oracle—a seer—wears glasses to look at Neo's palm, suggesting that she is like Orpheus and Tiresias, the blind seers of Greek tradition. In *Revolutions*, the motif is brought to closure, as Neo loses his physical eyes and for the first time truly "sees" the underlying structure of reality[30] not only in the Matrix, but outside of it as well. The point is made: the material world, on all levels, is not the supreme reality.

More than just a model Gnostic, however, Neo is like the Gnostic Christ. A clue to this formulation lies in Neo's name within the Matrix: *Thomas* Anderson. This first name reverberates with the most famous Gnostic gospel, the Gospel of Thomas, Thomas being the twin brother of Jesus in Gnostic tradition. That is, Neo is not the "Christ" familiar to most viewers, but as Thomas he is a twin, a Gnostic Christ. In *The Matrix*, Neo is "saved" through *gnosis*, or secret knowledge about the unreality of sensory perception; this is the knowledge he and the crew of the *Nebuchadnezzar* apparently pass on to others within the Matrix. Neo learns about the true structure of reality and about his own true identity, allowing him to break the rules of the material world, which he now perceives to be an illusion. That is, he learns that "the mind makes it [the Matrix] real," though it is not ultimately real. At the end of the first film, Neo implies he will tell others what he knows (while "Wake Up" by Rage Against the Machine plays in the background). In this sense, Neo functions like a Gnostic redeemer, a figure from another realm who enters the material world (the Matrix) in order to impart saving knowledge about humankind's true identity and the true structure of reality, thereby setting free anyone able to understand the message. Finally, by the end of the trilogy, Neo has learned

---

30. Quantum packets, light energy, the divine substructure of the universe.

that even the materiality of Zion and the Machine City is unreal; it too is a simulation, or a matrix.

As Morpheus predicts in the first film, Neo is eventually able to defeat the Agents because they must adhere to the rational laws of the Matrix, while his human mind allows him to bend or break these rules.[31] Mind, then, is not equated in the film merely with rational intelligence; otherwise artificial intelligence would win every time, and the Architect would not need to be balanced by the Oracle (*Reloaded* and *Revolutions*). Rather, the concept of "mind" in the film appears to point to the capacity for imagination, for intuition, or, as the phrase goes, for "thinking outside the box."

However, in the film series as a whole, it is not only humans, but the Oracle as well, who possess this divine spark that permits a perception of *gnosis* that is greater than the rational knowledge achievable by AI and machine programs in general.[32] In both the first and third films, Neo's luminous transfigurations, which overcome the "darkness" of Agent Smith, are achievable only by an enlightenment that is nonrational. For instance, in *The Matrix*, Neo must ignore sensory perception and the apparent fact that he is dying. By contradiction, in *Revolutions*, he must give up fighting Smith and cease to cling to his life. He is taught this latter lesson by the Oracle's presence from deep within Smith,[33] and as the Architect tantalizingly suggests in *Reloaded*, some things are only comprehensible by "a lesser Mind," that is, by a nonrational wisdom such as that represented by the intuitive Oracle. Any entities capable of *gnosis* in the films, whether they be Neo and Trinity or programs such as the Oracle and Sati, may achieve their highest potential as beings in the universe.

31. In Gnosticism, "Mind," or the Greek *nous* is a deity, such as in the text "Thunder, Perfect Mind," *Nag Hammadi Library*, 295–303.

32. In the original version of this article that appeared in the *Journal of Religion and Film* as well as on the Warner Bros. official *Matrix* Web site, we argued on the basis of the first film that the divine spark, which provides the capacity for Gnostic perception, was uniquely possessed by humans. After viewing *Revolutions*, the Oracle and perhaps other programs must be included in those having this characteristic.

33. This image in itself evokes the basic Gnostic myth. Smith acts as a Creator, that is, Yaldabaoth, in replicating himself repeatedly. However, the Oracle, as Sophia, is literally the spark of light that resides deep within him, inadvertently being spread throughout his creation.

Overall, then, the system portrayed in *The Matrix* parallels Gnostic Christianity in terms of key figures, metaphorical language, and the delineation of humanity's fundamental problem (a dream world of simulated reality) as well as its solution (waking up from illusion). But given that Gnosticism presumes an entire unseen realm of divine beings, where is God in the films? In other words, when Neo becomes sheer light and Sati becomes co-creator in the Matrix, are these symbols for the power of a transcendent divinity, or for human and machine potential? The series leaves it up to the viewer, and in the end it must be said that if there is some implied divinity in the films,[34] God remains transcendent, like the divinity of the ineffable, invisible supreme God of Gnosticism, except where it is immanent in the form of the divine spark active in creation.[35]

Buddhism in *The Matrix*

When asked by a fan if Buddhist ideas influenced them in the production of the movie, the Wachowski brothers offered an unqualified yes.[36] Indeed, Buddhist ideas pervade the film and appear in close proximity with

34. A viewer asked the Wachowski brothers, "What is the role [of] faith in the movie? Faith in oneself first and foremost—or in something else?" They answered, "Hmmmm . . . that is a tough question! Faith in one's self, how's that for an answer?" ("Wachowski chat"). This reply hardly settles the issue.

35. Specifically, divine immanence is implied in the characters of Neo (the Gnostic redeemer/messiah) and Morpheus and Trinity, both of whom are named for gods. As a godhead, this trio does not quite make sense in terms of traditional Christianity. However, the trio is quite interesting in the context of Gnosticism, which portrays God as Father, Mother, and Son, a trinity in which the Holy Spirit is identified as female, e.g., Apocryphon of John 2:9–14. For further reading on female divinities in Gnosticism, see Pagels, *The Gnostic Gospels*, 48–69.

36. The brothers maintain that "there's something uniquely interesting about Buddhism and mathematics, particularly about quantum physics, and where they meet. That has fascinated us for a long time" ("Wachowski chat"). In the *Time* interview with Richard Corliss (see note 9), Larry Wachowski explains that he and Andy became fascinated "by the idea that math and theology are almost the same. They begin with a supposition you can derive a whole host of laws or rules from. And when you take all of them to the infinity point, you wind up at the same place: these unanswerable mysteries really become about personal perception. Neo's journey is affected by all these rules, all these people trying to tell him what the truth is. He doesn't accept anything until he gets to his own end point, his own rebirth." The films illustrate this close relationship through their representation of the Matrix as a corporate network of human conceptions (or *samsara*) that are translated into software codes that reinforce one another.

the equally strong Christian imagery. Almost immediately after Neo is identified as "my own personal Jesus Christ," this appellation is given a distinctively Buddhist twist. The same hacker says: "This never happened. You don't exist." From the stupa-like[37] pods which encase humans in the horrific mechanistic fields to Cypher's selfish desire for the sensations and pleasures of the Matrix, Buddhist teachings form a foundation for much of the films' plots and imagery.[38]

Even the title of the film evokes the Buddhist world view. The Matrix is described by Morpheus as "a prison for your mind." It is a dependent "Construct" made up of the interlocking digital projections of billions of human beings who are unaware of the illusory nature of the reality in which they live and are completely dependent on the hardware attached to their real bodies and the elaborate software programs created by AI. The Construct embodies the Buddhist idea of *samsara*, which teaches that the world in which we live our daily lives is illusory, constructed from the sensory projections formulated from our own desires. When Morpheus takes Neo into the Construct to teach him about the Matrix, Neo learns that the way in which he had perceived himself in the Matrix was nothing more than "the mental projection of [his] digital self." The "real" world, which we associate with what we feel, smell, taste, and see, "is simply electrical signals interpreted by your brain." The world, Morpheus explains, exists "now only as part of a neural interactive simulation that we call the Matrix." In Buddhist terms, we could say that "because it is empty of self or of what belongs to self, it is therefore said: 'The world is empty.' And what is empty of self and what belongs to self? The

37. A *stupa* is a hemispherical or cylindrical mound or tower serving as a Buddhist shrine.

38. Of course, the most transparent reference to Buddhist ideas in the first film occurs in the waiting room at the Oracle's apartment, where Neo is introduced to the "Potentials." The screenplay describes the waiting room as "at once like a Buddhist temple and a kindergarten class." One of the children, clad in the garb of a Buddhist monk, explains to Neo the nature of ultimate reality: "There is no spoon." One cannot help wondering if this dictum only holds within the Matrix or if there is in fact "no spoon" even in the "real" world beyond it. In *Reloaded*, the intriguing gift of a spoon from the now-freed orphan to Neo as he is about to board a ship may be one hint that the world in which Zion exists may in fact also be within a matrix, since it is only within a matrix, or *samsara*, that one needs to realize the illusory nature of material objects such as spoons.

eye, material shapes, visual consciousness, impression[s] on the eye—all these are empty of self and of what belongs to self."[39] According to the core teachings of Buddhism and according to *The Matrix* films as well, the perception of reality that is based upon sensory experience, ignorance, and desire keeps humans locked in illusion until they are able to recognize the false nature of reality and relinquish their mistaken sense of identity.

Drawing on the Buddhist doctrine of dependent co-origination, the films present reality within the Matrix as a conglomerate of the illusions of all humans caught within its snare. Similarly, Buddhism teaches that the suffering of human beings is dependent upon *samsara*, a cycle of ignorance and desire which locks humans into a repetitive cycle of birth, death, and rebirth. The principle is stated in a short formula in the *Samyutta-nikaya*:

> If this is that comes to be;
> from the arising of this that arises;
> if this is not that does not come to be;
> from the stopping of this that is stopped.[40]

The idea of dependent co-origination is poignantly illustrated in the film through the illusion of the Matrix. The viability of the Matrix's illusion depends upon the belief by those enmeshed in it that the Matrix itself is reality. AI's software program is, in and of itself, no illusion at all. Only when humans interact with its programs do they become enmeshed in a corporately created illusion, the Matrix, or *samsara*, which reinforces itself through the interactions of those beings involved within it. Thus the Matrix's reality only exists when actual human minds subjectively experience its programs.[41]

---

39. *Samyutta-nikaya* IV, 54. In Edward Conze, ed., *Buddhist Texts through the Ages* (New York: Philosophical Library, 1954), 91.

40. *Samyutta-nikaya* II, 64–65. In Conze, *Buddhist Texts through the Ages*.

41. The entire process depends upon human ignorance, so that almost all who are born within the Matrix are doomed to be born, to die, and to reenter the cycle again. When asked about the films' depiction of the liquefaction of humans, the Wachowskis replied that this black ooze is "what they feed the people in the pods, the dead people are liquefied and fed to the living people in the pods." Tongue in Buddhist cheek, the

The problem, then, can be seen in Buddhist terms. Humans are trapped in a cycle of illusion, and their ignorance of this cycle keeps them locked in it, fully dependent upon their own interactions with the programs, the illusions of sensory experience which these provide, and the sensory projections of others. These projections are strengthened by humans' enormous desire to believe that what they perceive to be real is in fact real. This desire is so strong that it overcomes Cypher, who can no longer tolerate the "desert of the real" and asks to be reinserted into the Matrix. As he sits with Agent Smith in an upscale restaurant smoking a cigar with a large glass of brandy, Cypher explains his motives:

> You know, I know this steak doesn't exist. I know that when I put it in my mouth, the Matrix is telling my brain that it is juicy and delicious. After nine years, you know what I realize? Ignorance is bliss. (*Matrix*)

Cypher knows that the Matrix is not real and that any pleasure he experiences there is illusory. Yet for him, the "ignorance" of *samsara* is preferable to enlightenment. Denying the reality that he now experiences beyond the Matrix, he uses the double negative: "I don't want to remember nothing. Nothing. And I want to be rich. Someone important. Like an actor." Not only does Cypher want to forget the "nothing" of true reality, but he also wants to be an "actor," to add another level of illusion to the illusion of the Matrix that he is choosing to reenter.[42] The draw of *samsara* is so strong that not only does Cypher give in to his cravings, but Mouse also may be said to have been overwhelmed by the lures of *samsara*, since his death is at least in part due to distractions brought on by his sexual fantasies about the "woman in the red

---

brothers explained this reembodiment: "Always recycle! It's a statement on recycling" ("Wachowski chat"). Even in the "real world" beyond the Matrix, the human plight is depicted as an interdependent cycle of birth, death, and "recycling." This dialogue also pointed to the "reality" (or the "matrix") that we ourselves inhabit. In our world, and in the world of Joe Pantoliano, he is an actor. Therefore, the world of which both the actor Joe Pantoliano and we are now a part may be seen as the matrix into which he has been successfully re-inserted. Thus the film itself may be seen as a part of the software program of our own matrix.

42. For a fuller discussion of multiple tiers of reality in recent films, see Frances Flannery-Dailey, "Robot Heaven and Robot Dreams: Ultimate Reality in *A.I.* and Other Recent Films," *Journal of Religion and Film* 7, no 2 (October 2003).

dress" which occupy him when he is supposed to be standing watch (*Matrix*).

Whereas Cypher and Mouse represent what happens when one gives in to *samsara*, the rest of the *Nebuchadnezzar*'s crew epitomizes the restraint and composure praised by the Buddha. Instead of brandy, cigars, and steak, the crew regularly ingests Tastee-Wheat, reminiscent of a "bowl of snot." In contrast to the pleasures that Cypher enjoys in the Matrix, Neo and the crew must be content with the "single-celled protein combined with synthetic aminos, vitamins, and minerals" which Dozer claims is "everything the body needs" (*Matrix*). Clad in threadbare clothes, subsisting on gruel, and sleeping in bare cells, the crew is depicted enacting the Middle Way taught by the Buddha, allowing neither absolute asceticism nor indulgence to distract them from their work.[43]

The duality between the Matrix and the reality beyond it sets up the ultimate goal of the rebels, which is to free all minds from the Matrix and allow humans to live out their lives in the real world beyond. In making this point, the filmmakers draw on both Theravada and Mahayana Buddhist concepts.[44] The Theravada ideal of the *arhat*, the "worthy one" who achieves enlightenment through individual effort, is made clear by Morpheus, who acts as Neo's initial guide to reality. As Morpheus explains, "[N]o one can be told what the Matrix is. You have to see it for yourself" (*Matrix*). Morpheus tells Neo that he must make the final shift in perception entirely on his own, saying: "I'm trying to free your mind, Neo.

43. Take, for example, this quote from the *Sabbasava-sutta*: "A *bhikku* [monk], considering wisely, lives with his eyes restrained.... Considering wisely, he lives with his ears restrained ... with his nose restrained ... with his tongue ... with his body ... with his mind restrained.... a *bhikku*, considering wisely, makes use of his robes—only to keep off cold, to keep off heat ... and to cover himself decently. Considering wisely, he makes use of food—neither for pleasure nor for excess ... but only to support and sustain this body" (quoted in Walpola Sri Rahula, *What the Buddha Taught* [New York: Grove Weidenfeld, 1974], 103).

44. James Ford has argued that the film especially embodies ideas drawn from the Yogacara school of Buddhism. Instead of pointing to that which is absolutely different than the world as *nirvana*, Yogacarins point to the world itself, and through the processes enacted in meditation come to the realization that "all things and thought are but Mind-only. The basis of all our illusions consists in that we regard the objectifications of our own mind as a world independent of that mind, which is really its source and substance" (from Edward Conze, *Buddhism* [New York: Philosophical Library, 1959], 167).

But I can only show you the door. You're the one that has to walk through it." For Theravada Buddhists, "man's emancipation depends on his own realization of the Truth, and not on the benevolent grace of a god or any external power as a reward for his obedient good behavior."[45] In the *Dhammapada*, the Buddha urges the one seeking enlightenment to "free thyself from the past, free thyself from the future, free thyself from the present. Crossing to the farther shore of existence, with mind released everywhere, no more shalt thou come to birth and decay."[46] Morpheus suggests to Neo, "There's a difference between knowing the path and walking the path," just as the Buddha taught his followers, "You yourselves should make the effort; the Awakened Ones are only teachers."[47] As one already on the path to enlightenment, Morpheus is only a guide; ultimately Neo must recognize the truth for himself. This doctrine appears again when the Kid claims that Neo saved him (see *Animatrix*, "Kid's Story"), only to have Neo respond: "You saved yourself" (*Reloaded*).

At the same time, *The Matrix* also embraces ideas found in Mahayana Buddhism, especially in the ideal manifested by *bodhisattvas*, those who willingly remain in *samsara* and postpone their own final enlightenment in order to help liberate others and to act as guides.[48] The crew members of the *Nebuchadnezzar* epitomize this compassion. Rather than remain

---

The Matrix exists only in the minds of the human beings who inhabit it, so that in *The Matrix*, as in Yogacara, "The external world is really Mind itself" (Conze, *Buddhism*, 168). Yet a problem arises when one realizes that, for the Yogacara school, the mind is the ultimate reality, a realization based on the idea that with enlightenment, *samsara* and *nirvana* become identified. By contrast, the first film in *The Matrix* series insists on a clear distinction between *samsara* (the Matrix) and *nirvana* (that which lies beyond it), and at least suggests that there exists some form of physical reality beyond the Matrix. Because *The Matrix* maintains at least a superficial duality between the Matrix and the realm beyond it, Yogacara is of limited help in making sense of the Buddhist elements in the film, nor is it especially helpful in supporting the idea that beyond the Matrix and beyond the *Nebuchadnezzar* one may find an ultimate reality or realities not yet realized by humans. The possible collapse in *Reloaded* and *Revolutions* of a distinction between the Matrix (*samsara*) and what lies beyond it (*nirvana*?) may make perspectives such as these more applicable.

45. Rahula, *What the Buddha Taught*, 2.

46. Quoted in Rahula, *What the Buddha Taught*, 135.

47. Quoted in Rahula, *What the Buddha Taught*, 133.

48. The Buddha's compassion serves as the primary model for Mahayana Buddhists, since they point out that he remained in *samsara* in order to help others to achieve enlightenment through his teachings and his exemplary life.

outside of the Matrix where they are safer, they choose to reenter it repeatedly as ambassadors of knowledge with the ultimate goal of freeing the minds and eventually also the bodies of those who are trapped within the Matrix's digital web. Overall, then, the films blend the Mahayana ideal of the *bodhisattva* with the Theravada ideal of the *arhat,* presenting the crew as concerned for those still stuck in the Matrix and willing to reenter the Matrix to help them, while simultaneously arguing that final realization is an individual process.

Although the crew members of the *Nebuchadnezzar* each embody the ideals of the *bodhisattva* (with the obvious exception of Cypher), the filmmakers set Neo apart as unique, suggesting that while the crew may be looked at as *arhats* and *bodhisattvas,* Neo can also be seen as a Buddha. Neo's identity as Buddha, or the "Awakened One," is reinforced not only through the anagram of his name, The One, but also through the myth that surrounds him. The Oracle has foretold the return of one who has the ability to manipulate the Matrix. As Morpheus explains, the return of this man "would hail the destruction of the Matrix, end the war, bring freedom to our people. That is why there are those of us who have spent our entire lives searching the Matrix, looking for him" (*Matrix*). Neo, Morpheus believes, is a reincarnation of that man and, like the Buddha, he will be endowed with extraordinary powers to aid in the enlightenment of all humanity. Indeed, judging from the welcome that Neo receives from others in Zion (*Reloaded*), many do revere him and look to him for answers.

The idea that Neo can be seen as a reincarnation of the Buddha is reinforced by the prevalence of birth imagery in the film directly related to him. At least four incarnations are perceptible in the first film alone. The first birth takes place in the prehistory of the film, in the life and death of the first enlightened one who was able to control the Matrix from within. The second consists of Neo's life as Thomas Anderson, seen waking up in the initial scene of the first film. The third begins when Neo emerges, gasping, from the gel of the eerily stupa-like pod in which he has been encased, and is unplugged and dropped through a large black tube which can easily be seen as a birth canal.[49] He emerges at the bottom

---

49. The screenplay describes Neo as "floating in a womb-red amnion" in the power plant.

bald, naked, and confused, with eyes that Morpheus tells him have "never been used" before. Having "died" to the world of the Matrix, Neo has been "reborn" into the world beyond it. Neo's fourth life begins after he dies and is "reborn" again in the closing scenes of the film, as Trinity resuscitates him with a kiss.[50] At this point, Neo perceives not only the limitations of the Matrix, but also the limitations of the world of the *Nebuchadnezzar*, since he overcomes death in both realms. Like the Buddha, Neo's enlightenment grants him omniscience within *samsara/* the Matrix, and he is no longer under its power, nor is he subject to birth, death, and rebirth within AI's mechanical Construct.[51]

The ending of *Revolutions* points to two additional incarnations for Neo. First, within the Matrix, Neo, as light, suffuses all of the humans whom Smith has embodied. Second, Neo is meanwhile permanently fused with the computer mainframe. Neo's two new forms of existence powerfully point toward an interconnectedness that is at once traditionally Buddhist, in that all things are perceived as unified, and also quintessentially modern, in that Neo is united not only with other organic beings through the Matrix, but also with machines. Neo's identity as The One is thus fulfilled in its richest sense, as he is The One who is all things. He has achieved the monistic vision of the cosmos that was granted to the Buddha himself when, in his final stage of awakening, he could see and experience the suffering and joy of all living things, from all times, simultaneously.

50. In the original screenplay, Trinity does not kiss Neo but instead "pounds on his chest," thereby precipitating his resuscitation. The screenplay states directly: "It is a miracle." This fourth "life" can be viewed as the one to which the Oracle refers in her predictions that Neo was "waiting for something" and that he might be ready in his "next life, maybe." This certainly appears to be the case, since Neo rises from the dead and defeats the agents.

51. These four "lives" suggest that Neo is nothing other than The One foretold by the Oracle, the reincarnation of the first "enlightened one," or Buddha, who "had the ability to change whatever he wanted, to remake the Matrix as he saw fit." Buddhist teachings allow that those who have been enlightened are endowed with supernatural powers, since they recognize the world as illusory and so can manipulate it at will. Yet supernatural powers are incidental to the primary goal, which is explained in the very first sermon spoken by the Buddha: "The Noble Truth of the cessation of suffering is this: It is the complete cessation of that very thirst, giving it up, renouncing it, emancipating oneself from it, detaching oneself from it" (*Dhammacakkappavattana-sutta*, quoted in Rahula, *What the Buddha Taught*, 93).

Neo's compassion for humans has been evident since the first film, but his respect and consideration for machines has widened with the realization that the Oracle is a program (*Reloaded*) and through meeting Rama-Khandra, Kamala, and Sati in Mobil Avenue, an encounter that teaches him that programs can love (*Revolutions*). Thus, his eventual oneness with both humans and machines fulfills a Buddha-like awareness. In this sense, the Buddhist framework of the films has been transformed to encompass a much broader vision, tailored to a contemporary audience's postmodern anxieties about the relationship of technology to human life, and suggesting that our religious vision should be challenged to include all forms of mechanical "life" and artificial intelligence.

Neo, like the Buddha, seeks to be free from the Matrix and to teach others how to free themselves from it, and his "superman" powers are engaged to that end. As one who can overcome the limitations of the Matrix, and also as the only human being capable of ending the war between the humans and the machines, Neo represents the actualization of the Buddha-nature, one who cannot only recognize the "origin of pain in the world of living beings," but who can also envision "the stopping of the pain," enacting "that course which leads to its stopping."[52] In this sense, he is more than his *bodhisattva* companions and offers the hope of awakening and freedom for all humans, both those still trapped in the Matrix and those in Zion. Moreover, if we are to take seriously the films' Buddhist message as it applies to artificial intelligence, the programs and machines also appear to be thirsty for an end to suffering, and Neo's message is not only for humans, but for all sentient beings.

Although the films conclude with Neo's union with all, for much of the trilogy the Buddhist doctrine of transcending *samsara* for *nirvana* does not function perfectly. According to the teachings of Buddhism, *nirvana* manifests a complete loss of the notion of self, so that conditional reality fades away to the point that what remains, if anything, cannot be described. However, in his reentry into the Matrix, Neo consistently retains his "residual self-image" and the "mental projection of [his] digital self." Also, upon his initial "enlightenment" in the first film, Neo does not finds

52. *Buddhacarita* 1:65, in E. B. Cowell, trans., *Buddhist Mahayana Texts: Sacred Books of the East*, vol. 49 (Oxford: Oxford University Press, 1894).

himself in a *nirvana* that is nowhere (or no "where"), nor does he simply live out his life in the Matrix while blissfully aware of its illusions. Instead, Neo arrives, fully embodied, in a different *place*, a "where," with an intact, if somewhat confused, material sense of self that strongly resembles his "self" within the Matrix. It may be right that the Matrix "cannot tell you who you are," but who you are seems to be at least in some sense related to who you think you are in the Matrix.

One might rightly object that some strands of Buddhism that developed out of Mahayana Buddhism, such as Zen, collapse the distinction between *samsara* and *nirvana*, so that the achievement of *nirvana* simply enacts a radical shift in perspective for the *bodhisattva*, who remains "in" *samsara*, while simultaneously realizing its limitations. In this case, Neo's awakening to a material realm would not necessarily pose a tension with *nirvana*. This perspective, however, does not fully explain the desire of Morpheus and the others to escape from the Matrix, which, if they were fully enlightened, would no longer be a prison, but merely a conflation of *samsara* and *nirvana*. In other words, the continuing suffering experienced by the crew members throughout the trilogy because of their clinging to individual identity suggests that, whatever *nirvana* is, it has not been fully realized.

The Wachowskis' interest in Buddhist philosophy is integral to the overall project, made evident through the deliberate incorporation of Buddhist ideas not just in the trilogy of films, but also in the associated comic books, video games, and animated movie shorts. Mandalas, geometric iconographic representations common in Buddhist ritual, recur throughout the animated shorts in *Animatrix*. Since mandalas visually represent various levels of cosmic energy and reality, they can serve in *Animatrix* as reminders of the impermanence of material reality, also calling the viewer's attention to the mediated nature of the animated images. Other Buddhist images appear in the video game *Enter the Matrix*, which includes a scene situated in a Zen garden, and in the associated comic by Dave Gibbons called "Butterfly."

It is important to note that media representations of Buddhism must be carefully distinguished from Buddhism itself, and a gulf sometimes exists between the two in the *Matrix* project. The scene in the Zen garden illustrates this point well. As Ghost is meditating in Zen fashion in a Zen garden, he is disturbed by a stone flung at him by Trinity. The official guidebook for *Enter the Matrix* invites players to respond to Trinity's stone with a fight, noting that the objects in the Zen garden are all "breakable" and that players can watch them "crumble to the ground by throwing Trinity through them."[53] Although the guide describes this sparring as "friendly" and "penalty-free," the juxtaposition of destruction with Zen Buddhist meditation is problematic from the point of view of Zen meditation itself, which has peace as its goal.[54]

Clearly, the trilogy does not neatly recapitulate all of the central insights of Buddhism, and in fact makes a disturbing alteration to what could be considered its central tenet. The Buddhist doctrine of *ahimsa*, compassion or non-injury to all living beings, is overtly contradicted in the film.[55] For the majority of the film, violence is directly linked to salvation, since there seems to be no way that the crew can succeed without the help of weaponry. When Tank asks Neo and Trinity what they need for their rescue of Morpheus "besides a miracle," their reply is instantaneous: "Guns—lots of guns." The Wachowskis could easily have presented the "deaths" of the agents as nothing more than the ending of that particular part of the software program. Instead, the brothers have purposefully chosen to portray humans as innocent victims of the violent deaths of the agents. That is, although the perpetrators of violence within the Matrix may understand that their actions are not real, the victims do not share this realization, and thus they "really" die in the Machine City, blatantly contradicting *ahimsa*.

Reloaded includes several scenes that not only gratify the audience's desire for violence, but also seem to supersaturate it. The scene commonly called the "burly brawl," in which hundreds or thousands of replicated

53. Doug Walsh, *Enter the Matrix: Official Strategy Guide* (New York: Pearson Education, 2003), 150–51.

54. The association of Buddhism with a long tradition of martial arts cannot excuse frivolous violence, since traditional martial arts are characterized by violence only as a response to external aggression, using only the minimum amount of force necessary to repel an enemy.

55. See, for example, in the *Dhammapada*: "Of death are all afraid. Having made oneself the example, one should neither slay nor cause to slay" (verse 129), in *Dhammapada*, trans. John Ross Carter and Mahinda Palihawadana (New York: Oxford University Press, 1987), 35.

Agent Smiths battle Neo in a courtyard, begs the question of why Neo doesn't simply fly away, free from the fray, as he does at its conclusion. The extended car-chase scene, culminating in a monstrous explosion, lasts far longer than many people in the audience would wish. Similarly, fully a third of *Revolutions* comprises graphic scenes of the war between humans and machines. This overloading of violent images *may* suggest that the Wachowskis are deliberately exploring how much violence is too much. A rejection of physical violence may even be implied, since while the inhabitants of Zion wage battle with their bodies and weaponry, only Neo's nonviolent self-sacrifice finally brings an end to the war. However, after a cumulative six to seven hours of bullets, brawls, and bombshells, that message is lost on most audience members.

According to the world views of both Gnostic Christianity and Buddhism referenced by *The Matrix* project, the realization of true reality involves complete freedom from entrapment in the material realm and offers peace of mind. Just as a Buddhist desires to overcome *samsara* and realize *nirvana* and the Gnostic comes to understand that the material world is a dream, the wise viewer will overcome the worlds of illusion presented by the films, transcending the thoughtless violence that characterizes so much modern media.

What Is the Matrix?

Viewing the *Matrix* films from a Gnostic Christian or Buddhist perspective, the overwhelming message seems to be "Wake up!" Gnosticism, Buddhism, and the films all agree that ignorance enslaves us within an illusory material world and that liberation comes through enlightenment with the aid of a teacher or guide figure. Yet, when we ask the question "To what do we awaken?" the films sometimes appear to diverge sharply from both Gnosticism and Buddhism. Both of these traditions maintain that when humans gain enlightenment, they leave behind the material world, or at least a dependence upon the material world as normally perceived. The Gnostic ascends at death to the *pleroma*, the divine plane of spiritual, nonmaterial existence, and the enlightened one in Buddhism achieves *nirvana*, a state which cannot be described in language, but which is characterized by a realization that ultimate reality is not dependent on material reality. By contrast, the real world presumed in the trilogy seems to be a wholly material, technological world, in which humans battle machines, each side employing technology such as cell phones, computers, software training programs, and advanced weaponry.[56] Thus, "waking up" in *The Matrix* is leaving behind the Matrix and awakening to a dismal cyberworld, which is the real material world.

Or perhaps not. The scene of the Construct-loading program provides several cinematic clues that suggest that the version of reality that Morpheus shows the newly freed Neo may be suspect. Morpheus, whose name is taken from the Greek god of dreams, shows the "real" world to Neo as a video image on a television bearing the logo *Deep Image.* Throughout the first film, reflections in mirrors and in Morpheus's glasses, as well as images on television monitors, seem to be symbols for multiple levels of illusion and possibility, rather than for concrete reality.[57] This interpretation seems to be secured in *Reloaded* by the multiple *televised* space-time vectors in the Architect's room. But if television represents only what is possible rather than what is actual, Morpheus's initial explanation of the state of things is unreliable. Indeed, in the Construct-loading scene, the camera zooms up to and then inside of the picture on this *Deep Image* television in a way that places the viewer's point of view within the image, that is, in a simulated reality. In addition, as the viewer's point of view passes through the screen, it "morphs" in the same fashion as do certain objects in the unreal Matrix (e.g., buildings and surveillance monitors). Moreover, Neo's act of viewing "reality" in a television program takes place while Neo and Morpheus stand within a Construct-loading program in which Neo is warned not to be tricked by appearances. Finally, although he has just articulated that sense perception is not a reliable source for establishing reality, Morpheus erringly bases his construction of history and reality on physical sight, noting: "For a long

56. The Wachowskis themselves acknowledged that it is "ironic that Morpheus and his crew are completely dependent upon technology and computers, the very evils against which they are fighting" ("Wachowski chat").

57. This is especially true in the "red pill/blue pill" scene where Neo first meets Morpheus, and Neo is reflected differently in each lens of Morpheus's glasses. The Wachowskis noted that one reflection represents Thomas Anderson, and one represents Neo ("Wachowski chat").

time I wouldn't believe it, and then I saw the fields [of humans grown for energy] with my own eyes.... And standing there, I came to realize the obviousness of the truth."[58]

This scene also offers a subtle clue that Jean Baudrillard's *Simulacra and Simulation* (which was required reading for the films' cast members), should be referenced as a help to decipher Morpheus's version of reality. Baudrillard's work makes a cameo appearance in *The Matrix* as the book on Neo's shelf that is actually a secret container, open to a page entitled "On Nihilism" and otherwise empty except for a collection of hacking disks. On the first page of this book, Baudrillard discusses a fable by Borges describing a map that perfectly touches all parts of the land beneath. According to Baudrillard, our current age is informed by the map alone, such that "today it is the [geographical] territory whose shreds slowly rot across the extent of the map."[59] In other words, the signs of the real are substituted for the real, and the simulation is perceived as reality, just as the Matrix stands for reality for those within it and just as most viewers readily accept the false reality of images invented in film and other media.

Baudrillard calls this unreal, "hyperreal" state, symbolized by the map, *the desert of the real.* But Morpheus applies Baudrillard's phrase for the hyperreal, "the desert of the real," not to the Matrix, but to his renditions of reality and history existing outside of the Matrix. Thus, Morpheus's

---

58. A viewer asked the pertinent question of the Wachowskis: "Do you believe that our world is in some way similar to *The Matrix*, that there is a larger world outside of this existence?" They replied: "That is a larger question than you actually might think. We think the most important sort of fiction attempts to answer some of the big questions. One of the things that we had talked about when we first had the idea of *The Matrix* was an idea that I believe philosophy and religion and mathematics all try to answer. Which is, a reconciling between a natural world and another world that is perceived by our intellect" ("Wachowski chat").

59. Despite Morpheus's usage of "desert of the real," Baudrillard's description of the hyperreal clearly provides inspiration for the Matrix: "The real is produced from miniaturized cells, matrices, and memory banks, models of control—and it can be reproduced an indefinite number of times from these.... it no longer measures itself against either an ideal or negative instance. It is no longer anything but operational.... It is a hyperreal, produced from a radiating synthesis of combinatory models in a hyperspace without atmosphere." Jean Baudrillard, *Simulacra and Simulation*, trans. S. F. Glaser (Ann Arbor: University of Michigan Press, 1994), 2.

explanations to Neo bear no necessary relation to truth, and may even be nihilistic with respect to the possibility of a transcendent realm. Neo has not viewed *reality*, but only a *construct* of reality, from within a Construct-loading program. Every character in the trilogy is living on Baudrillard's map, both from the viewpoint of the story *and* from the viewpoint of the audience, since of course the trilogy is film and not reality. Morpheus's use of the phrase "the desert of the real" teaches that in viewing the films we, like the inhabitants of the original Matrix, have imbibed a hyperreal simulation of a world and nothing more.[60]

However, by also invoking Gnosticism and Buddhism, among other religious traditions, and placing these traditions in dialogue with secular philosophical perspectives, the films attempt to overcome Baudrillard's postmodern malaise with the hope of something more. Whereas for Baudrillard, the proliferation of worlds of illusion has no point,[61] for religious traditions like Gnosticism and Buddhism, the multiplication of worlds and of perspectives serves as a hint that the world we inhabit is not the ultimate one, that unity, mindful awareness, and true knowledge are possible. The variety of religious lenses in *The Matrix* project offers a way to transcend the superficial layers in the films by suggesting that there are levels of metaphysical reality beyond those we can ordinarily perceive, to which we ourselves have the possibility of awakening.

60. An even more subtle clue to the unreliability of Morpheus's rendition of reality lies in the centrality of the character of Sati, who appears as a principal shaper of the new Matrix at the end of *Revolutions*. In Hindu tradition, Sati is the first wife of Shiva the Destroyer God. In order to honor her husband, who has been humiliated by her father, Sati immolates herself, saying she will be reborn into a better family in her next incarnation. (Is the tenderness that Rama-Khandra shows to Sati evidence that she has indeed been reborn to a more loving family?) Shiva is so deeply grieved that he carries her body throughout the universe, whereupon another Hindu god, Vishnu, out of compassion, cuts her body into pieces that fall upon India, the site of each piece becoming sacralized as a site of pilgrimage. See David R. Kinsley, *Hindu Goddesses* (Berkeley: University of California Press, 1998), 38. The image of Sati's corpse lying across the holy land brings to mind the very first page of *Simulacra and Simulation* and Baudrillard's discussion of the map of Borges, employed there as an image of the desert of the real (Baudrillard, 1–2). Thus, the focus on Sati at the end of the third film sends us back to the first film and the Construct-loading scene, forming a giant referential loop, or *revolution*, that undermines the guiding constructions of reality in the trilogy.

61. Baudrillard, *Simulacra and Simulation*, 2, 4, 6.

Further Reading

For more on *The Matrix* and religion, see Frances Flannery-Dailey and Rachel L. Wagner, "Stopping Bullets: Constructions of Bliss and Problems of Violence," in *Jacking in to the Matrix Franchise*, ed. M. Kapell and W. G. Doty (New York: Continuum, 2004), 97–114. In this piece we briefly examine the presence of Christianity, Gnosticism, Buddhism, Hinduism, Taoism, and Baudrillard in the entire *Matrix* project, noting problems that arise as the various religious and philosophical traditions are subsumed under a violent version of apocalyptic Christianity. We also argue that the trilogy attempts to be self-critical in terms of both violence and media/advertising, with mixed success.

We also recommend Donna Bowman, "The Gnostic Illusion: Problematic Realized Eschatology in *The Matrix Reloaded*," *Journal of Religion and Popular Culture* 4 (Summer 2003), available at www.usask.ca/relst/jrpc/articles4.html. As far as we know, this cogent piece is the only existing discussion of Pauline theology and "realized eschatology" in the second film. Also, basing her article on the second film, she disagreed with part of our thesis, which actually allowed us to rethink and—we hope—to better our argument on Gnosticism in the trilogy in this final incarnation of our article "Wake Up!"

For more on Gnosticism in general, the following is an indispensable introduction: Elaine Pagels, *The Gnostic Gospels* (New York: Random House, 1979, repr. 1989). More difficult but excellent sources include Gershom Scholem, *Jewish Gnosticism, Merkabah Mysticism, and Talmudic Tradition* (New York: Jewish Theological Seminary of America, 1960); Bentley Layton, *The Gnostic Scriptures* (New York: Doubleday, 1995); and Kurt Rudolph, *Gnosis: The Nature and History of Gnosticism* (San Francisco: HarperSanFrancisco, 1987). The authoritative scholarly collection of Gnostic texts may be found in James M. Robinson, ed., *The Nag Hammadi Library*, rev. ed. (New York: HarperCollins, 1990; reprint of original Brill edition, 1978). The Gnostic texts themselves are engaging, surprising, and still generally unexplored in comparison to canonical Christian texts.

A basic collection of Buddhist texts may be found in Edward Conze, ed., *Buddhist Texts through the Ages* (New York: Philosophical Library,

1954). Our favorite basic introduction to Buddhism remains Walpola Sri Rahula, *What the Buddha Taught* (New York: Grove Weidenfeld, 1974); for Zen Buddhism, read D. T. Suzuki, *An Introduction to Zen Buddhism* (New York: Grove, 1964).

For more on religion and film, see John Lyden, *Film as Religion: Myths, Morals, and Rituals* (New York and London: New York University Press, 2003). Lyden not only explores the religious in film, but also how film itself functions in its cultural reception as religion.

APPENDIX: SELECTIONS FROM CLASSIC TEXTS

Plato (427?–347 B.C.) was arguably the first great systematic philosopher of the Western tradition and is still considered by many to be the greatest philosopher of all time. Inspired by Socrates (469–399 B.C.), who would become the main character in dialogues written by Plato, he argued passionately that most people are in an extreme state of ignorance regarding reality and that a journey of self-discovery and self-knowledge is required in order to escape this ignorance. In the excerpt from his *Republic* that is included here, we see his metaphorical description of our plight in his moving portrait of the Cave. Partridge's chapter considers the many parallels between the story Plato tells here and the situation described in *The Matrix*.

Plato, from *The Republic*

Next, I said, compare the effect of education and of the lack of it on our nature to an experience like this: Imagine human beings living in an *514* underground, cavelike dwelling, with an entrance a long way up, which is both open to the light and as wide as the cave itself. They've been there since childhood, fixed in the same place, with their necks and legs fettered, able to see only in front of them, because their bonds prevent them from turning their heads around. Light is provided by a fire burning far above and behind them. Also behind them, but on higher ground, there is a path *b* stretching between them and the fire. Imagine that along this path a low wall has been built, like the screen in front of puppeteers above which they show their puppets.

I'm imagining it.

Then also imagine that there are people along the wall, carrying all kinds of artifacts that project above it—statues of people and other animals,

c   made out of stone, wood, and every material. And, as you'd expect, some of
515 the carriers are talking, and some are silent.

It's a strange image you're describing, and strange prisoners.

They're like us. Do you suppose, first of all, that these prisoners see anything of themselves and one another besides the shadows that the fire casts on the wall in front of them?

How could they, if they have to keep their heads motionless throughout
b   life?

What about the things being carried along the wall? Isn't the same true of them?

Of course.

And if they could talk to one another, don't you think they'd suppose that the names they used applied to the things they see passing before them?[1]

They'd have to.

And what if their prison also had an echo from the wall facing them? Don't you think they'd believe that the shadows passing in front of them were talking whenever one of the carriers passing along the wall was doing so?

I certainly do.

c   Then the prisoners would in every way believe that the truth is nothing other than the shadows of those artifacts.

They must surely believe that.

Consider, then, what being released from their bonds and cured of their ignorance would naturally be like if something like this came to pass. When one of them was freed and suddenly compelled to stand up, turn his head, walk, and look up toward the light, he'd be pained and dazzled and unable to see the things whose shadows he'd seen before. What do you
d   think he'd say, if we told him that what he'd seen before was inconsequential, but that now—because he is a bit closer to the things that are and is turned towards things that are more—he sees more correctly? Or, to put it another way, if we pointed to each of the things passing by, asked him what each of them is, and compelled him to answer, don't you think he'd

---

1. Reading *parionta autous nomizein onomazein*. E.g. they would think that the name "human being" applied to the shadow of a statue of a human being.

be at a loss and that he'd believe that the things he saw earlier were truer than the ones he was now being shown?

Much truer.

And if someone compelled him to look at the light itself, wouldn't his eyes hurt, and wouldn't he turn around and flee towards the things he's *e* able to see, believing that they're really clearer than the ones he's being shown?

He would.

And if someone dragged him away from there by force, up the rough, steep path and didn't let him go until he had dragged him into the sunlight, wouldn't he be pained and irritated at being treated that way? And when he came into the light, with the sun filling his eyes, wouldn't *516* he be unable to see a single one of the things now said to be true?

He would be unable to see them, at least at first.

I suppose, then, that he'd need time to get adjusted before he could see things in the world above. At first, he'd see shadows most easily, then images of men and other things in water, then the things themselves. Of these, he'd be able to study the things in the sky and the sky itself more easily at night, looking at the light of the stars and the moon, than during the day, looking at the sun and the light of the sun. *b*

Of course.

Finally, I suppose, he'd be able to see the sun, not images of it in water or some alien place, but the sun itself, in its own place, and be able to study it.

Necessarily so.

And at this point he would infer and conclude that the sun provides the seasons and the years, governs everything in the visible world, and is in some way the cause of all the things that he used to see. *c*

It's clear that would be his next step.

What about when he reminds himself of his first dwelling place, his fellow prisoners, and what passed for wisdom there? Don't you think that he'd count himself happy for the change and pity the others?

Certainly.

And if there had been any honors, praises, or prizes among them for the one who was sharpest at identifying the shadows as they passed by and who best remembered which usually came earlier, which later, and *d* which simultaneously, and who could thus best divine the future, do you think that our man would desire these rewards or envy those among the prisoners who were honored and held power? Instead, wouldn't he feel, with Homer, that he'd much prefer to "work the earth as a serf to another, one without possessions,"[2] and go through any sufferings, rather than share their opinions and live as they do?

e I suppose he would rather suffer anything than live like that.

Consider this too. If this man went down into the cave again and sat down in his same seat, wouldn't his eyes—coming suddenly out of the sun like that—be filled with darkness?

They certainly would.

And before his eyes had recovered—and the adjustment would not be quick—while his vision was still dim, if he had to compete again with the
517 perpetual prisoners in recognizing the shadows, wouldn't he invite ridicule? Wouldn't it be said of him that he'd returned from his upward journey with his eyesight ruined and that it isn't worthwhile even to try to travel upward? And, as for anyone who tried to free them and lead them upward, if they could somehow get their hands on him, wouldn't they kill him?

They certainly would.

b This whole image, Glaucon, must be fitted together with what we said before. The visible realm should be likened to the prison dwelling, and the light of the fire inside it to the power of the sun. And if you interpret the upward journey and the study of things above as the upward journey of the soul to the intelligible realm, you'll grasp what I hope to convey, since that is what you wanted to hear about. Whether it's true or not, only the god knows. But this is how I see it: In the knowable realm, the form of the good is the last thing to be seen, and it is reached only with difficulty. Once one has seen it, however, one must conclude that it is the cause of all that is
c correct and beautiful in anything, that it produces both light and its source in the visible realm, and that in the intelligible realm it controls and provides truth and understanding, so that anyone who is to act sensibly in private or public must see it.

---

2. *Odyssey* 11.489–90. The shade of the dead Achilles speaks these words to Odysseus, who is visiting Hades. Plato is, therefore, likening the cave dwellers to the dead.

I have the same thought, at least as far as I'm able.

Come, then, share with me this thought also: It isn't surprising that the ones who get to this point are unwilling to occupy themselves with human affairs and that their souls are always pressing upwards, eager to spend their time above, for, after all, this is surely what we'd expect, if indeed things fit the image I described before.   *d*

It is.

What about what happens when someone turns from divine study to the evils of human life? Do you think it's surprising, since his sight is still dim, and he hasn't yet become accustomed to the darkness around him, that he behaves awkwardly and appears completely ridiculous if he's compelled, either in the courts or elsewhere, to contend about the shadows of justice or the statues of which they are the shadows and to dispute about the way these things are understood by people who have never seen justice itself?   *e*

That's not surprising at all.

No, it isn't. But anyone with any understanding would remember that *518* the eyes may be confused in two ways and from two causes, namely, when they've come from the light into the darkness *and* when they've come from the darkness into the light. Realizing that the same applies to the soul, when someone sees a soul disturbed and unable to see something, he won't laugh mindlessly, but he'll take into consideration whether it has come from a brighter life and is dimmed through not having yet become accustomed to the dark or whether it has come from greater ignorance into greater light and is dazzled by the increased brilliance. Then he'll declare the first soul happy in its experience and life, and he'll pity the latter—but *b* even if he chose to make fun of it, at least he'd be less ridiculous that if he laughed at a soul that has come from the light above.

What you say is very reasonable.

If that's true, then here's what we must think about these matters: Education isn't what some people declare it to be, namely, putting knowledge into souls that lack it, like putting sight into blind eyes.   *c*

They do say that.

But our present discussion, on the other hand, shows that the power to learn is present in everyone's soul and that the instrument with which each learns is like an eye that cannot be turned around from darkness to light without turning the whole body. This instrument cannot be turned around from that which is coming into being without turning the whole soul until it is able to study that which is and the brightest thing that is,

d namely, the one we call the good. Isn't that right?

Yes.

Then education is the craft concerned with doing this very thing, this turning around, and with how the soul can most easily and effectively be made to do it. It isn't the craft of putting sight into the soul. Education takes for granted that sight is there but that it isn't turned the right way or looking where it ought to look, and it tries to redirect it appropriately.

532 Then isn't this at last, Glaucon, the song that dialectic sings? It is intelligible, but it is imitated by the power of sight. We said that sight tries at last to look at the animals themselves, the stars themselves, and, in the end, at the sun itself.[13] In the same way, whenever someone tries through argument and apart from all sense perceptions to find the being itself of each thing and doesn't give up until he grasps the good itself with un-

b derstanding itself, he reaches the end of the intelligible, just as the other reached the end of the visible.

Absolutely.[3]

And what about this journey? Don't you call it dialectic?

I do.

Then the release from bonds and the turning around from shadows to statues and the light of the fire and, then, the way up out of the cave to the sunlight and, there, the continuing inability to look at the animals, the plants,

c and the light of the sun, but the newly acquired ability to look at divine images in water and shadows of the things that are, rather than, as before, merely at shadows of statues thrown by another source of light that is itself a shadow in relation to the sun—all this business of the crafts we've mentioned has the power to awaken the best part of the soul and lead it upward to the study of the best among the things that are, just as, before, the clearest thing

d in the body was led to the brightest thing in the bodily and visible realm.

René Descartes (1596–1650) is considered by many to be the father of modern Western philosophy. This excerpt includes the first two sections from his great

---

13. See 516a–b.

work *The Meditations.* Here we see him introduce both the skeptical possibility that one might be dreaming and the more radical skeptical worry that an evil intelligence might be controlling one's perceptions and even one's thoughts. Almost every chapter in this collection addresses his ideas to some degree, though you will find Descartes's arguments explicitly discussed in Grau's chapter.

René Descartes, *Meditations on First Philosophy: In Which Are Demonstrated the Existence of God and the Distinction between the Human Soul and the Body*

First Meditation

WHAT CAN BE CALLED INTO DOUBT   Some years ago I was struck by the large number of falsehoods that I had accepted as true in my childhood, and by the highly doubtful nature of the whole edifice that I had subsequently based on them. I realized that it was necessary, once in the course of my life, to demolish everything completely and start again right from the foundations if I wanted to establish anything at all in the sciences that was stable and likely to last. But the task looked an enormous one, and I began to wait until I should reach a mature enough age to ensure that no subsequent time of life would be more suitable for tackling such inquiries. This led me to put the project off for so long that I would now be to blame if by pondering over it any further I wasted the time still left for carrying it out. So today I have expressly rid my mind of all worries and arranged for myself a clear stretch of free time. I am here quite alone, and at last I will devote myself sincerely and without reservation to the general demolition of my opinions.

But to accomplish this, it will not be necessary for me to show that all my opinions are false, which is something I could perhaps never manage. Reason now leads me to think that I should hold back my assent from opinions which are not completely certain and indubitable just as carefully as I do from those which are patently false. So, for the purpose of rejecting all my opinions, it will be enough if I find in each of them at least some reason for doubt. And to do this I will not need to run through them all individually, which would be an endless task. Once the foundations of a building are undermined, anything built on them collapses of its own accord; so I will go straight for the basic principles on which all my former beliefs rested.

Whatever I have up till now accepted as most true I have acquired either from the senses or through the senses. But from time to time I have found that the senses deceive, and it is prudent never to trust completely those who have deceived us even once.

Yet although the senses occasionally deceive us with respect to objects which are very small or in the distance, there are many other beliefs about which doubt is quite impossible, even though they are derived from the senses—for example, that I am here, sitting by the fire, wearing a winter dressing-gown, holding this piece of paper in my hands, and so on. Again, how could it be denied that these hands or this whole body are mine? Unless perhaps I were to liken myself to madmen, whose brains are so damaged by the persistent vapours of melancholia that they firmly maintain they are kings when they are paupers, or say they are dressed in purple when they are naked, or that their heads are made of earthenware, or that they are pumpkins, or made of glass. But such people are insane, and I would be thought equally mad if I took anything from them as a model for myself.

A brilliant piece of reasoning! As if I were not a man who sleeps at night, and regularly has all the same experiences while asleep as madmen do when awake—indeed sometimes even more improbable ones. How often, asleep at night am I convinced of just such familiar events—that I am here in my dressing-gown, sitting by the fire—when in fact I am lying undressed in bed! Yet at the moment my eyes are certainly wide awake when I look at this piece of paper; I shake my head and it is not asleep; as I stretch out and feel my hand I do so deliberately, and I know what I am doing. All this would not happen with such distinctness to someone asleep. Indeed! As if I did not remember other occasions when I have been tricked by exactly similar thoughts while asleep! As I think about this more carefully, I see plainly that there are never any sure signs by means of which being awake can be distinguished from being asleep. The result is that I begin to feel dazed, and this very feeling only reinforces the notion that I may be asleep.

Suppose then that I am dreaming, and that these particulars—that my eyes are open, that I am moving my head and stretching out my hands— are not true. Perhaps, indeed, I do not even have such hands or such a body at all. Nonetheless, it must surely be admitted that the visions which come in sleep are like paintings, which must have been fashioned in the likeness of things that are real, and hence that at least these general kinds of things—eyes, head, hands and the body as a whole—are things which are not imaginary but are real and exist. For even when painters try to create sirens and satyrs with the most extraordinary bodies, they cannot give them natures which are new in all respects; they simply jumble up the limbs of different animals. Or if perhaps they manage to think up something so new that nothing remotely similar has ever been seen before—something which is therefore completely fictitious and unreal—at least the colours used in the composition must be real. By similar reasoning, although these general kinds of things—eyes, head, hands and so on—could be imaginary, it must at least be admitted that certain other even simpler and more universal things are real. These are as it were the real colours from which we form all the images of things, whether true or false, that occur in our thought.

This class appears to include corporeal nature in general, and its extension; the shape of extended things; the quantity, or size and number of these things; the place in which they may exist, the time through which they may endure, and so on.

So a reasonable conclusion from this might be that physics, astronomy, medicine, and all other disciplines which depend on the study of composite things, are doubtful; while arithmetic, geometry and other subjects of this kind, which deal only with the simplest and most general things, regardless of whether they really exist in nature or not, contain something certain and indubitable. For whether I am awake or asleep, two and three added together are five, and a square has no more than four sides. It seems impossible that such transparent truths should incur any suspicion of being false.

And yet firmly rooted in my mind is the long-standing opinion that there is an omnipotent God who made me the kind of creature that I am. How do I know that he has not brought it about that there is no earth, no sky, no extended thing, no shape, no size, no place, while at the same time ensuring that all these things appear to me to exist just as they do now? What is more, just as I consider that others sometimes go astray in cases where they think they have the most perfect knowledge, how do I know that God has not brought it about that I too go wrong every time I add two and three or count the sides of a square, or in some even simpler matter, if that is imaginable? But perhaps God would not have allowed me to be deceived in this way, since he is said to be supremely good. But if it were inconsistent with his goodness to have created me such that I am deceived all the time, it would seem equally foreign to his goodness to allow me to be deceived even occasionally; yet this last assertion cannot be made.

Perhaps there may be some who would prefer to deny the existence of so powerful a God rather than believe that everything else is uncertain. Let us not argue with them, but grant them that everything said about God is a fiction. According to their supposition, then, I have arrived at my present state by fate or chance or a continuous chain of events, or by some other means; yet since deception and error seem to be imperfections, the less powerful they make my original cause, the more likely it is that I am so imperfect as to be deceived all the time. I have no answer to these arguments, but am finally compelled to admit that there is not one of my former beliefs about which a doubt may not properly be raised; and this is not a flippant or ill-considered conclusion, but is based on powerful and well thought-out reasons. So in future I must withhold my assent from these former beliefs just as carefully as I would from obvious falsehoods, if I want to discover any certainty.

But it is not enough merely to have noticed this; I must make an effort to remember it. My habitual opinions keep coming back, and, despite my wishes, they capture my belief, which is as it were bound over to them as a result of long occupation and the law of custom. I shall never get out of the habit of confidently assenting to these opinions, so long as I suppose them to be what in fact they are, namely highly probable opinions—opinions which, despite the fact that they are in a sense doubtful, as has just been shown, it is still much more reasonable to believe than to deny. In view of this, I think it will be a good plan to turn my will in completely the opposite direction and deceive myself, by pretending for a time that these former opinions are utterly false and imaginary. I shall do this until the weight of preconceived opinion is counter-balanced and the distorting influence of habit no longer prevents my judgment from perceiving things correctly. In the meantime, I know that no danger or error will result from my plan, and that I cannot possibly go too far in my distrustful attitude. This is because the task now in hand does not involve action but merely the acquisition of knowledge.

I will suppose therefore that not God, who is supremely good and the source of truth, but rather some malicious demon of the utmost power and cunning has employed all his energies in order to deceive me. I shall think that the sky, the air, the earth, colours, shapes, sounds and all external things are merely the delusions of dreams which he has devised to ensnare my judgment. I shall consider myself as not having hands or eyes, or flesh, or blood or senses, but as falsely believing that I have all these things. I shall stubbornly and firmly persist in this meditation; and, even if it is not in my power to know any truth, I shall at least do what is in my power, that is, resolutely guard against assenting to any falsehoods, so that the deceiver, however powerful and cunning he may be, will be unable to impose on me in the slightest degree. But this is an arduous undertaking, and a kind of laziness brings me back to normal life. I am like a prisoner who is enjoying an imaginary freedom while asleep; as he begins to suspect that he is asleep, he dreads being woken up, and goes along with the pleasant illusion as long as he can. In the same way, I happily slide back into my old opinions and dread being shaken out of them, for fear that my peaceful sleep may be followed by hard labour when I wake, and that I shall have to toil not in the light, but amid the inextricable darkness of the problems I have now raised.

Second Meditation

THE NATURE OF THE HUMAN MIND, AND HOW IT IS BETTER KNOWN THAN THE BODY   So serious are the doubts into which I have been thrown as a result of yesterday's meditation that I can neither put them out of my mind nor see any way of resolving them. It feels as if I have fallen unexpectedly into a deep whirlpool which tumbles me around so that I can neither stand on the bottom nor swim up to the top. Nevertheless I will make an effort and once more attempt the same path which I started on yesterday. Anything which admits of the slightest doubt I will set aside just as if I had found it to be wholly false; and I will proceed in this way until I recognize something certain, or, if nothing else, until I at least recognize for certain that there is no certainty. Archimedes used to demand just one firm and immovable point in order to shift the entire earth; so I too can hope for great things if I manage to find just one thing, however slight, that is certain and unshakable.

I will suppose then, that everything I see is spurious. I will believe that my memory tells me lies, and that none of the things that it reports ever happened. I have no senses. Body, shape, extension, movement and place are chimeras. So what remains true? Perhaps just the one fact that nothing is certain.

Yet apart from everything I have just listed, how do I know that there is not something else which does not allow even the slightest occasion for doubt? Is there not a God, or whatever I may call him, who puts into me the thoughts I am now having? But why do I think this, since I myself may perhaps be the author of these thoughts? In that case am not I, at least, something? But I have just said that I have no senses and no body. This is the sticking point: what follows from this? Am I not so bound up with a body and with senses that I cannot exist without them? But I have convinced myself that there is absolutely nothing in the world, no sky, no earth, no minds, no bodies. Does it now follow that I too do not exist? No: if I convinced myself of something then I certainly existed. But there is a deceiver of supreme power and cunning who is deliberately and constantly deceiving me. In that case I too undoubtedly exist, if he is deceiving me; and let him deceive me as much as he can, he will never bring it about that I am nothing so long as I think that I am something. So after considering everything very thoroughly, I must finally conclude that this proposition, *I am, I exist*, is necessarily true whenever it is put forward by me or conceived in my mind.

But I do not yet have a sufficient understanding of what this 'I' is, that now necessarily exists. So I must be on my guard against carelessly taking something else to be this 'I', and so making a mistake in the very item of knowledge that I maintain is the most certain and evident of all. I will therefore go back and meditate on what I originally believed myself to be, before I embarked on this present train of thought. I will then subtract anything capable of being weakened, even minimally, by the arguments now introduced, so that what is left at the end may be exactly and only what is certain and unshakable.

What then did I formerly think I was? A man. But what is a man? Shall I say 'a rational animal'? No; for then I should have to inquire what an animal is, what rationality is, and in this way one question would lead me down the slope to other harder ones, and I do not now have the time to waste on subtleties of this kind. Instead I propose to concentrate on what came into my thoughts spontaneously and quite naturally whenever I used to consider what I was. Well, the first thought to come to mind was that I had a face, hands, arms and the whole mechanical structure of limbs which can be seen in a corpse, and which I called the body. The next thought was that I was nourished, that I moved about, and that I engaged in sense-perception and thinking; and these actions I attributed to the soul. But as to the nature of this soul, either I did not think about this or else I imagined it to be something tenuous, like a wind or fire or ether, which permeated my more solid parts. As to the body, however, I had no doubts about it, but thought I knew its nature distinctly. If I had tried to describe the mental conception I had of it, I would have expressed it as follows: by a body I understand whatever has a determinable shape and a definable location and can occupy a space in such a way as to exclude any other body; it can be perceived by touch, sight, hearing, taste or smell, and can be moved in various ways, not by itself but by whatever else comes into contact with it. For, according to my judgment, the power of self-movement, like the power of sensation or of thought, was quite foreign to the nature of a body; indeed, it was a source of wonder to me that certain bodies were found to contain faculties of this kind.

But what shall I now say that I am, when I am supposing that there is some supremely powerful and, if it is permissible to say so, malicious deceiver, who is deliberately trying to trick me in every way he can? Can I now assert that I possess even the most insignificant of all the attributes which I have just said belong to the nature of a body? I scrutinize them, think about them, go over them again, but nothing suggests itself; it is tiresome and pointless to go through the list once more. But what about the attributes I assigned to the soul? Nutrition or movement? Since now I do not have a body, these are mere fabrications. Sense-perception? This surely does not occur without a body, and besides, when asleep I have appeared to perceive through the senses many things which I afterwards realized I did not perceive through the senses at all. Thinking? At last I have discovered it—thought; this alone is inseparable from me. I am, I exist—that is certain. But for how long? For as long as I am thinking. For it could be that were I totally to cease from thinking, I should totally cease to exist. At present I am not admitting anything except what is necessarily true. I am, then, in the strict sense only a thing that thinks; that is, I am a mind, or intelligence, or intellect, or reason—words whose meaning I have been ignorant of until now. But for all that I am a thing which is real and which truly exists. But what kind of a thing? As I have just said—a thinking thing.

What else am I? I will use my imagination. I am not that structure of limbs which is called a human body. I am not even some thin vapour which permeates the limbs—a wind, fire, air, breath, or whatever I depict in my imagination; for these are things which I have supposed to be nothing. Let this supposition stand; for all that I am still something. And yet may it not perhaps be the case that these very things which I am supposing to be nothing, because they are unknown to me, are in reality identical with the 'I' of which I am aware? I do not know, and for the moment I shall not argue the point, since I can make judgments only about things which are known to me. I know that I exist; the question is, what is this 'I' that I know? If the 'I' is understood strictly as we have been taking it, then it is quite certain that knowledge of it does not depend on things of whose existence I am as yet unaware; so it cannot depend on any of the things which I invent in my imagination. And this very word 'invent' shows me my mistake. It would indeed be a case of fictitious invention if I used my imagination to establish that I was something or other; for imagining is simply contemplating the shape or image of a corporeal thing. Yet now I know for certain both that I exist and at the same time that all such images and, in general, everything relating to the nature of body, could be mere dreams [and chimeras]. Once this point has been grasped, to say 'I will use my imagination to get to know more distinctly what I am' would seem to be as silly as saying 'I am now awake, and see some truth; but since my vision is not yet clear enough, I will deliberately fall asleep so that my dreams may provide a truer and clearer representation.' I thus realize that none of the things that the imagination enables me to grasp is at all relevant to this knowledge of myself which I possess, and that the mind must therefore be most carefully diverted from such things if it is to perceive its own nature as distinctly as possible.

But what then am I? A thing that thinks. What is that? A thing that doubts, understands, affirms, denies, is willing, is unwilling, and also imagines and has sensory perceptions.

This is a considerable list, if everything on it belongs to me. But does it? Is it not one and the same 'I' who is now doubting almost everything, who nonetheless understands some things, who affirms that this one thing is true, denies everything else, desires to know more, is unwilling to be deceived, imagines many things even involuntarily, and is aware of many things which apparently come from the senses? Are not all these things just as true as the fact that I exist, even if I am asleep all the time, and even if he who created me is doing all he can to deceive me? Which of all these activities is distinct from my thinking? Which of them can be said to be separate from myself? The fact that it is I who am doubting and understanding and willing is so evident that I see no way of making it any clearer. But it is also the case that the 'I' who imagines is the same 'I'. For even if, as I have supposed, none of the objects of imagination are real, the power of imagination is something which really exists and is part of my thinking. Lastly, it is also the same 'I' who has sensory perceptions, or is aware of bodily things as it were through the senses. For example, I am now seeing light, hearing a noise, feeling heat. But I am asleep, so all this is false. Yet I certainly *seem* to see, to hear, and to be warmed. This cannot be false; what is called 'having a sensory perception' is strictly just this, and in this restricted sense of the term it is simply thinking.

From all this I am beginning to have a rather better understanding of what I am. But it still appears—and I cannot stop thinking this—that the corporeal things of which images are formed in my thought, and which the sense investigate, are known with much more distinctness than this puzzling 'I' which cannot be pictured in the imagination. And yet it is surely surprising that I should have a more distinct grasp of things which I realize are doubtful, unknown and foreign to me, than I have of that which is true and known—my own self. But I see what it is: my mind enjoys wandering off and will not yet submit to being restrained within the bounds of truth. Very well then; just this once let us give it a completely free rein, so that after a while, when it is time to tighten the reins, it may more readily submit to being curbed.

Let us consider the things which people commonly think they understand most distinctly of all; that is, the bodies which we touch and see. I do not mean bodies in general—for general perceptions are apt to be somewhat more confused—but one particular body. Let us take, for example, this piece of wax. It has just been taken from the honeycomb; it has not yet quite lost the taste of the honey; it retains some of the scent of the flowers from which it was gathered; its colour, shape and size are plain to see; it is hard, cold and can be handled without difficulty; if you rap it with your knuckle it makes a sound. In short, it has everything which appears necessary to enable a body to be known as distinctly as possible. But even as I speak, I put the wax by the fire, and look: the residual taste is eliminated, the smell goes away, the colour changes, the shape is lost, the size increases; it becomes liquid and hot; you can hardly touch it, and if you strike it, it no longer makes a sound. But does the same wax remain? It must be admitted that it does; no one denies it, no one thinks otherwise. So what was it in the wax that I understood with such distinctness? Evidently none of the features which I arrived at by means of the senses; for whatever came under taste, smell, sight, touch or hearing has now altered—yet the wax remains.

Perhaps the answer lies in the thought which now comes to my mind; namely, the wax was not after all the sweetness of the honey, or the fragrance of the flowers, or the whiteness, or the shape, or the sound, but was rather a body which presented itself to me in these various forms a little while ago, but which now exhibits different ones. But what exactly is it that I am now imagining? Let us concentrate, take away everything which does not belong to the wax, and see what is left: merely something extended, flexible and changeable. But what is meant here by 'flexible' and 'changeable'? Is it what I picture in my imagination: that this piece of wax is capable of changing from a round shape to a square shape, or from a square shape to a triangular shape? Not at all; for I can grasp that the wax is capable of countless changes of this kind, yet I am unable to run through this immeasurable number of changes in my imagination, from which it follows that it is not the faculty of imagination that gives me my grasp of the wax as flexible and changeable. And what is meant by 'extended'? Is the extension of the wax also unknown? For it increases if the wax melts, increases again if it boils, and is greater still if the heat is increased. I would not be making a correct judgment about the nature of wax unless I believed it capable of being extended in many more different ways than I will ever encompass in my imagination. I must therefore admit that the nature of this piece of wax is in no way revealed by my imagination, but is perceived by the mind alone. (I am speaking of this particular piece of wax; the point is even clearer with regard to wax in general.) But what is this wax which is perceived by the mind alone? It is of course the same wax which I see, which I touch, which I picture in my imagination, in short the same wax which I thought it to be from the start. And yet, and here is the point, the perception I have of it is a case not of vision or touch or imagination—nor has it ever been, despite previous appearances—but of purely mental scrutiny; and this can be imperfect and confused, as it was before, or clear and distinct as it is now, depending on how carefully I concentrate on what the wax consists in.

But as I reach this conclusion I am amazed at how [weak and] prone to error my mind is. For although I am thinking about these matters within myself, silently and without speaking, nonetheless the actual words bring me up short, and I am almost tricked by ordinary ways of talking. We say that we see the wax itself, if it is there before us, not that we judge it to be there from its colour or shape; and this might lead me to conclude without more ado that knowledge of the wax comes from what the eye sees, and not from the scrutiny of the mind alone. But then if I look out of the window and see men crossing the square, as I just happen to have done, I normally say that I see the men themselves, just as I say that I see the wax. Yet do I see any more than hats and coats which could conceal automatons? I *judge* that they are men. And so something which I thought I was seeing with my eyes is in fact grasped solely by the faculty of judgment which is in my mind.

However, one who wants to achieve knowledge above the ordinary level should feel ashamed at having taken ordinary ways of talking as a basis for doubt. So let us proceed, and consider on which occasion my perception of the nature of the wax was more perfect and evident. Was it when I first looked at it, and believed I knew it by my external senses, or at least by what they call the 'common' sense—that is, the power of imagination? Or is my knowledge more perfect now, after a more careful investigation of the nature of the wax and of the means by which it is known? Any doubt on this issue would clearly be foolish; for what distinctness was there in my earlier perception? Was there anything in it which an animal could not possess? But when I distinguish the wax from its outward forms—take the clothes off, as it were, and consider it naked—then although my judgment may still contain errors, at least my perception now requires a human mind.

But what am I to say about this mind, or about myself? (So far, remember, I am not admitting that there is anything else in me except a mind.) What, I ask, is this 'I' which seems to perceive the wax so distinctly? Surely my awareness of my own self is not merely much truer and more certain than my awareness of the wax, but also much more distinct and evident. For if I judge that the wax exists from the fact that I see it, clearly this same fact entails much more evidently that I myself also exist. It is possible that what I see is not really the wax; it is possible that I do not even have eyes with which to see anything. But when I see, or think I see (I am not here distinguishing the two), it is simply not possible that I who am now thinking am not something. By the same token, if I judge that the wax exists from the fact that I touch it, the same result follows, namely that I exist. If I judge that it exists from the fact that I imagine it, or for any other reason, exactly the same thing follows. And the result that I have grasped in the case of the wax may be applied to everything else located outside me. Moreover, if my perception of the wax seemed more distinct after it was established not just by sight or touch but by many other considerations, it must be admitted that I now know myself even more distinctly. This is because every consideration whatsoever which contributes to my perception of the wax, or of any other body, cannot but establish even more effectively the nature of my own mind. But besides this, there is so much else in the mind itself which can serve to make my knowledge of it more distinct, that it scarcely seems worth going through the contributions made by considering bodily things.

I see that without any effort I have now finally got back to where I wanted. I now know that even bodies are not strictly perceived by the senses or the faculty of imagination but by the intellect alone, and that this perception derives not from their being touched or seen but from their being understood; and in view of this I know plainly that I can achieve an easier and more evident perception of my own mind than of anything else. But since the habit of holding on to old opinions cannot be set aside so quickly, I should like to stop here and meditate for some time on this new knowledge I have gained, so as to fix it more deeply in my memory.

George Berkeley (1685–1753) was bishop of Cloyne as well as a philosopher and is known today primarily for his "idealism"—a brilliant and extreme defense of empiricism that brings with it a denial of the existence of a mind-independent reality. This excerpt from his *Principles of Human Knowledge* offers a concise but illuminating summary of his position. His view is considered briefly in Chalmer's chapter and given a more thorough investigation in Mawson's contribution.

George Berkeley, from *Of the Principles of Human Knowledge*

Part I

1. It is evident to anyone who takes a survey of the objects of human knowledge, that they are either ideas actually imprinted on the senses, or else such as are perceived by attending to the passions and operations of the mind, or lastly ideas formed by help of memory and imagination, either compounding, dividing, or barely representing those originally perceived in the aforesaid ways. By sight I have the ideas of light and colours with their several degrees and variations. By touch I perceive, for example, hard and soft, heat and cold, motion and resistance, and of all these more and less either as to quantity or degree. Smelling furnishes me with odours; the palate with tastes, and hearing conveys sounds to the mind in all their variety of tone and composition. And as several of these are observed to accompany each other, they come to be marked by one name, and so to be reputed as one thing. Thus, for example, a certain colour, taste, smell, figure and consistence having been observed to go together, are accounted one distinct thing, signified by the name *apple*. Other collections of ideas constitute a stone, a tree, a book, and the like sensible things; which, as they are pleasing or disagreeable, excite the passions of love, hatred, joy, grief, and so forth.

2. But besides all that endless variety of ideas or objects of knowledge, there is likewise something which knows or perceives them, and exercises

divers operations, as willing, imagining, remembering about them. This perceiving, active being is what I call *mind, spirit, soul* or *myself*. By which words I do not denote any one of my ideas, but a thing entirely distinct from them, wherein they exist, or, which is the same thing, whereby they are perceived; for the existence of an idea consists in being perceived.

3. That neither our thoughts, nor passions, nor ideas formed by the imagination, exist without the mind, is what everybody will allow. And it seems no less evident that the various sensations or ideas imprinted on the sense, however blended or combined together (that is, whatever objects they compose) cannot exist otherwise than in a mind perceiving them. I think an intuitive knowledge may be obtained of this, by anyone that shall attend to what is meant by the term *exist* when applied to sensible things. The table I write on, I say, exists, that is, I see and feel it; and if I were out of my study I should say it existed, meaning thereby that if I was in my study I might perceive it, or that some other spirit actually does perceive it. There was an odour, that is, it was smelled; there was a sound, that is to say, it was heard; a colour or figure, and it was perceived by sight or touch. This is all that I can understand by these and the like expressions. For as to what is said of the absolute existence of unthinking things without any relation to their being perceived, that seems perfectly unintelligible. Their *esse* is *percipi*, nor is it possible they should have any existence, out of the minds or thinking things which perceive them.

4. It is indeed an opinion strangely prevailing amongst men, that houses, mountains, rivers, and in a word all sensible objects have an existence natural or real, distinct from their being perceived by the understanding. But with how great an assurance and acquiescence soever this principle may be entertained in the world; yet whoever shall find in his heart to call in question, may, if I mistake not, perceive it to involve a manifest contradiction. For what are the forementioned objects but the things we perceive by sense, and what do we perceive besides our own ideas or sensations; and is it not plainly repugnant that any one of these or any combination of them should exist unperceived?

5. If we throughly examine this tenet, it will, perhaps, be found at bottom to depend on the doctrine of *abstract ideas*. For can there be a nicer strain of abstraction than to distinguish the existence of sensible

objects from their being perceived, so as to conceive them existing unperceived? Light and colours, heat and cold, extension and figures, in a word the things we see and feel, what are they but so many sensations, notions, ideas or impressions on the sense; and is it possible to separate, even in thought, any of these from perception? For my part I might as easily divide a thing from itself. I may indeed divide in my thoughts or conceive apart from each other those things which, perhaps, I never perceived by sense so divided. Thus I imagine the trunk of a human body without the limbs, or conceive the smell of rose without thinking on the rose itself. So far I will not deny I can abstract, if that may properly be called *abstraction,* which extends only to the conceiving separately such objects, as it is possible may really exist or be actually perceived asunder. But my conceiving or imagining power does not extend beyond the possibility of real existence or perception. Hence as it is impossible for me to see or feel anything without an actual sensation of that thing, so is it impossible for me to conceive in my thoughts any sensible thing or object distinct from the sensation or perception of it.

6. Some truths there are so near and obvious to the mind, that a man need only open his eyes to see them. Such I take this important one to be, to wit, that all the choir of heaven and furniture of the earth, in a word all those bodies which compose the mighty frame of the world, have not any subsistence without a mind, that their being is to be perceived or known; that consequently so long as they are not actually perceived by me, or do not exist in my mind or that of any other created spirit, they must either have no existence at all, or else subsist in the mind of some eternal spirit: it being perfectly unintelligible and involving all the absurdity of abstraction, to attribute to any single part of them an existence independent of a spirit. To be convinced of which, the reader need only reflect and try to separate in his own thoughts the being of a sensible thing from its being perceived.

7. From what has been said, it follows, there is not any other substance than *spirit,* or that which perceives. But for the fuller proof of this point, let it be considered, the sensible qualities are colour, figure, motion, smell, taste, and such like, that is, the ideas perceived by sense. Now for an idea to exist in an unperceiving thing, is a manifest contradiction; for to have an idea is all one as to perceive: that therefore wherein colour, figure, and the

like qualities exist, must perceive them; hence it is clear there can be no unthinking substance or *substratum* of those ideas.

8. But say you, though the ideas themselves do not exist without the mind, yet there may be things like them whereof they are copies or resemblances, which things exist without the mind, in an unthinking substance. I answer, an idea can be like nothing but an idea; a colour or figure can be like nothing but another colour or figure. If we look but ever so little into our thoughts, we shall find it impossible for us to conceive a likeness except only between our ideas. Again, I ask whether those supposed originals or external things, of which our ideas are the pictures or representations, be themselves perceivable or no? If they are, then they are ideas, and we have gained our point; but if you say they are not, I appeal to anyone whether it be sense, to assert a colour is like something which is invisible; hard or soft, like something which is intangible; and so of the rest.

Robert Nozick (1938–2002) was a profoundly influential contemporary philosopher who is perhaps best known for his philosophical defense of political libertarianism. In the following brief excerpt from his first book, *Anarchy, State, and Utopia*, he presents a now-classic thought-experiment involving the possibility of plugging into a machine that can provide a simulation of *any* desired experience. Nozick argues that our hesitancy to plug in suggests that we ultimately value more than just pleasant experience. The connections between Nozick's scenario and the choice that Cypher must make in *The Matrix* are discussed in the chapters by Grau, McGinn, Dreyfus and Dreyfus, Pryor, Vasiliou, Hanley, and Warwick.

Robert Nozick, from *Anarchy, State, and Utopia*

The Experience Machine

Suppose there were an experience machine that would give you any experience you desired. Superduper neuropsychologists could stimulate your brain so that you would think and feel you were writing a great novel, or making a friend, or reading an interesting book. All the time you would be floating in a tank, with electrodes attached to your brain. Should you plug into this machine for life, preprogramming your life's experiences? If you are worried about missing out on desirable experiences, we can suppose that business enterprises have researched thoroughly the lives of many others. You can pick and choose from their large library or smorgasbord of such experiences, selecting your life's experiences for, say, the next two years. After two years have passed, you will have ten minutes or ten hours out of the tank, to select the experiences of your *next* two years. Of course, while in the tank you won't know that you're there; you'll think it's all actually happening. Others can also plug in to have the experiences they want, so there's no need to stay unplugged to serve them. (Ignore problems such as who will service the machines if everyone plugs in.) Would you plug in? *What else can matter to us, other than how our lives feel from the inside?* Nor should you refrain because of the few moments of distress between the moment you've decided and the moment you're plugged. What's a few moments of distress compared to a lifetime of bliss (if that's what you choose), and why feel any distress at all if your decision *is* the best one?

What does matter to us in addition to our experiences? First, we want to *do* certain things, and not just have the experience of doing them. In the case of certain experiences, it is only because first we want to do the actions that we want the experiences of doing them or thinking we've done them. (But *why* do we want to do the activities rather than merely to experience them?) A second reason for not plugging in is that we want to *be* a certain way, to be a certain sort of person. Someone floating in a tank is an indeterminate blob. There is no answer to the question of what a person is like who has long been in the tank. Is he courageous, kind, intelligent, witty, loving? It's not merely that it's difficult to tell; there's no way he is. Plugging into the machine is a kind of suicide. It will seem to some, trapped by a picture, that nothing about what we are like can matter except as it gets reflected in our experiences. But should it be surprising that what *we are* is important to us? Why should we be concerned only with how our time is filled, but not with what we are?

Thirdly, plugging into an experience machine limits us to a man-made reality, to a world no deeper or more important than that which people can construct. There is no *actual* contact with any deeper reality, though the experience of it can be simulated. Many persons desire to leave themselves open to such contact and to a plumbing of deeper significance.

This clarifies the intensity of the conflict over psychoactive drugs, which some view as mere local experience machines, and others view as avenues to a deeper reality; what some view as equivalent to surrender to the experience machine, others view as following one of the reasons *not* to surrender!

We learn that something matters to us in addition to experience by imagining an experience machine and then realizing that we would not use it. We can continue to imagine a sequence of machines each designed to fill lacks suggested for the earlier machines. For example, since the experience machine doesn't meet our desire to *be* a certain way, imagine a transformation machine which transforms us into whatever sort of person we'd like to be (compatible with our staying us). Surely one would not use the transformation machine to become as one would wish, and thereupon plug into the experience machine! So something matters in addition to one's experiences *and* what one is like. Nor is the reason merely that one's experiences are unconnected with what one is like. For the experience machine might be limited to provide only experiences possible to the sort of person plugged in. Is it that we want to make a difference in the world? Consider then the result machine, which produces in the world any result you would produce and injects your vector input into any joint activity. We shall not pursue here the fascinating details of these or other machines. What is most disturbing about them is their living of our lives for us. Is it misguided to search for *particular* additional functions beyond the competence of machines to do for us? Perhaps what we desire is to live (an active verb) ourselves, in contact with reality. (And this, machines cannot do *for* us.) Without elaborating on the implications of this, which I believe connect surprisingly with issues about free will and causal accounts of knowledge, we need merely note the intricacy of the question of what matters *for people* other than their experiences.

Hilary Putnam (1926-) is one of the leading philosophers working today. His writings have touched on a wide range of philosophical subjects, including moral theory, philosophy of mind, philosophy of language, logic, and epistemology. Reprinted here in its entirety is one of his most influential essays, "Brains in a Vat," in which he sketches out a scenario that is remarkably similar to the one presented in *The Matrix*. He then draws some surprising philosophical conclusions regarding the possibility of skeptical doubt. Grau offers an introductory discussion of Putnam's position, while Chalmers's chapter considers an alternative route by which one might arrive at conclusions similar to Putnam's.

Hilary Putnam, from *Reason, Truth, and History*

Brains in a Vat

An ant is crawling on a patch of sand. As it crawls, it traces a line in the sand. By pure chance the line that it traces curves and recrosses itself in such a way that it ends up looking like a recognizable caricature of Winston Churchill. Has the ant traced a picture of Winston Churchill, a picture that *depicts* Churchill?

Most people would say, on a little reflection, that it has not. The ant, after all, has never seen Churchill, or even a picture of Churchill, and it had no intention of depicting Churchill. It simply traced a line (and even *that* was unintentional), a line that *we* can 'see as' a picture of Churchill.

We can express this by saying that the line is not 'in itself' a representation of anything rather than anything else. Similarity (of a certain very complicated sort) to the features of Winston Churchill is not sufficient to make something represent or refer to Churchill. Nor is it necessary: in our community the printed shape 'Winston Churchill', the spoken words 'Winston Churchill', and many other things are used to represent Churchill (though not pictorially), while not having the sort of similarity to Churchill that a picture—even a line drawing—has. If *similarity* is not necessary or sufficient to make something represent something else, how can *anything* be necessary or sufficient for this purpose? How on earth can one thing represent (or 'stand for', etc.) a different thing?

The answer may seem easy. Suppose the ant had seen Winston Churchill, and suppose that it had the intelligence and skill to draw a picture of him. Suppose it produced the caricature *intentionally*. Then the line would have represented Churchill.

On the other hand, suppose the line had the shape WINSTON CHURCHILL. And suppose this was just accident (ignoring the improbability involved). Then the 'printed shape' WINSTON CHURCHILL would *not* have represented Churchill, although that printed shape does represent Churchill when it occurs in almost any book today.

So it may seem that what is necessary for representation, or what is mainly necessary for representation, is *intention.*

But to have the intention that *anything,* even private language (even the words 'Winston Churchill' spoken in my mind and not out loud), should *represent* Churchill, I must have been able to *think about* Churchill in the first place. If lines in the sand, noises, etc., cannot 'in themselves' represent anything, then how is it that thought forms can 'in themselves' represent anything? Or can they? How can thought reach out and 'grasp' what is external?

Some philosophers have, in the past, leaped from this sort of consideration to what they take to be a proof that the mind is *essentially nonphysical in nature.* The argument is simple; what we said about the ant's curve applies to any physical object. No physical object can, in itself, refer to one thing rather than to another; nevertheless, *thoughts in the mind* obviously do succeed in referring to one thing rather than another. So thoughts (and hence the mind) are of an essentially different nature than physical objects. Thoughts have the characteristic of *intentionality*—they can refer to something else; nothing physical has 'intentionality', save as that intentionality is derivative from some employment of that physical thing by a mind. Or so it is claimed. This is too quick; just postulating mysterious powers of mind solves nothing. But the problem is very real. How is intentionality, reference, possible?

MAGICAL THEORIES OF REFERENCE   We saw that the ant's 'picture' has no necessary connection with Winston Churchill. The mere fact that the 'picture' bears a 'resemblance' to Churchill does not make it into a real picture, nor does it make it a representation of Churchill. Unless the ant is an intelligent ant (which it isn't) and knows about Churchill (which it doesn't), the curve it traced is not a picture or even a representation of anything. Some primitive people believe that some representations (in particular, *names*) have a necessary connection with their bearers; that to know the 'true name' of someone or something gives one power over it. This power comes from the *magical connection* between the name and the bearer of the name; once one realizes that a name *only* has a contextual, contingent, conventional connection with its bearer, it is hard to see why knowledge of the name should have any mystical significance.

What is important to realize is that what goes for physical pictures also goes for mental images, and for mental representations in general; mental representations no more have a necessary connection with what they represent than physical representations do. The contrary supposition is a survival of magical thinking.

Perhaps the point is easiest to grasp in the case of mental *images*. (Perhaps the first philosopher to grasp the enormous significance of this point, even if he was not the first to actually make it, was Wittgenstein.) Suppose there is a planet somewhere on which human beings have evolved (or been deposited by alien spacemen, or what have you). Suppose these humans, although otherwise like us, have never seen *trees*. Suppose they have never imagined trees (perhaps vegetable life exists on their planet only in the form of molds). Suppose one day a picture of a tree is accidentally dropped on their planet by a spaceship which passes on without having other contact with them. Imagine them puzzling over the picture. What in the world is this? All sorts of speculations occur to them: a building, a canopy, even an animal of some kind. But suppose they never come close to the truth.

For *us* the picture is a representation of a tree. For these humans the picture only represents a strange object, nature and function unknown. Suppose one of them has a mental image which is exactly like one of my mental images of a tree as a result of having seen the picture. His mental image is not a *representation of a tree*. It is only a representation of the strange object (whatever it is) that the mysterious picture represents.

Still, someone might argue that the mental image is *in fact* a representation of a tree, if only because the picture which caused this mental image was itself a representation of a tree to begin with. There is a causal chain from actual trees to the mental image even if it is a very strange one.

But even this causal chain can be imagined absent. Suppose the 'picture of the tree' that the spaceship dropped was not really a picture of a tree, but the accidental result of some spilled paints. Even if it looked exactly like a picture of a tree, it was, in truth, no more a picture of a tree than the ant's 'caricature' of Churchill was a picture of Churchill. We can even imagine that the spaceship which dropped the 'picture' came from a planet which knew nothing of trees. Then the humans would still have mental images qualitatively identical with my image of a tree, but they would not be images which represented a tree any more than anything else.

The same thing is true of *words*. A discourse on paper might seem to be a perfect description of trees, but if it were produced by monkeys randomly hitting keys on a typewriter for millions of years, then the words do not refer to anything. If there were a person who memorized those words and said them in his mind without understanding them, then they would not refer to anything when thought in the mind, either.

Imagine the person who is saying those words in his mind has been hypnotized. Suppose the words are in Japanese, and the person has been told that he understands Japanese. Suppose that as he thinks those words he has a 'feeling of understanding'. (Although if someone broke into his train of thought and asked him what the words he was thinking *meant*, he would discover he couldn't say.) Perhaps the illusion would be so perfect that the person could even fool a Japanese telepath! But if he couldn't use the words in the right contexts, answer questions about what he 'thought', etc., then he didn't understand them.

By combining these science fiction stories I have been telling, we can contrive a case in which someone thinks words which are in fact a description of trees in some language *and* simultaneously has appropriate mental images, but *neither* understands the words *nor* knows what a tree is. We can even imagine that the mental images were caused by paint-spills (although the person has been hypnotized to think that they are images of something appropriate to his thought—only, if he were asked, he wouldn't be able to say of what). And we can imagine that the language the person is thinking in is one neither the hypnotist nor the person hypnotized has ever heard of—perhaps it is just coincidence that these 'nonsense sentences', as the hypnotist supposes them to be, are a description of trees in Japanese. In short, everything passing before the person's mind might be qualitatively identical with what was passing through the mind of a Japanese speaker who was *really* thinking about trees—but none of it would refer to trees.

All of this is really impossible, of course, in the way that it is really impossible that monkeys should by chance type out a copy of *Hamlet*. That is to say that the probabilities against it are so high as to mean it will never really happen (we think). But it is not logically impossible, or even physically impossible. It *could* happen (compatibly with physical law[s] and, perhaps, compatibly with actual conditions in the universe, if there are lots of intelligent beings on other planets). And if it did happen, it would be a striking demonstration of an important conceptual truth; that even a large and complex system of representations, both verbal and visual, still does not have an *intrinsic,* built-in, magical connection with what it represents—a connection independent of how it was caused and what the dispositions of the speaker or thinker are. And this is true whether the system of representations (words and images, in the case of the example) is physically realized—the words are written or spoken, and the pictures are physical pictures—or only realized in the mind. Thought words and mental pictures do not *intrinsically* represent what they are about.

THE CASE OF THE BRAINS IN A VAT   Here is a science fiction possibility discussed by philosophers: imagine that a human being (you can imagine this to be yourself) has been subjected to an operation by an evil scientist. The person's brain (your brain) has been removed from the body and placed in a vat of nutrients which keeps the brain alive. The nerve endings have been connected to a super-scientific computer which causes the person whose brain it is to have the illusion that everything is perfectly normal. There seem to be people, objects, the sky, etc.; but really all the person (you) is experiencing is the result of electronic impulses traveling from the computer to the nerve endings. The computer is so clever that if the person tries to raise his hand, the feedback from the computer will cause him to 'see' and 'feel' the hand being raised. Moreover, by varying the program, the evil scientist can cause the victim to 'experience' (or hallucinate) any situation or environment the evil scientist wishes. He can also obliterate the memory of the brain operation, so that the victim will seem to himself to have always been in this environment. It can even seem to the victim that he is sitting and reading these very words about the amusing but quite absurd supposition that there is an evil scientist who removes people's brains from their bodies and places them in a vat of nutrients which keep the brains alive. The nerve endings are supposed to be connected to a super-scientific computer which causes the person whose brain it is to have the illusion that . . .

When this sort of possibility is mentioned in a lecture on the Theory of Knowledge, the purpose, of course, is to raise the classical problem of scepticism with respect to the external world in a modern way. (*How do you know you aren't in this predicament?*) But this predicament is also a useful device for raising issues about the mind/world relationship.

Instead of having just one brain in a vat, we could imagine that all human beings (perhaps all sentient beings) are brains in a vat (or nervous systems in a vat in case some beings with just a minimal nervous system already count as 'sentient'). Of course, the evil scientist would have to be outside—or would he? Perhaps there is no evil scientist, perhaps (though this is absurd) the universe just happens to consist of automatic machinery tending a vat full of brains and nervous systems.

This time let us suppose that the automatic machinery is programmed to give us all a *collective* hallucination, rather than a number of separate unrelated hallucinations. Thus, when I seem to myself to be talking to you, you seem to yourself to be hearing my words. Of course, it is not the case that my words actually reach your ears—for you don't have (real) ears, nor do I have a real mouth and tongue. Rather, when I produce my words, what happens is that the efferent impulses travel from my brain to the computer, which both causes me to 'hear' my own voice uttering those words and 'feel' my tongue moving, etc., and causes you to 'hear' my words, 'see' me speaking, etc. In this case, we are, in a sense, actually in communication. I am not mistaken about your real existence (only about the existence of your body and the 'external world', apart from brains). From a certain point of view, it doesn't even matter that 'the whole world' is a collective hallucination; for you do, after all, really hear my words when I speak to you, even if the mechanism isn't what we suppose it to be. (Of course, if we were two lovers making love, rather than just two people carrying on a conversation, then the suggestion that it was just two brains in a vat might be disturbing.)

I want now to ask a question which will seem very silly and obvious (at least to some people, including some very sophisticated philosophers), but which will take us to real philosophical depths rather quickly. Suppose this whole story were actually true. Could we, if we were brains in a vat in this way, *say* or *think* that we were?

I am going to argue that the answer is 'No, we couldn't'. In fact, I am going to argue that the supposition that we are actually brains in a vat, although it violates no physical law, and is perfectly consistent with everything we have experienced, cannot possibly be true. *It cannot possibly be true,* because it is, in a certain way, self-refuting.

The argument I am going to present is an unusual one, and it took me several years to convince myself that it is really right. But it is a correct argument. What makes it seem so strange is that it is connected with some of the very deepest issues in philosophy. (It first occurred to me when I was thinking about a theorem in modern logic, the 'Skolem-Löwenheim Theorem', and I suddenly saw a connection between this theorem and some arguments in Wittgenstein's *Philosophical Investigations.*)

A 'self-refuting supposition' is one whose truth implies its own falsity. For example, consider the thesis that *all general statements are false.* This is a general statement. So if it is true, then it must be false. Hence, it is false. Sometimes a thesis is called 'self-refuting' if it is *the supposition that the thesis is entertained or enunciated* that implies its falsity. For example, 'I do not exist' is self-refuting if thought by *me* (for any 'me'). So one can be certain that one oneself exists, if one thinks about it (as Descartes argued).

What I shall show is that the supposition that we are brains in a vat has just this property. If we can consider whether it is true or false, then it is not true (I shall show). Hence it is not true.

Before I give the argument, let us consider why it seems so strange that such an argument can be given (at least to philosophers who subscribe to a 'copy' conception of truth). We conceded that it is compatible with physical law that there should be a world in which all sentient beings are brains in a vat. As philosophers say, there is a 'possible world' in which all sentient beings are brains in a vat. (This 'possible world' talk makes it sound as if there is a *place* where any absurd supposition is true, which is why it can be very misleading in philosophy.) The humans in that possible world have exactly the same experiences that *we* do. They think the same thoughts we do (at least, the same words, images, thought-forms, etc., go through their minds). Yet, I am claiming that there is an argument we can give that shows we are not brains in a vat. How can there be? And why couldn't the people in the possible world who really *are* brains in a vat give it too?

The answer is going to be (basically) this: although the people in that possible world can think and 'say' any words we can think and say, they cannot (I claim) *refer* to what we can refer to. In particular, they cannot think or say that they are brains in a vat (*even by thinking 'we are brains in a vat'*).

TURING'S TEST   Suppose someone succeeds in inventing a computer which can actually carry on an intelligent conversation with one (on as many subjects as an intelligent person might). How can one decide if the computer is 'conscious'?

The British logician Alan Turing proposed the following test: let someone carry on a conversation with the computer and a conversation with a person whom he does not know. If he cannot tell which is the computer and which is the human being, then (assume the test to be repeated a sufficient number of times with different interlocutors) the computer is conscious. In short, a computing machine is conscious if it can pass the 'Turing test'. (The conversations are not to be carried on face to face, of course, since the interlocutor is not to know the visual appearance of either of his two conversational partners. Nor is voice to be used, since the mechanical voice might simply sound different from a human voice. Imagine, rather, that the conversations are all carried on via electric typewriter. The interlocutor types in his statements, questions, etc., and the two partners—the machine and the person—respond via the electric keyboard. Also, the machine may *lie*—asked 'Are you a machine', it might reply, 'No, I'm an assistant in the lab here'.)

The idea that this test is really a definitive test of consciousness has been criticized by a number of authors (who are by no means hostile in principle to the idea that a machine might be conscious). But this is not our topic at this time. I wish to use the general idea of the Turing test, the general idea of a *dialogic test of competence*, for a different purpose, the purpose of exploring the notion of *reference*.

Imagine a situation in which the problem is not to determine if the partner is really a person or a machine, but is rather to determine if the partner uses the words to refer as we do. The obvious test is, again, to carry on a conversation, and, if no problems arise, if the partner 'passes' in the sense of being indistinguishable from someone who is certified in advance to be speaking the same language, referring to the usual sorts of objects, etc., to conclude that the partner does refer to objects as we do.

When the purpose of the Turing test is as just described, that is, to determine the existence of (shared) reference, I shall refer to the test as the *Turing Test for Reference.* And, just as philosophers have discussed the question whether the original Turing test is a *definitive* test for consciousness, i.e., the question of whether a machine which 'passes' the test not just once but regularly is *necessarily* conscious, so, in the same way, I wish to discuss the question of whether the Turing Test for Reference just suggested is a definitive test for shared reference.

The answer will turn out to be 'No'. The Turing Test for Reference is not definitive. It is certainly an excellent test in practice; but it is not logically impossible (though it is certainly highly improbable) that someone could pass the Turing Test for Reference and not be referring to anything. It follows from this, as we shall see, that we can extend our observation that words (and whole texts and discourses) do not have a necessary connection to their referents. Even if we consider not words by themselves but rules deciding what words may appropriately be produced in certain contexts—even if we consider, in computer jargon, *programs for using words*—unless those programs themselves *refer to something extralinguistic* there is still no determinate reference that those words possess. This will be a crucial step in the process of reaching the conclusion that the Brain-in-a-Vat Worlders cannot refer to anything external at all (and hence cannot say *that* they are Brain-in-a-Vat Worlders).

Suppose, for example, that I am in the Turing situation (playing the 'Imitation Game', in Turing's terminology) and my partner is actually a machine. Suppose this machine is able to win the game ('passes' the test). Imagine the machine to be programmed to produce beautiful responses in English to statements, questions, remarks, etc., in English, but that it has no sense organs (other than the hookup to my electric typewriter), and no motor organs (other than the electric typewriter). (As far as I can make out, Turing does not assume that the possession of either sense organs or motor organs is necessary for consciousness or intelligence.) Assume that not only does the machine lack electronic eyes and ears, etc., but that there are no provisions in the machine's program, the program for playing the Imitation Game, for incorporating inputs from such sense organs, or for controlling a body. What should we say about such a machine?

To me, it seems evident that we cannot and should not attribute reference to such a device. It is true that the machine can discourse beautifully about, say, the scenery in New England. But it could not recognize an apple tree or an apple, a mountain or a cow, a field or a steeple, if it were in front of one.

What we have is a device for producing sentences in response to sentences. But none of these sentences is at all connected to the real world. *If one coupled two of these machines and let them play the Imitation Game with each other, then they would go on 'fooling' each other forever, even if the rest of the world disappeared!* There is no more reason to regard the machine's talk of apples as referring to real world apples than there is to regard the ant's 'drawing' as referring to Winston Churchill.

What produces the illusion of reference, meaning, intelligence, etc., here is the fact that there is a convention of representation which *we* have under which the machine's discourse refers to apples, steeples, New England, etc. Similarly, there is the *illusion* that the ant has caricatured Churchill, for the same reason. But we are able to perceive, handle, deal with apples and fields. Our talk of apples and fields is intimately connected with our *nonverbal* transactions with apples and fields. There are 'language entry rules' which take us from experiences of apples to such utterances as 'I see an apple', and 'language exit rules' which take us from decisions expressed in linguistic form ('I am going to buy some apples') to actions other than speaking. Lacking either language entry rules or language exit rules, there is no reason to regard the conversation of the machine (or of the two machines, in the case we envisaged of two machines playing the Imitation Game with each other) as more than syntactic play. Syntactic play that *resembles* intelligent discourse, to be sure; but only as (and no more than) the ant's curve resembles a biting caricature.

In the case of the ant, we could have argued that the ant would have drawn the same curve even if Winston Churchill had never existed. In the case of the machine, we cannot quite make the parallel argument; if apples, trees, steeples and fields had not existed, then, presumably, the programmers would not have produced that same program. Although the machine does not *perceive* apples, fields, or steeples, its creator-designers did. There is *some* causal connection between the machine and the real world apples, etc., via the perceptual experience and knowledge of the creator-designers. But such a weak connection can hardly suffice for reference. Not only is it logically possible, though fantastically improbable, that the same machine *could* have existed even if apples, fields, and steeples had not existed; more important, the machine is utterly insensitive to the *continued* existence of apples, fields, steeples, etc. Even if all these things *ceased* to exist, the machine would still discourse just as happily in the same way. That is why the machine cannot be regarded as referring at all.

The point that is relevant for our discussion is that there is nothing in Turing's test to rule out a machine which is programmed to do nothing *but* play the Imitation Game, and that a machine which can do nothing *but* play the Imitation Game is *clearly* not referring any more than a record player is.

BRAINS IN A VAT (AGAIN)   Let us compare the hypothetical 'brains in a vat' with the machines just described. There are obviously important differences. The brains in a vat do not have sense organs, but they do have *provision* for sense organs; that is, there are afferent nerve endings, there are inputs from these afferent nerve endings, and these inputs figure in the 'program' of the brains in the vat just as they do in the program of our brains. The brains in a vat are *brains;* moreover, they are *functioning* brains, and they function by the same rules as brains do in the actual world. For these reasons, it would seem absurd to deny consciousness or intelligence to them. But the fact that they are conscious and intelligent does not mean that their words refer to what our words refer. The question we are interested in is this: do their verbalizations containing, say, the word 'tree' actually refer to *trees*? More generally: can they refer to *external* objects at all? (As opposed to, for example, objects in the image produced by the automatic machinery.)

To fix our ideas, let us specify that the automatic machinery is supposed to have come into existence by some kind of cosmic chance or coincidence (or, perhaps, to have always existed). In this hypothetical world, the automatic machinery itself is supposed to have no intelligent creator-designers. In fact, as we said at the beginning of this chapter, we may imagine that all sentient beings (however minimal their sentience) are inside the vat.

This assumption does not help. For there is no connection between the *word* 'tree' as used by these brains and actual trees. They would still use the word 'tree' just as they do, think just the thoughts they do, have just the images they have, even if there were no actual trees. Their images, words, etc., are qualitatively identical with images, words, etc., which do represent trees in *our* world; but we have already seen (the ant again!) that qualitative similarity to something which represents an object (Winston Churchill or a tree) does not make a thing a representation all by itself. In short, the brains in a vat are not thinking about real trees when they think 'there is a tree in front of me' because there is nothing by virtue of which their thought 'tree' represents actual trees.

If this seems hasty, reflect on the following: we have seen that the words do not necessarily refer to trees even if they are arranged in a sequence which is identical with a discourse which (were it to occur in one of our minds) would unquestionably *be about trees* in the actual world. Nor does the 'program', in the sense of the rules, practices, dispositions of the brains to verbal behavior, necessarily refer to trees or bring about reference to trees through the connections it establishes between words and words, or *linguistic* cues and *linguistic* responses. If these brains think about, refer to, represent trees (real trees, outside the vat), then it must be because of the way the 'program' connects the system of language to *non-verbal* inputs and outputs. There are indeed such non-verbal inputs and outputs in the Brain-in-a-Vat world (those efferent and afferent nerve endings again!), but we also saw that the 'sense-data' produced by the automatic machinery do not represent trees (or anything external) even when they resemble our tree-images exactly. Just as a splash of paint might resemble a tree picture without *being* a tree picture, so, we saw, a 'sense datum' might be qualitatively identical with an 'image of a tree' without being an image of a tree. How can the fact that, in the case of the brains in a vat, the language is connected by the program with sensory inputs which do not intrinsically or extrinsically represent trees (or anything external) possibly bring it about that the whole system of representations, the language-in-use, *does* refer to or represent trees or anything external?

The answer is that it cannot. The whole system of sense-data, motor signals to the efferent endings, and verbally or conceptually mediated thought connected by language entry rules to the sense-data (or what-ever) as inputs and by language exit rules to the motor signals as outputs, has no more connection to *trees* than the ant's curve has to Winston Churchill. Once we see that the *qualitative similarity* (amounting, if you like, to qualitative identity) between the thoughts of the brains in a vat and the thoughts of someone in the actual world by no means implies sameness of reference, it is not hard to see that there is no basis at all for regarding the brains in a vat as referring to external things.

THE PREMISES OF THE ARGUMENT   I have now given the argument promised to show that the brains in a vat cannot think or say that they are brains in a vat. It remains only to make it explicit and to examine its structure.

By what was just said, when the brain in a vat (in the world where every sentient being is and always was a brain in a vat) thinks 'There is a tree in front of me', this thought does not refer to actual trees. On some theories that we shall discuss it might refer to trees in the image, or to the electronic impulses that cause tree experiences, or to the features of the program that are responsible for those electronic impulses. These theories are not ruled out by what was just said, for there is a close causal connection between the use of the word 'tree' in vat-English and the presence of trees in the image, the presence of electronic impulses of a certain kind, and the presence of certain features in the machine's pro-gram. On these theories the brain is *right*, not *wrong* in thinking 'There is a tree in front of me.' Given what 'tree' refers to in vat-English and what 'in front of' refers to, assuming one of these theories is correct, then the truth-conditions for 'There is a tree in front of me' when it occurs in vat-English are simply that a tree in the image be 'in front of' the 'me' in question—in the image—or, perhaps, that the kind of electronic impulse that normally produces this experience becoming from the automatic machinery, or, perhaps, that the feature of the machinery that is supposed to produce the 'tree in front of one' experience be operating. And these truth-conditions are certainly fulfilled.

By the same argument, 'vat' refers to vats in the image in vat-English, or something related (electronic impulses or program features), but cer-tainly not to real vats, since the use of 'vat' in vat-English has no causal connection to real vats (apart from the connection that the brains in a vat wouldn't be able to use the word 'vat', if it were not for the presence of one particular vat—the vat they are in; but this connection obtains between the use of *every* word in vat-English and that one particular vat; it is not a special connection between the use of the *particular* word 'vat' and vats). Similarly, 'nutrient fluid' refers to a liquid in the image in vat-English, or something related (electronic impulses or program features). It follows that if their 'possible world' is really the actual one, and we are really the brains in a vat, then what we now mean by 'we are brains in a vat' is that *we are brains in a vat in the image* or something of that kind (if we mean anything at all). But part of the hypothesis that we are brains in a vat is that we aren't brains in a vat in the image (i.e., what we are 'hallucinating' isn't that we are brains in a vat). So, if we are brains in a vat, then the sentence 'We are brains in a vat' says something false (if it says anything). In short, if we are brains in a vat, then 'We are brains in a vat' is false. So it is (necessarily) false.

The supposition that such a possibility makes sense arises from a combination of two errors: (1) taking *physical possibility* too seriously; and (2) unconsciously operating with a magical theory of reference, a theory on which certain mental representations necessarily refer to certain external things and kinds of things.

There is a 'physically possible world' in which we are brains in a vat—what does this mean except that there is a *description* of such a state of affairs which is compatible with the laws of physics? Just as there is a tendency in our culture (and has been since the seventeenth century) to take *physics* as our metaphysics, that is, to view the exact sciences as the long-sought description of the 'true and ultimate furniture of the universe', so there is, as an immediate consequence, a tendency to take 'physical possibility' as the very touchstone of what might really actually be the case. Truth is physical truth; possibility physical possibility; and necessity physical necessity, on such a view. But we have just seen, if only in the case of a very contrived example so far, that this view is wrong. The existence of a 'physically possible world' in which we are brains in a vat (and always were and will be) does not mean that we might really, actually, possibly *be* brains in a vat. What rules out this possibility is not physics but *philosophy*.

Some philosophers, eager both to assert and minimize the claims of their profession at the same time (the typical state of mind of Anglo-American philosophy in the twentieth century), would say: 'Sure. You have shown that some things that seem to be physical possibilities are really *conceptual* impossibilities. What's so surprising about that?'

Well, to be sure, my argument can be described as a 'conceptual' one. But to describe philosophical activity as the search for 'conceptual' truths makes it all sound like *inquiry about the meaning of words*. And that is not at all what we have been engaging in.

What we have been doing is considering the *preconditions* for *thinking about, representing, referring to*, etc. We have investigated these preconditions *not* by investigating the meaning of these words and phrases (as a linguist might, for example) but by *reasoning a priori*. Not in the old 'absolute' sense (since we don't claim that magical theories of reference are *a priori* wrong), but in the sense of inquiring into what is *reasonably* possible *assuming* certain general premises, or making certain very broad theoretical assumptions. Such a procedure is neither 'empirical' nor quite '*a priori*', but has elements of both ways of investigating. In spite of the fallibility of my procedure, and its dependence upon assumptions which might be described as 'empirical' (e.g., the assumption that the mind has no access to external things or properties apart from that provided by the senses), my procedure has a close relation to what Kant called a 'transcendental' investigation; for it is an investigation, I repeat, of the *preconditions* of reference and hence of thought—preconditions built into the nature of our minds themselves, though not (as Kant hoped) wholly independent of empirical assumptions.

One of the premises of the argument is obvious: that magical theories of reference are wrong, wrong for mental representations and not only for physical ones. The other premise is that one cannot refer to certain kinds of things, e.g., *trees*, if one has no causal interaction at all with them, or with things in terms of which they can be described. But why should we accept these premises? Since these constitute the broad framework within which I am arguing, it is time to examine them more closely.

THE REASONS FOR DENYING NECESSARY CONNECTIONS BETWEEN REPRESENTATIONS AND THEIR REFERENTS   I mentioned earlier that some philosophers (most famously, Brentano) have ascribed to the mind a power, 'intentionality', which precisely enables it to *refer*. Evidently, I have rejected this as no solution. But what gives me this right? Have I, perhaps, been too hasty?

These philosophers did not claim that we can think about external things or properties without using representations at all. And the argument I gave above comparing visual sense-data to the ant's 'picture' (the argument via the science fiction story about the 'picture' of a tree that came from a paint-splash and that gave rise to sense-data qualitatively similar to our 'visual images of trees', but unaccompanied by any *concept* of a tree) would be accepted as showing that *images* do not necessarily refer. If there are mental representations that necessarily refer (to external things) they must be of the nature of *concepts* and not of the nature of images. But what are *concepts*?

When we introspect we do not perceive 'concepts' flowing through our minds as such. Stop the stream of thought when or where we will, what we catch are words, images, sensations, feelings. When I speak my thoughts out loud I do not think them twice. I hear my words as you do. To be sure it feels different to me when I utter words that I believe and when I utter words I do not believe (but sometimes, when I am nervous, or in front of a hostile audience, it feels as if I am lying when I know I am telling the truth); and it feels different when I utter words I understand and when I utter words I do not understand. But I can imagine without difficulty someone thinking just these words (in the sense of saying them in his mind) and having just the feeling of understanding, asserting, etc., that I do, and realizing a minute later (or on being awakened by a hypnotist) that he did not understand what had just passed through his mind at all, that he did not even understand the language these words are in. I don't claim that this is very likely; I simply mean that there is nothing at all unimaginable about this. And what this shows is not that concepts *are* words (or images, sensations, etc.), but that to attribute a 'concept' or a 'thought' to someone is quite different from attributing any mental 'presentation', any introspectible entity or event, to him. Concepts are not mental presentations that intrinsically refer to external objects for the very decisive reason that they are not mental presentations at all. Concepts are signs used in a certain way; the signs may be public or private, mental entities or physical entities, but even when the signs are 'mental' and 'private', the sign itself apart from its use is not the concept. And signs do not themselves intrinsically refer.

We can see this by performing a very simple thought experiment. Suppose you are like me and cannot tell an elm tree from a beech tree. We still say that the reference of 'elm' in my speech is the same as the reference of 'elm' in anyone else's, viz., elm trees, and that the set of all beech trees is the extension of 'beech' (i.e., the set of things the word 'beech' is truly predicated of) both in your speech and my speech. Is it really credible that the difference between what 'elm' refers to and what 'beech' refers to is brought about by a difference in our 'concepts'? My concept of an elm tree is exactly the same as my concept of a beech tree (I blush to confess). (This shows that the determination of reference is social and not individual, by the way; you and I both defer to experts who *can* tell elms from beeches.) If someone heroically attempts to maintain that the difference between the reference of 'elm' and the reference of 'beech' in *my* speech is explained by a difference in my psychological state, then let him imagine a Twin Earth where the words are switched. Twin Earth is very much like Earth; in fact, apart from the fact that 'elm' and 'beech' are interchanged, the reader can suppose Twin Earth is exactly like Earth. Suppose I have a *Doppelganger* on Twin Earth who is molecule for molecule identical with me (in the sense in which two neckties can be 'identical'). If you are a dualist, then suppose my *Doppelganger* thinks the same verbalized thoughts I do, has the same sense-data, the same dispositions, etc. It is absurd to think his psychological state is one bit different from mine: yet his word 'elm' represents *beeches*, and my word 'elm' represents elms. (Similarly, if the 'water' on Twin Earth is a different liquid—say, XYZ and not H_2O—then 'water' represents a different liquid when used on Twin Earth and when used on Earth, etc.) Contrary to a doctrine that has been with us since the seventeenth century, *meanings just aren't in the head.*

We have seen that possessing a concept is not a matter of possessing images (say, of trees—or even images, 'visual' or 'acoustic', of sentences, or whole discourses, for that matter) since one could possess any system of images you please and not possess the *ability* to use the sentences in situationally appropriate ways (considering both linguistic factors—what has been said before—and non-linguistic factors as determining 'situational appropriateness'). A man may have all the images you please, and still be completely at a loss when one says to him 'point to a tree', even if a lot of trees are present. He may even have the image of what he is supposed to do, and still not know what he is supposed to do. For the image, if not accompanied by the ability to act in a certain way, is just a *picture*, and acting in accordance with a picture is itself an ability that one may or may not have. (The man might picture himself pointing to a tree, but just for the sake of contemplating something logically possible; himself pointing to a tree after someone has produced the—to him meaningless—sequence of sounds 'please point to a tree'.) He would still not know that he was supposed to point to a tree, and he would still not *understand* 'point to a tree'.

I have considered the ability to use certain sentences to be the criterion for possessing a full-blown concept, but this could easily be liberalized. We could allow symbolism consisting of elements which are not words in a natural language, for example, and we could allow such mental phenomena as images and other types of internal events. What is essential is that these should have the same complexity, ability to be combined with each other, etc., as sentences in a natural language. For, although a particular presentation—say, a blue flash—might serve a particular mathematician as the inner expression of the whole proof of the Prime Number Theorem, still there would be no temptation to say this (and it would be false to say this) if that mathematician could not unpack his 'blue flash' into separate steps and logical connections. But, no matter what sort of inner phenomena we allow as possible *expressions* of thought, arguments exactly similar to the foregoing will show that it is not the phenomena themselves that constitute understanding, but rather the ability of the thinker to *employ* these phenomena, to produce the right phenomena in the right circumstances.

The foregoing is a very abbreviated version of Wittgenstein's argument in *Philosophical Investigations*. If it is correct, then the attempt to understand thought by what is called 'phenomenological' investigation is fundamentally misguided; for what the phenomenologists fail to see is that what they are describing is the inner *expression* of thought, but that the *understanding* of that expression—one's understanding of one's own thoughts—is not an *occurrence* but an *ability*. Our example of a man pretending to think in Japanese (and deceiving a Japanese telepath) already shows the futility of a phenomenological approach to the problem of *understanding*. For even if there is some introspectible quality which is present when and only when one *really* understands (this seems false on introspection, in fact), still that quality is only *correlated* with understanding, and it is still possible that the man fooling the Japanese telepath have that quality too and *still* not understand a word of Japanese.

On the other hand, consider the perfectly possible man who does not have any 'interior monologue' at all. He speaks perfectly good English, and if asked what his opinions are on a given subject, he will give them at length. But he never thinks (in words, images, etc.) when he is not speaking out loud; nor does anything 'go through his head', except that (of course) he hears his own voice speaking, and has the usual sense impressions from his surroundings, plus a general 'feeling of understanding'. (Perhaps he is in the habit of talking to himself.) When he types a letter or goes to the store, etc., he is not having an internal 'stream of thought'; but his actions are intelligent and purposeful, and if anyone walks up and asks him 'What are you doing?' he will give perfectly coherent replies.

This man seems perfectly imaginable. No one would hesitate to say that he was conscious, disliked rock and roll (if he frequently expressed a strong aversion to rock and roll), etc., just because he did not think conscious thoughts except when speaking out loud.

What follows from all this is that (a) no set of mental events—images or more 'abstract' mental happenings and qualities—*constitutes* understanding; and (b) no set of mental events is *necessary* for understanding. In particular, *concepts cannot be identical with mental objects of any kind*. For, assuming that by a mental object we mean something introspectible, we have just seen that whatever it is, it may be absent in a man who does understand the appropriate word (and hence has the full-blown concept), and present in a man who does not have the concept at all.

Coming back now to our criticism of magical theories of reference (a topic which also concerned Wittgenstein), we see that, on the one hand, those 'mental objects' we *can* introspectively detect—words, images, feelings, etc.—do not intrinsically refer any more than the ant's picture does (and for the same reasons), while the attempts to postulate special mental objects, 'concepts', which *do* have a necessary connection with their referents, and which only trained phenomenologists can detect, commit a *logical* blunder; for concepts are (at least in part) *abilities* and not occurrences. The doctrine that there are mental presentations which necessarily refer to external things is not only bad natural science; it is also bad phenomenology and conceptual confusion.

CONTRIBUTORS

David J. Chalmers is professor of philosophy, ARC Federation Fellow, and director of the Centre for Consciousness at the Australian National University. He is author of *The Conscious Mind: In Search of a Fundamental Theory*. He is especially interested in consciousness, artificial intelligence, metaphysics, and meaning.

Andy Clark is a philosopher and cognitive scientist in the School of Philosophy, Psychology, and Language Sciences at Edinburgh University. He is the author of five books, including *Being There: Putting Brain, Body and World Together Again* and *Natural-Born Cyborgs: Minds, Technologies and the Future of Human Intelligence*. He is especially interested in robotics, neural control systems, and the role of the body and the world in thought.

Julia Driver currently teaches at Dartmouth College. Her main research interests are in ethical theory and moral psychology, and she has published a book (*Uneasy Virtue*) and a variety of articles in the area of normative ethical theory. She is co-editor of the normative ethics section of *The Stanford Encyclopedia of Philosophy*.

Hubert L. Dreyfus was educated at Harvard and teaches philosophy at the University of California, Berkeley. His research interests bridge the analytic and continental traditions in twentieth-century philosophy. He has written books on Heidegger (*Being-in-the-World*) and on artificial intelligence (*What Computers (Still) Can't Do*). Dreyfus recently published *On the Internet* and is working on a book with Charles Taylor tentatively entitled *Retrieving Realism*.

Stephen D. Dreyfus was a film major at the University of California, Santa Cruz. He is a graduate of the Video Symphony School for digital editing and has been assistant editor on several small films.

Frances Flannery-Dailey received her Ph.D. from the University of Iowa and is assistant professor of religion at Hendrix College in Conway, Arkansas. She teaches courses on the Bible, religion and culture, and Judaism. She is author of *Dreamers, Scribes, and Priests: Jewish Dreams in the Hellenistic and Roman Eras* (2004).

Christopher Grau was educated at Johns Hopkins University and New York University. In addition to editing the "Philosophy and *The Matrix*" section of *The Matrix* Web site, Grau is assistant professor of philosophy at Florida International University in Miami. He has previously taught at Dartmouth College, Johns Hopkins University, Brooklyn College, and the University of Maryland, Baltimore County. His current research involves the ethical ramifications of theories of personal identity.

Richard Hanley was educated at Sydney University and the University of Maryland, College Park. He is the author of *The Metaphysics of Star Trek* (reprinted in paperback as *Is Data Human?*) and is co-editor of the forthcoming *Blackwell Guide to the Philosophy of Language*. He works on metaphysics, philosophy of language, and ethics and dabbles in time-travel fiction; he is gainfully employed in the Philosophy Department at the University of Delaware.

Colin McGinn was educated at Oxford University. He has written widely on philosophy and philosophers in publications such as the *New York Review of Books*, *London Review of Books*, *New Republic*, and *New York Times Book Review*. McGinn has written fourteen books, including *The Making of a Philosopher*; *The Mysterious Flame*; *The Character of Mind*; *Ethics, Evil and Fiction*; and the novel *The Space Trap*. He is currently a professor of philosophy at Rutgers University.

Michael McKenna received his Ph.D. from the University of Virginia in 1993. He is an associate professor of philosophy in the Department of Philosophy and Religion at Ithaca College. McKenna has published various articles on the topics of free will and moral responsibility. He is currently working on a book devoted to a communication-based account of morally responsible agency. McKenna teaches courses in metaphysics, moral and political philosophy, and philosophy in film.

Tim Mawson was educated at Oxford University and has never left; he is currently a fellow and tutor in philosophy at St. Peter's College. His main area of research interest is the philosophy of religion, but he has also published on the history of philosophy and ethics.

John Partridge is assistant professor of philosophy at Wheaton College in Norton, Massachusetts. He was educated at the College of William and Mary and Johns Hopkins University. He has published articles on ancient philosophy and the history of ethics.

James Pryor was educated at Princeton and teaches philosophy at New York University. He has published on the epistemology of perception and works primarily on philosophical issues concerning the mind and knowledge.

Iakovos Vasiliou is associate professor of philosophy at Brooklyn College, City University of New York. He has previously taught at Cornell, Johns Hopkins, and Georgia State University. He has published articles on Plato, Aristotle, and Wittgenstein and is currently working on a book on moral epistemology in Plato and Aristotle.

Rachel Wagner was educated at Wake Forest University and the University of Iowa. She is currently the Hundere Teaching Fellow of Religion and Culture at Oregon State University. There she teaches courses on religion and film, Islam and media, and pluralism and religious diversity. Her current research focuses on the analysis of religion and violence in film and other popular media.

Kevin Warwick is a professor of cybernetics at the University of Reading, UK. His book *In the Mind of the Machine* gives a warning of a future in which machines are more intelligent than humans. In 1998 and 2002, he received surgical implants which shocked the scientific community. The second of these linked his nervous system to the Internet. His experiments are reported in his autobiography *I, Cyborg*.

INDEX